# AFRICAN AMERICANS AND CIVIL RIGHTS

# Social Issues in American History Series

*Immigration*

*Women's Rights*

*African Americans and Civil Rights:
From 1619 to the Present*

# AFRICAN AMERICANS AND CIVIL RIGHTS

## FROM 1619 TO THE PRESENT

by
**Michael L. Levine**

*Social Issues in American History Series*

Oryx Press
1996

*The rare Arabian Oryx is believed to have inspired the myth of the unicorn. This desert antelope became virtually extinct in the early 1960s. At that time several groups of international conservationists arranged to have 9 animals sent to the Phoenix Zoo to be the nucleus of a captive breeding herd. Today the Oryx population is over 1000, and over 500 have been returned to the Middle East.*

© 1996 by Michael L. Levine
Published by The Oryx Press
4041 North Central at Indian School Road
Phoenix, Arizona 85012-3397

Cover photograph courtesy of United Press International. Illustrations on pages 11, 45, 81, 101, and 117 courtesy of The Bettmann Archive. Illustration on page 28 courtesy of the Rare Books and Manuscripts Division; The New York Public Library; Astor, Lenox and Tilden Foundations. Photographs on pages 72, 126, 134, 157, and 175 courtesy of the Portrait Collection; Prints and Photographs Division; Schomburg Center for Research in Black Culture; The New York Public Library; Astor, Lenox and Tilden Foundations. Illustrations on pages 138, 161, 184, 193, and 238 courtesy of UPI/Bettmann. Photographs on pages 185 and 190 courtesy of UPI/Bettmann Newsphotos. Photograph on page 236 courtesy of the Congressional Black Caucus. Photograph on page 244 courtesy of Reuters/Bettmann.

Published simultaneously in Canada
Printed and bound in the United States of America

∞ The paper used in this publication meets the minimum requirements of the American National Standard for Information Sciences—Permanence of Paper for Printed Library Materials, ANSI Z39.48-1984.

*Library of Congress Cataloging-in-Publication Data*
Levine, Michael L.
  African Americans and civil rights : from 1619 to the present / by Michael L. Levine.
    p. cm. — (Social issues in American history series)
  Includes bibliographical references (p. ) and index.
  ISBN 0-89774-859-X
    1. Afro-Americans—History. 2. Afro-Americans—Civil rights—History. 3. Afro-Americans—Legal status, laws, etc. 4. Racism—United States—History. 5. Civil rights movement—United States—History. 6. United States—Race relations. I. Title.
  II. Series: Social issues in American history.
E185.L45    1996
973'.0496073—dc20
                                                              96-8923
                                                                CIP

# CONTENTS

•••••••••

# PREFACE

● ● ● ● ● ● ● ● ●

Beginning in the seventeenth century, Africans were brought forcibly to British North America because British and European settlers needed laborers. Soon, blacks—people of full or partial African descent—found themselves occupying a special and inferior status. The majority were slaves, but even so-called free blacks were deprived of most rights on racial grounds. And although the civil rights revolution of the 1960s brought about great changes, troubled race relations in the United States remain a central fact of life as blacks seek, finally, to achieve full equality.

*African Americans and Civil Rights* surveys the oppression of blacks in America and the gains made against racism by blacks and their allies, from the beginning of American history to the present. It is hoped that the volume will help high school students, college students, and members of the general public to understand the cruel history of race relations in America.

As the title suggests, this book emphasizes the legal and political status of black Americans. But that status is closely linked to the role of blacks in the economy. Therefore, slavery, sharecropping and tenant farming, industrial labor, and the postindustrial economy all receive attention as they relate to African Americans. The volume, however, in no way claims to be a complete history of blacks in America. For example, the huge black contribution to the arts and popular culture is not discussed. Other works do take a comprehensive approach, and the most popular among them is by John Hope Franklin and Alfred A. Moss, Jr.: *From Slavery to Freedom: A History of African Americans* (7th edition, 1994).

*African Americans and Civil Rights* is based upon broad reading in the huge secondary literature on black history. At the end of this work, a long list of suggested readings in that literature is provided. Because memoirs and autobiographies are often self-serving and can mislead the beginning reader, almost all of the books listed are works by historians or other specialists. Biographical sketches of important persons in black history are also provided. The great majority are black, but some are not. A chronology section lists important events in African American history. Finally, a glossary is included to define terms used in the book that may be unfamiliar to readers, and to explain the significance of important civil rights laws, court rulings, organizations, and agencies.

# CHAPTER 1

# West Africa,
# the Atlantic Slave Trade,
# and the Americas

## THE CIVILIZATIONS OF WEST AFRICA

From the 1490s to the late 1800s, western European and American ships brought millions of slaves to the Americas from Africa—in particular, from the part of Africa south of the Sahara Desert, once known as black Africa. Because Europeans had not enslaved one another for some time, they looked for reasons to justify treating Africans differently. The most important justification was the claim that the darker-skinned Africans were inferior to the lighter-skinned Europeans. As one "proof" of inferiority, Europeans argued that the peoples of Africa were at a very low stage of development. They were, Europeans contended, living in primitive, barbaric societies in a constant state of mindless, random violence.

A look at the history of Africa south of the Sahara—and especially of West Africa, where most of the American slaves originated—shows clearly that this claim was false. Hundreds of years before Europeans began sailing down the African coast, West Africans had established flourishing kingdoms and empires with civil services, powerful armies, productive economies, systems of law, large cities, skilled artisans, outstanding schools, and many other features associated with civilized societies.

### The Iron Age

The civilizations of West Africa emerged as the Iron Age replaced the Stone Age, starting around 500 B.C. and spreading to almost all of the continent before A.D. 1000. West Africans replaced stone weapons and tools with much more durable and effective iron ones. With stone tools, farmers could grow only enough food for themselves. But with superior iron implements, they could produce a food surplus. Once this happened, not everyone had to be a farmer. Some could be craftspersons, using materials such as earth, wood, metals, minerals, ivory, and animal skins. Other people could mine below the earth's surface for metals and minerals. Trade became possible, because surplus food, precious metals, and manufactured goods could be sent elsewhere in exchange for things not found or produced at home. Centers of trade grew from villages into towns and even cities.

By tying together places that previously had no links, trade also paved the way for the creation of large political states controlling entire regions. Iron weapons promoted this development by making it possible for groups with such weapons to conquer societies without them. As a result, kingdoms and empires replaced traditional village groups ruled by local clans and kinship groups. These powerful kingdoms and empires were better able to organize trade, defend trade routes, and promote manufacturing.

One final ingredient was important in the emergence of West African civilizations: the conquest of North Africa (Africa north of the Sahara) by Muslim Arabs. Inspired by the new religion of Islam, Arabs invaded Africa from the Arabian peninsula to the east. They entered Egypt in A.D. 639 and, moving westward, had conquered all of North Africa by the early eighth century. The Arabs ended the disunity and warfare that had previously existed in North Africa, which made possible an expansion of the trade route system that crossed the Sahara. At the north end of the trade routes were the North African Arabs and Berbers (a group that lived in North Africa before the Arab conquest). The routes crossed the Sahara to the darker-skinned peoples living in the savannah (a type of grassland) of West Africa just south of the desert. The routes continued southward to the tropical forestlands of the Guinea coastal region (from modern Sierra Leone eastward to modern Cameroon) and to the coast itself. Growing trade meant growing wealth in the savannah, which advanced the development of West African civilizations. So did the spread of Islam south of the Sahara, which began in the tenth century. Islam was based on belief in a single God, Allah. By replacing previous West African religious systems based on local deities, Islam helped unite people over a large area, which in turn made it easier to establish governments over a wide territory.

## Kingdoms and Empires

The first major empire of West Africa was Ghana, centered in the savannah in modern Mali and Mauritania, about 500 miles northwest of the modern nation of Ghana. It rose around the fourth century A.D. and began expanding rapidly in the eighth or ninth century as the trade with Muslim North Africa grew. Its power rested on the control of north-south trade routes along which salt, cattle, horses, cloth, and metalwork moved southward from North Africa and the Sahara, and gold, slaves, ivory, kola nuts, beads, and cloth moved northward from the Guinea forestland and especially from the Gold Coast (modern Ghana). Kumbi, ancient Ghana's capital, was a major trading center with a population around 15,000. Ghana's rulers practiced traditional African religion, which sometimes included a number of gods but always recognized one as the Supreme Being, a shapeless spirit

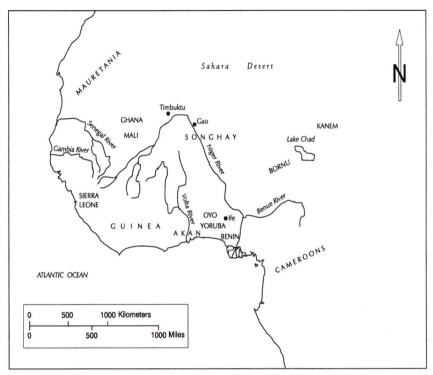

Some kingdoms and empires in West Africa: ninth through sixteenth centuries.

that had created the others and was present everywhere. But to improve Ghana's relations with its Arab Muslim trading partners to the north, Ghana's rulers allowed the empire's Muslim subjects to build their own city.

The Ghana Empire reached its peak in the eleventh century. According to an Arab geographer named al-Bakri, its ruler in the 1060s was a man named Tenkamenin. Al-Bakri claimed that Tenkamenin had 200,000 soldiers at his disposal. Tenkamenin reportedly lived in a lavish castle decorated by sculptors and artists, with temples and a prison on the royal grounds. Al-Bakri wrote in 1067 that when Tenkamenin held court to listen to his subjects' grievances, "he sits in a pavilion around which stand his horses caparisoned [clothed] in cloth of gold; behind him stand ten pages holding shields and gold-mounted swords; and on his right hand are the sons of the princes of his empire, splendidly clad with gold plaited into their hair." However, this splendor did not last for long. Muslims from the northwest invaded Ghana in 1076, a blow from which the empire never recovered.

Farther east, in the ninth or tenth century, the empire of Kanem-Bornu developed in the savannah around Lake Chad. As with Ghana, Kanem-Bornu's domination of important trade routes was crucial to its growth. From the north came salt and copper. From the south, in the eastern part of the Guinea region (in modern Nigeria), came forest products and cotton goods. Late in the eleventh century, a ruler named Hume converted to Islam, more to promote trade with Islamic North Africa than out of religious belief. Most merchants and many urban dwellers became Muslims, but not the people of the countryside, who kept their traditional African religion. This pattern occurred in other West African empires led by Islamic rulers, who responded by combining Islam with the old beliefs in forming the official state religion.

In the 1300s or 1400s, the capital shifted from Kanem, northeast of Lake Chad, to Bornu, southwest of the lake. The empire reached its peak under Idris Alooma, who ruled from 1580 to 1617. In his time Kanem-Bornu was almost 1,000 miles wide from east to west, had diplomats in Cairo and Tripoli on the North African coast, and maintained friendly relations with the Ottoman Turks in Istanbul (at the southeast tip of Europe, about 2,000 miles from Lake Chad).

To the west of Kanem-Bornu, Mali—another state in the savannah—became the successor to the Ghana Empire. The Mali Empire, also based on control of trade, arose around the Upper Niger River under Sundiata, who ruled from 1230 to 1265. His successors adopted Islam, and in 1324 a ruler named Mansa Musa made a famous pilgrimage to Mecca, the holy city of Islam on the Arabian peninsula. Accompanied by an escort of some 80,000 people, he became re-nowned for the gold he gave as presents along his route. Mansa Musa brought back Muslim scholars, legal experts, architects, and others who helped him make Mali into one of the great centers of the Muslim world. He had a university built at Timbuktu (in modern Mali), which drew students from Africa north and south of the Sahara and from the Middle East as well. Mosques were built in Timbuktu and elsewhere. Under Mansa Musa, brick began to replace clay as a building material. His reputation extended into Europe, where a 1375 atlas of Africa included a drawing of Mansa Musa—described as "Lord of the Blacks"—sitting on a throne as the merchants of North Africa flocked toward the trading centers of his empire.

The Mali Empire had a more effective government than either Ghana or Kanem-Bornu. Literacy was spreading among the ruling elite, and Mansa Musa was reported to have secretaries and permanent government offices. His reign was remembered as an era of peace and prosperity. Around 15 years after his death in 1337, a traveler named Ibn Battuta could still report that "there is complete security in their country. Neither traveler nor inhabitant in it has anything to fear from robbers or men of violence." During Mansa Musa's reign, the Mali Empire reached its maximum size, stretching more than 1,300 miles from the Atlantic coast of modern Senegal to the western border of modern Nigeria. In the 1400s the empire began to decline when it came under attack from several groups, particularly the Songhay people.

The Songhay lived in and around the major trading city of Gao, on the Middle Niger River in modern Mali. Their state, which adopted Islam in the eleventh century, was originally part of the Mali Empire. But in the late 1400s a Songhay king named Sunni Ali broke free of the empire and began conquering the surrounding territory. This process continued under Askia Muhammad Turay into the early 1500s and under Askia Dawud into the mid-1500s.

The Songhay Empire, with its capital at Gao, became the greatest of the West African kingdoms. It covered much of the same territory as Mali, but was larger. Songhay also had a more developed system of government. The empire was divided into districts, each with a royally appointed governor. Officials received long-term appointments, and the work of professional administrators and civil servants was based more on fixed rules and less on the personal decisions of the king. This made it possible for the Songhay Empire to move toward a system of justice in which everyone was judged by the same standards. Songhay also had a professional army and even a professional navy, which operated on the Niger River.

Following in the footsteps of Mali king Mansa Musa, Askia Muhammad Turay made a pilgrimage to Mecca in 1495 and gave away gold during the journey. Like Mansa Musa, he returned with Muslim scholars and advisers and tried to apply Islamic law; as in previous centuries, however, the farmers of West Africa resisted Islam, as did many city dwellers outside the urban elite. Askia revived culture and education in Timbuktu and the other cities where it had once flourished under Mali rule. During Askia's reign, African writers began publishing books, including works on history and Islam. But the Songhay Empire eventually fell victim to military attack. Invaders from Morocco, on Africa's northwest coast, defeated Askia Ishaq II near Gao in 1591, leading to the empire's collapse.

By the year 1200 at the latest, kingdoms similar to those in the grasslands had appeared farther south, within and just above the tropical forests of the Guinea region just north of the coast. In the center of the region lay the Akan states in what became known as the Gold Coast (modern Ghana). Farther east lay Yorubaland, and still farther east was the Benin Empire on the Lower Niger River.

Much less is known of these states than of those to the north, because the Arab travelers who wrote about the grasslands states did not enter the forestlands. Except for Benin, Europeans did not penetrate the forestlands until the nineteenth century. Still, a picture of the region can be pieced together for the 1500s, during the early days of European trade with the Guinea coast. The Akan states, going back to the thirteenth century, rested their power on control of the major gold mines of West Africa. Yorubaland to the east could boast of fertile soil and skilled craftsworkers, whose products included sculptures of bronze, terracotta (fired clay), and stone. In the sixteenth century, the Oyo group among the Yoruba people traded surplus food and the works of its artisans northward to the savannah. In exchange the Oyo received horses, which their kings used to build a powerful cavalry for conquering their neighbors. The Oyo state used a number of advanced ideas for creating a strong government in the 1500s. One was to send a group of permanent administrators to run the conquered territories. Another was to give each member of the king's council specific areas of responsibility.

In the Benin Empire farther east, the kings strengthened their rule in the 1400s and 1500s by shifting power from hereditary local chiefs to officials appointed by the kings themselves. Trade grew increasingly important in the 1500s. The king controlled most of it and amassed great wealth. In 1602 a Dutch traveler in Benin's royal city of Ife reported what he saw:

> The town seemeth to be very great, when you enter into it, you go into a great broad street, not paved . . . which goeth right out and never crooks . . . it is thought that street is [three miles long]. . . . When you are in the great street . . . you see many streets on the sides thereof, which also go right forth. . . . The houses in this town stand in good order, one close and even with the other, as the houses in Holland stand. . . .

Other travelers were equally impressed.

## West African Slavery

West Africa, then, was obviously not the primitive, barbaric place that some Europeans claimed in order to justify the Atlantic slave trade. In fact, West Africa and Europe were in many ways at similar stages of development. When they came into contact in the 1400s, and for several centuries afterward, they were about equal in power—some historians claim the African states were stronger. How, then, could the Europeans carry away millions of Africans to the Americas? The answer is that West Africa had both slavery and a slave trade of its own, and its rulers were eager to sell slaves to the Europeans.

Most if not all civilizations have had systems of slavery in their early phases, including Egypt, the Near East, Greece, Rome, China, India, the Islamic world, and Europe. In the West African savannah and tropical forests, slavery emerged after the start of the Iron Age, centuries before the Europeans came into direct contact with West Africa in the 1400s. Slaves were one of the commodities that the West Africans sent north on the trade routes to North Africa, along with gold, ivory, and other goods. A common way of enslaving people in West Africa was through military conquest; soldiers taken prisoner of war were enslaved, as were some civilians of the defeated states. Raids and kidnapping by strong states against weak ones were also employed to obtain slaves. In times of famine, people might become slaves voluntarily just to survive. Sometimes, slavery was a punishment for crime. Most slaves within any West African society, however, came from outside that society.

In West Africa, being a slave did not mean losing all rights. Slaves could marry, own property, and act as witnesses. Also, slaves were not social outcasts. They were adopted into the families that owned them, and they became members of the community. Many slaves were agricultural workers, domestic servants, and rank-and-file soldiers. Some were used as human sacrifices when an important person died. Others, though, held important positions as government officials and military officers. Some slave men married their masters' daughters; more often, slave women married their masters.

The millions of Africans sold to western slave traders experienced a different form of slavery in the Americas. There, slavery became associated with dark skin, which became a permanent badge of inferiority. Color bias meant that even freed slaves in the Western Hemisphere had lower status and fewer opportunities than slaves in Africa.

## ACQUIRING SLAVES FOR THE AMERICAS

The European Age of Discovery began when Portuguese ships started sailing down the West African coast after 1415, seeking a trade route to Asia. In 1441 the Portuguese raided the northwest African coast above the Senegal River in modern Mauritania, bringing a small group of Africans back to Europe as slaves. This was the first time that Europeans had carried African slaves directly from Africa—previously, Europe had received small numbers of African slaves indirectly through the trade across the Sahara Desert into North Africa. During the second half of the fifteenth century, the Portuguese carried back to Europe several thousand African slaves a year, most of whom were used as household workers in Portugal and Spain. Toward the end of the 1400s, though, the growing population there reduced the need for African labor.

After Christopher Columbus arrived in the Americas in 1492, however, a huge new market for African slave labor emerged in the European colonies of the Western Hemisphere. The slave trade from Africa became highly profitable, and traders from most western European nations competed to control it, with their governments' support. The Portuguese dominated the trade until the early 1600s, when the Dutch became the major traders. The English and French controlled the lion's share of the trade in the late 1600s and the 1700s. As the slave trade declined during the 1800s, control came into the hands of Portugal and Brazil, Portugal's former colony.

At first the Portuguese obtained slaves along the West African coast through raids. By the mid-1450s, however, they realized that the African states were strong enough to prevent raiding on a massive scale. From then on, the Portuguese, and later other Europeans, worked in partnership with coastal African rulers. The Europeans gave gifts to these rulers as a kind of payment for the right to participate in the slave trade. With the agreement of the rulers, the Europeans built forts and castles along the coast, where a few Europeans settled to act as middlemen with the Africans.

But Africans ran the trade, selecting the slaves and bringing them to the Europeans' ships. At first, coastal rulers supplied the slaves. But as the European demand grew in the seventeenth and eighteenth centuries, the supply began to come from the interior. Inland rulers acquired slaves in familiar ways: through trade, raids, and war. However, they now did so on a much greater scale than before, because the Atlantic trade was much larger than the traditional slave trade across the Sahara. In exchange for slaves, the Europeans gave them gold, iron, beads, copperware, brassware, alcohol, guns, gunpowder, and many other items.

The inland rulers sent their slaves to the coast. There, the European slave traders, or slavers, collected slaves in two ways. Agents of the larger traders bought slaves from African merchants on the coast and had them ready when their employers' ships arrived. Traders without agents sent their ships along the coast to pick up slaves at various locations until their holds were full, which could take weeks or even months. The great majority of slaves were obtained on the West

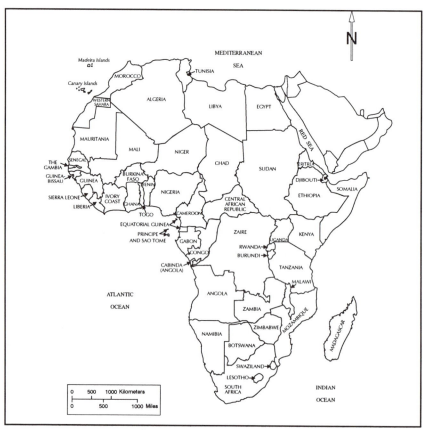

The nations of contemporary Africa.

African coast: from Senegambia (the area between the Senegal and Gambia
Rivers) in the north, to modern Angola in the south. In the nineteenth century,
Portuguese and Brazilian traders brought slaves from the East African coast at
modern Mozambique. The trade was heaviest in Senegambia, in Angola, and in
between along the Guinea coast.

How many captives were carried off from Africa on ships bound for the
Americas? Historians have long debated this question, and estimates have ranged
from less than 10 million to around 15 million. Twelve million is now widely
regarded as a fair estimate. But the number surviving the voyage to the Western
Hemisphere was much lower. A look at the ordeal suffered by the Africans sent
across the Atlantic will show why.

## THE SLAVES' JOURNEY:
## FROM AFRICAN CAPTURE TO AMERICAN LANDING

Before being sent from inland to the coast, the slaves chosen for sale to the
Europeans were chained together to prevent escape. An English observer reported

that they were tied together by leather thongs around their necks and marched in groups of 30 to 40, one behind another, about a yard apart. The forced march to the western shores of the continent normally took weeks, during which the slaves were usually undernourished. Many slaves from the interior highlands quickly caught the unfamiliar diseases of the coastal region, especially malaria. At the shore, they frequently spent weeks in overcrowded enclosures or barracks while waiting for European ships. There they often received spoiled food and contaminated water. When Europeans came, the slaves were brought outside, where every part of their bodies could be carefully examined for defect or disease. Then the Europeans chose which individuals they wanted. Those rejected were sometimes beaten or even killed by their African owners, but most were put into household service in Africa. About two-thirds of those purchased were males, and the great majority were between 14 and 35 years old. The captives were then branded with a hot iron to identify their owners. They were chained together in pairs at the wrist and ankle and had their heads shaved; then, naked, they were rowed out to the slave ships. All the while they were terrified, often believing that the Europeans were red cannibals who were going to eat them.

## On Board the Ships

When the slaves walked onto the ships, many were already ill or malnourished and certainly not fit for the horrors of the ocean voyage, known as the Middle Passage. The women and children were normally left on deck or placed in cabins and generally were free to wander about the ship. Sometimes, though, they were placed in holds below deck. The women were considered fair game for sexual assault by the ships' officers and often the crew as well. Some of those who resisted were beaten to death.

The male slaves were sent below deck to the hold, hundreds of them crowded into a small space. For security reasons, they were chained together and to the ship. A typical hold was five feet high, but it was often divided by a horizontal platform so that the ship could carry more slaves. In such cases, the men occupied a space less than two and one-half feet high. When the hold was six feet high, two platforms were sometimes used, giving the slaves less than two feet of height. According to an eighteenth-century captain of the British Royal Navy, each man was typically allotted a floor space 6 feet long by 16 inches wide. This made it nearly impossible to move. Those women and children who were kept in the holds received less space. All slaves had their hair and nails cut weekly so that they would not injure one another in struggles for floor space. They usually slept on bare wooden boards, unsmoothed by planing; sometimes the rough wood wore their elbows down to the bone.

The men were brought on deck in fair weather to get some air and to be fed. There, the crews forced them to dance, believing it was good for their mental and physical health. Those who refused were lashed, while those who obeyed might have their flesh torn away by the iron shackles around their ankles. In bad weather they had to stay below deck all day, where the air ports used for ventilation were shut to keep out the rain and rough seas, making the hold suffocatingly hot.

Each day the slaves ate two meals. Commonly, one meal consisted of African food and the other of European. The Africans disliked some of the European-style meals so much that they frequently refused to eat them. The inadequate food rations were cut when bad weather or calm seas lengthened the journey; sometimes the sicker slaves were thrown overboard so the crew and remaining slaves could have larger rations. Near the end of the journey, food rations were usually increased to improve the slaves' appearance before they were sold. The slaves received a pint of water a day—a totally insufficient amount, especially in the hot, stifling holds.

Experts on the slave trade used to believe that overcrowding was the major cause of slave deaths during the Middle Passage. Actually, overcrowding was not strongly linked to the rate of death, although it made shipboard life miserable. Major causes of death were undernourishment and malnourishment by virtue of insufficient or contaminated food, which either caused deaths directly or made slaves more vulnerable to disease. Other major reasons for death were dehydration from the inadequate water rations and diseases. Of all the diseases, smallpox—a European illness unknown in Africa—was the biggest killer. Dysentery and various fevers were also common. A less frequent but significant cause of death was suicide. Many slaves suffered from severe depression; some refused to eat, jumped overboard, or hanged themselves. The longer the ocean crossing, the more deaths occurred. The average crossing took about 60 days, but the length of individual voyages varied greatly, depending on the century, the points of departure and arrival, the type of ship, and the weather.

How many captives died during the Middle Passage? The death rate was highest during the 1500s and 1600s, at around 25 percent of all the slaves. The earliest ships were the slowest, with voyages ranging from 40 days to more than 4 months. The ships had been built as cargo vessels, and no adjustments were made for their new task of transporting people. Captains often miscalculated the amount of food and water needed. During the 1700s, the mortality rate declined to between 10 and 15 percent. By then major traders used ships built especially for the slave trade. Treated better before boarding the ships, the slaves could more easily resist disease. Medical care also improved. For example, slaves were sometimes given smallpox inoculations. Much more important, ship captains had learned from experience how much food and water to carry. In the nineteenth century, the death rate fell to around 5 percent. The British navy was trying to eliminate the trade; to escape the naval vessels, slavers used faster ships, which cut travel time and thereby reduced shipboard deaths.

It is impossible to be sure how many of the 12 million African slaves shipped to the Americas died before arrival, but a fair estimate would be around 1.5 million. Many slaves also died in Africa during the forced march to the coast or while imprisoned at the shore. They never became part of the 12 million shipped out, and because they did not appear in written records, their numbers cannot even be

African captives stage a mutiny aboard an eighteenth-century slave ship. Most revolts aboard "slavers" occurred before the ships left the African coast. Judging by the background, that seems to have been the case here.

estimated. But they were victims of the slave trade as surely as those who died aboard ship.

Slave ship crews were afraid of their resentful human cargoes and therefore designed iron shackles, chains, obstructions, and other security measures against slave violence. Every day the sailors searched the holds to make sure the slaves were not gathering pieces of metal or wood. Despite all obstacles, slaves sometimes managed to stage mutinies. Fear of being eaten at the voyage's end gave them a powerful motive to rebel. The majority of mutinies occurred while the ships were still along the African coast, and they happened most often when the slaves were on deck. Male slaves did most of the fighting, but female slaves sometimes participated. Since the women did not wear shackles and were usually free to wander the ship, they were able to offer other forms of assistance. Sometimes they gave the men information about the number of sailors on deck. In some cases, the women helped by stealing weapons. Some mutinies succeeded, especially when the crews were weakened by tropical diseases. But few revolts occurred on the open sea, because the Africans did not have ocean navigating skills.

## Arrival and Sale

When the slave ships finally arrived on American shores, the captives were sold in various ways. Sometimes the slaves had already been bought in Africa on behalf of an individual or a group of individuals and no further sale was necessary. Otherwise, the captain might give the slaves to a factor, who then sold them on a retail basis in exchange for a commission on each sale. When the captain himself sold the slaves, two methods were used. One was by auction, conducted onshore. Usually the unhealthy slaves were sold that way. The healthy slaves were sold in a "scramble." The captain and the purchasers agreed on standard prices for the men, women, boys, and girls. The slaves were brought on deck and the buyers gathered on the dock. At the sound of gunfire, the purchasers charged onto the ship to claim the slaves they wanted. Many of the terrified slaves believed that they were about to be eaten, as they had feared from the beginning.

## SLAVERY IN THE AMERICAS

The first African slaves came to the Western Hemisphere in 1494, just two years after Columbus's first voyage to the Americas. But by 1600, fewer than 300,000 Africans had arrived. During the first century of European settlement, Native American labor was employed more widely than African labor. As a rule, the more American Indians present in an area, the smaller the number of African slaves. Also, the plantation system, which eventually employed large numbers of slaves as agricultural workers, was just emerging. In the mid-1500s, sugar plantations began to appear in the provinces of Bahia and Pernambuco in northeastern Brazil, a Portuguese colony. From then on, Brazil would be a leading importer of African slaves. But the plantation system did not spread widely through the Americas until the 1600s. Many Africans imported in the 1500s were used in Spanish America as assistants and soldiers to the conquistadors and as household servants.

In the 1600s, four or five times more African slaves arrived than in the previous century. One reason was the decimation of the American Indian population. When the Europeans arrived in the 1490s, from 80 to 100 million people lived in the Western Hemisphere. By 1600 the Native American population had declined to around 10 million, an astounding 90 percent decline. European diseases and wars of conquest were the major causes of American Indian deaths. The number of European settlers was not nearly great enough to exploit the economic potential of the Americas, so a new source of labor was sought. Africans were readily available, and they resisted European diseases much better than Native Americans. Also, the demand for labor increased greatly in the 1600s: during the 1500s only Spain and Portugal had made major colonization efforts, but in the 1600s the English, French, Dutch, and other northern European peoples began making serious efforts to establish their own colonies.

The creation of new colonies meant a vast expansion of the plantation system, especially in the Caribbean. On the English island of Barbados, sugar plantations emerged in the 1640s. Soon after, the English colony of Jamaica adopted sugar cultivation, and after 1660 the English islands in the Caribbean exported more sugar than Brazil. These islands soon had a huge number of African slaves. Sugar plantations began to dominate the economies of the French Caribbean islands of Guadeloupe and Martinique in the last decades of the century. The colonies of British North America (later known as the United States) began importing large numbers of African slaves in the late 1600s. The climate was too cold for sugar cultivation, but in Virginia and Maryland, slave labor was used on tobacco plantations, and in Carolina, slaves toiled to produce rice and indigo, the source of a blue dye.

Slave imports peaked in the 1700s. At least 6 million African slaves came to the Americas during that century, around half of all African slaves imported there. The demand grew in most areas where slavery had already taken root. Also, new markets for slaves developed. In 1697 the French acquired the previously Spanish colony of Saint Domingue (later known as Haiti) in the Caribbean. By 1740 it had become the leading sugar producer of the French colonies, which by the mid-1700s were rivaling the English islands in sugar production. During the 1690s, gold was discovered in Minas Gerais and Goias, interior provinces of Brazil. Soon slaves began streaming in to work the mines.

Until the late 1700s, African slavery was not a major part of Spanish America's economy; Spain concentrated on mining in its colonies and used mostly Native American labor. But in the late 1700s, Spain began encouraging sugar cultivation on Cuba in the Caribbean; soon that island was one of the most important slave importers. At the same time, Spain started promoting sugar, indigo, cacao, rice, and cotton plantations in Colombia, Venezuela, and Ecuador. Also, during the 1790s, cotton production began expanding rapidly in South Carolina and Georgia, then the southernmost states of the United States; as a result slave imports, largely suppressed in the era of the American Revolution, experienced a small revival.

For a combination of humanitarian and economic reasons, the slave trade and slavery itself came to an end in the 1800s. The decline began in the 1790s with a slave revolt on Saint Domingue that wrecked its sugar-based economy. Meanwhile, a movement against the traffic in slaves developed in Britain, which banned the trade within its empire in 1807. With British encouragement, most other northern European colonies followed suit. Subsequently, Britain's navy tried to intercept slave ships. The United States abolished the overseas slave trade in 1808. The wars for independence in Spanish America from 1810 to 1825 led to the emancipation of slaves in those colonies that became nations. Britain abolished slavery in its empire in 1834, the French followed in 1848, and the United States emancipated its slaves in 1865, after a bloody civil war.

The major importers of slaves in the nineteenth century were Cuba (a Spanish possession until 1898) and Brazil (which became independent of Portugal in 1822). By the mid-1800s Cuba was the world's leading sugar producer. But emancipation began in 1870 and was virtually completed within 20 years. In the 1830s, coffee plantations were spreading rapidly in Brazil, first around Rio de Janeiro and then farther south in the vicinity of São Paulo. Meanwhile, though, sugar production declined in Brazil's northeast. An antislavery movement grew during the 1880s, and in 1888 Brazil became the last area in the Western Hemisphere to free its slaves.

Of all the African slaves imported into the Americas, 40 percent went to Brazil, more than 40 percent to the Caribbean, 10 percent to the Spanish mainland colonies, and 5 percent to the United States. The highest mortality rates for slaves occurred on the sugar plantations of the Caribbean and Brazil and in the gold mines, particularly those in Brazil. During the sugar harvest, slaves had to work up to 20 hours a day. Gold mining required the slaves to stand in freezing cold water, which led to a quick deterioration in their health. It is no wonder that around 80 percent of all imported slaves went to Brazil and the Caribbean islands: replacement slaves were always needed.

The United States had the lowest slave mortality rate. Because of the cooler climate, disease took a smaller toll than in tropical regions. Unlike the Caribbean, the United States had few absentee landowners, which may have meant better treatment for the slaves. More importantly, while work on tobacco, rice, and cotton plantations in the United States was difficult enough, it was not quite as hard as on sugar plantations. In Brazil and the Caribbean the young, mostly male slaves were simply worked to death on the sugar plantations and replaced by new imports. Because slaves in the United States lived longer, more of them had children. As a result, the United States was the only slave society in the Americas where the slave population increased as a result of births rather than from more importation. Although only about 5 percent of the approximately 12 million African slaves brought to the Americas went to the United States, by 1825 slaves there accounted for more than one-third of all bondpeople in the Western Hemisphere.

No country in the Americas gave slaves reparations upon emancipation. As a consequence, most freed slaves had to become agricultural laborers, sharecroppers, and tenants. They generally became trapped in a cycle of perpetual debt to landowners—who often were their former masters. Entering the mainstream of society was very difficult, more so in the United States than anywhere else. While slaves in the United States probably had the highest living standard and clearly had the lowest death rate in the Americas, that nation also had the strictest color barrier. In Latin America there was a hierarchy of color status; the lighter a person's skin, the higher his or her status. Those who had one African grandparent (quadroons) or one African great-grandparent (octoroons) had more rights than those with more African ancestry. Also, legalized racial segregation never existed in Latin America.

In the United States, all those with visible African ancestry were usually placed in the same category and called, at various times, Negroes, colored people, blacks, Afro-Americans, or African Americans. During most of U.S. history, all were treated as belonging at the bottom of society, with no or few rights. In the late nineteenth century, the southern states began imposing a full-fledged legal system of segregation upon them, covering almost every area of life.

The remainder of this volume will examine the history of people with African ancestry in the United States, from the nation's beginning as British colonies to the mid-1990s. In particular, the focus will be upon the history of their oppression and the political struggle to end it.

# CHAPTER 2

# The Colonial Era: 1619–1763

## VIRGINIA

At the end of August 1619, a Dutch ship from the West Indies arrived at Jamestown, capital of Virginia, the earliest successful English colony in North America. The vessel left behind 20 Africans, the first permanent black residents in what would become the United States. Over the next few decades, more Africans were brought to the colony, but in small numbers. By 1650, the black population was only about 400, compared with nearly 19,000 whites.

The status of most early black arrivals seems to have been the same as that of white indentured servants. These were Europeans who agreed to work in America for a master without pay over a number of years; in exchange, the master paid the cost of their transportation to America. At the end of their terms—which averaged around seven years—the servants became free. The blacks reaching Virginia in 1619 apparently were sold as indentured servants, and records show that as late as 1665, some newly arrived blacks became servants.

A small group of blacks even became landholders after completing their obligations as indentured servants. Richard Johnson arrived in Virginia in 1651 and was an indentured servant for three years. Under Virginia's "headright" system, he received 100 acres of land from the colony for bringing two people into Virginia. A relative of his, Anthony Johnson, not only received 250 acres in 1651 for transporting five people into the colony; he also acquired a black servant named John Casor.

### The Emergence of Slavery

After around 1640, however, indentured blacks found that their status was declining. Their masters were forcing them to work terms of 20 years or longer or, more and more often, for their entire lives. Although slavery had become estab-lished in the Spanish and Portuguese colonies to the south by 1600, the English settlers of Virginia had come to America without any intention of using slave labor. Yet they eventually did just that. Why did it happen?

First, the cultivation of tobacco—the colony's major crop—required large numbers of unskilled laborers. White indentured servants did not completely meet this need. Land was abundant in America; therefore, servants usually could acquire their own farms at the end of their terms instead of continuing to work for their former masters as free laborers. To make matters worse, after 1660 the flow of white servants from England declined as birth rates there went down and wages went up. And of those who did come in the late seventeenth century, many went to new colonies such as Pennsylvania and Carolina. To compensate, the colonists imported more blacks into Virginia—mostly from the West Indies and Africa. The black population increased from 950 in 1660 to 16,000 in 1700. In 1730, blacks numbered 30,000. Thirty years later, the figure was 141,000 (around 41 percent of the entire population), the largest number (though not the highest percentage) of all the British North American colonies.

Second, by around 1640 whites began to realize that black servants were easier to exploit than whites. Uprooted from their native societies, new black arrivals found themselves in an unfamiliar land; furthermore, they came from many different groups and spoke many different languages. Therefore, they were not in a position to resist white authority effectively.

Third, prejudice enabled whites to justify slavery. In most of western Europe, slavery had died out hundreds of years before. But as we have seen, many Europeans believed that the African societies from which blacks came were backward and barbarous. Europeans could convince themselves that while it was wrong to enslave whites, it might be justifiable in the case of an "inferior" people such as blacks.

In sum, masters had the financial motive, the power, and the excuse to manipulate and intimidate blacks into longer service than whites. According to court records, for example, in 1675 a black indentured servant named Philip Cowen complained in court that his master, Charles Lucas, "not being willing that he should enjoy his freedom, did with threats and a high hand and by confederacy with some other persons" force Cowen to sign a 20-year indenture after he had completed his original term. Others were browbeaten into working for still longer terms, until lifetime service became the rule rather than the exception.

Responding to this development, Virginia's legislature began passing laws to define the basic characteristics of slavery and to regulate the conditions under which slaves lived. Slavery in Virginia and elsewhere in Britain's North American provinces had three basic traits that set it apart from indentured servitude: (1) it was lifelong; (2) it was a status that passed from generation to generation; and (3) it was based on race.

A 1661 bill adopted by Virginia's assembly was the first in that colony to legally recognize lifetime service. It declared "that in case any English servant shall run away in company with any negroes who are incapable of makeing satisfaction by addition of time," the English servant must make up the blacks' lost time as well as her or his own. Apparently, the runaway blacks could not make up their lost time because they were already serving for life. By recognizing the existence of such blacks, the law indirectly gave the legislature's approval to lifelong service. The legislature established the hereditary nature of slavery the following year, when it declared that the children of women serving for life would also serve for life.

Soon after, slavery was established on a racial basis. An early justification of enslavement claimed that it was a way of converting "heathens" to Christianity. But a 1667 law stated that baptism would not alter the legal status of slaves—black slaves would remain slaves whether they were heathen or Christian. Legislation of 1670 and 1682 imposed slave status on virtually all blacks arriving in Virginia. No longer would Africans brought to Virginia become indentured servants and eventually become free. A 1670 law barred free blacks from having white servants or slaves.

Clearly, then, slavery had little to do with religious belief and everything to do with race—or, more specifically, with being black. The enslavement of American Indians, members of another nonwhite group, was permitted by the legislature in the 1670s. But Indian slavery was intended mostly for prisoners of war, not for Indians in general. Besides, Virginia abolished Indian slavery in 1691, and it was eventually abolished in all the colonies. Only for blacks, then, was slavery considered the normal condition. With blackness becoming a badge of subordinate status, all blacks—even the shrinking number still free by 1700—came to be regarded as lowly and inferior. And so, for example, in 1692 whites were prohibited from marrying any black, slave or not. Just as prejudice against blacks had helped to create the institution of slavery, so slavery in turn strengthened prejudice against blacks.

## Controlling the Slaves

Meanwhile, legislation defining the specific conditions of slavery was passed. Like the other colonial assemblies, Virginia's legislature defined slaves both as property and as persons. Masters could sell or give away slaves as they wished; it did not matter if this meant the breakup of slave families, which were not legally recognized outside New England anyway. Among the few laws protecting slaves were those requiring masters to provide sufficient food and clothing and prohibiting them from inflicting punishment causing loss of life or limb.

But even the slaves' right to live was seriously qualified. A law of 1669 stated that if a slave was killed while resisting "moderate" corporal punishment by the master—which usually meant whipping—the master could not be charged with a felony. After all, the reasoning went, why would masters intentionally destroy their own property? A 1723 law added a modification: the master could be indicted for murder if one credible witness testified that the killing was intentional. But a white was not likely to testify against another white on such a matter. And even if slaves and free blacks had the courage to testify against slave owners, they could not: a 1705 law prohibited them from giving testimony against whites.

Slaves' lives were threatened from another direction as well. A 1672 law permitted persons pursuing runaway slaves to kill them for resisting seizure. Legislation of 1705 replaced the right to kill such slaves with the right to apply severe physical punishment. But in practice, Virginia's government may still have winked at the killing of runaways. In 1729 the governor's council agreed to pardon a plantation overseer convicted of whipping to death a fugitive slave. The council stated that execution of the overseer would "in all probability stir up the Negro's to a contempt of their Masters and Overseers, which may be attended with dangerous consequences to this colony." In other words, keeping the slaves in fear of their white superiors was more important than protecting their lives.

As the slave population grew, fear of revolts constantly haunted whites, although no major rebellion occurred in colonial Virginia. This fear accounted for many of the laws that regulated the lives of slaves. A 1680 measure limited their movement: to leave the home plantation, a slave needed a signed pass from his or her master. That same year, slaves were prohibited from carrying clubs, swords, or any other weapons (except on the frontier, where the ability to hunt and to defend oneself were matters of survival). An order of the governor's council in 1690 barred militia officers from enlisting blacks. (In emergencies, however, Virginia and other colonies sometimes overlooked such restrictions.)

With the slave population still growing rapidly in the early eighteenth century, new measures to control bondpeople were passed. In 1726 the legislature authorized the militia to break up unusual slave gatherings. An act of 1738 established special patrols of one officer and four militiamen in each county. They were to visit plantation slave quarters and places suspected of hosting illegal slave gatherings.

Whites believed that swift and severe punishment for disobedient slaves was the best way to control them. To accomplish this, the assembly established special courts for slaves accused of crimes punishable by death. These courts had several special features, all to the disadvantage of slave defendants: there was no jury; a confession or the oath of two witnesses was sufficient for conviction; and until 1748 the tribunal of judges did not have to be unanimous to convict. Also, as in most colonies, slaves often received harsher penalties than did free persons for the same crime. To make sure that masters did not try to protect their property by concealing the crimes of their slaves, legislation of 1705 gave owners of executed slaves compensation for their full value.

## Free Blacks

White Virginians, like whites in all colonies, regarded free blacks as a danger to society. Whites complained that they fenced goods stolen by slaves and hid fugitive slaves. Whites feared that in a slave rebellion, free blacks would side with those of their own race. Governor William Gooch stated early in the eighteenth century that free blacks "always did, and ever will, adhere to and favour the slaves."

Whites felt that the fewer free blacks, the better. And since masters rarely had moral reservations about slavery during the colonial period, they did not often free their bondpeople. Of the few they did free, many were their children, born of sexual relations with female slaves—relations usually forced upon slave women. When there was a genuine, mutual relationship between a master and a slave mistress, he sometimes freed her.

Those few masters who wanted to free slaves were hampered by legislation. A 1691 law required masters manumitting (freeing) their slaves to send them out of the colony. After 1723, masters could not free their slaves at all without the permission of the governor and council. Not only did the authorities limit manumission, they even turned it into a weapon for controlling slaves by occasionally freeing one as a reward for "good" behavior. In 1710, for example, the assembly freed a slave named Will for exposing "a conspiracy of divers [various] Negroes for levying war in this colony."

The few free blacks in Virginia—perhaps 1 or 2 percent of the black population in 1750—were actually far from free. Unlike slaves, they had the right to trial by jury and the right to own property. But from 1670 on they could not have white servants, and beginning in 1692 they were barred from marrying whites. During the seventeenth century, free blacks held some minor positions in government. For example, during the 1650s one served as a beadle, who administered corporal punishment at the order of the court. But a law of 1705 barred free blacks from holding public office.

Following reports of a planned slave rebellion, the legislature in 1723 further restricted the rights of free blacks. They lost the right to vote and, with some exceptions, to carry firearms. They were barred from meeting with slaves (although full enforcement clearly was impossible). In the militia they could serve only as musicians and menial laborers. In the legislation establishing special slave patrols, no distinction was made between slaves and free blacks. Thus, the right of free blacks to assemble and to have privacy in their own homes could be invaded whenever the patrols suspected any unusual activities among them. Other laws, too, restricted the rights of free blacks by failing to distinguish between them and slaves, simply referring to "Negroes."

Perhaps even more important than any specific restriction was the fact that whites often assumed that all blacks were slaves; this meant that free blacks always faced the danger of losing what rights they had. For example, if free blacks traveled to areas where they were unknown, they might be challenged to produce the pass required of a slave. In such circumstances in all the colonies, the burden of proof was on free blacks to prove they were free. Some whites took advantage of this situation to enslave free blacks.

In Virginia and the other colonies, furthermore, free blacks were social outcasts. By the end of the seventeenth century, they had little more chance than slaves to associate with whites on an equal basis, and they could achieve only the most limited economic success.

# MARYLAND

Maryland was a tobacco colony like Virginia, and the development of slavery was similar in the two colonies. Maryland was settled in 1633, and by 1640 the black population consisted of both indentured servants and slaves. As in Virginia, the declining supply of white indentured servants increased the demand for black labor in the late seventeenth century. The black population grew from 300 in 1650 to 3,200 in 1700, or nearly 11 percent of the total population, and to 12,500 in 1720, almost 19 percent. By 1760 the proportion was 30 percent.

Legislation passed in 1663 recognized lifetime service, two years later than in Virginia. Beginning in 1664, a series of laws dictated that the status of slavery was inherited. A 1664 law branded as slaves all blacks entering the colony from then on. A 1671 measure assured slaveholders that baptism would not make slaves free—as in Virginia, slavery was to be a matter of race, not religion.

After the basic ground rules concerning who was a slave had been laid down, slave control legislation was passed. A 1692 act prohibited anyone from conducting business with slaves without the master's permission. This was to stop the slaves' practice of stealing their masters' property and then selling or bartering it. A 1695 law required slaves to carry a pass signed by the master or overseer when leaving the master's property. Legislation passed in 1715 imposed a fine on persons entertaining slaves or otherwise keeping them from their masters.

Using the argument that blacks were more "barbarous" (more violent and irrational) than whites, the colonists claimed that special steps had to be taken to control slave crime. To speed up punishment, a 1717 law allowed a single justice of the peace to try slaves accused of minor offenses. In 1729 the assembly argued that blacks, not having a sense of shame, were not deterred from murder by ordinary punishment. Therefore, it provided especially cruel penalties for slaves who either killed a person in authority over them or committed arson. First, the offending slave's hand was to be cut off. Then, the slave would be hanged. Finally, the body would be beheaded, quartered, and displayed in a public place as an example to other slaves. Punishment considered brutal by later standards was applied to whites as well as blacks in the colonial era, but racism and the fear of slave violence made blacks the most common victims of such extreme measures.

Maryland also acted to speed up the trial of slaves accused of crimes punishable by death. Unlike Virginia, Maryland did not set up special courts that deprived slaves of trial by jury. But while others accused of capital crimes had to be tried in the colonywide Provincial Court, beginning in 1751 slaves could be tried in any of the lower county courts.

Possibly reacting to reports of a slave conspiracy in Virginia, Maryland adopted several slave control measures in 1723. Escaped slaves resisting capture could be killed without penalty. Courts were to appoint constables, where needed, to break up "unruly" gatherings of slaves. These constables were to search all places where such meetings might be held. They could administer up to 39 lashes to any slaves away from home without passes from their masters. This provision—which also existed in other colonies—is significant because it gave public officials the right to punish slaves without any trial or hearing. The constables could call upon anyone to assist them, and those refusing could be fined. This provision, too, is significant. It shows that slave control was considered so important that all citizens had a responsibility in the matter. Also in 1723, the assembly made plantation owners responsible for sending home, with a whipping if needed, any visiting slave with no pass.

Until 1752 Maryland had no laws limiting masters' right to free their slaves. And its 1752 law was not nearly as strict as Virginia's. It required that freed slaves be sound of mind and body and be under 50 years old, so that they would not become public burdens. In addition, the law provided that masters on their deathbeds could not free their slaves. Apparently it was feared that they would not use good judgment while they were dying. Maryland seemingly had a higher proportion of free blacks than Virginia. A 1755 census found that free blacks made up about 4 percent of Maryland's black population, about twice as much as in Virginia.

The status of free blacks in Maryland was about the same as in its sister tobacco colony. They could own property and were entitled to a trial by jury. Maryland's law, in contrast to Virginia's, did not prevent free blacks from voting, but since there is no evidence that they actually did vote, it may be that local custom prevented them from doing so. By a 1680 law, free blacks, like slaves, could not serve in the militia. Legislation enacted in 1717 prohibited free blacks as well as slaves from testifying against whites.

A Maryland law of 1715 reveals a great deal about the shaky status of free blacks. It stated that whites held on suspicion of being runaway indentured servants should be released if no one claimed them after six months. Blacks suspected of being runaway slaves, on the other hand, were not to be released. Ultimately, those unclaimed could be sold at auction as slaves to the highest bidder. Free blacks were assumed to be slaves unless they could prove otherwise, and so were always on the brink of enslavement.

## THE CAROLINAS AND GEORGIA

In Virginia and Maryland, slavery evolved gradually from indentured servitude. But it existed from the very beginning in the colony of Carolina (divided into North and South Carolina in 1712) established south of Virginia under a charter from the English king in 1663. The reason was that many of Carolina's founders and early settlers were from the English island of Barbados in the Caribbean, where black slaves had worked on large sugar plantations since the 1640s. In 1663, the year of the charter, Carolina's proprietors offered land to those whites bringing slaves into the colony. Carolina's Fundamental Constitutions of 1669 gave the slave owner "absolute power and authority over his negro slaves."

Like tobacco, Carolina's major crops—rice and the indigo plant, a source of blue dye—required large quantities of cheap labor. Therefore, slaves were imported in great numbers from early on; in the first decade of the eighteenth century, blacks outnumbered whites. In 1760 South Carolina, the area of Carolina most favorable for rice and indigo, had a population of 57,000 blacks, or 61 percent of the total. No other British colony on the North American mainland had a black majority.

The great number of blacks made white Carolinians more fearful of slave plots and revolts than any other colonists in British North America. The situation was even more dangerous because Carolina lay close to both Spanish-controlled Florida and French-controlled Louisiana. If Carolina were invaded from those territories, the slaves—perhaps incited by France and Spain—might rebel. Even in peacetime, slaves sometimes escaped to Florida, and the Spanish usually refused to return them.

Therefore, Carolina adopted extremely oppressive slave control measures. Its 1696 slave code was borrowed from the slave laws of Barbados, which were known for being particularly brutal. North American slave codes generally required masters to provide their slaves with sufficient food and clothing, but the Carolina code contained no such requirements. Slaves who ran away or struck their masters might be subjected to physical punishment such as whipping and branding—or even castration, a powerful symbol that was the ultimate way for whites to show black men that they were impotent, or powerless. On the other hand, a white person who intentionally killed a slave would have only to pay a fine. Carolina's masters gained a reputation for harsh treatment of slaves. That reputation was certainly not altered by this report made by a visitor from Georgia in the mid–eighteenth century:

> Mr. Hill, a dancing-master in Charlestown, whipped a female slave so long that she fell down at his feet, in appearance dead; but when, by the help of a physician, she was so far recovered as to show some signs of life, he repeated the whipping with equal rigour, and concluded the punishment by dropping scalding wax upon her flesh: her only crime was overfilling a tea-cup!

To assure swift and severe justice, Carolina—like Virginia—created special courts for slaves, beginning with the slave code of 1690. When before these tribunals, bondpeople did not receive a trial by jury. In addition, the votes of just three of the court's five members were needed to convict slaves of crimes punishable by death.

In 1720 South Carolina's first major slave rebellion plot was discovered, and some of the participants were hanged or burned to death. Ten years later, reports circulated that another conspiracy had been uncovered. In 1733, the South Carolina assembly questioned a number of slaves believed to be involved in a conspiracy, but the matter was dropped for lack of evidence. Feeling under continual threat of slave rebellion, white South Carolinians strengthened their restrictions on slaves. Charlestown, a haven for runaway slaves, was considered especially exposed to rebellion. A 1721 law applying only to that town authorized watchmen to stop any black; those blacks outdoors after 9:00 P.M. were to be held until the following morning. A 1737 act required blacks on the streets of

Charlestown after 8:00 P.M. in winter and 9:00 P.M. in summer to carry either a lantern with a lighted candle or a pass stating their business.

During the 1720s and 1730s, the assembly passed bills to strengthen the slave patrols in the countryside. Perhaps because of rising fear of a slave revolt, during the 1730s the heads of executed slaves were sometimes displayed publicly to frighten bondpeople. To make sure slaves "knew their place," South Carolina in 1735 adopted a law that apparently was unique in the colonial era. Complaining that some slaves were wearing "clothes much above the condition of slaves," the measure specified that their clothing should be of only the cheapest materials.

In one respect South Carolina law gave slaves opportunities not available in most other colonies. Because of the danger of Spanish and French attack as well as the threat of Indian wars, the colony's militia regulations permitted the recruitment of slaves as combat troops during emergencies. A 1704 law required masters to furnish slaves to the militia when so directed. A more detailed law of 1708 provided that the number of slaves recruited must not exceed the number of whites. But it also stated that any slave who killed or captured an enemy soldier would be freed, and that slaves disabled by wounds suffered in combat would be freed and supported for life from the public treasury. The slaves played their greatest military role in the Yamassee War of 1715, a major Indian conflict that for a while threatened to destroy the colony. Governor Charles Craven reported that 200 slaves were recruited. Militia laws of 1720 and 1739 again permitted the recruitment of slaves.

In 1739 South Carolina experienced the Stono Rebellion, the largest slave revolt in British North America (see "Slave Resistance," page 32). Afterward, the colony's already strict laws were tightened still further. A new slave code of 1740 outlawed slave gatherings, strengthened slave patrols, and banned the sale of alcohol to slaves. It also imposed larger fines upon masters unable to control disobedient slaves and gave larger rewards to slaves who revealed slave conspiracies. Furthermore, it enlisted slaves to deal corporal punishment to other slaves. This made it possible to punish slaves more quickly while also pitting the slaves against one another.

The 1740 code also imposed the death penalty on slaves who fled with intent to leave the colony (and perhaps to aid the Spanish or French). Slaves who ran away within the colony also faced drastic retaliation. Each time a slave tried to escape, the punishment got harsher. For the first attempt, it was 40 lashes and the brand "R" on the left cheek. By the fourth offense, the branding was repeated, the left ear was cut off, and males were castrated. Finally, South Carolina became the only colony (except for Georgia) to outlaw teaching slaves to write.

Free blacks, of course, found no welcome in South Carolina. Beginning in 1722, they had to leave the colony within a year after being freed. Starting in 1740, in reaction to the Stono Rebellion, slaves could be freed only by a special act of the assembly. Free blacks probably accounted for no more than 1 percent of the total black population of eighteenth-century South Carolina. Beginning in 1721, free blacks could neither vote nor hold public office. Racial intermarriage was banned the following year. Stop-and-search regulations imposed on slaves by the pass and patrol laws were also applied to free blacks. And the 1740 slave code brought free blacks under the authority of the special courts established for slaves in 1696.

## North Carolina

North Carolina, settled mostly by Virginians, had a smaller slave population than most of the other southern colonies. In 1760 there were 34,000 slaves, making up 30 percent of the population. Slaveholding was most common in the northeast, a tobacco-growing region, and in the southeast, where rice and the indigo plant were raised. In contrast to Virginia, Maryland, South Carolina, and, later, Georgia, North Carolina did not have many large slave owners. Therefore, the slaveholding class was not as politically powerful there as in those other colonies. Despite that, North Carolina applied many of the same harsh slave regulations.

Laws passed in 1715 and 1741 created special courts for slaves accused of serious crimes. The later law provided for trial by a panel of two justices of the peace and four slaveholding landowners. Like the earlier measure, it made no provision for jury trial. Traditional practice barred blacks—both slave and free— from testifying against whites. A 1746 law confirmed this tradition. Legislation adopted in 1715 created a pass system similar to those of the other southern colonies. Patrols to search slave quarters on a regular basis were created in 1753. As elsewhere, the system of justice was merciless to blacks considered dangerous to the slave system or to society. Legislation passed in 1715 allowed those who killed runaway slaves to escape punishment if they simply swore that they had been acting in self-defense.

North Carolina's laws attempted to keep down the number of free blacks. A 1715 measure required emancipated slaves to leave the colony within six months. A 1723 law provided that free blacks reentering North Carolina would be sold into servitude for seven years. In 1741, masters were prohibited from freeing their slaves on their own. From then on, only slaves performing a special service to society, as determined by the county courts, could be freed. Those manumitted could remain in the colony.

## Georgia

Of the 13 colonies, Georgia was established last. Settled in 1733, it began as a humanitarian project for the resettlement of Englishmen imprisoned for debt. Because Georgia was planned as a society of white small landowners, slavery was banned. In fact, South Carolina, its northern neighbor, had exactly the kind of slave-based social system that Georgia's founders did not want. But as Georgians watched some South Carolinians get rich from slave labor, pressure for permitting slavery in Georgia increased.

The ban on slavery was lifted in 1751. Just nine years later, blacks made up 37 percent of the colony's 9,500 people, and the social order was becoming sharply divided into rich and poor whites, with the slaves at the bottom. Many settlers came in from South Carolina with their slaves. Because of their political influence and because Georgians, like them, feared that the nearby Spanish and French might incite slave rebellions, the colony in 1755 adopted a harsh slave code based largely on South Carolina's 1740 code. It permitted any white to challenge any slave to show a pass and to "moderately correct such slave" if none was produced; if the slave resisted, "such slave may be lawfully killed." The code tried to prevent communication among slaves by making it illegal to teach slaves to write and by prohibiting the use of drums or horns in the slave quarters. The code established special slave courts similar to those in South Carolina. Also as in South Carolina, blacks could be recruited into the militia to help repel attacks from Florida and Louisiana. Those who showed courage in battle were to be freed, but blacks were limited to one-quarter of the total force. In 1757 the legislature established a slave watch in Savannah and patrols in the countryside.

The very few free blacks of colonial Georgia lived in Savannah. The law made little distinction between them and slaves. As in South Carolina after the Stono Rebellion, free blacks were tried before the same special tribunals as bondpeople. Most other laws regulating slaves also applied to free blacks. Furthermore, every free black was required to have a white guardian. But no legal restrictions were imposed upon manumission.

## THE MIDDLE COLONIES

The middle colonies—New York, New Jersey, Pennsylvania, and Delaware—had far fewer slaves than the southern provinces. The reason was that the soil and climate were generally not suitable for plantation crops like tobacco, rice, and indigo; therefore, not as many agricultural laborers were needed as in the southern colonies. Many of the slaves in the middle colonies did perform agricultural labor, usually on small farms. However, many others worked as domestics; in various crafts; in the iron, maritime, and other industries; and as unskilled urban laborers. Despite the relatively small number of slaves in these colonies, slave laws were harsh.

### New York

Founded by the Dutch in 1624, New Netherland had a relatively mild form of slavery under which many bondpeople were freed. The slaves, though they never numbered more than about 600, played an important role in the economy, particularly as agricultural laborers on Hudson Valley estates. After the English conquered the colony in 1664 and renamed it New York, the slave population grew quickly. New York's 16,000 slaves in 1760 made up about 14 percent of the entire populace, the highest proportion in the northern colonies.

Under English rule, the slave laws were in many ways as severe as the regulations in the plantation colonies. Flogging was a mandatory punishment for slaves who committed minor offenses, and towns were required by law to appoint "negro whippers." For theft, the punishment was flogging and branding. For assaulting a white, a slave could be sentenced to any penalty short of death or dismemberment.

In 1712 a short-lived slave rebellion in New York City resulted in the deaths of nine whites (see "Slave Resistance," page 32). The colonial assembly responded by establishing special tribunals consisting of three justices of the peace and five landowners to try slaves charged with crimes punishable by death. The master could ask for a jury trial (since it was his property that might be destroyed), but the slave had no say in the matter. The defense had no right to challenge the jurors or freeholders. Additionally, in order to terrify the slave population, the court could execute convicted slaves in any way it chose. Slaves were sometimes burned to death, impaled, hung by chains to starve, or killed by other frightening methods. Slaves who committed minor crimes (carrying a weapon or assembling illegally, for example) also appeared in special courts, in which one or two justices of the peace issued a verdict without a jury.

As in the South, slaves in New York could not make contracts or testify against whites and were legally barred from owning property. But there and in the other northern colonies, slaves by custom were permitted to acquire and dispose of property—in fact, masters often willed some of their possessions to slaves. The law did not recognize slave marriages. Some were recorded in church registers, but this in no way limited the masters' right to break up slave families. Slaves were prohibited from gathering in groups of more than four (the number was later reduced to three) except when on the master's business.

Although the colony as a whole did not have a pass system, many localities required them; in some areas, anyone could stop slaves and whip those without passes from their master. A number of localities had slave curfews. In New York City, slaves over the age of 14 had to be off the streets by sunset unless accompanied by a member of their master's family. Punishment on the spot, without any court proceeding, was sometimes practiced by local law enforcement officials. In New York City, it apparently was the custom to dunk drunk and disorderly slaves into the harbor and then force them to drink a solution of salt water and lamp oil.

When rumors of slave insurrection circulated in the colony, all bondpeople were in danger. One of the worst slave scares in the colonies was the so-called Negro Plot of 1741 in New York City. First, a series of fires occurred in the fort, the barracks, the chapel, and the governor's house. Then a white servant, Mary Burton, made wild accusations connecting these incidents to a supposed slave plot; finding that she was believed, she named more and more people, black and white. In the climate of hysteria that prevailed, 14 slaves were burned at the stake, 18 were hanged (along with 4 whites), and 72 were deported from the colony. As the panic spread beyond the city, other bondpeople were affected. In Kingston, New York, for example, a slave was hanged for assault, a crime usually punished by flogging.

New York imposed one major restriction on the freeing of slaves. Masters had to post a large bond for each one, the money to be used if the slave became a public charge. This precaution was necessary, the law stated, because "it is found by

# A
# JOURNAL

### OF THE

# PROCEEDINGS

### IN

## The Detection of the Conspiracy

#### FORMED BY

Some *White* People, in Conjunction with *Negro* and other *Slaves*,

#### FOR

### Burning the City of *NEW-YORK* in AMERICA,

#### And Murdering the Inhabitants.

Which Conspiracy was partly put in Execution, by Burning His Majesty's House in Fort GEORGE, within the said City, on Wednesday the Eighteenth of *March*, 1741. and setting Fire to several Dwelling and other Houses there, within a few Days succeeding. And by another Attempt made in Prosecution of the same infernal Scheme, by putting Fire between two other Dwelling-Houses within the said City, on the Fifteenth Day of *February*, 1742 ; which was accidentally and timely discovered and extinguished.

### CONTAINING,

I. A NARRATIVE of the Trials, Condemnations, Executions, and Behaviour of the several Criminals, at the Gallows and Stake, with their *Speeches* and *Confessions* ; with Notes, Observations and Reflections occasionally interspersed throughout the Whole.

II. AN APPENDIX, wherein is set forth some additional Evidence concerning the said Conspiracy and Conspirators, which has come to Light since their Trials and Executions.

III. LISTS of the several Persons (Whites and Blacks) committed on Account of the Conspiracy ; and of the several Criminals executed; and of those transported, with the Places whereto.

### By the Recorder of the City of NEW-YORK.

*Quid faciant Domini, audent cum talia Fures?* Virg. Ecl.

### NEW-YORK:

Printed by *James Parker*, at the New Printing-Office, 1744.

Published in 1744, this book contains the courtroom proceedings and other matters connected to a slave conspiracy scare in New York City in 1741, known as the Negro Plot. "Negro and other slaves" in the book title means slaves of pure African descent and those of partial African ancestry.

Experience, that the free Negroes of this colony are an Idle slothful people." The poverty of free blacks, however, is better explained by the fact that New York, like all of the colonies, treated them as outcasts and fenced them in with numerous restrictions. New York, for example, prohibited free blacks from owning real estate, a severe limitation in an era when farming was the most common occupation. Many of the slave laws applied to all people of African descent; therefore, free blacks found themselves hemmed in by many of the same limitations on movement, assembly, and other freedoms that restricted the slaves.

## New Jersey

In New Jersey, separate governments in the east and west existed from 1675 until the unification of the colony in 1702. West Jersey was controlled by Quakers who had misgivings about slavery, and the fundamental law of that colony stated that all residents should be as far as possible "free from oppression and slavery." That did not stop the importation of slaves. But during most of New Jersey's colonial history, slaves were much less numerous in western New Jersey than in the eastern half. Overall, some 6,600 blacks constituted about 7 percent of New Jersey's population in 1760.

New Jersey's slave laws rivaled New York's in their harshness. In 1695 special slave tribunals were established in East Jersey; in 1713 a separate system like New York's was established for all of New Jersey. (It was abolished in 1768.) As in New York, these courts could impose especially painful methods of execution to terrorize the slave population, and in 1735 and 1741 slaves were burned to death for committing arson. Slave gatherings could not exceed five people. A 1704 law stated that for small thefts, blacks must pay with 40 lashes; for larger thefts, the punishment was 40 lashes and branding with a "T." In the same year, castration was specified as a punishment for some crimes. As in New York, masters were required to post large bonds for each slave they freed, and free blacks were not permitted to own real estate.

## Pennsylvania and Delaware

The colony of Pennsylvania was established in 1682 by William Penn, a leading English Quaker. An enlightened man in many respects, Penn believed in freedom of religious conscience and in fair dealing with the Indians. But unlike some of his fellow Quakers, he did not object to slavery. In fact, in 1685 he told the steward of his Pennsylvania estate to use slaves instead of indentured servants, "for then a man has them for life." Slaves apparently resided in Philadelphia as early as 1684. In 1720, the slave population in Pennsylvania, concentrated in Philadelphia and vicinity, numbered around 2,000, or between 6 and 7 percent of the whole population. By 1760 blacks were only about 2.5 percent of the overall population. The decline resulted partly from a large inflow of British and German servants after 1720.

Pennsylvania's slave laws were about as severe as those of New York and New Jersey. An act of 1700 was the colony's first statute to acknowledge slavery. The law established special juryless courts for slaves and imposed harsher penalties on slaves than on free persons. Slaves could be executed for murder, burglary, or the rape of white women, while free people could be executed only for murder. Twenty-five years later, the colonial assembly prohibited bondpeople from traveling more than 10 miles from home, required them to be at home after 9:00 P.M., and barred them from meeting in groups of more than 4. These restrictions could not always be enforced, but their existence indicates as much disregard for the rights of slaves as in the southern colonies. For major theft, culprits received 39 lashes and a "T" brand on the face, just as in New Jersey, but in Pennsylvania they could also be deported out of the colony.

The laws of Pennsylvania were not friendly toward free blacks either. Unlike New York and New Jersey, Pennsylvania did not bar them from owning real estate. However, they were judged by the same special courts as were slaves and suffered the same discriminatory penalties. Free blacks had to carry passes proving their free status. The law declared that a free black who should "loiter and mispend his or her Time" could be bound out as an apprentice, making free blacks a source of unpaid labor. (In the nineteenth century, some of the states passed similar laws.) Worse, those breaking the law by marrying whites could be sold by a court into slavery; other crimes considered serious could result in the same fate. Free blacks did not even have control over their own children; the law provided for the binding out of their offspring as indentured servants until the age of 24 (for males) or 21 (for females), another method for obtaining free labor that was to be used more widely in the next century.

Originally part of Pennsylvania and known as the Lower Counties, Delaware was given its own legislature in 1702. Its black population was greater than Pennsylvania's. By 1710 there were some 500 blacks out of 3,600 people (14 percent); in 1760, Delaware's 1,700 blacks made up only 5 percent of the whole, but that was still twice Pennsylvania's percentage. This tiny colony's slave code did not differ sharply from those of the other middle colonies.

## NEW ENGLAND

In New England the institution of slavery appeared very soon after European settlers arrived. In Massachusetts, founded in 1630, slavery existed as early as 1638, and the first law recognizing slavery was passed in 1641. (A law of 1670 extended the status of slavery to the children of slaves.) In Connecticut, first settled in the mid-1630s, slaves were already present in 1639. New Hampshire, settled in the late 1630s, had slavery by 1645. In Rhode Island, founded in 1636, slavery may have taken longer to emerge, but a 1652 law banning it soon proved completely ineffective.

Although slavery established itself quickly in New England, it never developed deep roots in the region. For one thing, the stony soil was not favorable for large-scale agriculture. For another, the Puritans who settled New England were a close-knit group suspicious of all outsiders. So even though Boston's merchants were the leading North American slave traders in the seventeenth century—to be over-taken in the eighteenth by the traders of Newport, Providence, and Bristol, all in Rhode Island—New Englanders did not actually buy many slaves for themselves.

In 1715 about 158,000 whites and 4,200 blacks lived in New England. On the eve of the American Revolution, blacks numbered 16,000 out of 659,000 persons, or 2.4 percent of the population. Rhode Island had the greatest proportion of blacks, more than 6 percent. In Connecticut the proportion was just above 3 percent, in Massachusetts just under 2 percent, and in New Hampshire around 1 percent. As in the middle colonies, many of the slaves worked as domestics, laborers, and craftsmen. They dwelled mostly in and around towns and cities, but in eastern Connecticut and the Narragansett Bay area of Rhode Island, some large agricultural estates had as many as a few dozen slaves.

## The Rights of Blacks

Slaves in New England had more rights than elsewhere. The region's judicial system was fairer to them. In almost all cases, slaves were tried in the same courts as whites and had the right to a bill of indictment, the right to a jury trial, the right to challenge jurors, and the right to testify against whites. (It appears, however, that no blacks served on juries.) When slaves were convicted of crimes, punish-ment was most often, though not always, based on the crime itself and not on race or condition of servitude.

Slaves had the right to file suits—even to sue their masters for excessive punishment, which some slaves did. Slaves could legally acquire, hold, and transfer property. Frank, a slave belonging to Silas Carpenter of Providence, Rhode Island, bought a piece of land from Ephraim Carpenter in 1694. They could also make contracts. In Massachusetts, John Saffin and his slave, Adam, made a written agreement in 1694 giving Adam his freedom on condition of six more years of loyal service. Slave marriages were not only legal but encouraged. As with free persons, slave spouses could not be compelled to testify against each other.

## The Oppression of Blacks

But slaves faced many of the same oppressive conditions, restrictions, and punish-ments found elsewhere. Although slave marriages had legal standing, masters still had complete freedom to break up slave families by sale or gift. Special slave curfews were imposed everywhere. A Connecticut law of 1690 required slaves to be off the streets by 9:00 P.M. Nine o'clock curfews were also passed in Massachu-setts in 1703, in Rhode Island the same year, and in New Hampshire in 1714. Restrictions were more severe where blacks were most numerous. In 1742 Boston, which then was home to about one-third of the blacks residing in Massachusetts, barred slaves from Boston Common after sunset. In 1705, Massachusetts imposed a severe whipping on any slave who struck a white person. In Connecticut, the mere threat to strike a white meant a flogging. As elsewhere, New England slaves who committed crimes considered especially serious were sometimes punished brutally. Some convicted of arson, for example, were burned to death.

The very nature of slavery meant that bondpeople had to receive special punishment. For some crimes free people paid fines; but slaves, most of whom had little or no wealth, paid with a flogging. So in New England, as in the other colonies, slaves endured corporal punishment more often than free people.

Rhode Island had the most severe slave laws in New England, probably because it had the highest proportion of slaves. There, special courts were established to try slaves accused of stealing, one of the few examples of special slave courts in New England. The wealthy town of South Kingstown, Rhode Island, which was about one-third black in 1755, had among the harshest regulations in the region. To prevent conspiracies among blacks, a 1718 regulation stated that if a slave was found in the home of a free black, both were to be whipped. In 1723 all outdoor social gatherings of blacks were banned.

The social barriers between the races were as strong in New England as anywhere. Although their slave regulations were relatively mild, the Puritans believed that blacks were an inferior race and that slavery was a punishment for sin. Racial intermixture was offensive to them; one reason they favored slave marriages was to strengthen separation of the races. In the region, only Massachusetts actually banned racial intermarriage. But in all of New England, adultery was punished more severely when a white and a black were involved.

As in the other regions, free blacks in New England did not receive treatment equal with whites. The laws often lumped them with slaves so that curfews and other restrictions applied to them. Free blacks were taxed, but there is no evidence that they voted until after the Revolution. New England alone had public schools in the colonial era, but free blacks apparently could not attend them. In South Kingstown, they could not own livestock; in Boston they could not own pigs. Everywhere their employment opportunities were limited, partly because of the hostility of white laborers and artisans. And although exclusively black ghettos did not emerge until the late nineteenth century, free blacks were forced to live in the worst parts of town—near the docks, along the rivers, and in the alleys.

## SLAVE RESISTANCE

Even in its relatively mild New England form, slavery was a thoroughly oppressive system. Slaves had to endure a lifetime of unpaid service. They were at the mercy of their masters; the law hardly ever intervened to protect them. Slaves could be sold or given away at any time; a slave who had spent a lifetime in one place might suddenly be sent to a strange, distant location, far from family and friends. And slaves knew that in all probability their children would suffer the same fate.

Slaves had no vote and thus no representation; they were completely outside the colonial political system and had few white sympathizers within it. And so, although they occasionally petitioned the colonial legislatures for relief, slaves usually had to act outside the political process to improve their lot. Their efforts took many different forms, the most extreme being violent rebellion.

Around midnight or one o'clock on the night of Sunday, April 6, 1712, about two dozen slaves gathered in an orchard in New York City, seeking freedom and revenge against their masters. They were armed with guns, pistols, knives, swords, axes, and other weapons. The plotters were led by Akans from West Africa's Gold Coast, who were known for their great physical bravery. (The British called them Cormantees.) After two of them, known to us only as John and Cuffee, created a decoy by setting fire to a building, they all hid. When people came to put out the fire, the slaves attacked, killing nine whites and wounding seven. Escaping whites, however, spread word of the revolt. Soon, Governor Robert Hunter fired the guns of the city's fort to call the citizens to arms and then sent out a detachment of troops. By the end of the day, all of the rebels had either been captured or committed suicide.

The most serious slave uprising of the colonial era was the Stono Rebellion in South Carolina. Before dawn on Sunday, September 9, 1739, around 20 slaves met near the western fork of the Stono River, less than 20 miles from the capital of Charlestown (later spelled Charleston). Led by a slave named Jemmy, they broke into a storehouse and stole guns, ammunition, and other military supplies. They then began to move southward on the road to Georgia and St. Augustine, the capital of Spanish Florida. Along the way they attacked whites, killing 10, and burned buildings. Apparently, they were trying to damage the slave system while escaping to Spanish-controlled territory.

As they marched, some slaves willingly joined them; others were forced to join so that they would not report the uprising to the authorities. By 11:00 A.M. their number had grown to more than 50. But then they had a stroke of bad luck. By pure coincidence, Lieutenant Governor William Bull, riding on horseback, came within sight of the rebels. After seeing them, he rushed to spread the alarm. At around 4:00 P.M. the slaves were attacked by a force of armed whites. Many slaves died, and others fled. Over the next week, most of the fugitives were captured, but some remained free for months. All told, from 20 to 25 whites died; the black death toll was at least twice that, including those who were executed.

From New England through Georgia, slave conspiracies were frequently reported. Some were real and others were imagined by fearful whites. Few reached the stage of actual armed revolt. But slaves found many other ways to resist bondage. Arson was one form of violence used by slaves. Other individual acts of violence against whites occurred regularly. In 1729 a slave in Marlborough, Massachusetts, was hanged for killing his owner and her two children. Six years later, the Scarlett family of Pennsylvania died after a slave put ratsbane in a skillet of chocolate. In South Carolina a slave named Dolly poisoned her master. Cases of poisonings were not unusual, possibly because in West Africa a class of women and men had special knowledge of how to use herbs as medicine. In America, these specialists were sometimes described as doctors by their masters. (They were also called obeahs, from the Akan word *obayifo*, or witch.) Apparently, some of them used their expertise to retaliate against whites.

Running away was the most common form of resistance to slavery. Almost every issue of most colonial newspapers carried advertisements for fugitive slaves. Among the most common reasons for flight were harsh punishment and a desire to rejoin family and friends after having been sold to a distant place. Slaves often overcame monumental obstacles and took great risks to escape. A New York City newspaper observed that slaves sometimes returned to their old neighborhoods from as far away as Virginia or South Carolina. During 1764 in Georgia, a 16-year-old runaway girl was captured and handcuffed, yet she escaped again. A slave in Pelham Manor, New York, fled with his wife and four children, although bringing them with him greatly increased his chance of being captured. Some slaves chose death over captivity. One who escaped from Coventry, Rhode Island, was about to be captured when, it was reported, he "cut his own throat and soon after expired."

Probably more than two-thirds of all fugitives were men. Women slaves were not often given tasks that took them off the plantation, and so they were less familiar with the surrounding terrain than were the men. Also, since the women nursed their children and provided most of their care, they were more reluctant than the men to leave the children behind; furthermore, they realized that taking their children would greatly reduce the chance of successful escape. Many women tried a middle way between becoming fugitives and staying at home. When feeling a desire to escape the plantation—just after or before a whipping, for example—they fled for short periods of time, remaining in the neighborhood, and then returned.

Some slaves, like the Stono rebels, sought freedom by escaping the British colonies entirely and going to Native American communities, to French Canada, or to Spanish Florida. In 1738 news spread that Spain was granting freedom to any slaves from British America who reached Florida. In November of that year, a group of more than 60 slaves fled from Port Royal, South Carolina, and made it to Spanish territory.

Unskilled agricultural workers, or field hands, may have been the most oppressed slaves, but they were not the only ones to attempt flight. Skilled artisans and craftspeople, with a higher standard of living and more freedom than plantation workers, were just as interested in escape. The authorities knew that any slave might take any chance to flee. That was the reason for the pass system and for the patrols not only on plantations but on the coast and frontier.

Stealing was common, which is why the colonies prohibited free people from trading with slaves. Some slaves intentionally damaged their masters' farm equipment or personal property. Others verbally abused their masters. Passive types of resistance—such as working slowly and carelessly, "misunderstanding" instructions, and pretending to be ill or insane—were often used. These methods were safer than open defiance because the risk of punishment was less.

Some masters gave their slaves the chance to hire themselves out during their free time; slaves paid fees to their masters and kept whatever else they earned. The eagerness with which many slaves took this opportunity showed their desire to escape the tight restrictions of slavery. Often, slaves hired themselves out without their masters' knowledge, perhaps neglecting their assigned tasks in doing so. With the money they earned, slaves sometimes bought their freedom. Then, they frequently continued to save money so they could buy their wives, children, and friends out of slavery.

## ANTISLAVERY ACTIVITY

In 1700 Samuel Sewall, a prominent Massachusetts judge, wrote a tract called *The Selling of Joseph*. In it he condemned slavery, stating: "It is most certain that all Men, as they are the sons of *Adam*, are Co-heirs, and have equal right unto Liberty, and all other outward Comforts of Life."

However, white opposition to slavery during the colonial period was very rare. Except for Sewall, almost all antislavery activity—until near the end of the colonial era—came from a Protestant denomination called the Society of Friends. The Society's members, whom outsiders called Quakers, were known for their support of humanitarian reforms.

In 1688 Quakers in Germantown, Pennsylvania, drew up the first antislavery appeal in British North America. "There is a saying," they wrote,

> that we should do to all men like as we will be done ourselves; making no difference of what generation, descent, or colour they are . . . to bring men hither, or rob and sell them against their will, we stand against. . . . Ah! do consider well this thing, you who do it, if you would be done at this manner— and if it is done according to Christianity!

But even most Quakers did not agree with their Germantown brethren at that time. However, antislavery views spread among Quakers in the early 1700s, thanks to the work of individuals including Elihu Coleman of Nantucket, Rhode Island; Benjamin Lay of Abington, Pennsylvania; and especially John Woolman, a farmer and tailor from Mount Holly, New Jersey. Their arguments all came down to one simple principle: that all persons are equal under God—or, as Woolman wrote, "Did not He who made us make them?"

Under the influence of such people, the Society of Friends began to act against slavery. Leading the way was the Philadelphia Yearly Meeting, which had authority over Pennsylvania and New Jersey, the colonies with the most Quakers. In 1715 it condemned the slave trade and warned Friends not to participate in it. Progress was slow, and not until 1730 did the Meeting warn against buying slaves imported by the traders. In 1758 it finally called upon all Pennsylvania and New Jersey Quakers to free their slaves.

Other meetings followed Philadelphia's example. The Virginia Meeting condemned the slave trade in 1722 and in 1740 instructed its members not to participate in slave patrols. In 1760 the New England Yearly Meeting condemned the slave trade, and in 1773 it asked the Quakers of that region to free their bondpeople. The New York Meeting called for emancipation in the 1770s, as did the Maryland, Virginia, and North Carolina Meetings.

For most of the colonial period, Quakers stood almost alone in their condemnation of slavery. That began to change in the 1760s, when the colonists launched a struggle with Britain over colonial rights that led to the American Revolution.

# CHAPTER

# The Era of the American Revolution: 1764 – 1820

## FREEDOM, SLAVERY, AND THE AMERICAN REVOLUTION

U ntil the 1760s, Britain did not interfere greatly with the affairs of its American colonies; it hoped that they would simply grow and prosper on their own. But after defeating France in the Seven Years' War (1756–1763), the mother country decided to strengthen its control over its possessions and obtain more revenue from them. Beginning in 1764, Britain adopted tax laws and other measures to achieve these goals.

The colonists were alarmed. Influenced by English Whig and European Enlightenment philosophers, they believed that certain rights belonged to all (or at least all white men) by birth; they sometimes called these rights "natural rights." Among them was freedom, or the right of persons to control their own destiny. Britain's rulers, they feared, wanted to deprive them of their freedom. Many colonists expressed this fear by stating that the mother country wished to impose "slavery" upon them. As early as 1764, for example, Virginia political leader Richard Bland warned that British interference in colonial affairs could leave the colonists as bad off as "galley slaves in Turkey or Israelites under an Egyptian bondage." Five years later George Washington helped write the Virginia Resolves, which charged England with "endeavoring . . . to fix the shackles of slavery upon us."

Some of the colonists who denounced Britain's attempts to "enslave" them began to see a contradiction between their defense of freedom and their ownership of slaves. In 1768, a letter to a Philadelphia newspaper asked, "How suits it with the glorious cause of Liberty to keep your fellow men in bondage, men equally the work of your great Creator, men formed for freedom as yourselves." Six years later, a Massachusetts man exclaimed, "Blush . . . ye trifling patriots! who are making a vain parade of being for the liberties of mankind, who are thus making a mockery of your profession by trampling on the sacred rights and privileges of Africans." From New England as far south as North Carolina, many colonial leaders condemned slavery. Benjamin Rush of Pennsylvania assailed it in *On Slave-Keeping* (1773), as did Thomas Jefferson of Virginia (a slave owner himself) in *A Summary View of the Rights of British America* (1774) and the Reverend Samuel Hopkins of Rhode Island in *A Dialogue Concerning the Slavery of Africans* (1776).

In the early colonial era, slaves had occasionally petitioned for their freedom. But as the Revolution approached, they realized that white opposition to slavery was growing and so began petitioning more often. In January 1773, a group of Massachusetts slaves petitioned the governor and legislature in highly emotional terms, observing that neither they nor their children would ever be able "to possess or enjoy any Thing, no not even *Life itself,* but in a manner as the *Beasts that perish.* We have no Property! We have no Wives! No Children! We have no City! No country!" Some slaves used the colonists' own language (for example, referring to "natural rights") in an effort to influence them. In May 1774 another group of Massachusetts slaves wrote: "Your Petitioners apprehind we have in common with all other men a naturel right to our freedoms without Being depriv'd of them by our fellow men as we are a freeborn Pepel and have never forfeited this Blessing by aney compact or agreement whatever."

In addition to their appeals, blacks could point to their contributions to the American cause. The story of Crispus Attucks is one of the earliest and best-known examples. Attucks ran away from his master in Framingham, Massachusetts, in 1750 and subsequently worked as a seaman on ships out of Boston harbor. In March 1770 he took center stage in the struggle between Britain and her North American colonies. The stationing of British troops in Boston had aroused great resentment among the populace. On March 5, Attucks led a crowd of Bostonians who challenged Captain Thomas Preston and the British soldiers under his command. Several soldiers fired into the crowd. Attucks apparently was the first to fall; he and four others died, and Attucks soon was hailed as an American who had sacrificed himself for the cause of liberty.

Would white Americans—faced with their own condemnations of bondage, black appeals for freedom, and black involvement in the American cause— translate their antislavery words into deeds? There was some evidence that they would. As early as 1767, a bill to abolish slavery was introduced in Massachusetts. In 1771 and 1774, bills banning the slave trade were passed by the Massachusetts legislature but were vetoed by the British governor. Rhode Island and Connecticut, the only colonies that chose their own governors, limited the slave trade in 1774. That year the Continental Congress called for a halt of slave imports and a boycott of merchants who continued to import them. True, this was part of a general economic boycott aimed at influencing Britain's colonial policy. But in 1776 Congress removed the prohibition on most imports while keeping the ban on slaves, indicating that the embargo on the slave trade was based on a higher principle than simply placing economic pressure on Britain. Finally, 1775 saw the creation in Philadelphia of the Society for the Relief of Free Negroes Unlawfully Held in Bondage, the first antislavery society in the colonies.

But whites were far from unanimous on the subject of slavery. Thomas Jefferson's Declaration of Independence (1776) made a ringing statement: "We hold these truths to be self-evident, that all men are created equal, that they are endowed by their Creator with certain unalienable Rights, that among these are Life, Liberty and the pursuit of Happiness." To some white Americans, this was an antislavery statement. But others disagreed. Jefferson's first version of the Declaration accused Britain's King George III of having forced a cruel slave trade upon the United States. But the delegates to the Continental Congress from South Carolina and Georgia—where slavery was most profitable—objected; they believed that to condemn the slave trade suggested criticism of slavery itself. The condemnation was omitted in the Declaration's final version.

Not only were white Americans divided over slavery, racism was already deeply ingrained in their thinking. Therefore, they had to decide not only whether blacks should be slave or free, but whether free blacks should have the same rights as whites. And so the decades during and just after the American Revolution were very important in shaping the destiny of blacks in the United States.

## THE REVOLUTIONARY WAR

Before examining how far white Americans would go in applying to blacks their Revolutionary-era enthusiasm for freedom, we should survey the impact on blacks of the American Revolution itself. As the war went on, more and more blacks became involved in the fighting. By the end of the conflict, the lives of thousands of them had been reshaped.

During the Revolution's first two years (1775–1776), only a few blacks served in the state forces and in George Washington's Continental Army. Americans were reluctant to put guns in the hands of slaves. Also, most white Americans believed that blacks lacked the courage and discipline to make good soldiers. On July 9, 1775, an order issued from General Washington's headquarters prohibited the recruitment of blacks into the army. (Those already serving could remain.) A gathering of Washington and his top officers on October 8, 1775, confirmed this policy.

But on November 7, 1775, Lord Dunmore, the British governor of Virginia, issued a proclamation that shocked Americans by offering freedom to all slaves who would join his forces. Soon, slaves were flocking to British lines. They were organized into a unit known as Lord Dunmore's Ethiopian Regiment. By December 1, 300 slaves were in uniform, wearing sashes reading "Liberty to Slaves." When Dunmore's fleet left Virginia's waters for New Jersey in August 1776, about 800 slaves had reached his forces.

Dunmore's proclamation persuaded General Washington to reverse partially the Continental Army's recruitment policy. To keep free blacks from going to the enemy, in December 1775 he authorized his recruiters to enlist them. During the same month, Virginia's Revolutionary legislature offered a pardon to any slave returning from Dunmore's camp. Suddenly, white Americans found that their struggle for freedom was forcing them to compete with the British for the loyalty of blacks.

However, it was not until mid-1777 that blacks were allowed into the army and the state militias in significant numbers; at that time, growing shortages of manpower forced a change of policy. To fill their Continental Army quotas, the New England states began seriously recruiting free blacks. In 1777 Connecticut's legislature permitted the recruitment of slaves. Rhode Island proposed recruiting an all-slave black regiment for the army in 1778, and Washington gave his approval. During that year, Massachusetts began mustering slaves. In 1779 the Continental Congress approved the enlistment of bondmen.

By the end of 1780, most of the northern states and Maryland were recruiting not only free blacks but slaves, many of whom received their freedom for enlisting. Officially, Virginia accepted only free blacks, but in reality slaves were mustered as well. Delaware and North Carolina followed policies similar to Virginia's, admitting free blacks and, occasionally, slaves. Only South Carolina and Georgia refused to enlist any blacks at all.

Meanwhile, in 1779, British commander in chief Henry Clinton repeated Lord Dunmore's offer of freedom in exchange for military service. Southern slaves went over to the British standard by the thousands. During the war, British ships leaving the United States carried off some 20,000 blacks.

On the American side, blacks both slave and free served not only in the Continental Army but also in the Continental Navy and the state navies. Because blacks had been employed in fishing fleets, on coastal vessels, and in the British Royal Navy during the colonial period, they were accepted more readily into the naval services than the army. They even served in the South Carolina and Georgia navies. There and in Virginia and Maryland, blacks commonly were used as pilots. Blacks were also accepted for service on privateers—privately owned vessels commissioned by American authorities to harass British shipping.

Both armies usually assigned blacks to menial tasks like working as orderlies, waiters, cooks, teamsters, foragers, and drum or fife players. In the Continental Navy, blacks usually held the lowliest positions, working as captains' boys and powder boys (carrying powder to the guns).

When blacks got a chance to serve in combat roles, they disproved racist stereotypes by fighting with bravery and skill. Some fought on the patriot side at the battle of Lexington and Concord (April 19, 1775), the first armed conflict of the war. One was Peter Salem, a freeman in a company of minutemen from Framingham, Massachusetts. At the battle of Bunker Hill (June 17, 1775) were Bazillai Lew and Salem Poor. Poor, a freeman in the Massachusetts militia, fought with such bravery that 14 officers present during the battle signed a petition urging the state legislature to reward him. Prince Whipple, a slave from New Hampshire, was one of George Washington's oarsmen in the famous crossing of the Delaware River on December 25, 1776.

Jack (or Tack) Sisson was among 40 volunteers who captured British major general Richard Prescott near Newport, Rhode Island, in July 1777. He steered one of the boats there and then broke down the door of Prescott's house while the other soldiers surrounded it. Edward Hector was one of the few blacks to serve in an artillery unit. During a retreat at the battle of Brandywine (September 1777), he braved enemy fire to gather up some of the arms left by his comrades and to save his own ammunition wagon. At Henry's Point, Virginia, in 1781, a slave named George Latchom helped Colonel John Cropper slow down a British advance, which enabled the Virginia militia to retreat. Then, when Colonel Cropper became trapped in a marsh as the British approached, Latchom pulled him out and carried him away. In gratitude, Cropper bought Latchom from his master and then freed him.

The all-black First Rhode Island Regiment of the Continental Army was formed in 1778. Later that year in the battle of Rhode Island, it turned back three assaults by Hessian troops, inflicting heavy casualties on them. Another all-black group was a Massachusetts unit called the Bucks of America, but little is known about it. In 1779 French forces helped the Americans in fighting around Savannah, Georgia. Part of the French contingent was a brigade called the Volunteer Chasseurs, made up of 545 blacks from the French colony of Saint Domingue (later Haiti).

Some blacks, not officially in either side's forces, fought as irregulars. A man named Tye worked for the British in and around Monmouth County, New Jersey. He led a band of about 25 whites and blacks that made raids against the Americans. Some blacks operated as spies. James Armistead Lafayette spied on Benedict Arnold's camp at Portsmouth, Virginia, after Arnold had gone over to the British. A double agent, Lafayette worked for the Americans but convinced the British he was working for them. A free black named Benjamin Whitcuff spied for the British in New Jersey for two years before he was caught. Finally arrested by the Americans and sentenced to be hanged, Whitcuff was saved by British troops at the last minute, when he was already swinging from the rope!

The Revolutionary War gave some blacks the opportunity to win their freedom and to display their valor and skill. But those freed were only a small fraction of the black population, and the number of blacks given a chance to fight was too small to make a major dent in white prejudice. In the long term, the ideas behind the Revolution changed black lives much more than did the war itself.

## THE NORTH

During the era of the American Revolution, all of the northern states adopted measures against the slave trade and took steps to abolish slavery. Of course, the northern economies had always been much less dependent on slavery than those of the South. And at the end of the colonial period, that dependence was declining as large numbers of European immigrants arrived at northern ports. Yet slavery was still profitable for those who owned slaves, and the influence of Revolutionary ideals was crucial to the emancipation of bondpeople in the North.

The American colonies—and, after independence, the states—began to restrict the slave trade in the 1770s. By the late 1780s, each northern state had barred the importation of slaves into its ports for sale (although not all of them prohibited their citizens from importing slaves into other states or elsewhere in the Western Hemisphere).

Some northern states also softened some of the harsher features of slavery. In 1779 Rhode Island banned the sale of slaves out of state without the slaves' consent. In 1780 Pennsylvania required that slaves be tried in the same courts as whites (although slaves still could testify only against other slaves). In 1788 the state prohibited slave sales that would separate family members by more than 10 miles. During the same year, New York gave slaves the right to a jury trial in cases involving crimes punishable by death. At the same time it abolished the terroristic penalties applied in colonial times, such as burning at the stake; slaves tried for major offenses would now receive the same punishment as whites. Also in 1788, New Jersey outlawed the selling of slaves outside the state without their approval, gave blacks the same rights in court as whites, ended the system of harsher punishments for slaves, and required masters to teach their slaves to read by age 21.

Yet far more important were the measures taken in all northern states to end slavery. Most of the states decided to postpone a decision on emancipation until after the Revolution. One exception was the newly created state of Vermont, whose 1777 constitution abolished bondage. Another was Pennsylvania, which in February 1780 adopted a law providing for the gradual abolition of slavery. It actually represented a compromise with the slaveholders: no slave then alive was freed by the measure, but all slaves born after passage of the act would become free at age 28.

After the Revolutionary War, the pace of emancipation picked up. In 1783, Massachusetts chief justice William Cushing, ruling in a suit brought by slave Quork Walker against his master, ruled that "the idea of slavery is inconsistent with . . . [the Massachusetts] constitution . . . and there can be no such thing as perpetual servitude of a rational creature." The decision was based on the assertion in the state's 1780 constitution that "all men are born free and equal." Recognizing from then on that the state's courts would rule favorably on freedom suits brought by slaves, masters often did not even challenge such suits. The upshot was that by 1790, there were no slaves remaining in Massachusetts.

The 1783 New Hampshire state constitution declared that "all men are born equal and independent" and have natural rights, "among which are enjoying and defending life and liberty." As in Massachusetts, these words, as interpreted by the courts, apparently speeded up the end of slavery. In 1800 there were eight slaves in New Hampshire, and by 1810 there were none.

In January 1784, the Connecticut legislature passed a gradual emancipation measure similar to Pennsylvania's. All slaves born after March 1, 1784, would become free at age 25. Rhode Island followed with a similar law in February 1784.

All male slaves born after March 1, 1784, would become free at age 21; female slaves born after that date would obtain their freedom at 18.

New York and New Jersey were the last northern states to put slavery on the road to extinction; not surprisingly, they were the northern states with the largest numbers of slaves. The New York Manumission Society, created in 1784, worked for gradual abolition with the support of leading New Yorkers such as John Jay and Alexander Hamilton. The New Jersey Society for Promoting the Abolition of Slavery was established in 1793. These organizations distributed abolitionist literature, sponsored debates on slavery, awarded prizes for antislavery articles, petitioned legislatures, and pressured state officials. But in both states, gradual abolition bills went down to defeat again and again during the 1780s and 1790s.

By the end of the century, though, public opinion had reached the point where action could be taken. As a New York City resident wrote in his diary for 1797, "within 20 years the opinion of the injustice of slaveholding has become almost universal." In 1799 the New York legislature approved a law giving slaves born after July 4, 1799, their freedom at the age of 28 for males and 25 for females. (In 1817 a New York law provided that slaves born *before* July 4, 1799, would be free as of July 4, 1827.) In 1804 New Jersey passed legislation to free slaves born after July 4, 1804—males at 25 and females at 21.

These measures soon eliminated slavery as a significant institution in the North. By 1790, 78 percent of New England's blacks were free. By 1820, there were only 145 slaves in that region out of 21,000 blacks. In the middle states (New York, New Jersey, and Pennsylvania), 72 percent of all blacks were still slaves in 1790, but by 1820 the figure was only 20 percent. (Delaware remained a slave state.) Also, Congress in 1787 passed the Northwest Ordinance, prohibiting the introduction of slaves into the area north of the Ohio River and east of the Mississippi. As a consequence, Ohio, Indiana, Illinois, Michigan, and Wisconsin eventually entered the Union as free states.

Of the more than 1.5 million slaves in the United States in 1820, only 18,000 lived in the North—just 1.2 percent of the total. A national institution at the beginning of the Revolution, slavery was now restricted to the southern states. This was one of the major, although little remembered, accomplishments of the Revolutionary era; had slavery remained legal in all of the states, its total elimination from American life later on would almost surely have been more difficult.

Acting in the American Revolution's spirit of liberty, the northern states also expanded somewhat the rights of free blacks during the last quarter of the eighteenth century. Pennsylvania in 1780 abolished its special courts for free blacks and slaves. That year the state also permitted free blacks to testify against whites and removed the prohibition against interracial marriage. None of the northern state constitutions established a color bar for voting, and free blacks voted in all of those states. (In some northern colonies, free blacks had been prevented from voting by custom rather than law, but that custom seems to have faded away after independence.) Furthermore, the northern abolition societies established several schools for free blacks and helped some find employment.

Yet free blacks were far from equal. Not only did they still face many legal handicaps, but racial prejudice and hostility dogged them in every aspect of their lives. As in the colonial period, they were excluded from the most desirable types of employment, forced to live in the worst urban neighborhoods, and often subject to public abuse.

Furthermore, there were signs that things might get worse. After 1790, the memory of Revolutionary ideals was fading. In addition, the growth in the number of free blacks seems to have strengthened white racism. By 1800, many white churches were forcing blacks to sit in the back or in the gallery. Integrated private schools were either closing or becoming segregated. During the 1790s, a French traveler noted that a New York hospital placed whites and blacks in separate wards and that in Philadelphia's prisons, whites and blacks ate apart.

The right of blacks to vote came under attack after 1800. In 1802, Ohio entered the Union as a free state but barred free blacks from voting. Five years later, New Jersey took the vote away from them, and in 1818 Connecticut adopted a constitution that did the same. In 1804 and 1807, Ohio tried to discourage black immigration by requiring blacks arriving in the state to post a $500 bond. This trend toward intensified discrimination continued in the following decades.

## THE UPPER SOUTH

Some of the nation's most prominent political leaders of the Revolutionary era came from the states of the Upper South—Virginia, Maryland, North Carolina, and Delaware. Virginia alone produced Thomas Jefferson, George Washington, James Madison, George Mason, and Patrick Henry, among others. Although nearly all owned slaves, the great majority regarded slavery as an evil. They would have agreed with John Iredell of North Carolina, who said in 1788 that the abolition of slavery was "an event which must be pleasing to every generous mind and every friend of human nature." They believed that slavery was in clear conflict with the American Revolution's ideals of liberty. Jefferson, a slave owner, felt this so strongly that he feared God would punish America. In his *Notes on Virginia* (1784), he condemned slavery and then wrote: "Indeed I tremble for my country when I reflect that God is just . . . [and] that his justice cannot sleep for ever."

Others in the Upper South opposed slavery on religious grounds. During the 1780s and 1790s, an evangelical religious revival emerged in the region, particularly among Methodists and Baptists. The revival promoted the spirit of Christian equality; blacks and whites often worshiped together, and blacks often preached to these mixed congregations. In 1780 the ruling body of the Methodist Church declared: "Slavery is contrary to the laws of God . . . [and] contrary to the dictates of conscience and pure religion." Methodists (along with Quakers) helped establish abolition societies from Delaware to North Carolina. In 1789 the General Committee of Virginia Baptists denounced slavery and urged Baptists to use all legal means to eliminate it.

Changing economic conditions in parts of the Upper South also encouraged antislavery opinion. In the older, more settled areas, tobacco cultivation had caused major soil erosion by the end of the colonial period. Meanwhile, grain prices were rising on the international market, so many planters switched from tobacco to wheat and corn. But grain did not require as much labor as tobacco did; moreover, grain required labor at a higher level of skill, best obtained from free laborers. And so the planters who had more slaves than they needed no longer regarded slavery as an essential economic institution.

These political, religious, and economic developments lay behind laws designed to ease the conditions of slavery, make manumission easier, and protect the rights of free blacks. In 1780 the Maryland legislature opened up the state militia to free blacks. By 1800 slaves and free blacks were being tried in the same courts as whites. Also, an 1809 law reformed Maryland's system of criminal punishment. Most of the extreme physical punishments that had been applied to slaves in the colonial era—such as dismemberment and burning—were eliminated. Flogging alone remained.

Virginia's legislature made manumission easier. From 1782 on, masters—for the first time since 1723—could free their slaves without permission from the government. Delaware followed Virginia's example in 1787, and the new Upper South slave state of Kentucky did so in 1792. A 1786 Virginia statute made it easier for slaves to win freedom suits; the law gave slaves suing for freedom all the rights of free persons in court. Four years later, the state's slave courts were required to provide an attorney for the slave at the master's expense. In 1788

A black woman and her son are seized in this print published in 1817. The number of free blacks grew in the states of the North and Upper South in the late eighteenth and early nineteenth centuries. Some of them were kidnapped by organized gangs and sold as slaves in other states, usually in the Deep South.

Virginia applied the death penalty to anyone trying to enslave free blacks. This was a response to a serious problem: as the number of free blacks in the northern and the Upper South states multiplied, a kidnapping business emerged in which free blacks were seized and sold as slaves in another state.

The economic developments that created slave surpluses in parts of Maryland and Virginia had much less impact in North Carolina, so reform there did not go as far. For example, the colonial law requiring masters to obtain county court approval before freeing their slaves remained in force. (The new slave state of Tennessee adopted a similar policy.) However, some steps were taken to protect the state's blacks. In 1779 North Carolina—like Virginia nine years later—imposed the death penalty on those attempting to kidnap free blacks. In 1791 the killing of a slave was made a crime punishable by death. (Previously, the penalty had been a year's imprisonment for the first offense.) Legislation giving slaves the right to a jury trial for serious crimes cleared the legislature in 1793.

## Why Slavery Was Not Abolished

Some antislavery advocates had hoped that the Upper South states would move on from these measures to gradual abolition laws like those passed in the North. But this was not to be. There were basic differences between the two regions. In the North, slavery had never been a crucial part of the economy. In the Upper South, it was a vital economic institution during the colonial era and remained so afterward. In some sections of the region, such as coastal Virginia, slavery was on the decline. But in areas of Virginia's interior that had been settled later, tobacco cultivation and the use of slaves was increasing, not decreasing. The Upper South had too great a stake in the slave system to let it go.

Another basic distinction between the North and the Upper South was that many more blacks resided in the latter region. In 1790, blacks made up only 1.7 percent of New England's population and 5.3 percent of the middle states' inhabitants. But the figures were 21.6 percent for Delaware, 34.7 percent for Maryland, 40.9 percent for Virginia, and 26.8 percent for North Carolina. Virginia alone had 305,000 blacks, compared to 67,000 in all of the northern states.

Whites in the North may have been just as racially prejudiced as those of the Upper South. In both regions, pro- and antislavery whites alike generally regarded blacks as inherently unintelligent, lazy, sexually loose, and inclined to crime and violence. When faced with the accomplishments of blacks such as poets Jupiter Hammon of New York and Phillis Wheatley of Massachusetts, mathematician Benjamin Banneker of Maryland, and merchant Paul Cuffee of Massachusetts, whites either minimized their accomplishments or argued that they were rare exceptions to the rule.

In the North, racial prejudice did not prevent the elimination of slavery, because the number of free blacks resulting from abolition would be small. But in the Upper South, abolition would create more than 500,000 free blacks. Whites could not imagine living with hundreds of thousands of "uncivilized," "barbarous" blacks unrestrained by the chains of servitude. In 1805, Nathaniel Macon, a U.S.

representative from North Carolina, said, "No one rejects the evil [of slavery] more than I do, but what to do with it is the question." What he really meant was: What would be done with the free black population that would result from abolition? It was this problem that made emancipation seem impossible even for those whites who, like Thomas Jefferson, hated the institution.

Even without the general abolition of slavery, the number of free blacks was increasing; because of relaxed manumission laws, the surplus of slaves, and the influence of Revolutionary ideals, many more individual slaveholders freed their slaves than had done so in the colonial period. Between 1790 and 1810, the number of free blacks in the Upper South increased from 30,000 to 93,000, or from 5 to 13 percent of the region's blacks.

But the growing number of manumissions was a self-limiting process, because as the free black population grew, so did the racial fears of whites. The result was a reversal of the trend toward making manumission easier and expanding black rights. The reversal was strengthened by fear that the growing number of free blacks, seen as dangerous and undesirable on their own account, also would encourage unrest and rebellion among the slaves. Two events, one in the Caribbean and one in Virginia, deepened this fear. Inspired by the French Revolution, the free mulattoes of the French colony of Saint Domingue began a revolt in 1791; later in the year, the colony's black slaves joined in. Fighting continued until 1804, when Saint Domingue became the independent Republic of Haiti. Southerners heard firsthand accounts of violence and destruction when thousands of refugees (mostly whites and their slaves) arrived in southern ports in 1793.

Another development sparked fear of revolt even more, since it occurred at home. During the summer of 1800, a group of Virginia slaves headed by Gabriel Prosser, a blacksmith, plotted an insurrection. They planned to march hundreds of slaves into the capital of Richmond at midnight on August 30. There, they would burn down the warehouse district, seize weapons, and kill whites with the aim of inspiring a revolt throughout the region. The conspiracy was centered in the Richmond area, but the revolt's organizers recruited followers from as far away as Charlottesville, about 75 miles northwest. However, drenching rains on the night of August 30 made roads and bridges impassable, and the slaves could not march. The authorities learned of the plot from two slave informants. Within 6 weeks, from 20 to 30 conspirators, including Prosser, had been tried and executed. But although it had failed, the size and scope of Gabriel's Plot sent shock waves throughout the South.

## Tighter Restrictions on Free Blacks

Frightened by the expanding free black population and the menace of slave insurrection, the Upper South legislatures began imposing stricter controls on blacks. Some measures, such as strengthening slave patrols, were aimed at bondpeople. But the major targets of restrictive legislation were free blacks, who were seen as inciters of slave unrest. Virginia in 1798 prescribed 39 lashes for free blacks who hid runaway slaves. Maryland in 1806 ordered the punishment of free blacks merely for being present at disorderly meetings of slaves. Virginia in 1793 required urban free blacks to register with local town clerks and prohibited whites from hiring those not registered. Maryland adopted essentially the same registration system in 1805, as did Tennessee in 1806. Other controls included an 1801 Virginia statute prohibiting free blacks—even those with papers proving their free status—from moving from county to county or from town to town, on penalty of being arrested as vagrants.

Many other special burdens were imposed upon free blacks in the early nineteenth century. Maryland in 1805 required every free black vendor of wheat, corn, or tobacco to obtain a certificate of good character from a justice of the peace and to renew it each year. Other Upper South regulations excluded free blacks from some trades. Virginia abolished poll taxes in 1787 but in 1813 adopted a new one that applied only to free blacks. Also in Virginia, free blacks, but not whites, could be compelled to serve long terms of labor for nonpayment of taxes and fines.

Increasingly, voting regulations excluded free blacks. The new slave state of Kentucky permitted blacks to vote under its 1792 constitution but excluded them under the 1799 charter that replaced it. Delaware deprived free blacks of the suffrage in 1792. In 1783 a Maryland law denied voting rights to free blacks born after its passage, and in 1810 the state excluded all free blacks from the polls. Virginia never lifted its colonial-era ban on black suffrage. That left North Carolina and Tennessee as the only Upper South states permitting blacks to vote after 1810.

The Upper South states also took steps to keep the free black population as small as possible. In 1793 Virginia barred free black migration into the state. Two years later, both Maryland and North Carolina required those arriving from other states to post large bonds. An 1806 Maryland statute required most free blacks visiting from out of state to leave after two weeks. Ten years earlier, a Maryland law had made it possible to expel from the state those free blacks without visible means of support.

Other laws sought to limit the free black population by restricting manumission. In 1795 North Carolina provided that slaves could not be freed unless they were able to post large bonds guaranteeing their good behavior, which few slaves could do. In Maryland and Virginia, white lawyers—often members of local abolition societies—frequently helped slaves to sue for their freedom. To discourage this practice, a 1791 Maryland act made those assisting in freedom suits liable for the master's expenses and court costs if the suit was lost. In 1795 Virginia provided that a slave could use only court-appointed lawyers and that if the slave lost the suit, those assisting her or him would be fined $100. A 1798 statute barred members of abolition societies from sitting on juries in freedom suits. In 1806 Virginia required all slaves freed in the future to leave the state within 12 months. Neighboring states sought to protect themselves from the consequences of Virginia's action: within a year, Delaware, Kentucky, and Maryland had passed laws forbidding free blacks entering those states from becoming permanent residents.

With so much concern about the presence of free blacks, it is no wonder that interest in colonizing them grew—impractical though colonization might have been from both a financial and an organizational standpoint. Thomas Jefferson, James Madison, and other prominent figures of the region proposed or supported colonization plans during the 1770s, 1780s, and 1790s. Interest in such plans increased as the fear of blacks grew, and in December 1800—just a few months after Gabriel's Plot—the Virginia legislature urged the federal government to buy land outside of the United States for the resettlement of free blacks. Many leaders of the American Colonization Society—founded by prominent whites in 1816 to establish and settle a black colony in Africa—were from the Upper South, including Henry Clay of Kentucky and John Randolph of Virginia.

The growing hostility toward free blacks was expressed not only through laws but in the practices of everyday life. Segregation of free blacks and whites had always existed to a degree, but it had not been widely applied—if only because there were few free blacks until the late 1700s. In the first decade of the nineteenth century, the practice began to spread. It became more common at sites such as public baths, parks, places of entertainment, hospitals, jails, and cemeteries. In 1812 Paul Cuffee, a shipbuilder and merchant and one of the leading free blacks of New England, was refused service at a Baltimore tavern. "When I arrived in Baltimore," he wrote, "they utterly refused to take me in at the tavern or to get me dinner unless I would go back among the servants." Racially mixed congregations, which had often existed among Methodists and Baptists in the late eighteenth century, were condemned and ridiculed in the early nineteenth century. Racial segregation was usually not a matter of law but of custom or of rules laid down by the owners of public accommodations such as inns and theaters.

Clearly, the trend during and just after the Revolution toward easing the plight of blacks had been sharply reversed. The Upper South entered the nineteenth century with a growing commitment to human bondage and racial oppression.

## THE LOWER SOUTH

In contrast to parts of the Upper South, slavery in the Lower or Deep South became more rather than less profitable during the Revolutionary era. Rice continued to be a money-making crop in late-eighteenth-century South Carolina and Georgia, reaching its highest level of production in the early 1790s. Cultivation of the indigo plant declined in the 1780s, but great increases in cotton planting more than made up for it. (In the Upper South, the growing season was too short for cotton.) The increasing demand for cotton fiber to supply the expanding textile industries of Britain, western Europe, and, later, the northern United States fueled the spread of cotton plantations. Eli Whitney's cotton gin, invented in 1793, made it much easier to meet growing demand by mechanically removing seeds from the cotton plant—by hand, the process had been very slow.

Because of Whitney's invention, the cotton plantation—and slavery along with it—spread more rapidly into the interior of South Carolina and Georgia. The process was also speeded along because cotton—like tobacco but unlike rice—required only a small investment and could be grown on small plots. The number of slaves in South Carolina nearly doubled between 1790 and 1810. Expansion was so rapid that South Carolina, which had banned the international slave trade in 1787, reopened it in 1803.

In the 1790s, cotton farming expanded farther westward into the Mississippi Territory, out of which the states of Mississippi (1817) and Alabama (1819) were later created. After the Louisiana Purchase of 1803, slaves were brought into the Louisiana Territory to work on cotton and sugar plantations. Between 1792 and 1810, U.S. cotton production increased from 6,000 to 178,000 bales a year.

After the War of 1812 (1812–1815), booming cotton and sugar markets speeded up the development of what was then called the Southwest. Between 1810 and 1820, the slave population of Alabama and Mississippi increased from 17,000 to 75,000. In the state of Louisiana, which entered the Union in 1812, the slave population grew from 35,000 to 69,000 over the same period.

Enjoying economic prosperity, whites in the Deep South never wavered in their support of slavery. As we have seen, South Carolina and Georgia forced Thomas Jefferson to delete his condemnation of the slave trade from the Declaration of Independence. At the Constitutional Convention of 1787 (see the following section), their delegates were the strongest supporters of slavery. The ideals of the Revolution may have had some ripple effect on the treatment of blacks in the Deep South, however. In the 1780s, whites seem to have been more reluctant to break up slave families and to impose harsh punishment. Also, manumissions increased slightly. But no abolition societies existed in the region, and no real loosening of the laws relating to manumission, slave control, or free blacks occurred. In 1790, free blacks in South Carolina and Georgia numbered just 2,200, or 1.5 percent of the black population; 20 years later, the number was still only 6,400, or 2.1 percent of all blacks.

As in the Upper South, Gabriel's Plot and the revolution in Saint Domingue led South Carolina and Georgia to tighten their already strict controls on blacks. South Carolina's colonial restrictions on manumission had been allowed to expire. But starting in 1800, masters wishing to free their slaves had to obtain permission from a panel of one magistrate and five freeholders. In the same year, South Carolina prohibited free blacks from migrating into the state. Also in 1800, gatherings of slaves behind locked doors for educational purposes were banned, even if whites were present. At the same time, all black gatherings for religious or educational instruction between sunset and sunrise were banned.

In the colonial period, Georgia had not limited manumission, but an 1801 law required masters to get approval from the legislature. Beginning in 1793, free blacks entering Georgia had to register with local authorities and present character references. In 1810 free blacks were simply barred from entering the state. Starting in 1818, all of Georgia's free blacks had to register annually, obtain a certificate of freedom, and select a white guardian. Meanwhile, as in the Upper South, separation of the races in South Carolina and Georgia became increasingly common.

# THE CONSTITUTION AND THE FEDERAL GOVERNMENT

Southern opinion concerning slavery and blacks made itself felt at the national level, both in the Constitutional Convention of 1787 and, subsequently, in the federal government. The delegates from South Carolina and Georgia fought vigorously at the convention to defend the interests of slave owners, and the northern delegates were willing to compromise with them. As a result the U.S. Constitution, although it never actually used the word *slavery*, recognized the institution of human bondage in three of its clauses.

The delegates debated whether slaves should be counted in determining a state's representation in Congress. Northern delegates believed that since slaves were property, they should not be counted, while the South Carolina and Georgia delegates insisted that they should. The result was the "three-fifths compromise" of Article I, Section 2, of the Constitution. It provided that three-fifths of the slave population would be counted for the purpose of calculating both a state's representation and its taxes.

The great majority of delegates wanted to outlaw United States participation in the international slave trade, against which most states had already acted. But South Carolina and Georgia were adamantly opposed (probably with support from some of the North Carolina delegates) and threatened to reject the Constitution if it was banned. Again, a compromise was reached: Article I, Section 9, provided that Congress could not abolish the trade until 1808.

Once the northern delegates had recognized the legitimacy of slavery by the "three-fifths" and slave trade compromises, it was a foregone conclusion that they would agree to a clause for the return of fugitive slaves who crossed state lines. And so Article IV, Section 2, guaranteed masters the right to have fugitive slaves returned to them from other states.

The actions of the new federal government established under the Constitution followed the same pattern; on matters related to slavery and race, Congress and the executive branch both tended to yield to southern white opinion. Congressional legislation of 1790, for example, provided for the naturalization of white aliens only; it contained no provision for black foreigners to become citizens. In 1792, a law allowed only whites to enroll in the federal militia.

The Fugitive Slave Act of 1793 was passed by Congress to implement the constitutional provision on runaway slaves. Masters or their agents could seize a black person and then take him or her to any state or federal judge to prove ownership. The black man or woman had no right to receive a trial by jury, to testify, or to present witnesses. Some have said that this law virtually legalized kidnapping, since those claiming ownership of a black person had a smaller burden of proof than in any other type of judicial case.

When Congress admitted Kentucky (1792) and Tennessee (1796) into the Union as slave states, very few legislators objected. A proposal in 1798 to bar slavery in the Mississippi Territory received only a few votes. That year the secretaries of war and of the navy excluded blacks from the Marine Corps and from naval ships (although during the naval war with France [1798–1800] and the War of 1812 with England [1812–1815], blacks served with distinction in both the army and navy). In 1802 President Thomas Jefferson signed a law denying free blacks the vote in the nation's new capital, Washington, D.C. Congress acted similarly in 1808 with regard to the Mississippi and Indiana Territories. Two years later, blacks were prohibited from carrying the U.S. mail.

Of the few federal actions that worked in favor of blacks, most were related to the slave trade. Congress in 1807 passed legislation outlawing the importing of slaves into the United States beginning January 1, 1808—the earliest date possible under the Constitution. Yet even here the victory was not complete, since Congress rejected a provision that would have freed those blacks imported illegally. Instead, the matter was left to the states. Since such slaves would be coming to the southern states, their chance for freedom was small.

Why did northerners give in to southern interests time after time? One reason was to prevent conflict that might threaten the new country's existence. Another was racial prejudice against blacks. An additional reason was a belief that slavery would eventually die out. Some opponents of slavery felt that the slave labor system was too inefficient to survive. Others thought that with the elimination of the slave trade, the supply of slaves would be inadequate.

But these beliefs proved to be false. Slavery became increasingly profitable and spread rapidly in the Lower South. And there was no slave shortage; the slave surplus in some parts of the Upper South, the kidnapping of free blacks from the Upper South and North, illegal imports of blacks, and the natural increase of the slave population provided an adequate number of bondpeople for the new planta-tions of the Deep South.

After the great cotton boom began in 1815, the plantation system moved rapidly into the Mississippi and Louisiana Territories. No one could believe any longer that slavery would soon disappear by itself. The result was growing tension between North and South. Northerners now had two great fears: one was that slave labor would, wherever it spread, replace or impoverish free labor; the other was that the slave states would multiply and eventually dominate the federal government. Therefore, northerners would no longer let the slave system go unchallenged.

But just as northern opinion was hardening against slavery, southern opinion was uniting in support of it. The economic success of the plantation system gave slavery a new legitimacy in the minds of southerners. Previously, even those southerners who defended slavery had acknowledged that it was an evil, although perhaps a necessary one for controlling blacks. But starting in 1818, southerners in Congress began to emphasize the supposedly beneficial aspects of slavery while refusing to admit its immorality. Furthermore, because the spread of slavery in the Lower South gave the Upper South a market for its surplus slaves, the Upper South states defended the expansion of the slave system as strongly as did the Deep South states. The two regions of the South had differed in their attitudes toward slavery in the early years of the Revolutionary era; now they were coming together in its defense.

A major political conflict between North and South erupted in 1819, when Missouri applied for admission to the Union as a slave state. Northerners were alarmed. Concerned as they were over slavery's extension westward within the Lower South, they were even more disturbed as it moved northward out of that region and into the milder climate of Missouri. Therefore, strong northern opposition to Missouri's proslavery constitution arose in Congress. The southern states leaped to its defense—led, significantly, by Virginia, politically the most important Upper South state. With the North now determined to restrict slavery and the South increasingly opposed to any restrictions, the battle over Missouri would be just the first of a series of sectional crises.

## BLACK PROTEST, BLACK INSTITUTIONS

During the Revolutionary era, blacks began to make their voices heard on a regular basis. For one thing, the American Revolution created a more tolerant climate for dissent. Another reason was the increasing number of free blacks. Despite all restrictions imposed on them, free blacks were in a far better position than slaves to speak out.

Throughout the country, free blacks asserted their claim to equal rights. Beginning in the late 1770s, Massachusetts shipbuilder-merchant Paul Cuffee and his brother John refused to pay taxes because they could not vote. In their 1780 petition to the legislature, they used the slogan made famous by white Americans: "No taxation without representation." (After Massachusetts adopted its 1780 constitution, blacks began to vote.) Seven years later Prince Hall, Boston's leading free black, and other free blacks objected to their children's exclusion from the city's free school system.

Protest occurred in the South, too. Free blacks in South Carolina petitioned in 1783 against a special poll tax levied on them, claiming it reduced them to a state "but small removed from slavery." Eight years later Peter Mathews, a butcher, and other free black shop owners and craftspersons in Charleston, South Carolina, petitioned for the right to testify against whites. They pointed out that unless allowed to do so, they could not collect debts owed them by whites. These petitions were unsuccessful.

By and large, free blacks could vote only in states where they were few in number, and the overwhelming majority of whites opposed racial equality. Therefore, black petitions had little influence upon the state legislatures and other agencies of government.

More effective than black protest were the institutions that free black communities created during the Revolutionary era. Denied equal rights and facing a trend toward separation of the races, free blacks recognized that they would have to depend on their own resources to advance their welfare. The organizations they created became the centers of black life, the engines for black advancement, and the source of black leadership.

Starting in the 1780s, blacks began to form mutual aid and self-improvement societies. They assisted the poor and sick and promoted self-respect by setting high moral standards for their members. They also tried to combat racism by showing whites that blacks could be good, responsible citizens.

The first such association was the African Union Society of Newport, Rhode Island, founded in 1780. In 1787 Richard Jones and Absalom Jones founded the Free African Society of Philadelphia. That year, Prince Hall obtained a charter from the British Masons to establish in Boston the first black Masonic lodge in America. In the next decade, free blacks established the Brown Fellowship Society in Charleston (1790), the African Society of Providence (Rhode Island) (1793), and the African Society of Boston (1796); by 1797 Hall had established black Masonic lodges in Philadelphia and Providence. The New York African Society for Mutual Relief was founded in 1810.

Black churches were even more important than the mutual aid societies. They were havens where blacks could express their grief and their hopes and where they could claim spiritual equality with whites. They also served as centers of black community and social life. And black preachers were by far the most important source of community leadership.

In the late eighteenth century, evangelical Methodist and Baptist churches in the Upper South sometimes accepted blacks with full rights and with a nonracial seating policy. Furthermore, black preachers, slave and free, often preached to mixed and even all-white congregations. But most churches in the South never accepted blacks on an equal basis, if they accepted them at all, and so black churches began to emerge. In the mid-1770s, David George in Silver Bluff, South Carolina, and George Liele in Savannah, Georgia, established the first ones. By 1800, there were a number of black Baptist churches serving both slaves and free blacks. Also, free and slave black preachers ministered to slaves on the plantations.

Blacks also established their own places of worship in the North. In 1787 Richard Allen, a former slave, led blacks out of St. George's Episcopal Church in Philadelphia over the issue of separate seating. Subsequently, Allen established the Bethel African Methodist Church, which by 1810 had nearly 500 members. Other African Methodist churches formed in Baltimore; Wilmington, Delaware; Salem, New Jersey; and Attleboro, Pennsylvania. In 1816, they united to form the first black denomination in the United States, the African Methodist Episcopal (AME) church, with Allen as its bishop. Meanwhile, black churches were also forming in New York, Boston, and elsewhere as blacks left white churches that denied them equal rights.

The abolition societies established some schools for free blacks; the best known was the African Free School, founded in 1787 by the New York Manumission Society. But most schools for blacks were established by blacks themselves, and the majority were connected to churches. These schools were essential for free blacks, since the number of integrated private schools began declining in the 1790s, and most public school systems, like those of Philadelphia and Boston, continued to exclude blacks.

No significant opposition to black institutions emerged in the North. After Gabriel's Plot of 1800, however, southern whites began to regard independent black organizations as subversive. Some southern black churches were forced to close—most whites wanted blacks to worship in separate churches, but under white control and with white ministers.

Black schools, too, came under attack. The school of black leader Daniel Coker thrived in Baltimore, but the experience of Christopher McPherson in Virginia was very different. When McPherson, a free black, attempted to establish a school for blacks in Richmond in 1811, one obstacle after another was placed in his way. He was badgered by the police. The editor of a Richmond newspaper, under pressure from local whites, refused to run his advertisement. When McPherson persisted, he was jailed and finally sent to the Williamsburg Lunatic Asylum. Under such pressure, few black schools could carry on.

## AMERICA OR AFRICA?

As blacks began speaking up for their rights more often, some said that the only way they could live in full dignity was to leave the United States entirely and settle in Africa. In 1773, several slaves told the Massachusetts legislature that if they could purchase their freedom, they would "leave the province . . . as soon as we can, from our joynt labours procure money to transport ourselves to some part of the coast of *Africa*, where we propose a settlement." In 1787, 73 Massachusetts blacks, including Prince Hall, petitioned the legislature. Noting "the very disagreeable and disadvantageous circumstances" of their existence, they asked the legislature to help them obtain funds for settling in Africa.

In the early nineteenth century, Paul Cuffee came to a similar conclusion, stating that blacks would "never become a people until they com out from amongst the white people. . . ." As a prosperous businessman, he could act on his belief. In 1811, Cuffee went to Sierra Leone on the West African coast to explore the possibilities for establishing a colony. Four years later, he brought 38 settlers there. Subsequently, Cuffee was an adviser to the white-run American Colonization Society.

Most free blacks opposed colonization. When the American Colonization Society was formed in December 1816, many feared they would be forced to leave the country. A group of free blacks in Richmond declared in January 1817 that they would prefer being "colonized in the most remote corner of the land of our nativity, to being exiled."

During the same month, a meeting of some 3,000 free blacks—the largest gathering of blacks in American history to that point—was held at Richard Allen's Philadelphia church to express opposition to colonization. They believed that the colonization society wanted to ship out free blacks in order to secure the slave system. (Many of the society's supporters had exactly that goal.) Although the gathering was chaired by James Forten, a supporter of colonization at the time, it resolved that "we will never separate ourselves voluntarily from the slave population of the country; they are our brethren by the ties of consanguinity [blood], of suffering, and of wrong." The signers also stated that they were "entitled to participate in the blessings of [America's] luxuriant soil," which their "blood and sweat manured." Appealing to the ideals of the Revolution, they asserted that "any measure or system of measures, having a tendency to banish us from her bosom, would not only be cruel, but in direct violation of those principles, which have been the boast of this republic."

Disagreement over colonization was the first stage of a debate within the black community about whether to separate from white America. It divided those who, like the participants in the Philadelphia gathering, placed their hopes in the American Revolution's ideals of freedom from those who believed that its ideals would never be applied to blacks. This division would continue, in various forms, through the nineteenth and twentieth centuries.

# CHAPTER 4

# The Antebellum Years: 1820 –1860

## NINETEENTH-CENTURY SLAVERY

In 1850 about 3.2 million slaves lived in the 15 southern slave states, making up about one-third of the southern population. The great majority of them—about 2.5 million—were directly involved in agriculture, raising the lion's share of the staple crops grown in the region. About 350,000 grew tobacco, mostly in Maryland, Virginia, North Carolina, Kentucky, and Tennessee; 150,000 raised sugar in Louisiana; 125,000 cultivated rice in South Carolina and Georgia; and 60,000 raised hemp, primarily in Kentucky. But 1,815,000, by far the greatest number, were involved in cotton farming, mostly in the 8 Lower South states of South Carolina, Georgia, Florida, Alabama, Mississippi, Louisiana, Texas, and Arkansas.

As we have seen, the cultivation of cotton spread rapidly through the Lower South during the first two decades of the nineteenth century. With the flourishing of the American and European textile industries, the demand for cotton continued to grow rapidly in the years between 1820 and the Civil War. As a result, southern production increased from less than half a million bales in 1820 to roughly 5.4 million bales in 1860. By 1840 the South was producing more than 60 percent of the world's supply of cotton, accounting for over half the value of U.S. exports. Cotton prices dropped sharply during economic depressions beginning in 1819 and 1837, but in general the cotton economy prospered in the pre–Civil War decades.

It is a matter of debate whether slavery was the most profitable system possible for farming the South's staple crops. But slave masters clearly profited from slavery in the antebellum (pre–Civil War) years. That is why the price of slaves rose; at Charleston the cost of young male field hands increased from $850 in 1818 to

$1,200 in 1860, while in New Orleans the price rose from $1,000 in 1818 to $1,800 in 1860. Demand was so great in the Lower South that by 1860, slaves were 45 percent of the population. In 1860 they made up 57 percent of the population in South Carolina and 55 percent in Mississippi. In Louisiana, Alabama, Florida, and Georgia, over 40 percent of the population was slave. On the eve of the Civil War, 2.4 million of the South's nearly 4 million slaves lived in the Lower South.

Slavery often was less profitable in the Upper South than in the Lower South's Cotton Kingdom. Slaveholders in the Upper South—especially in the older states on the Atlantic coast—continued an earlier trend of converting from tobacco to wheat and other food crops; as a result, they had too many slaves. But the demand was so great in the Deep South that Upper South slaveholders could sell their bondpeople there at a handsome price. In Richmond the price of young male hands grew from $700 in 1818 to $1,300 in 1856. Many slaves bought by domestic slave traders there and in Baltimore, Washington, D.C., and Norfolk were later sold in New Orleans, Montgomery, and other Deep South locales. Some Upper South slave owners simply moved to the Lower South with their slaves.

## Farm and Plantation Slaves

Masters throughout the South were profiting from their slaves. But what did slavery mean for the slaves themselves? What kind of lives did they live? The great majority of them performed agricultural labor as either full- or part-time field hands. At midcentury, half of all slaveholders owned 5 or fewer slaves, and only 12 percent owned more than 20. But the latter group owned over half of all slaves. About half the slaves worked on large farms known as plantations.

On the small farms, the master usually worked in the field right alongside the slaves. But on the plantations, the division of labor was much more complicated. Masters never performed physical labor in the fields. On the larger plantations, they often did not even manage the estate, instead hiring overseers to supervise operations. The great majority of overseers were white, but once in a while a trusted slave was given that position. Masters selected slaves to be slave drivers, whose job was to see that the other slaves did their work. Often, the masters separately appointed a female slave to be forewoman over her sister slaves. On most plantations, the slaves were divided into groups called gangs, each gang working through the entire day under the supervision of a driver. On the rice plantations along the Georgia and South Carolina coasts, however, the task system was used. The driver assigned each slave his or her particular tasks, and the slaves worked individually rather than in groups. Slaves who finished their work early could take the rest of the day off.

Not all plantation slaves were field hands. The larger the plantation, the more specialized the labor force. On the big plantations, many slaves worked as domestic servants, craftspersons (blacksmiths, carpenters, weavers, etc.), nursemaids, millers, gardeners, coachmen, and so on. The jobs of seamstress, cook, and midwife were reserved for women. Most of these occupations required considerable skill, giving slaves an opportunity to develop their abilities and to take pride in their work. However, on all but the largest estates, every slave was sent into the fields when a great deal of labor was required—at cotton picking and sugar harvesting time, for example. The gap between house and field slaves, therefore, was not as great as has often been imagined.

Slaves generally worked from sunrise to sunset, and sometimes even after dark. On Sundays they were off. They worked longer hours than did free blacks after the Civil War and probably more than did the northern industrial workers of the antebellum years. Though all crops had slack periods, there was usually ample work to do. Since the planting and harvesting cycles for cotton and corn came at different times, cotton growers generally raised corn as well. Also, large numbers of livestock—especially hogs and cattle—were raised in the South, and tending them was another responsibility of the slaves.

Female slaves were routinely sent into the fields, where they often joined the male slaves in performing such heavy tasks as plowing, digging ditches, and cutting down trees—work usually considered inappropriate for white women. From the fifth through ninth months of pregnancy, however, slave women usually received lighter tasks like pulling weeds, hoeing, and weaving. It was easier for slave women than slave men to escape work by pretending to be ill, because the masters did not want to destroy the slave women's ability to bear children. But overall, the women had heavier work burdens than the men: in addition to their full-time jobs in the fields or in the master's house, they provided most of the care for their children and did the household work in the slave dwellings.

In addition to their long hours each week, slaves labored for more years than did free people. Children were sent into the fields well before adolescence. As early as five or six years old, they might begin performing small tasks like carrying water. At around 10 or 12 they became field hands, although they were usually not considered full or prime hands until 18. Not only did women field hands work almost to the end of pregnancy, although at lighter tasks; after childbirth, they were quickly sent back to the field while still nursing. When slaves became too old to work in the fields, they were given other tasks. Only the extremely old and the totally disabled escaped labor.

In the antebellum years, the slaves' diet was usually adequate in quantity but lacking in variety, consisting primarily of corn and pork in most of the South—for an adult, about a peck (eight quarts) of cornmeal and four pounds of pork a week. Molasses was also provided frequently. Less often, slaves might be given such items as sweet potatoes, peas, squash, coffee, beef, and poultry. Women received extra food during pregnancy. Most masters allowed slaves to have their own garden plots, where vegetables could be grown. If they had the time, male slaves and, much less often, female slaves hunted, trapped, and fished. Women working as domestic slaves in the master's house usually managed to bring back some food for their families—if necessary, by stealing.

The clothing of the average male field hand was hardly above the bare minimum. It consisted of two suits of clothes, one for summer and one for winter, made of cheap fabric called "Negro cloth." In addition to work clothes, women field hands had one dress for special occasions. Shoes were generally provided only for cold weather, and they were of poor quality; children often received no shoes at all. Household slaves sometimes had the advantage of receiving the whites' old clothing. Slaves suffered most in the winter, when they wore flimsy coats and went without gloves or socks.

On the plantations, some slaves lived in reasonably comfortable frame houses made of brick, clapboard, or shingles. Others resided in well-constructed log houses covered with weatherboarding. But most lived in small wooden shacks, about 15 feet square, made of roughly cut and poorly fitted clapboard. On the larger plantations, these houses were built in parallel rows forming a "street." Usually, each slave family had a cabin to itself. These poorly built huts were cold in winter, hot in summer, and leaky in rain. Few had windows or floors. Furniture was scarce and privacy nonexistent in the one-room dwellings (although some slaves added partitions or lean-tos for privacy). Slaves on small farms usually lived in the attics of the master's house or in outbuildings.

Hard as the slaves' lot was, conditions probably improved from the eighteenth to the nineteenth centuries. By the nineteenth century the overwhelming majority of slaves were native-born, English-speaking Christians. They seemed less alien to whites, and so less threatening, than their African-born ancestors who had arrived in the colonial period. Therefore, masters could more easily sympathize with their needs. Also, once the international slave trade was banned in 1808, masters had an incentive to treat slaves better: they could not legally be replaced with imports from abroad. Furthermore, beginning in the 1830s a new northern abolitionist movement began an aggressive campaign against slavery that emphasized the brutality of slaveholders (see "The New Abolitionist Movement," page 67). This probably encouraged a number of masters to end some of the slave system's worst abuses so that they could better defend their system of bondage.

In addition, the masters' view of the institution of slavery changed with time. In the eighteenth century, they tended to see slavery simply as a labor system, a way of getting work done, and they regarded the slaves simply as uncivilized barbarians who needed to be strictly controlled. But as time went by, slavery became for masters not just a form of labor but the basis for a way of life to which they were accustomed and attached. They began to idealize slavery as a paternalistic or patriarchal social system in which they, as "fathers," had an obligation to make sure that their slaves, or "children," were well cared for. Some masters probably upgraded the slaves' living standards, thought twice about using the whip, and gave at least some consideration to the slaves' interests before selling them.

But this point can be carried too far. A system under which one person owned another was unjust and oppressive by its nature. Furthermore, slaves still were overworked and underrewarded. Whippings were the usual form of punishment. Slave women usually had no choice but to submit to the sexual advances of their masters; normally, all that they could do was hope for some relief from the burdens of bondage in exchange. Slave men, meanwhile, were humiliated by their inability to prevent the rape of their wives and mothers. Perhaps as many as 30 percent of slave families were separated by sale. Finally, the comparison of slaves to children perpetuated racism and was used to justify slavery.

## Industrial and Urban Slaves

Not all slaves worked on farms or plantations. Hundreds of thousands worked in industries or in urban centers. At midcentury about 200,000 slaves—a little more than 1 in 20—were industrial slaves. Most of them worked in the countryside, in villages, or in small towns. The largest group was the 16,000 slaves employed in lumbering. About 6,000 slaves worked in Virginia's tobacco factories. Some 7,000 labored in the ironworks of Virginia and Maryland, while others were used in textile factories, mostly in South Carolina and Georgia. Around 2,000 were used in coal mining. In the transportation industry, slaves built and operated ships and trains.

Although industrial work was hard and dangerous, slaves often preferred it to agricultural labor. For one thing, the work was more rewarding because it frequently required ingenuity and initiative. Also, slaves often received material incentives, such as money for working extra hours, supervising others, or doing skilled work. Finally, industrial slaves were usually less closely supervised than those in agriculture, both during and after work.

More than 140,000 slaves lived in southern urban centers in 1860; Charleston with 13,900, New Orleans with 13,300, and Richmond with 11,700 had the most. These slaves worked as domestic servants, carriage drivers, draymen, bricklayers, carpenters, painters and plasterers, tailors, printers, fishermen, common laborers, among many other occupations. But as a percentage of city populations, slaves were declining in the 1850s. That was partly because some employers began using white migrants from the North and immigrants from Europe. Another reason was the sharp rise in cotton prices during that decade, which increased the demand for field hands.

Urban slaves were the most fortunate (or least unfortunate) bondpeople. Like industrial slaves, they received bonus pay for overwork. More importantly, they had the greatest freedom. Upon leaving their masters' homes, urban slaves entered a bustling world where they came into contact with other slaves and free blacks and with a variety of black institutions ranging from self-help organizations and churches to restaurants and grogshops owned by free blacks or, occasionally, by slaves. Here was a world in which they could participate without whites' supervision, and often even without their knowledge. Some urban industrialists did not provide housing; instead, they gave cash housing allowances to their bondpeople, who were free to find their own lodging. These slaves normally stayed at boardinghouses run by free blacks. Many slaves were allowed to hire themselves out. They looked for employment on their own and gave their masters a part of their pay. Since workers were in short supply during the antebellum period, the slaves could often obtain very favorable terms for their work.

Some urban slaves had even more freedom. A group known as free slaves were owned by white masters who simply let them live as if they were free. In many cases these masters wanted to free their bondpeople but faced state laws either prohibiting manumission or requiring freed slaves to leave the state. Sometimes a "free slave" was owned by a black relative. For example, a free black man might buy his slave wife from her master and keep her in legal slavery so she would not have to leave the state. Other free slaves were fugitives who escaped the farms and plantations of the South, went to the region's large cities, and blended into the urban population. Probably more slaves gained their freedom that way than by escaping to the North.

## NINETEENTH-CENTURY SLAVES: STRATEGIES OF RESISTANCE

In theory, whites had almost absolute power over their slaves. But in reality, bondpeople found many ways, well short of open revolt, of pressuring masters to treat them better. By the antebellum period, masters and slaves on the South's farms and plantations had developed unspoken understandings about their mutual obligations. If the masters failed to fulfill their responsibilities, slaves often found ways of persuading them to do so. A Mississippi planter understood this: he warned an overseer that if he did not feed the slaves adequately, they would steal. Other reactions to mistreatment included staging work slowdowns, doing work badly, and destroying tools and other property. On an Alabama plantation, the slaves tricked the master into firing a harsh overseer by covering up the weeds in the cotton fields instead of chopping them out. As a former slave said, "White folks do as they please, and the darkies do as they can." By doing as they could, slaves got better treatment and preserved their self-respect.

As in the colonial period, many slaves became fugitives. Some went off to find family members who had been sold away. Others ran off in anger after being whipped. Still others left to seek their freedom outside the South. From the Upper South, some reached the free states. From the western states of the Deep South, some escaped to Mexico. Others found refuge with Native Americans in the Florida swamps or in the Great Dismal Swamp in Virginia and North Carolina. Some fled to the cities of the South.

### The Slave Communities

But slaves did more than react to abusive treatment on a day-by-day basis or resort to running away. By the nineteenth century, they had forged their own semi-independent societies within which they developed rules, values, a sense of self-respect, and a spirit of solidarity that helped them to survive both physically and psychologically. And in doing so, the slaves did not simply draw on the culture of the dominant white society. Rather, they blended American and West African practices and values, so that by the early nineteenth century they had created an African American culture that met their needs.

Slave families are an excellent example of how bondpeople developed their own values and practices to suit their circumstances. Slave marriages were not recognized by the dominant white society. Furthermore, masters often violated male-female slave relationships by raping the females. Also, man and woman could suddenly be separated by sale.

Yet slave families survived these obstacles. Regardless of the law, slaves formed families, and the two-parent family prevailed. Adapting to the facts of life, slaves considered it acceptable for a husband and wife to remarry if they were separated. The slaves also preserved the West African tradition of large, extended families strongly bound by mutual obligation. These values helped to preserve slave families. For example, when the master broke up a family so that children were separated from their parents, the youngsters were raised by other relatives—or, if there were no blood relatives, strangers would step in to act as "grandparents," "aunts," and "uncles." The slave family's survival in a society that did not recognize it, and in fact did much to undermine it, was a remarkable achievement.

The slaves' religion gave them strength to carry on despite their oppression. They adopted the Christian religion but stressed those aspects of Christianity that had special importance for them. These included the Christian belief that all were equal before God, regardless of earthly status, and that every life was, therefore, significant; that all those with faith, whatever their position in society, could attain salvation; and that salvation would finally bring relief from the trials of earthly existence. The slaves readily identified with the Israelites of the Bible, enslaved and downtrodden but eventually finding freedom.

The slaves added elements of African religion to their religious practices. These included the communal call-and-response style of worship, drumming, and clapping, all of which strengthened slave solidarity. West African-style conjurers and magicians played a role in African American religion. Though condemned and ridiculed by whites, they had a high status in the slave community.

As we have seen, whites generally did not care for independent black worship; they preferred that blacks listen to white preachers. But even when masters tried to prevent slaves from holding their own services, bondpeople managed to assemble on their own, even going into the woods or swamps if necessary. By shaping their own religious practices, slaves asserted an independent spiritual identity that enabled them to be free from within although enslaved from without.

Slaves asserted themselves in other ways. Storytellers were important people within the slave community, and their stories often had hidden messages. The stories of Brer Rabbit and Brer Fox, based on the African tradition of "trickster" tales, told of how the weak could triumph over the strong by using their wits. These stories relieved the anger that slaves felt toward their masters by providing at least imaginary victories; they also offered guidance on how to survive in an unfriendly world.

Musicians, too, were important people among the slaves. Their music was mostly improvised and group oriented. Group singing, possibly based on African practice, fostered the union of the individual with the slave community and was another way of promoting solidarity. Work songs, with their rhythms adjusted to the labor being performed, eased the burden of toil. Songs often contained messages of protest and, particularly in the case of spirituals, of hope.

## Slave Revolts

Attempts to overthrow the system were less common in the nineteenth century than before, and there were no major revolts after 1831, at least none that are well documented. One reason is that the development of the slave community increased bondpeople's ability to resist the psychological pain of slavery and so decreased the likelihood of rebellion. Another is that treatment of the slaves improved somewhat in the nineteenth century. Also, in the nineteenth century a larger proportion of slaves were married than before (men outnumbered women until the late eighteenth century), and slaves with family attachments had more to lose should a revolt fail.

Nevertheless, two significant revolts were organized in the antebellum period. One was the Denmark Vesey conspiracy. In 1800 Vesey won $1,500 in a lottery and purchased his freedom. Later he earned a good living as a carpenter in Charleston, South Carolina. Hating slavery and slaveholders, Vesey was not satisfied to live in comfort. For several years he agitated among the slaves, urging them to resist oppression. In 1821 Vesey, an intelligent and well-read man, built a revolutionary organization. As his assistants, he chose blacks who were respected in the community, including slave artisans, officials in the African Methodist Episcopal church, and an African-born sorcerer, Gullah Jack. Recruits were found in Charleston and the surrounding area, and weapons were collected. Up to 9,000 slaves may have been involved.

A slave army was to attack six strategic points in Charleston on July 14, 1822. But during the last week of May, a slave revealed the existence of a plot, although he did not know any details. While the authorities tried to discover who the leaders were, Vesey—aware that they knew of a conspiracy—moved up the day of the revolt to June 16. But the plot was broken up before he could strike. Vesey was arrested on June 22. On July 2, he was tried and hanged. Ultimately, more than 130 blacks were arrested and 35 were hanged.

Nine years later a slave revolt occurred in Southampton County, Virginia. Nat Turner was a devoutly religious slave preacher who gave no obvious sign of being discontent. But from early in his life, Turner believed that he had been chosen by God to liberate his people. In February 1831 he interpreted a solar eclipse as a sign to act. Turner selected four lieutenants and set July 4, 1831, as the day for his uprising. He became ill and had to postpone it. But on August 13, when the sun seemed to have a strange greenish-blue tint, Turner decided to stage the revolt on August 21.

The rebels' strategy was first to terrorize the countryside by killing all the whites they met and then to spare those who surrendered. Beginning with only seven men armed with just a broad-axe and a hatchet, the rebels first killed Turner's master and his family. Within a day their numbers had grown to about 70, and they had killed 60 whites. Troops soon gathered; they killed more than 100 blacks, many of whom had not played any part in the rebellion. A Richmond newspaper reported that "men were tortured to death, burned, maimed and subjected to nameless atrocities. The overseers were called upon to point out any slaves whom they distrusted; and if any tried to escape they were shot down." The point was not just to put down the rebellion but to terrorize blacks so there would be no future revolts. Most of the surviving participants were tried in September and October and either executed or sent out of the state. Turner himself escaped capture until October 30. On November 11 he was executed.

The South was stunned by the uprising. It was not just the number of whites killed, but the fact that the insurgents had been led by a seemingly obedient, pious slave. In fact, before Turner was executed, he described his owner as "a kind master . . . in fact, I had no cause to complain of his treatment of me." If this slave could not be trusted, which ones could? In fact, as we have noted, the Vesey and Turner episodes by no means represented typical slave behavior, especially in the antebellum years. But these events—along with the growth of sectional conflict and the emergence of a new, militant abolitionist movement—made southerners more fearful than ever of rebellions. The result was a further tightening of laws for controlling slaves and free blacks.

## NORTH VERSUS SOUTH, 1820–1850

During the first half of the nineteenth century, friction between the North and South over the issue of slavery became the central issue of American politics. As we have seen, the rapid spread westward of the Cotton Kingdom after 1815 alarmed many northerners. Suddenly, it no longer seemed likely that the "peculiar institution," as slavery was sometimes called, would die out on its own. Therefore, northern political leaders were no longer willing to give in to the South on slave-related issues.

This became clear in 1819, when Missouri applied for admission to the Union as a slave state. It was one thing for slavery to extend into Deep South states such as Mississippi and Alabama. But it was another matter when slavery moved north into Missouri, an area with a temperate climate and at roughly the same latitude as the free states of Ohio, Indiana, and Illinois. If slavery was permitted in Missouri, it might sweep through all the western territories. Many northern white farmers and workers feared they would have no economic future in the West if slavery became the dominant labor system there. Another concern was that the slaveholders would have greater power in Washington, D.C., if the territories entered the Union as slave states. A much smaller number of people concerned themselves with the moral implications of slavery's expansion.

In 1820 a New York congressman proposed to admit Missouri only if it provided for the gradual abolition of slavery. This measure passed in the House, where most members came from free states. But the Senate, half of whose members represented slave states, voted to admit Missouri as a slave state without conditions. A compromise was worked out, with Speaker of the House Henry Clay of Kentucky playing a key role. Missouri was admitted as a slave state with no restrictions. To maintain the equal balance in the Senate, Maine—which had been part of Massachusetts—was admitted as a free state. Also, slavery was barred from that part of the Louisiana Purchase north of latitude 36 degrees, 30 minutes.

The slavery issue temporarily faded into the background, partly because for 25 years the United States did not acquire new territory to disturb the balance established by the Missouri Compromise. However, the issue would not die. With a growing majority of the American people living in the free states, southerners increasingly saw themselves as a minority whose way of life was threatened by hostile northern politicians and a new abolitionist movement that emerged in the 1830s (see "The New Abolitionist Movement," page 67). By then John C. Calhoun of South Carolina had developed a nullification doctrine to protect southern interests. It claimed that a state could declare federal laws void within its borders. Northerners, not surprisingly, rejected the doctrine.

In 1836 the House of Representatives adopted the so-called gag rule for handling the growing number of antislavery petitions it was receiving. The rule provided for tabling (removing from consideration) such petitions instead of sending them to a committee, which was the usual procedure. It was backed by southern congressmen with the support of some of their northern colleagues, who wanted to avoid divisive debate. But the rule was denounced by abolitionists and others as violating the constitutional right of petition. Opponents of the rule, led by John Quincy Adams, repealed it in 1845.

In the 1820s and 1830s, southern states with major ports on the Atlantic and Gulf coasts passed laws for the jailing of free black sailors while their ships were in port. This reflected the southern fear of free blacks as instigators of slave rebellions. Since many of those arrested were from the free states, protest against these laws came from the North. In the 1830s presidents Andrew Jackson and Martin Van Buren encouraged postmasters to stop the delivery of abolitionist literature to the South. Some in the North contended that this policy, along with the gag rule, showed that slavery, based on repression, threatened the liberties of all.

On the other hand, southerners were disturbed by the attempts of some northern states to prevent enforcement of the Fugitive Slave Act of 1793. In 1826, for example, Pennsylvania passed a measure banning the seizure and removal of slaves from the state, in effect annulling the law. An 1841 New York law gave fugitive slaves the right to trial by jury, although the federal law did not. The Supreme Court, in *Prigg v. Pennsylvania* (1842), declared such laws unconstitutional. But the decision also said that the states did not have to help enforce the federal law. Some northern states then barred state officials from carrying it out. Actions such as these convinced a growing number of southerners that the North sought to destroy slavery and dominate the South.

Even more alarming to southerners was the support some northerners expressed for slave violence. In 1841, a slave ship called the *Creole* was carrying slaves from Virginia to New Orleans. The slaves revolted, gained control of the vessel, and sailed it to the Bahamas. Representative Joshua Giddings of Ohio expressed sympathy for the slaves' actions. Censured by the House of Representatives, he resigned, ran again, and won reelection.

War with Mexico in 1846 resulted in U.S. acquisition of vast amounts of land in the West and Southwest, which revived the issue of whether slavery should be allowed in the territories. Many northerners supported the Wilmot Proviso. Introduced in Congress in 1846, it would have barred slavery from all territories won from Mexico. Endorsed by 14 northern state legislatures and passed by the House, it was defeated in the Senate. For southerners, the broad support among the free states for the Wilmot Proviso was further evidence of northern hostility to slave state interests. The emergence in 1848 of the Free Soil Party, opposed to any expansion of slavery outside of the existing slave states, further aroused southern anxiety.

In 1850 Henry Clay helped work out still another arrangement between North and South, known as the Compromise of 1850. California, part of the territory acquired from Mexico, entered the Union as a free state. The rest was divided into the New Mexico and Utah territories, with no federal restrictions on slavery. The slave trade in the District of Columbia was outlawed. Finally, the Fugitive Slave Act of 1850 offered even stronger protection than the 1793 Fugitive Slave Act for slaveholders seeking to recapture their escaped chattel. However, this compromise by no means ended sectional conflict. For one thing, it left unclear whether territorial governments had the right to prohibit slavery. For another, some in the North interfered with enforcement of the new fugitive slave law. For these and other reasons, conflict between North and South would intensify, not lessen, during the 1850s.

## THE NEW ABOLITIONIST MOVEMENT

The abolitionist movement of the Revolutionary era was in decline by 1800—in the North because steps had been taken to abolish slavery there, and in the Upper South because its white inhabitants feared living with a large population of free blacks. Except for a brief revival in the Upper South during the 1820s and early 1830s, abolitionism disappeared forever in the southern states.

During the 1830s, however, a new abolitionist movement emerged in the North. It was linked to a religious revival and was part of a larger crusade for reform causes including temperance, peace, and women's rights. The new abolitionism was different from the old movement in many respects. The Revolutionary-era abolitionists strongly condemned slavery, but they did not launch harsh attacks on slaveholders. Also, they favored a moderate approach: gradual emancipation with compensation for owners. Some supported colonization. The new abolitionists, however, were not known for their moderation. To them, slavery was a sin and slaveholders were sinners. They opposed gradualism and colonization and demanded the immediate and unconditional end of slavery. Like the eighteenth-century abolitionists, however, the great majority opposed the use of violence.

The new abolitionism began with the publication on January 1, 1831, of the first issue of the *Liberator*, an antislavery newspaper edited by the fiery William Lloyd Garrison of Massachusetts. In it Garrison took the militant tone that characterized the movement, stating that on the subject of slavery "I do not wish to think, to speak, or write with moderation. . . . I am in earnest—I will not equivocate—I will not excuse—I will not retreat a single inch—AND I WILL BE HEARD." In 1832 he founded the New England Anti-Slavery Society. The following year Garrison was a founder of the American Anti-Slavery Society, an organization that he did not control but did strongly influence.

Other white antislavery leaders included Arthur and Lewis Tappan, New York merchants; former Alabama slave owner James Birney, living in Cincinnati; Wendell Phillips, a Boston aristocrat and an outstanding orator; Sarah and Angelina Grimké of Philadelphia, daughters of a South Carolina slaveholder; and feminists such as Lucretia Mott. Theodore Dwight Weld, the leading abolitionist in the West, promoted antislavery sentiment among the students at Lane Seminary and then Oberlin College, both in Ohio; many of them went on to help slaves escape through the Underground Railroad (see page 71).

Garrison and his followers, whose influence was strongest in New England, stressed the strategy of moral persuasion. They believed that through such methods as lecturing and distributing literature, the abolitionists would be able rouse the North against slavery and eventually shame the South into abolishing it. They rejected political activity, believing that their moral crusade would be corrupted by the compromises required in the world of politics. In 1840 abolitionists who disagreed with Garrison over political participation and other issues withdrew from the American Anti-Slavery Society and, led by Lewis Tappan, established the American and Foreign Anti-Slavery Society. These political abolitionists, as they were known, supported James Birney for president in 1840 and 1844 as the candidate of the antislavery Liberty Party; in 1848 many endorsed the Free Soil ticket.

## Black Abolitionists

Blacks had not been a part of the Revolutionary-era abolitionist movement, but they were very much part of the new one. Even before Garrison began the new movement, blacks had formed a number of antislavery groups in the North; the Massachusetts General Colored Association, created in 1826, may have been the earliest one. *Freedom's Journal*, founded by John Russwurm and Samuel E. Cornish in 1827 as the first black newspaper in the United States, was a voice against slavery. In 1829 David Walker, a free black in Boston, published *Walker's Appeal*, a bold, harsh, uncompromising call for emancipation that urged slaves to use violence if necessary. "Strike for your lives and liberties," he wrote. "Let every slave throughout the land do this, and the days of slavery are numbered. You cannot be more oppressed than you have been. . . . *Rather die freemen than live to be slaves.*" Soon copies of the *Appeal* were circulating in the South, to the horror of whites. In 1830, 40 black leaders held a national convention in Philadelphia to discuss the struggle against slavery and ways to improve the status of northern blacks. What came to be known as the colored convention movement held national gatherings annually through 1835, and occasionally afterward, to coordinate strategy. Many state and local conventions were also held.

Blacks, then, were ready to participate in the new abolitionist movement, although whites played the dominant role. Three of the 63 delegates to the founding convention of the American Anti-Slavery Society in 1833 were black, and 6 blacks served on the organization's board of managers, the most prominent among them Robert Purvis. Blacks were also involved in the organization of various state affiliates. Four black women signed the charter of the Female Anti-Slavery Society, founded in 1833. Separate black auxiliaries were also formed. But because many black abolitionists did not favor separate black organizations, they were not necessarily closed to whites. (One was named the Lexington [Massachusetts] Abolition Society of Colored Persons and Whites Who Feel Desirous to Join.)

Especially before 1850, abolitionists were extremely unpopular in the North. White abolitionists were often victims of violence: In 1834 a New York mob destroyed Lewis Tappan's house; Garrison came close to being lynched by a Boston mob in 1835; and Elijah P. Lovejoy was killed in Alton, Illinois, in 1837. Yet black abolitionists faced an even greater likelihood of attack, since they challenged racist stereotypes of blacks as submissive and fearful. So, for example, when Garrison and black abolitionist Frederick Douglass attended a meeting in Harrisburg, Pennsylvania, in 1847, it was Douglass who became the target for thrown objects.

Despite the dangers, black abolitionists persisted and played significant roles in the movement. Robert Purvis of Philadelphia, son of a wealthy white merchant and a free black woman, was a founder of the American Anti-Slavery Society and served as president of the Pennsylvania Anti-Slavery Society from 1845 to 1850. Charles Lenox Remond of Salem, Massachusetts, became an active member of the Massachusetts Anti-Slavery Society in 1838 and was its first black lecturer. Although she did not have an official title, Sojourner Truth, a former New York slave, played a unique role in the movement. Although illiterate, she was a mesmerizing antislavery lecturer, known for her sharp insights and her quick retorts to male hecklers.

Other prominent black abolitionists included Henry Bibb, an escaped slave from Kentucky who became an antislavery lecturer; William Wells Brown, a fugitive from the same state who became a historian, novelist, and antislavery speaker; Charles B. Ray of New York, editor of the *Colored American*; Martin R. Delany, a free black whose family moved from western Virginia to Chambersburg, Pennsylvania, and who became a physician and antislavery writer; James W. C. Pennington, a fugitive slave from Maryland who became a Congregational minister in Hartford, Connecticut; Samuel Ringgold Ward, a New York schoolteacher and Congregational minister; and Henry Highland Garnet, a Maryland slave who fled to New York and became a Presbyterian minister.

But the most famous black abolitionist was Frederick Douglass. A Maryland slave, he escaped to the North in 1838. After coming to the attention of Garrison in 1841, he went on the abolitionist lecture circuit. With his imposing six-foot-plus physique, rousing voice, and great command of language, he became one of the movement's best orators. In 1845 the *Narrative of the Life of Frederick Douglass*, his account of his life as a slave, was published. Since the publicity from his book would make his former master aware of where he lived, Douglass spent two years abroad to avoid recapture. Returning in 1847, he founded an abolitionist newspaper, the *North Star* (later known as *Frederick Douglass's Paper*), in Rochester, New York.

During the 1830s the great majority of black abolitionists were enthusiastic and hopeful about the new abolitionist movement. Willing to follow the lead of Garrison, who dominated the white movement during that decade, they joined him in opposing political activity and the use of force. Many were also critical of separate black antislavery organizations, arguing along with Garrison that they fostered prejudice and segregation.

By the late 1830s, however, some blacks were coming to believe that their race should take a more independent stand within the movement. They had become somewhat disillusioned by the discovery that many white abolitionists were racially prejudiced and did not believe in full equality for blacks. Some black abolitionists complained, for example, that most of them served as fieldworkers and lecturers while very few were given positions of leadership. Then the 1840 split in the abolitionist movement, by reducing Garrison's authority, gave blacks more leeway to express their own independent views.

Just a few weeks after the split, for example, debate over separate black organizations broke out in two black newspapers, the pro-Garrison *National Anti-Slavery Standard* and Charles Ray's *Colored American*, which was critical of the Garrisonians. After the *Standard* declared, "We oppose all exclusive action on the part of colored people except where the clearest necessity demands it," Samuel Ringgold Ward replied in the *Colored American*. Noting that a large number of whites in the movement "best loved the colored man at a distance," he argued that so long as this was the case, blacks had to organize on their own. His white friends would understand this, Ward wrote, "had they worn a colored skin . . . as I have in this pseudo-republic."

During the 1840s some black abolitionists—though only a minority—began to look favorably upon violence as a way of ending slavery; in doing so they defied the nonviolent stand of nearly all their white associates. In 1840 Charles Lenox Remond stated that war between the United States and Britain over their Canadian-U.S. boundary dispute might be desirable; by weakening the Union, he reasoned, it could lead to a slave rebellion. In 1843 Henry Highland Garnet questioned whether slavery could be defeated by moral force alone; some bloodshed, he felt, would probably be necessary. When Garrison's *Liberator* attacked him both for that and for his support of the abolitionist Liberty Party, Garnet argued that by demanding conformity within the movement the Garrisonians were trying to turn abolitionism into "abject slavery."

Frederick Douglass began to distance himself from Garrison after 1847, when he left New England—Garrison's stronghold—and moved to Rochester, New York, to publish the North Star. In an 1849 speech, he surprised a Boston audience by stating that he would "welcome the intelligence to-morrow, should it come, that the slaves had risen in the South. . . ." Two years later Douglass completed his break by endorsing political action. (However, he remained a firm advocate of racial integration and an opponent of exclusively black institutions.)

Perhaps the strongest statement of black independence was made by Martin R. Delany—known as the father of black nationalism—in his Condition, Elevation, Emigration and Destiny of the Colored Race (1852). While praising the work of white abolitionists, he complained that they "presumed to think for, dictate to, and know better what suited colored people, than they know for themselves." He urged blacks to develop more confidence in their own efforts and depend less on whites.

## The Underground Railroad

Despite growing differences between blacks and whites within the antislavery crusade, they worked together on the most dramatic project of the abolitionist movement: the Underground Railroad. More than 3,000 men and women of both races forged an organization to help bondpeople escape to the free states. "Conductors," most of them black, went into the South to help slaves who wanted to flee. The most famous was Harriet Tubman, a Maryland slave who escaped to freedom in 1849. She went back south at least 15 times, bringing back some 300 slaves and gaining a reputation as the "Black Moses." Tubman was short and slight of build, but her appearance was deceptive; she was a resourceful, tough, and fearless woman who eventually had $40,000 worth of rewards on her head in the South. When slaves lost their courage and asked to turn back, she pulled out a gun and threatened to shoot them. This tactic helps explain her reputation for bringing all of her charges to freedom.

Other black conductors included Josiah Henson, a slave who had escaped to Canada, and Leonard A. Grimes, a free black in Washington, D.C. Whites also served as conductors. Levi Coffin, a Quaker known as the "president" of the railroad for his organizing work over a 35-year period, also went south to speed slaves on their way. Others were Calvin Fairbank, an Oberlin graduate, and John Fairfield, a Virginian from a slave-owning family.

The slaves were sent northward by train, by boat, and when necessary, by foot. Most came from the border states of Delaware, Kentucky, and Maryland. Many clever methods of deception were employed: male slaves, for example, dressed as the opposite sex were given white babies to carry so that they could claim to be nurses, and one slave was even shipped northward in a crate. In an emergency, the quick-thinking Tubman hid escaping slaves under a wagonload of manure after giving them straws for breathing.

Harriet Tubman, photographed in her later years, was a conductor on the Underground Railroad during the 1850s and a Union scout and spy during the Civil War. She won fame for her bravery and resourcefulness.

Along their escape routes, slaves stopped at "stations," or safe houses, where white and black "stationmasters" gave them food and lodging. Because of fugitive slave legislation, stations were needed in the North as well as the South. Slaves often moved quickly from one station to another to put a distance between themselves and the slave states, some ending their journey only upon reaching

Canada. Many abolitionists served as either northern stationmasters or members of vigilance committees, which protected the ex-slaves from recapture, advised them of their rights, and helped them start their new lives in the North.

## THE SOUTH REACTS

From about the 1820s on, southerners believed that their way of life was under a growing threat: the Denmark Vesey conspiracy, David Walker's *Appeal,* and the Nat Turner rebellion aroused fear of insurrection from within, while growing sectional tensions and abolitionist attacks appeared to threaten slavery from without. The southern states responded by imposing new restrictions on slaves and free blacks.

In 1831, the Turner Rebellion terrified the South, and the fact that Turner was a literate slave who had drawn inspiration by reading the Bible promoted the belief that literate bondpeople were more likely to be troublemakers than illiterate ones. Between 1831 and 1834 Virginia, South Carolina, Georgia, and Alabama outlawed the teaching of slaves to read or write. (Louisiana had done so in 1830 in reaction to David Walker's *Appeal,* and Mississippi had acted before 1820.) In 1833 Georgia even barred slaves from doing any tasks at printing shops that might help them become literate. An 1835 North Carolina measure allowed private teaching but banned public instruction. Kentucky, Tennessee, and Maryland did not prohibit the education of slaves, but in some areas public opinion prevented it.

Since Turner was a preacher, his revolt intensified the southern fear that black religious leaders spread sedition and that religious meetings could become gatherings for plotting revolt. In 1831 Maryland barred slaves from attending religious meetings except those conducted by a licensed white clergyman or his agent, while Virginia prohibited preaching by slaves and nighttime religious gatherings. That year the Mississippi legislature ruled that slaves could preach only on their home plantations and with their master's permission.

To prevent poisonings, Georgia in 1835 ordered druggists not to employ slaves in the compounding, dispensing, or selling of medicines. With abolitionists helping slaves to flee the South, Maryland—which bordered on free territory—passed laws to check fugitives. An 1838 law made escape a felony. An 1849 measure raised from 5 to 15 years the maximum penalty for encouraging or helping a fugitive. To reduce the danger of slave conspiracies, Nashville, Tennessee, in 1837 banned slave meetings not supervised by whites.

But free blacks were the primary targets of white southerners. As we have seen, whites believed that free blacks—who numbered about 240,000 in the South by 1850—incited dissatisfaction among the slaves. And even when they did not, whites believed that their very existence promoted discontent by showing slaves that they had an alternative to bondage.

Furthermore, in the nineteenth century, southerners increasingly claimed that slavery was an ideal social system for blacks as well as whites; blacks, they claimed, could not take care of themselves and so needed masters to care for them.

Therefore, any accomplishments of free blacks were a challenge to the South's justification for slavery; if blacks could succeed as free people, how could whites argue that slavery was the best arrangement for them? Consequently, free blacks made white southerners very uncomfortable. (One southern white said, "I like a nigger . . . but I hate a damned free nigger.")

## Free Blacks Face New Forms of Oppression

By 1820 the slave states had already imposed many types of burdensome laws upon free blacks. They were assumed to be slaves unless they could prove otherwise. Their movement was restricted. They could not vote in most states. They paid special taxes, were barred from many occupations, could not testify against whites, and received greater punishments than whites for the same offenses. Yet new ways were found to curtail their freedom after 1820.

Some states made it illegal to teach free blacks, as well as slaves. Many prohibited free blacks from preaching. These laws sought not just to reduce the number of black subversives, but also to prevent the establishment of independent black institutions, such as schools and churches, that would give free blacks some measure of liberty and initiative. Since around 1800, attempts had been made to close black churches and schools, but more by pressure than by legislation. From the 1830s on, many slave states banned them by law. Other institutions also came under attack; Maryland in 1843 tried to uproot black fraternal organizations by barring free blacks from belonging to secret societies.

During the 1830s, the only two southern states still permitting free blacks to vote withdrew that right: Tennessee in 1834 and North Carolina in 1835. Restrictions on their right to carry weapons were tightened. In 1806, for example, Virginia had required free blacks to obtain a special license for carrying firearms; in 1832 it barred them entirely from owning guns. In 1843 the city of Augusta, Georgia, prohibited them from even carrying canes, clubs, or sticks unless they were blind. Five years afterward Virginia barred free blacks from owning dogs in some counties—they, too, could be used as weapons.

The practice of segregation—or Jim Crow, as it came to be known after a stereotyped black man in a nineteenth-century song-and-dance routine—was expanded. As we have seen, segregation spread after about 1800. During the period from 1820 to 1860, it was applied to new institutions as they emerged. These included railroads, railroad stations, parks, museums, theaters, libraries, benevolent societies, and workingmen's associations. New Orleans required separate brothels for blacks and whites. By the Civil War, segregation had spread into nearly every facet of life in the South. Also, legislation requiring segregation became more common in the antebellum years. But these laws applied mostly to government-owned facilities. Otherwise, Jim Crow remained primarily a matter of custom and private business practice rather than of law (and was not always rigidly enforced).

After 1820 most Lower South states imposed a new type of supervision upon free blacks: each was required to choose a white guardian to supervise his or her affairs. Such laws were only occasionally enforced, though. The Deep South states also became known for laws aimed at the free black seamen entering the ports of Atlantic and Gulf states. Spurred by Denmark Vesey's conspiracy in Charleston, the South Carolina legislature passed the Seamen's Act in 1822. It required Charleston's sheriff to arrest free blacks aboard incoming merchant vessels until the ships departed; the purpose was to prevent them from roaming the city and inciting the slaves. Alabama, Georgia, and Louisiana passed similar laws for their ports.

Other oppressive measures attempted to extract cheap labor from free blacks— especially in the Upper South states, where over 80 percent of free blacks lived. Most Upper South states permitted judges to place free black children of supposedly unfit parents with white families as apprentices. Normally, apprenticeship laws required that apprentices be educated and taught a skilled trade with which they could then earn a living. With regard to blacks, however, the law imposed no such requirements, and the children were simply used to perform menial tasks without pay. Also, in some states free blacks delinquent in paying taxes or private debts were leased out as laborers, usually to farmers but also to canal and railroad companies.

Maryland and Delaware had the largest proportions of free blacks in their populations—11 percent and 22 percent, respectively, in 1840. That is probably why they made the greatest attempts to subject free blacks to forced labor. Maryland in 1840 authorized sheriffs to hire out for a year all free black vagrants— individuals without visible means of support or good work habits. (White vagrants merely served short terms in jail or the poorhouse.) If they were unemployed 10 days after the year expired, they could be hired out again for another year, and so on. Seven years later Delaware passed a similar bill. These laws sought to deprive free blacks of their independence. They also provided employers with low-wage labor; the free blacks who were hired out got wages far lower than the going rate on the open market. These laws threatened all free blacks, because racially prejudiced white officials were the ones deciding who was a vagrant.

In 1831 Maryland reacted to the Turner Rebellion by adopting a law that promoted the colonization of free blacks in Africa. This measure was unique because it provided for the expulsion of free blacks who did not leave voluntarily. The expulsion clause, passed at the urging of slaveholders, went unenforced—but not out of sympathy for free blacks. First, the legislature was unwilling to spend the huge amount that would have been needed for colonization. Second, the labor of the state's 52,000 free blacks—the highest number in any state—was important for Maryland's rural and urban economies.

Virginia, with the second-greatest number of free blacks in the South, adopted a unique law of its own in 1848. Many southern states passed legislation to restrict education for free blacks and to keep down their numbers by requiring newly freed slaves to leave the state, by barring free black migration into the state, and by other methods. But Virginia managed to combine the two goals in a spiteful piece of legislation that barred free blacks who left the state for educational purposes from ever returning.

## Free Blacks' Struggle for Survival

Free blacks tried to improve their hard lot in a number of ways. Many went to the free states—by 1860, southern-born persons made up one-third of Philadelphia's blacks and over one-quarter of Boston's. More would have gone except that many blacks saw little difference between the racism in the slave states and the racism in the free states (see the following section). Others went to Africa at the urging of the white-controlled colonization movement, which gained renewed support from whites after the Turner Rebellion. About 15,000 blacks left the country, most going to Africa, where they established the nation of Liberia.

The great majority of free blacks remained in the South, using their limited options to ease their hardships. One option *not* available to them was political protest. Not only were they denied the vote, but from the late 1830s on, any expression of opposition to the existing order by either blacks or whites was treated as virtual treason. Free blacks could, however, move to the region's cities and towns, where it was easier to escape white supervision. By 1860, one-third of the South's free blacks lived in urban areas, compared to just 15 percent of whites. These blacks often managed to establish their own churches, schools, and other institutions despite the law.

In urban areas and to a lesser extent in the countryside, free blacks could ignore some discriminatory laws simply by avoiding the authorities—laws such as those ordering free blacks to register with local government or to leave the state after being manumitted. These measures were poorly enforced most of the time. But blacks never knew when enforcement would tighten, as it usually did when rumors of slave revolts were circulating. And even when discriminatory laws went unenforced by the government, free blacks still had to worry about vigilante groups, such as the South Carolina Association in Charleston and the Raleigh Regulators in North Carolina, as well as groups formed on the spur of the moment. They enforced racial subordination through whipping, dunking, and other forms of violence. So while free blacks had some room to maneuver, they remained a highly subjugated group.

Economically, free blacks had sharply restricted opportunities. In rural areas they often worked in the fields alongside the slaves. Many rural free black women did agricultural work along with the men, but frequently they served as seamstresses, cooks, housekeepers, and laundresses. Males sometimes worked as boatmen and fishermen. Urban free blacks were better off, even though whites generally restricted them to occupations offering the least prestige and money. Typically the men worked as factory hands, waiters, longshoremen, and day laborers. The women performed household work or were peddlers. Yet rising prices for slaves increased the demand for free blacks as an alternative source of labor, which drove up their wages.

Despite all the roadblocks in their way, some free blacks did well for themselves. For example, the number of black landowners increased greatly during the antebellum years. A small black elite in the Deep South even managed to establish plantations, complete with black slaves. A free black in King George County,

Virginia, owned 71 slaves; two in St. Landry Parish, Louisiana, owned 84 each. This elite tried to mimic the ways of white planters, and they shunned their fellow blacks. Below them was a larger middle-class group of small businessmen and artisans. Some, including a number of barbers and caterers, developed a white clientele, but to keep the white customers, they had to deny service to their fellow blacks. Most, however, operated within the black community and provided its leadership before, during, and immediately after the Civil War.

## BLACKS IN THE FREE STATES

Blacks in the North were spared some of the restrictions imposed on free blacks in the slave states. Northern blacks, for example, could legally speak, write, and organize against racism. Also, the southern laws that compelled free blacks to perform low- or no-wage labor were generally absent in the free states. But the great majority of northern whites believed that blacks were an inferior race and supported discrimination against them. Northern blacks, who numbered 196,000 in 1850—about 1.5 percent of the North's population—were victimized by bigotry in almost all aspects of their lives.

In the antebellum years, northern blacks actually lost ground in the fight for the right to vote. After 1819 every new state entering the Union excluded blacks from the voting rolls. Meanwhile, some states that had previously given blacks the vote restricted it or took it away. For example, New York in 1820 limited black suffrage to those owning land worth at least $250. In 1837, Pennsylvania deprived all blacks of the vote. By 1860 only five northern states—Massachusetts, Rhode Island, Vermont, New Hampshire, and Maine—gave blacks equal suffrage rights with whites, and only 6 percent of all northern blacks lived in those states.

Some northern states followed the slave states in depriving blacks of basic courtroom rights. Ohio, Indiana, Illinois, Iowa, and California prohibited blacks from testifying against whites. (Ohio in 1856 and California in 1861 repealed those laws.) Most northern states prohibited blacks from serving on juries. Four free states—Indiana, Illinois, Iowa, and Oregon—banned black migration onto their soil. Others tried to exclude them by requiring incoming blacks to post large bonds.

Although generally not imposed by law, segregation was widespread. White public opinion—even among some abolitionists—overwhelmingly supported it. Among the places that were segregated were churches, schools, public transportation vehicles, theaters, lecture halls, restaurants, hotels, resorts, jails, hospitals, and cemeteries. Segregation also existed in housing: blacks usually could not buy homes in the more attractive locations. However, they were not yet segregated into all-black ghettos.

Public schools were one place where segregation was mandated by government. Many state and local governments that had made no provision for black education before 1820 established segregated schools afterward. The black schools were inferior to white schools: the buildings were frequently run down, the teachers were poorly trained, less money was spent on them than on white schools, and only the most basic subjects were taught.

Private attempts to improve education for blacks were often blocked by white prejudice. In 1834 the Noyes Academy in Canaan, New Hampshire, opened as an integrated school with 28 whites and 14 blacks. Townspeople feared that if they tolerated an integrated school, blacks would flood into Canaan. And so on July 4, 1835, some 300 local whites, using about 100 oxen, dragged the building away and left it in ruins. Even all-black private schools aroused white anger when they drew blacks from outside the community. In 1831, plans to establish a black college in New Haven, Connecticut, were abandoned after the town meeting condemned the proposal by a vote of 700 to 4. In April 1833, Prudence Crandall, a Quaker, opened a school for black girls in Canterbury, Connecticut, that drew students from a number of northern states. But intimidation and harassment—including window breaking, attempted arson, and pistol shots—forced the school to close in September 1834.

Blacks left white-controlled churches that discriminated against them, and formed their own. Frederick Douglass, an opponent of separate black institutions, condemned the black churches in 1848 as "negro pews [separate pews for blacks in white-controlled churches], on a higher and larger scale" and urged blacks to fight for equality in the white churches. That year black abolitionist Henry Bibb stated, "I see no more use in having a colored church exclusively than having a colored heaven and a colored God." But in the case of churches, most blacks favored separation. Black churches were the most powerful and effective institutions in their communities. Also, the religion of these churches, like slave religion, drew on the unique black experience in Africa and America to meet the special spiritual needs of their members.

After 1840 blacks, working with white abolitionists, began to fight back against discrimination. However, they had only limited success, and most of it was in Massachusetts, where the abolitionist movement was strongest. The Massachusetts law against racial intermarriage was repealed in 1843. Frederick Douglass and other black abolitionists demonstrated against discrimination by sitting in whites-only railroad cars, from which they were thrown out by force. Finally, though, Massachusetts railroad companies ended their Jim Crow policy in the early 1840s. In the mid- and late 1840s, most towns and cities in Massachusetts, including Boston, ended school segregation. Progress also came in higher education. Western Reserve and Oberlin, both in Ohio, began admitting blacks in the 1830s. Later, Princeton, Amherst, Union College, the Oneida Institute, and a number of professional schools became integrated.

Blacks often faced harassment and mob violence. When in white neighborhoods, blacks frequently became the targets of taunts and insults. In 1829 and 1841, Cincinnati mobs attacked blacks, forcing many to flee the city. In 1842 whites in Philadelphia attacked a black parade marking the abolition of slavery in the British West Indies eight years earlier. Many blacks were assaulted or had their homes destroyed. Mob attacks occurred in other cities, too. Often the authorities did little or nothing to stop the violence.

Northern blacks—like free blacks in the South—were usually restricted to the lowest-paying and most menial work. Beginning in the 1830s, heavy immigration from Ireland meant that blacks faced increasing competition even for undesirable jobs. White, and especially Irish, workers saw blacks as competitors and sometimes used violence against them, especially during depressions, when jobs were scarce. Trade unions usually excluded blacks, and so the latter did not hesitate to serve as strikebreakers.

Still, a growing number of northern blacks overcame all obstacles and achieved economic success. These included doctors, lawyers, businesspeople, farmers, and craftsmen. Most of them served the black community, but some—such as barbers and restauranteurs—built up lists of white customers. To keep them, these black entrepreneurs had to turn away black customers, just as in the South.

## THE 1850s AND THE ROAD TO CIVIL WAR

During the 1850s the North and South drifted farther apart as each felt increasingly threatened by the other. The Fugitive Slave Act of 1850 made it easier for masters to recover escaped slaves and for kidnappers to falsely identify northern blacks as escaped slaves. As under the previous fugitive slave law, blacks could not testify or present witnesses to show that they did not belong to the person claiming them. But unlike under the old law, slaves were brought before a special commissioner, not a judge. The commissioner was not bound by any of the rules that protected defendants in normal court proceedings. Also, the commissioner would receive a higher fee for ruling in favor of the claimant than for ruling in favor of the alleged fugitive. Finally, the new law required citizens of the North to help capture runaways.

Many northerners who had felt little sympathy for abolitionism before were repelled by the law. Blacks and whites worked together to prevent slavecatchers, as they were called, from coming North to seize blacks. Southerners regarded this resistance as further evidence of a northern desire to destroy slavery. Spurred by the new fugitive slave law, Harriet Beecher Stowe wrote the antislavery novel *Uncle Tom's Cabin*, published in 1852. The leading character, Uncle Tom, was a saintly slave who rose above bitterness and a desire for revenge, despite all of the injustices he suffered. (Later, the meaning of "Uncle Tom" changed to signify blacks who were submissive and fawning toward whites and who served white rather than black interests.) Many of slavery's horrors were vividly depicted. The book's huge success in the North, where it was read by millions and performed as a play, strengthened southern hostility toward the North still more.

The Compromise of 1850 had temporarily quieted the controversy over whether slavery should be allowed in the territories. But the Kansas-Nebraska Act of 1854, introduced by Senator Stephen A. Douglas of Illinois, started up the conflict again. It provided that in the Kansas and Nebraska territories the issue of slavery would be settled by the territorial legislatures. Pro- and antislavery settlers rushed into the Kansas Territory, each side hoping to form a political majority. Soon warfare broke out in what became known as "Bleeding Kansas."

Many northerners were outraged because the Kansas-Nebraska Act repealed the Missouri Compromise, which had outlawed slavery in an area including Kansas and Nebraska. The law helped convince opponents of slavery in the Whig and Democratic parties to form the new Republican Party, which replaced the dying Whig organization. Most Republicans believed in white superiority and supported discrimination against blacks; many of its leaders, including Abraham Lincoln, favored colonization. Still, it was the first major American political party that was against slavery and that flatly opposed allowing slavery into the territories. White southerners regarded the Republicans as their mortal enemies.

The gap between North and South was widened by the Supreme Court's famous *Dred Scott v. Sanford* decision in 1857. The Court ruled that when the U.S. Constitution was drafted, blacks had not been considered part of the political community and that they had been regarded as "so far inferior, that they had no rights which the white man was bound to respect." Therefore, blacks could not be considered U.S. citizens. This ruling was of momentous importance for blacks, but whites were more interested in another part of the decision. The Court declared that Congress had no more power to ban slavery in the territories than it did in already existing states. Many northerners were outraged, because this ruling was in line with the most extreme proslavery views in the South. The *Dred Scott* opinion, along with the fact that the Democratic Party (which controlled the White House) was dominated by pro-southern elements, convinced many free-state whites that slaveholding interests were running the national government.

Two years later, it was the South's turn to be outraged. John Brown, a white abolitionist who had fought in "Bleeding Kansas," decided to use violence again. On October 16, 1859, he and about 20 armed followers, black and white, attacked the federal arsenal at Harper's Ferry, Virginia. They hoped their action would set off a slave revolt. However, they were quickly forced to surrender, and no revolt followed. Southerners were alarmed by the outpouring of northern admiration for Brown after the raid. This response convinced many southerners that slavery was in mortal danger as long as the South remained part of the Union.

That feeling spread further in 1860 after Republican candidate Abraham Lincoln was elected president without a single southern vote. Southern advocates of secession from the Union gained new strength. From December 1860 through the spring of 1861, 11 of the 15 slave states left the Union, and the Civil War began.

Because southerners felt increasingly threatened by the events of the 1850s, they passed ever more drastic laws to defend slavery. Hoping to reduce the number of free blacks, between 1855 and 1860 Virginia, Florida, Alabama, and other states passed laws allowing them to reenslave themselves. Very few free blacks took advantage of this offer, but whenever one did—to at least have the assurance of food, clothing, and shelter in a society extremely hostile to free blacks—southerners claimed that it demonstrated the great appeal of the slave system for blacks. Some states considered expelling free blacks. The Virginia legislature debated such a measure in 1853. It was not passed because of concerns that it

# FUGITIVE SLAVE BILL!

## HON. HENRY WILSON

### Will address the citizens on

## Thursday Evening, April 3,

At the

At 7 o'clock, on the all-engrossing topics of the day—the FUGI-TIVE SLAVE BILL, the pro-slavery action of the National Government and the general aspect of the Slavery question.

Let every man and woman, without distinction of sect or party, attend the meeting and bear a testimony against the system which fills the prisons of a free republic with men whose only crime is a love of freedom—which strikes down the habeas corpus and trial by jury, and converts the free soil of Massachusetts into hunting ground for the Southern kidnappers.

*Ashby, March 29, 1851.*

White & Potter's Steam Press—4000 Impressions per hour—Spring Lane, Boston.

A protest meeting against the Fugitive Slave Act of 1850 is announced. The speaker, Henry Wilson, was president of the Massachusetts state senate. The law made it easier for southern slave masters to retrieve runaways who had escaped to the North. The measure also required northern citizens to help retrieve runaways when the authorities requested them to do so.

would result in a labor shortage. In 1858 Arkansas actually passed a law requiring all free blacks to leave by January 1, 1860. Although the measure was never enforced, hundreds of free blacks fled the state because of it. Maryland in 1858 and Virginia in 1860 provided that free blacks who committed certain crimes could be sold into slavery. Also, between 1857 and 1860, Maryland, Alabama, Mississippi, and Arkansas banned manumission entirely.

As the 1850s progressed, black hopes for improving their condition in the United States grew dimmer. Between 15,000 and 20,000 northern blacks fled to Canada during the 1850s to escape possible reenslavement under the Fugitive Slave Act of 1850. Also, a growing number of blacks supported colonization. The leading black advocate was Martin R. Delany, who saw colonization as the only way for blacks to elevate themselves. Henry Highland Garnet, formerly an opponent of colonization, became a supporter. Frederick Douglass condemned an 1854 convention of black supporters of colonization, saying, "We are Americans. We are not aliens. We are a component part of the nation." But even Douglass, the foremost black advocate of integration, had softened his opposition a bit by early 1861.

The great majority of blacks continued to oppose colonization, but they became increasingly alienated and militant during the 1850s. Black leaders vowed to—and in fact did—resist the Fugitive Slave Act by force. Robert Purvis declared in 1850 that if a slavecatcher came after him, "I'll seek his life, I'll shed his blood." In his newspaper Frederick Douglass wrote that the remedy for the 1850 law was "a good revolver, a steady hand, and a determination to shoot down any man attempting to kidnap." After the *Dred Scott* decision, some black leaders asserted that they owed no further allegiance to the United States. Purvis said, "I would hail the advent of a foreign army on our shores, if that army provided liberty to me and my people in bondage." H. Ford Douglass stated, "I can hate this Government without being disloyal, because it has stricken down my manhood, and treated me as a saleable commodity."

Some blacks, anticipating a war over slavery, began practicing the use of firearms and studying military tactics. Since blacks could not join the state militias, some began forming their own military units in the North. At a Boston meeting to protest the Dred Scott decision in 1858, John R. Rock predicted that "sooner or later the clashing of arms will be heard in this country and the black man's services will be needed." His words proved prophetic: within a few years blacks would be fighting against the army of the secessionist slave states, sacrificing their lives to destroy the slave system.

# CHAPTER 5

......... 

# The Civil War and Reconstruction: 1861–1877

## EMANCIPATION AND BLACK MILITARY SERVICE

By February 1861 seven slave states, all in the Lower South, had seceded from the Union. During that month, delegates from those states met in Montgomery, Alabama, and formed the Confederate States of America. For president they chose Jefferson Davis of Mississippi, a former U.S. senator and secretary of war. Between February and June, four additional slave states left the Union. In the meantime, on April 12, 1861, Confederates had started the Civil War by firing on Fort Sumter, a federal military installation in Charleston Harbor.

President Abraham Lincoln's priorities were clear throughout the war. As he stated in 1862:

> My paramount object in this struggle is to save the Union and is not either to save or to destroy slavery. . . . What I do about slavery, and the colored race, I do because I believe it helps to save the Union; and what I forbear, I forbear because I do not believe it would help to save the Union.

Lincoln hated slavery. But like almost all Northern political leaders, he did not believe the Constitution gave him the authority to abolish it in the states. Therefore, the president would consider emancipation only if it seemed a military necessity.

Early in the war, President Lincoln gave no support to emancipation because, like many Northerners, he believed (or at least hoped) that the Confederacy could be defeated quickly and by conventional means—that is, with white troops. Also, he feared that any attempt to emancipate the slaves would prolong the war: first, because it would make the Confederate states fight harder; second, because it would antagonize pro-Union elements in the Confederacy; third, because it might undermine the loyalty of the five slave border states—Delaware, Maryland, Kentucky, Missouri, and the new state of West Virginia—that remained in the Union; and fourth, because many Northerners, especially workers, feared emancipation, believing that former slaves would flood the North and work for wages below existing rates. But in time, various developments pushed federal policy toward the emancipation of slaves and the use of black soldiers. (In the less race-conscious navy, blacks served almost from the beginning of the war.)

Just one month into the war, Northern military officers had to deal with slaves escaping to Union lines. In May 1861 General Benjamin F. Butler, who had captured territory in eastern Virginia around Fortress Monroe, refused to return slaves that had entered his lines. Butler claimed that because the Confederates were using slaves to build military fortifications, he could keep them as contraband property, subject to confiscation under the rules of war, instead of returning them under the Fugitive Slave Act. Since Butler's policy deprived the Confederacy of labor while adding labor to the Union side, Secretary of War Simon Cameron approved Butler's actions in late May. The importance of slave labor to the Confederacy was illustrated in July 1861 at the First Battle of Bull Run in Virginia: the fortifications that helped the Confederates win were built by slaves. Partly in response to Bull Run, Congress in August 1861 passed the First Confiscation Act, which declared that any property used to advance the rebellion, including slaves, was subject to seizure. In March 1862 Congress adopted an article of war that went farther: it barred officers from applying the Fugitive Slave Act to any contrabands under their control. The policy of confiscating slaves as contraband property did not give them their freedom, but it was the first step in that direction.

After Bull Run, Northerners began to realize that victory would not come easily; this recognition brought about changes in attitude toward the war. In late 1861 and 1862, a growing number of Northerners believed, first, that Southerners should pay the price of secession by losing their slaves, and second, that ex-slaves then should share the burden of battle. The stalemated military situation led to the war's first official act of emancipation, taken on August 30, 1861, by General John C. Frémont, Union commander of the Department of the West. Fighting Confederate guerrillas in Missouri, he declared a state of martial law and announced that all rebel property would be seized and the slaves freed. Lincoln quickly revoked the order, but the wide support for Frémont showed that Northern opinion was changing. In May 1862 General David Hunter, commander of the Department of the South, declared martial law, stated that all slaves in South Carolina, Georgia, and Florida were free, and began organizing blacks into the First South Carolina Volunteers. Again, Lincoln canceled the order.

But late in 1861, Lincoln began developing a program of emancipation. Moving with caution, though, he tried to avoid offending the slave states in the Union and public opinion in general. In November 1861 he sent an emancipation proposal to the Delaware legislature providing for gradual emancipation over a 30-year period, with compensation to masters paid partly by the federal government. In March 1862 he convinced Congress to offer financial help to any state that adopted a gradual emancipation plan. Lincoln felt that if just one of the Union slave states accepted, the others would follow. But none ever took the lead.

Lincoln also tried to develop a colonization plan to send slaves abroad after emancipation. Although Lincoln was not a man of hatred and his conduct toward blacks was always respectful, he shared many of the era's racial prejudices and believed that both blacks and whites would be better off apart. At Lincoln's request, Congress in April and July 1862 voted funds for colonizing freedpeople. In August he met with a delegation of blacks to promote colonization in Central America. Lincoln also encouraged colonization schemes in Haiti. But the great majority of blacks continued to reject colonization.

As the battlefield stalemate continued into 1862, Lincoln took decisive steps against slavery. In April, at his urging, Congress abolished slavery in Washington, D.C. Two months later Lincoln signed a bill ending slavery in the territories. Neither action violated his belief that the federal government could not abolish slavery in existing states: Washington, D.C., was a federal district, and the territories were not part of any state.

## The Emancipation Proclamation and Black Recruitment

By the summer of 1862, however, Lincoln was ready to go farther and attack slavery in the Confederate states. Developments in mid-1862 strengthened fears of a long war. By July, General George McClellan's campaign against Richmond, Virginia, the Confederate capital, had failed. The flow of Union volunteers had almost stopped. Although there was still much opposition, public opinion was moving rapidly in favor of freeing and then arming the slaves. On July 17, 1862, Congress passed the Second Confiscation Act, which freed all slaves belonging to persons supporting the rebellion. Four days later, Lincoln called his cabinet together and announced that he would issue a proclamation freeing all slaves in those states or parts of states still in rebellion on January 1, 1863. On September 22 Lincoln issued a preliminary proclamation in which he announced just that.

When Lincoln signed the Emancipation Proclamation on January 1, 1863, he justified it as a military necessity, not as an act of liberation, and he signed it as commander in chief of the armed forces, not as president. Because it was a military measure, the proclamation did not cover the border states that had stayed in the Union or the Union-occupied areas of Tennessee, Louisiana, and Virginia. These areas accounted for about 1 million slaves. Yet the proclamation did cover the approximately 3 million slaves in Confederate territory and was an invitation for them to cross over to the Union lines. However limited the scope of the proclamation, it clearly represented a death blow to the institution of slavery—provided that the North won the war.

Blacks understood this and celebrated joyously at meetings throughout the Union. At a gathering in Washington, D.C., a black man eloquently expressed the feelings of many:

> Once, the time was that I cried all night. What's the matter? What's the matter? Matter enough. The next morning my child was to be sold, and she

> was sold; and I never 'pected to see her no more till the day of judgment. Now, no more that! No more that! No more that! With my hands against my breast I was going to my work, when the overseer used to whip me along. Now, no more that! No more that! No more that!

Slaves in Confederate territory were not free to celebrate, but word of the proclamation spread among them.

The Emancipation Proclamation led directly to a policy of recruiting black soldiers. Some black units had already been organized. In September 1862, the first one had been mustered into the Union Army; made up of Southern free blacks, it was called the First Regiment Louisiana Native Guards. In August 1862 Secretary of War Simon Cameron authorized the creation of the first unit of former slaves. Called the First South Carolina Volunteers, it was commanded by Colonel Thomas Wentworth Higginson, a Massachusetts abolitionist. The unit was mustered in during November 1862. In Kansas, General James H. Lane formed the first unit of Northern blacks, known as the First Regiment of Kansas Colored Volunteers. It was mustered into the army in January 1863.

But only after the Emancipation Proclamation did the federal government and the states begin a serious drive to recruit blacks. Shortly after the proclamation, Lincoln ordered the enrollment of four regiments of black infantry and a battalion of black mounted scouts; recruitment headquarters were set up in New York and in New Orleans (captured in April 1862). In 1863 many Northern states began to form black fighting units. On orders from Washington, D.C., early in 1863 Northern military officers in the South began urging slaves to flee to Union lines; in the spring they began recruiting ex-slaves on a large scale. In May 1863, the War Department formed the Bureau of Colored Troops to supervise all matters relating to black units.

## BLACK SOLDIERS IN THE UNION CAUSE

Nearly 180,000 black troops served in the Union Army during the Civil War, almost three-quarters from the slave states. They served in 166 all-black units: 145 infantry, 7 cavalry, 12 heavy artillery, 1 light artillery, and 1 engineer. The units were led almost entirely by white commissioned officers; blacks served at lower levels as noncommissioned officers. Blacks participated in 449 engagements, of which some 40 were considered major. More than 37,000 were killed. In the navy, one-quarter of the 118,000 sailors were black. Sixteen black soldiers and at least four black sailors won Congressional Medals of Honor for bravery in combat.

An early test of black soldiers occurred at the battle of Port Hudson in May 1863, involving the First and Third Louisiana Native Guards. In the face of intense rebel fire, the black troops attacked rebel fortifications on the Lower Mississippi River a few miles above Baton Rouge, Louisiana. Pushed back twice, they attacked two times more. The battle plan was poorly designed, and the Union forces were defeated. But the bravery of the 900 black combatants, 600 of whom died, greatly impressed the Northern public. The New York Tribune (June 8, 1863) declared: "That heap of six-hundred corpses, lying there dark and grim and silent and within the Rebel works, is a better proclamation of freedom than even President Lincoln's. A race ready to die thus was never yet retained in bondage and never can be."

In June 1863, black troops fought in the battle of Milliken's Bend in Louisiana, about 20 miles north of Vicksburg, Mississippi. Ex-slaves, mostly from Louisiana and Mississippi, helped to hold a Union fortification by hand-to-hand bayonet fighting in some of the most intense combat of the entire war. Almost 40 percent of the black soldiers were killed or wounded. An eyewitness wrote, "This battle has significance. It demonstrates the fact that freed slaves will fight." Assistant Secretary of War Charles A. Dana commented that "the bravery of the blacks at Milliken's Bend completely revolutionized the sentiment of the army with regard to the employment of Negro troops."

In July 1863 the 54th Massachusetts Regiment, commanded by Colonel Robert Gould Shaw, won renown for its valor in an unsuccessful attempt to capture Fort Wagner on Morris Island near Charleston. The fort's defenders waited until the black soldiers were just 200 feet away and then opened up an intense fire, much heavier than expected. Even so, Shaw and some of his soldiers reached the parapet, although ultimately they had to retreat. Among the 1,515 Union dead and wounded, 247 were black. Black troops gave a good account of themselves in many other engagements. These included the battle of Olustee, 50 miles west of Jacksonville, Florida, in February 1864, and the battle of Nashville in December 1864. The greatest concentration of black troops during the war was in northern Virginia from mid-1864 to the end of the war in April 1865.

Despite the great contributions of black soldiers, they were not treated as equals. A Board of Examiners within the Bureau of Colored Troops selected the commissioned officers for black units. Although the board tried to select white officers who supported the use of black soldiers, it rarely selected blacks as high-ranking field officers. Black nationalist Martin R. Delany was the first black commissioned officer; he organized the 104th and 105th U.S. Colored Troops in the South. Two regiments of the Louisiana Native Guards were staffed by black officers. A number of black surgeons and chaplains also received commissions; but in general, blacks were commanded by whites, which promoted a black convention in January 1865 to appoint a committee "to inquire why we are commanded and cannot command."

Blacks received lower pay than whites. Under the Enlistment Act of July 1862, blacks received $10 a month, $3 of which was paid in clothing, leaving $7; whites received $13 a month plus clothing. In protest, the men of the 54th Massachusetts Regiment refused to accept any pay and on at least one occasion went into battle shouting "Three cheers for Massachusetts and $7 a month!" This and other protests moved Congress in 1864 to mandate equal pay for blacks. Blacks often were given outdated or badly made arms and equipment. More frequently than whites, they were assigned fatigue and garrison duty. Some black units did not have enough surgeons because white physicians did not want to serve black troops; consequently, black soldiers often were treated by less qualified medical workers. And though the Bureau of Colored Troops selected white officers carefully, some were abusive. In December 1863 black troops in the Louisiana Native Guards at Fort Jackson rebelled briefly after a white officer publicly whipped a black soldier for a minor infraction.

Another concern was abusive treatment by outraged Confederates, who regarded the use of black troops against them as an insult. It was Confederate policy to treat captured blacks as rebellious slaves and to sell them into slavery. But Lincoln's threat to retaliate by requiring Confederate prisoners to do hard labor forced the Confederates to back off. The Confederate side refused to exchange black prisoners. But, short of manpower, the Confederacy modified its policy in the spring of 1864, agreeing to exchange freeborn blacks.

Brutal treatment of black soldiers by Confederates was not the rule. But an outrageous exception occurred after Southern forces captured Fort Pillow, Tennessee, 50 miles north of Memphis, on April 12, 1864. Shouting, "kill the goddamned niggers," they went on a rampage in which 238 of the 262 black troops at the fort were killed.

Black troops played a greater role in the Civil War than in the American Revolution, and their performance was enough to modify the antiblack views of some whites. After the war, their valiant service for the Union became a strong argument in behalf of equal rights for blacks.

## NONMILITARY SERVICE FOR THE UNION

During the war, about 500,000 slaves fled to Union lines. About 200,000 worked for the army in nonmilitary capacities. Many were used as laborers to dig military entrenchments and erect fortifications. They also worked as longshoremen, constructed roads and bridges, and helped build and operate railroads. The escaped slaves knew their way around the areas where they had lived, so they made excellent foragers, locating food and other items needed by the army. The ex-slaves also served as teamsters, hostlers (taking care of horses and mules), waiters, cooks, and servants.

From the early days of the war, some of the fleeing slaves brought valuable information about Confederate troop movements and defenses. *Harper's Weekly* (December 7, 1861), discussing the intelligence received by the Union Army's General George McClellan, remarked that "the most reliable information he can get comes from fugitive slaves." Some fugitives were in a position to bring information of a special kind. When William A. Jackson, Jefferson Davis's coachman, came into Union lines in May 1862, he reported on conversations of the Confederate president with his military officers and others.

Both recently escaped slaves and free blacks were often used as spies and scouts. One was Mary Elizabeth Bowser, a former slave living in Richmond. A Union spy, Elizabeth Van Lew, managed to place Bowser in the Confederate White House as a servant of Jefferson Davis. Although well educated, Bowser pretended to be illiterate so that secret documents would not be kept away from her. While dusting the furniture, she read letters and military orders. While serving dinner to Jefferson Davis and his guests, she listened carefully to discussions about military matters. Never caught, she spied until the end of the war. Harriet Tubman, the heroine of the Underground Railroad, served as a scout and spy. She arrived at Hilton Head, South Carolina, in 1862. A small, stooped woman with a bandanna wrapped around her head, she made herself look like a plantation slave to avoid suspicion. Moving on ahead of the Second South Carolina Volunteers, she assured slaves of the good intentions of the federal troops (white Southerners made up horror stories about Union forces to frighten slaves), encouraged them to leave their plantations, and brought back information about rebel defenses.

A famous Civil War incident occurred in Charleston Harbor during the spring of 1862. Robert Smalls, a slave who was an experienced pilot, wanted to flee Confederate territory. He put his family on board the armed Confederate steamship *Planter* at night. Piloting the ship at a slow speed as if he were on a normal run and giving the appropriate signals at each checkpoint, he reached the Union fleet that was blockading the harbor. Smalls reportedly told Union sailors, "I thought the *Planter* might be of some use to Uncle Abe."

## HOW THE CONFEDERACY EMPLOYED THE SLAVES

Without any choice in the matter, slaves made great nonmilitary contributions to the Confederate war effort. They were the backbone of the South's agricultural labor force and also worked in industry. Without them, the Confederacy could not have put nearly as many soldiers in the field as it did. With whites off to war, slaves assumed additional responsibilities in the Southern economy; on the plantations, for example, they sometimes acted as overseers, in fact if not in name. Also, the Confederate and state governments contracted with masters to use slaves in the armed forces. In the army, they worked as teamsters, bakers, butchers, boatmen, drovers, shoemakers, waiters, orderlies, and so on. In Confederate hospitals they worked as nurses. As laborers they built fortifications and other military works.

Slaves simply did what they had to do, but many free blacks offered their services, often working as military laborers. Most probably volunteered to increase their incomes. Yet some donated money or goods to the Confederate cause, and others volunteered for combat. Three companies of free blacks were actually organized in Louisiana's militia in 1861, though none saw combat. One reason for this spirit of generosity may have been a sense of local patriotism. Another may have been a hope that helping the rebel cause might lead to better treatment.

As the war went on, the armed forces' need for labor increased until the system of voluntary contracts with masters proved inadequate. By the end of 1862, most Confederate states had authorized the armed forces to impress slaves. In March 1863 the Confederate congress passed similar legislation. Slaves did not like working for the army because it usually meant harder labor than they faced on the farm. Masters disliked impressment because they feared their slaves would be overworked, which they were, or might flee, as many did. In April 1864 the congress voted to compensate masters whose slaves died or escaped, but the payment was very low.

As the Confederacy's military position worsened, some Southern leaders suggested using slaves as soldiers. Inconceivable during the first two years of the war, the idea gained support after the fall of Vicksburg in July 1863 gave the Union complete control of the Mississippi River and divided the Confederacy in two. In the autumn of 1863, the Alabama legislature urged President Davis to utilize slaves on a trial basis. Around the end of 1863, Secretary of War James A. Seddon spoke up in favor of both using and emancipating them. In 1864 public support for Southern independence declined, as a growing number of whites came to feel that the war was being fought merely to protect the property of the planter aristocracy. The governors of North Carolina, South Carolina, Georgia, Alabama, and Mississippi met in October 1864 and recommended the use of slaves as soldiers. After Robert E. Lee, commanding officer of the army, and President Davis expressed support for such a plan, the congress in March 1865 gave its approval. Companies of blacks were raised, but the war ended in April before any of them could be used.

## ASSISTANCE TO FREEDPEOPLE AND ITS LIMITS

From the war's start, the slaves believed that the conflict would bring freedom, and they regarded the arrival of federal troops as the fulfillment of Old Testament prophecy. To discourage servants from fleeing to the Union Army, Southern propaganda portrayed the "Yankees" as monsters who would ruthlessly mistreat them and then sell them to the dreaded sugar plantations of the Caribbean. As Union forces approached an area, masters moved their slaves away from Northern lines, a practice known as "running the Negroes." Still, about 500,000 of them reached Union lines.

The expectations of the slaves were realized to a great degree. The Emancipation Proclamation of January 1863 led less than three years later to ratification of the Thirteenth Amendment, which abolished slavery entirely. In addition, former slaves received a considerable amount of assistance from the North during the war. The movement to aid freedpeople was led by the American Missionary Society, the New England Freedman's Aid Society, the National Freedmen's Relief Association, the Friends Association for the Relief of Colored Freedmen, and other philanthropic groups, black and white. Some 200,000 Northern women organized themselves to send food, clothing, and books to the ex-slaves.

The aid organizations also sent more than 1,000 teachers from the North, most of them women, to Union-occupied territory, where they taught more than 200,000 blacks. Among them were such accomplished women as Charlotte Forten, a black abolitionist from Philadelphia, and Annie Wittenmyer, a white woman from Iowa who later became the first president of the Women's Christian Temperance Union. Freedpersons, adults and children alike, flocked enthusiastically to the new schools. Blacks often established schools on their own. Just a few weeks after Union forces occupied Savannah, Georgia, two schools financed entirely by blacks were organized. Blacks in Little Rock, Arkansas, established the first free schools for either race in the state's history. In Natchez, Mississippi, black women founded three schools. Many black church basements in Washington, D.C., were used as schoolrooms.

What the freedpeople probably wanted most was freedom from white control, which meant having their own land instead of working on white plantations and farms. They voiced this hope with the expression, "forty acres and a mule." But the former slaves found that Northern officials had little interest in ending the Southern plantation system with its strict form of labor control. Union Army officers in charge of the fugitive slaves who flooded military camps were interested not in promoting the well-being of blacks but in winning the war. To help the Union cause, they used blacks as military laborers and later as troops. Also, the officers wanted to revive the local economy quickly. It was easier to do this by restoring the customary plantation system (minus slavery) than by experimenting with a completely new system by distributing land to the ex-slaves.

To bring things back to normal, the army drew up one-year labor contracts on behalf of blacks; these contracts were made with loyal Southern planters, who were allowed to keep their land, and with Northern purchasers of abandoned and confiscated land. The contract labor system was first applied on Louisiana's cotton and sugar plantations in 1862. Beginning in 1863 it was used in the Mississippi Valley between Natchez, Mississippi, and Memphis, Tennessee. By 1864 it had spread to all areas under Union control.

The contracts represented a step up from slavery. Blacks could decide for whom to work—although they had to choose someone. The agreements prohibited corporal punishment, and some planters were punished for whipping their workers. Under the contract system, families could not be divided.

But the system had many harsh features, some reminiscent of slavery. Blacks received very low wages—from two to three dollars a month for men and one dollar for women—less than they could have received by bargaining in a free labor market. Their contracts required them to work 10 hours each day for 26 days each month. Usually they worked under the old gang-labor system, supervised by overseers. The former slaves needed the landowners' permission to leave the plantation. Freedpersons who refused to work on the plantations were forced to work under even harsher conditions on public works or on plantations operated by the military.

The contracts were enforced by military agents, who often favored the planters. This made it possible for the landowners to cheat their black workers by not paying wages for work lost to bad weather; withholding benefits provided for in the contracts, including garden plots, medical care, and food for the ill and for children too young to work; and charging workers for food. Often the workers owed money to the planters at the end of the month.

Ex-slaves often rebelled against the contract system. Despite restrictions on their movement, many managed to leave the plantations for the cities. In Louisiana, black soldiers sometimes went into the plantations to get their relatives out. Plantation workers sometimes engaged in strikes and revolts. In Plaquemines Parish, Louisiana, hands stopped working because they had not been paid. In St. Martinsville, Louisiana, workers revolted against white authority in general and eventually clashed with local whites and Union troops in April 1863.

Only a few former slaves were able to buy or rent land. In coastal Virginia some plantation superintendents rented abandoned land to a small number of freedmen. But at the end of the war, most independent black farmers lost their land to returning whites. On the South Carolina Sea Islands, all whites fled before Union occupiers arrived in November 1861. A few blacks bought small plots of 5 to 20 acres. They were not, however, allowed by the military to buy 40-acre plots because then they would be self-sufficient; the result, it was feared, would be a shortage of black laborers on the large plantations.

After General William T. Sherman completed his march through Georgia, he issued an order in January 1865 that land extending from the coast to 30 miles inland, from Charleston southward into Florida, be distributed to blacks. However, this was a war measure to secure Union control of the southeastern coast. When the war ended a few months later, the plan was dropped and the freedpeople lost their land. In the Lower Mississippi Valley, a few hundred blacks leased land from the army, usually from 10 to 20 acres; few could afford to run larger farms.

The gains that many ex-slaves made during the war were undeniable. But most still depended on white planters for their economic survival instead of owning their own land. This situation would make it harder for Southern blacks to defend their claims for equal civil and political rights after the war was over.

## RACIAL CONFLICT IN THE WARTIME NORTH

Northern blacks were as enthusiastic about the war against the Confederacy as were their Southern brethren, especially after the Emancipation Proclamation. The war reversed the pessimism and anger they had felt during the 1850s. Martin R. Delany, who had advocated emigration, now organized regiments of black soldiers for the Union Army. During the late 1850s, black abolitionist Robert Purvis had condemned the U.S. government as "one of the basest, meanest, most atrocious despotisms that ever saw the face of the sun." But in May 1863 he said, "I am proud to be an American citizen."

Yet Northern racism persisted during the war, and the future of the region's blacks was just as clouded as the prospects of the freed slaves. Tensions ran particularly high between white and black workers. A number of blacks worked for themselves as artisans and craftspersons, but the exclusion of black wage workers from most types of employment forced many of them to accept menial work on almost any terms; therefore, they often undercut white wages and working conditions. White workers, failing to recognize that the source of the problem was racial bias, blamed blacks instead. So white workers often opposed emancipation, afraid that freedpeople would come to the North and take their jobs. Many of these whites were Copperheads, the term for Northern Democrats sympathetic to the Confederacy.

The fear of emancipation lay behind the Cincinnati race riot of July 1862, which began after the *Cincinnati Gazette* reported that fugitive slaves were replacing white workers as stevedores on local riverboats. Laborers, mostly Irish along with some Germans, rampaged through the black section of town, burning homes and beating people. For revenge, blacks marched into the Irish section and burned buildings. In August 1863, white workers attacked a tobacco factory in Brooklyn, New York, where black women and children were working. The whites drove them upstairs and set a fire, but a group of black men helped the victims to escape. In December 1862, black workers were attacked in Chicago. After shippers in Buffalo, New York, hired black longshoremen, white workers assaulted the black employees in July 1863, killing three and badly injuring seven. Elsewhere in the North, violence followed the use of blacks as strikebreakers.

But the most serious racial violence by far occurred in New York City. In March 1863, white longshoremen working on the piers of the Erie Railroad Company and the Hudson River Railroad went on strike for a wage of $1.50 a day. The railroads defeated both walkouts with the help of black replacements. During the same month, Congress passed a draft law. White workers were enraged at having to risk their lives for the freedom of blacks. They were further angered by a provision enabling men to avoid the draft by paying $300, then a large amount of money that only the well off could afford.

On July 12, 1863, New York's newspapers printed the names of the first men to be drafted. On the next morning, a mob attacked the draft office. Later in the day, thousands of workers assaulted stores, warehouses, factories, docks, and other property of the city's elite, as well as some of the mansions of the wealthy. But as the New York Draft Riots went on, they became most of all an attack on blacks. Blacks were hunted on the streets, and some were hanged from lampposts and trees. Children were thrown from windows or killed in front of their mothers. The Colored Orphan Asylum was burned down (although the children were rescued in time). The mobs also attacked blacks' homes and businesses that employed blacks. During the four days of rioting, many blacks fled for their lives, hiding under piers or seeking refuge in Central Park; others left the city, many never to return. At least 105 were killed.

One thing was clear in the wake of the riots. Racial hatred was deeply embedded in the hearts of Northern as well as Southern whites, and the road to full citizenship for blacks would be a difficult one everywhere.

## THE ROAD TO RADICAL RECONSTRUCTION

The defeat of the Confederacy raised this issue: On what terms should the rebel states be restored to the Union? Did they need to be reformed, or reconstructed, before they resumed their place? Or should they be readmitted almost as if secession had never occurred? The emancipation of the slaves—completed by the

ratification in December 1865 of the Thirteenth Amendment barring slavery—
raised another issue: What should be the status of the ex-slaves? Should blacks
have equal rights with white people? Or should they have a lower rank, some-
where between slavery and full freedom? The two issues were linked. Usually,
those favoring equal rights for blacks also believed that the Southern states had to
be radically reformed, because they knew that under the old rules of government,
white supremacy would continue. Those not supporting racial equality were
generally much less interested in remaking the Southern state governments.

In 1863 the Union Army occupied a significant amount of Confederate territory, so President Lincoln's thoughts turned toward the readmission of the rebel
states. Lincoln favored easy terms. For one thing, he believed leniency would
encourage Southerners to accept defeat, which would shorten the war. For
another, he did not believe that Southern society could be drastically changed by
outsiders. Also, Lincoln felt that his Republican Party could establish itself in the
South with the support of the Unionists who had opposed secession and of
secessionists now willing to declare their loyalty to the United States. Strict terms
of restoration, he feared, would offend those groups.

In December 1863, Lincoln announced his Ten Percent Plan. For the government of any ex-Confederate state to receive presidential recognition, only 10
percent of the qualified voters of 1860 would have to swear allegiance to the
United States. They could then elect delegates to draw up a new state constitution. Provided that the constitution abolished slavery, a new government could be
formed. Lincoln's plan made no provision for black legal or political rights; it
assumed that blacks would continue to play their traditional role as underlings.
Lincoln was somewhat flexible; in March 1864 he suggested that the "very
intelligent" blacks, especially those who had fought for the Union, might be
allowed to vote. But none of the four ex-confederate states that accepted Lincoln's
plan—Virginia, Tennessee, Louisiana, and Arkansas—made any arrangement for
black voting.

Congress had a voice in Reconstruction because only it could decide whether
the U.S. representatives and senators chosen by the former Confederate states
would be seated. None elected under the Ten Percent Plan ever were, because
many in the Republican Party, which controlled Congress, disliked the plan.
Congressional Republicans did not object to the plan's failure to defend black
rights—except for a few known as Radical Republicans, they did not concern
themselves greatly with that matter until after the war. But they feared that under
the Ten Percent Plan, Confederate supporters might dominate the new governments, and so they adopted a stricter plan: the Wade-Davis bill of July 1864,
which required that a *majority* of white male citizens must take an oath of
allegiance. Then, delegates to a constitutional convention would be elected. But
to vote for delegates or to be a delegate, one had to take another oath—the so-
called Ironclad Oath—that he had never voluntarily supported the Confederacy.
Then, the convention had to renounce secession and abolish slavery. But Lincoln
refused to sign the bill, so this plan was never applied.

## Reconstruction under President Johnson

After the assassination of President Lincoln in April 1865, Vice President Andrew Johnson replaced him. A pro-Union Democrat from eastern Tennessee, Johnson came from a modest background and despised the South's slaveholding elite—although he was also a racist with little sympathy for blacks. Many Republicans believed he would follow more radical policies than Lincoln's. As it turned out, though, their approaches were basically the same. In May 1865 he recognized the four state governments that had been formed according to Lincoln's plan. That month Johnson issued his own Reconstruction plan. It pardoned and restored the property (except for slaves) of Confederate supporters willing to take a loyalty oath, with two exceptions: major Confederate officials and persons with over $20,000 worth of property had to apply individually for pardons. Except for them, all who took the loyalty oath and who had been qualified to vote in 1860 (which meant whites only) were eligible to elect delegates to state conventions that would write new constitutions.

Johnson hoped and expected that Southern voters would reject their former leaders, who came mostly from the planter class, and establish governments that represented small farmers and artisans. But the fall 1865 elections gave planters and former Confederate officials control of most of the new governments. For example, South Carolina governor James Orr had sat in the Confederate senate; Louisiana governor James M. Wells, a sugar planter, had owned over 100 slaves before the war; and Mississippi governor Benjamin G. Humphreys had been a Confederate general. The majority of those sent to Congress had been Confederate officers. Alexander M. Stephens, chosen for the U.S. Senate by Georgia, had just a few months before been the vice president of the Confederacy! Many, including Stephens, were not even eligible to take the oath of allegiance under Johnson's plan. Had Johnson been more flexible, he might have scrapped or at least modified his plan, but he would not admit his errors. Instead, in December 1865, Johnson announced the end of Reconstruction and issued pardons to those just elected so they could take office.

The Johnson state governments tried to restore blacks to virtual slavery through laws known as Black Codes. The codes legalized marriages between blacks and permitted blacks to buy, own, and sell property and to sue or be sued, but prevented them from sitting on juries and from testifying against whites. Many of the codes required blacks to sign yearly labor contracts and provided for the punishment of those who left their plantations before their contracts expired—the goal was to prevent blacks from bargaining with other employers for better terms. South Carolina's law was especially oppressive, stating that blacks would work from dawn to dusk and could not leave the plantation or have visitors without the planter's permission.

Vagrancy laws like those of prewar Maryland and Delaware, apprenticeship laws enabling local authorities to take black children away from supposedly unfit parents and place them with white guardians, and laws permitting the leasing out of convicts all were designed to provide whites with free or cheap black labor (see

"The South Reacts," page 73). Also, the Johnson governments failed to protect blacks from acts of violence. Many were committed by militiamen, sometimes wearing old Confederate uniforms. More were committed by private citizens seeking to keep blacks down.

## Congress Takes Charge

But Southern whites made a political mistake by going so far. Most Northerners and the great majority of congressional Republicans rejected the idea that the Civil War, with all of its sacrifices, had been fought so that Confederate leaders could return to power, restore the old plantation system, and perhaps start another civil war. At the end of 1865, Congress refused to accept Johnson's declaration that Reconstruction was over and appointed a Joint Committee on Reconstruction to investigate conditions in the South. In April 1866 the panel rejected the seating of the U.S. representatives and senators elected under the Johnson governments.

Developments in the South, among other factors, drove many moderate Republicans in Congress toward the Radical camp, led by Pennsylvania representative Thaddeus Stevens and Massachusetts senator Charles Sumner. The Radicals wanted to sweep away the old planter class and establish a society in which everyone—or at least all males—had equal legal status and voting rights. Stevens stated: "This is not a 'white man's government.' To say so is political blasphemy, for it violates the fundamental principles of our gospel of liberty. This is man's government; the government of all men alike." Furthermore, the Radicals (and many others) felt that government owed a debt to blacks because of their invaluable services during the Civil War. Also, most of the Radicals had practical reasons for their views. They believed that black votes would make Republicans the dominant party in the South. Furthermore, they were trying to help their Northern business allies, who knew that a Republican South would be more receptive to Northern investment than a Democratic South committed to preserving the old plantation-dominated economy.

Unlike the Radicals, moderate Republicans were not yet ready to support voting rights for blacks. But by early 1866 most of them backed legislation promoting the social welfare of freedpeople and assuring them of equality before the law. In March 1865 Congress had created the Bureau of Refugees, Freedmen, and Abandoned Land—known as the Freedmen's Bureau—to help the former slaves adjust to freedom. In February 1866 Congress extended the bureau's life and expanded its responsibilities. The agency now could take control of legal cases involving blacks, because they were not getting equal justice in local Southern courts. A month later, Congress passed the Civil Rights Act of 1866, which gave national citizenship to all persons born in the United States (except American Indians). It also guaranteed citizens equal protection of person and property and authorized U.S. officials to safeguard these rights by bringing suit in federal courts. President Johnson vetoed both bills, but Congress overrode his vetoes.

Afraid that the Supreme Court might declare the Civil Rights Act unconstitutional, Congress included it in the Fourteenth Amendment, which was sent to the states for ratification in June 1866. The amendment included the act's definition of U.S. citizenship. It prohibited any state from depriving "any person of life, liberty, or property, without due process of law" or denying "any person within its jurisdiction the equal protection of the laws." For the first time in U.S. history, blacks were recognized as citizens with equal rights before the law. Another provision in the amendment was a compromise between Radical Republicans, who favored black suffrage, and moderates, who were still uncertain: it did not require states to give blacks the vote, but allowed Congress to reduce a state's congressional representation to the extent that the state deprived its male citizens of the vote (a provision that has never been used). The amendment also barred from state or national office those who had held public positions before the war and then supported the Confederacy; however, it allowed Congress to free individuals from this provision by a two-thirds vote.

Tennessee ratified the Fourteenth Amendment in 1866, and Congress seated its senators and representatives, completing the state's restoration to the Union. But between October 1866 and January 1867, the legislatures of the other 10 ex-Confederate states rejected the amendment. Once again Southern white resistance to change helped the Radicals in the North. In the fall 1866 congressional elections, the Radical Republicans swept to victory over candidates supported by President Johnson. Johnson became virtually powerless (although an attempt in Congress in 1868 to remove him from office by the impeachment process narrowly failed), and the Radicals dominated Congress.

Early in 1867 Congress gave the vote to blacks in Washington, D.C., and in the territories. Then, in the First Reconstruction Act of March 1867 and in three later acts, Congress spelled out its plan for Radical Reconstruction. The 10 unreconstructed ex-Confederate states (all ex-Confederate states but Tennessee) were to be divided into five military districts, each governed by an army officer. Each district commander was to register voters, including blacks but not including those Confederate supporters barred from holding public office under the Fourteenth Amendment. In each state these voters were to choose delegates to a state convention, which would write a constitution that must contain a clause guaranteeing the vote to all adult males. After the people ratified the constitution, they were to elect a state government. At its first session, the state legislature was to ratify the Fourteenth Amendment. Only then would the state's U.S. representatives and senators be seated in Congress.

By 1868 six states—North and South Carolina, Florida, Alabama, Louisiana, and Arkansas—had been restored to the Union after meeting these terms. Four states—Virginia, Georgia, Mississippi, and Texas—did not meet the terms before the Fourteenth Amendment became part of the U.S. Constitution in 1868. Congress then required those four states to meet an additional requirement: ratification of the Fifteenth Amendment, sent to the states by Congress in February 1869. It prohibited both the federal and state governments from denying anyone the vote "on account of race, color, or previous condition of servitude." By 1870 the four states had complied, and that year the Fifteenth Amendment was ratified by the required number of states.

Having established legal and political equality for blacks, most supporters of Radical Reconstruction believed their job was done. Some, however, felt that another step must be taken: granting land to the freedpeople. Thaddeus Stevens argued that blacks would not be able to defend their new rights without the economic independence that land ownership would give them; as landless laborers, he believed, they would be controlled by the planters for whom they worked. Outside of Congress, black leader Frederick Douglass made the same argument.

But only the most radical of the Radical Republicans felt that way. In 1866 and 1867 Stevens, Sumner, and Representatives George W. Julian of Indiana and Benjamin F. Butler of Massachusetts proposed legislation to break up the large plantations owned by Confederate supporters and give part of the land to blacks; Congress, however, rejected their proposals by wide margins. Moderate and some Radical Republicans believed that the right to vote would be enough to enable blacks to defend their civil rights. Furthermore, confiscation conflicted with their strong belief in property rights, which most Northerners shared. Also, these congressmen, like the great majority of Northerners, felt that people must work out their own economic futures without government aid; otherwise, they believed, people would lose their incentive to work. It is true that Congress supported the Freedmen's Bureau, which, as we will see, was a social welfare institution that gave ex-slaves a great deal of help. But the bureau was always meant to be a temporary agency. Giving blacks legal equality and the right to vote was the outer limit to which Congress would go.

## THE RECONSTRUCTED STATES

Even before the Southern states began forming governments under the Radicals' plan late in 1867, the ex-slaves were asserting their new freedom. Right after the war, many of them traveled a great deal. Some were looking for relatives who had been sold away. Others simply wanted to travel freely and see new places, a right they had been denied under the old pass system. Still others went to the cities looking for work.

Many Southern whites believed that all this movement stemmed from natural laziness and that most blacks did not want to work. In fact most did want to work, but they also wanted to have a say in *how* they worked. They opposed attempts by white landowners to restore the old gang-labor system on the plantations. The former slaves despised that system because it was easy for whites to supervise blacks closely when they were gathered in one or a few large gangs. Because of black resistance, many cotton planters began to break up large gangs into smaller squads, usually supervised by a squad member chosen by the freed slaves themselves. Under pressure from freedpeople, some planters had introduced a sharecropping system by 1866. Under this arrangement, each black family took responsibility for a piece of land and received a share of the crop grown on it; this system, even more than the squads, made white supervision difficult. By 1880 more blacks worked on a sharecropping basis than as wage laborers.

Meanwhile the First Reconstruction Act, passed by Congress in March 1867, emboldened blacks to take political action even before the creation of Radical Reconstruction governments under that law. In May 1867 the streetcars of New Orleans were integrated after a series of black demonstrations. Similar demonstrations at the same time in Charleston, Richmond, and Mobile were also successful.

With the help of the Freedmen's Bureau, blacks managed to advance in other ways immediately after the war. The bureau was created just before the end of the conflict to assist ex-slaves on the road to freedom—and to help poor whites as well. Under the direction of its commissioner, General Oliver O. Howard, the bureau distributed millions of rations. It also provided direct health care to hundreds of thousands and greatly expanded the South's hospital system. It worked with Northern humanitarian groups and Southern blacks to establish schools for both freedmen and whites, and by 1869 more than 3,000 schools were educating over 150,000 pupils. The bureau also helped to create the black colleges that sprang up right after the war, including Atlanta University and Virginia Union College in 1865; Fisk University in 1866; and Howard University, Morgan College, and Morehouse College in 1867.

In 1865 Freedmen's Bureau agents began handling grievances brought to them by blacks; the next year, it set up courts to help freedmen and planters settle contract disputes. The bureau's courts gave freedmen fairer hearings than they received in Southern courts. A sure sign that the bureau's courts were successful was the eagerness of the Johnson governments to get rid of them.

The Freedmen's Bureau was never meant to be more than a temporary agency, and in 1869 Congress provided for its termination. Therefore, blacks' chances of securing permanent justice would depend on the new Radical Reconstruction governments that were being established, starting in 1867, on an equal suffrage basis under the Reconstruction Acts of Congress.

By that time, blacks had already started organizing themselves politically. In 1866, they started joining local Union Leagues, which were Republican Party clubs. In 1867, when it became clear that blacks would win the right to vote, they poured into the leagues. The minority of Southern whites who were Republicans sometimes walked out to form their own leagues, but some chapters were integrated.

The Union Leagues represented a radical break with the past for Southern blacks. League meetings were often guarded by armed blacks, and unofficial black self-defense groups sometimes developed in connection with the leagues. Many blacks received a political education at Union League meetings, where political issues were discussed and Republican newspapers were read aloud. The leagues also organized political rallies and parades. Some leagues ran petition drives against racial injustices and nominated black candidates for office. Hundreds of thousands of freedpeople became politically aware thanks to the Union Leagues, and many black political leaders came out of the these organizations.

Thanks to the work of the leagues and to blacks' enthusiasm over their newly won right to vote, African Americans came out in large numbers to elect delegates to state conventions in 1867 and 1868. Their turnout varied from 70 percent in Georgia to almost 90 percent in Virginia. Almost all blacks voted for Republicans who supported Radical Reconstruction. Most whites backed the Democrats, the party of white supremacy. Others refused to vote in protest against black suffrage. A minority of whites supported Radical Reconstruction. Southern white Republicans belonged to two groups. Those called carpetbaggers were Northerners who had moved to the South after the Civil War. The other and much larger group, called scalawags, consisted of native Southerners. Most were opponents of secession: former Whigs looking for an alternative to the Democrats, small farmers hostile to the planter class, or businesspersons hoping for a new South free of planter control. The Republicans won a majority of delegates in all 10 ex-Confederate states subject to Radical Reconstruction. White Republican delegates outnumbered black Republican delegates in all conventions except in Louisiana, where blacks and whites were equal in number, and in South Carolina, where more blacks were chosen. Out of a total of 1,039 delegates elected, 267 were black. Many had been free blacks before the war, and many were preachers.

## The Radical Constitutions and Governments

The constitutions drawn up by the conventions were the most democratic in Southern history. They all guaranteed blacks equal civil and political rights; outlawed whipping as a punishment for criminals; ended imprisonment for debt; and eliminated property qualifications for voting, holding political office, and serving on juries. Most of the constitutions established fairer tax systems that placed more of the burden on landowners and less on the former slaves. The constitutions of Alabama, Arkansas, Louisiana, Mississippi, and Virginia took the vote away from large numbers of Confederate supporters.

Issues related to segregation were controversial. Black delegates wanted to require equal access to public transport and public accommodations (such as hotels and restaurants). Many white Republican delegates opposed such a step, regarding it as an attempt to impose social equality; only Louisiana's constitution mandated integration in those areas. Regarding schools, segregation had not been a significant issue in the antebellum period: for one thing, there had been few schools for either race; for another, almost 95 percent of blacks had been slaves. But because the new constitutions created the first state-supported school systems in Southern history, the matter of school integration was raised by black delegates. Blacks were not especially interested in having their children mix with white children, but they feared that in a segregated system, black schools would not get their fair share of government support. Again, however, white opposition was strong: only the Louisiana and South Carolina conventions—where black delegates were most numerous—banned segregated schools.

In the governments elected under the new constitutions, blacks held office at every level (although in numbers far below their proportion in the overall popula-

Among the first blacks elected to Congress were (seated, left to right): Sen. Hiram R. Revels (1869–1871, Miss.), Rep. Benjamin S. Turner (1871–1873, Ala.), Rep. Josiah T. Walls (1871–1877, Fla.), Rep. Joseph H. Rainey (1869–1879, S.C.), and Rep. Robert B. Elliot (1871–1875, S.C.); and (standing, left to right) Rep. Robert C. DeLarge (1871–1873, S.C.), and Rep. Jefferson H. Long (1869–1871, Ga.). All were Republicans.

tion). In the late 1860s and early 1870s, a high proportion of black public officials were freeborn; but by the mid-1870s, the proportion of freedpeople had begun growing, thanks in part to the education they received in the new school systems and the self-confidence it inspired. Two blacks sat in the U.S. Senate, both from Mississippi. In 1870 that state's legislature chose Hiram R. Revels, an African Methodist Episcopal minister from Natchez, to the Senate seat previously held by Jefferson Davis. He sat for the last year of Davis's unexpired term. In 1874 Mississippi's state legislators selected Blanche K. Bruce for a full, six-year U.S. Senate term. Bruce was a former slave who had held various local offices in Mississippi. During Radical Reconstruction, 14 blacks were elected by the voters to the U.S. House of Representatives: South Carolina sent 6, including Civil War hero Robert Smalls; Alabama chose 3; and North Carolina, Mississippi, Louisiana, Georgia, and Florida each sent 1.

At the state level, P. B. S. Pinchback of Louisiana became the first black governor in American history; he served for just one month while his predecessor was undergoing impeachment hearings. Oscar J. Dunn, P. B. S. Pinchback, and Caesar C. Antoine each served as lieutenant governor in Louisiana. Alonzo J. Ransier and Richard H. Gleaves served in South Carolina, and Alexander K. Davis held that post in Mississippi. Louisiana's Antoine Dubuclet and South Carolina's Francis L. Cardozo were state treasurers. One black held the post of superintendent of education in each of the states of Arkansas, Florida, Louisiana, and Mississippi. Mississippi had five black secretaries of state, Louisiana had two, and Florida had one.

More than 600 blacks sat in the Southern state legislatures during Radical Reconstruction—the majority of them former slaves—although nowhere except in the lower house of the South Carolina legislature did they ever make up a majority. As time went on, a growing number of blacks served as chairmen of legislative committees. John R. Lynch of Mississippi, later a U.S. representative, was elected speaker of the Mississippi house of representatives at the age of 24. At the local level, blacks served as mayors in a few cities and towns. Many more sat on town and city councils. Blacks frequently served as county supervisors and tax collectors. They also held many law-enforcement positions, including sheriff, judge, justice of the peace, city policeman, rural constable, and even police commissioner in Little Rock, Arkansas, and Tallahassee, Florida. This and the fact that blacks now served as jurors ensured them better justice than they had ever received before.

The state governments took many steps to benefit blacks and poor people in general. Never before had Southern state governments made serious efforts to provide decent school systems—although segregation prevailed in the great majority of schools under Radical Reconstruction. The number of children going to school in Florida tripled in four years; in South Carolina it more than quadrupled in eight years. Other public services such as hospitals, orphanages, asylums, roads, and bridges were greatly expanded. The legislatures adopted labor laws favoring workers. The apprenticeship and vagrancy laws of the Johnson-era governments were rewritten to prevent the exploitation of black labor.

Agricultural workers received protection. They were given first claim on the property of planters who could not meet their financial obligations. Legislatures outlawed the practice of firing farmworkers just before their contracts ran out to avoid paying their wages or share of the crop. Government-supported health care for the poor and free legal representation for the destitute were established. Legislatures passed reform laws enlarging the property rights of wives, holding white men financially responsible for the children they fathered with black women, and reducing the number of crimes punishable by death. The Black Codes, with their restrictions on the freedom of blacks, were repealed. Under Republican rule, local authorities gave blacks their fair share of jobs on government construction projects.

Yet just as there were limits to Radical Reconstruction at the federal level, so at the state level certain boundaries were not crossed. As we have seen, Louisiana's constitution required the integration of public transport and public accommodations, and many of the Southern states adopted laws of a similar nature. In some cities, blacks conducted successful campaigns to integrate streetcars. But in general the laws were not put into effect. Railroads often excluded blacks from first-class cars, and few blacks attempted to cross the color line at white-owned restaurants, hotels, and other businesses serving the public. Many blacks preferred their own separate facilities (although even they felt that blacks should not be segregated as a matter of policy). Others believed that it was useless to challenge the deep-seated white racial prejudices that lay behind segregation.

Like the federal government, most Southern states did little to promote land ownership for blacks. Many white Republicans in the South, like many Republican congressmen in Washington, D.C., believed that people should work out their own economic destinies without government help. However, South Carolina was an exception. The state created a commission to buy land and then sell it, allowing purchasers to pay over a long period of time. By the mid-1870s, some 14,000 black families—almost 15 percent of the state's black population—were settled on homesteads. The same percentage applies to Florida. There, blacks acquired more than 160,000 acres of land under Congress's Southern Homestead Act of 1866, which opened up public lands. But in the rest of the South, less than 5 percent of blacks had their own land.

However, the most significant characteristic of Radical Reconstruction was not its limits but the extent to which blacks advanced under it. Radical Reconstruction truly was radical, bringing profound change to the region. But its enemies were determined to undermine it, and it did not take them long to succeed.

## THE DECLINE OF RADICAL RECONSTRUCTION

A large majority of Southern whites—including the planter class, which still dominated the South's economy—opposed Radical Reconstruction, and many were prepared to use violence to bring down the Republican state governments. After 1865 white terrorist organizations sprang up. The Ku Klux Klan and the Knights of the White Camelia were the two most powerful groups; others included the White Brotherhood, the Council of Safety, the Constitutional Union Guard, and the Pale Faces. The Klan, founded in Tennessee in 1866, is the best known; its members wore white hoods and robes and rode on white horses draped with white sheets. Most members of these groups were of poor or modest means, but the organizations often had planter leadership and close ties to Democratic Party leaders. The goal of these secret societies was to reestablish Democratic control over the South and restore blacks to a subordinate position in society.

As the Radical governments were being established in 1868, these terrorist groups began committing acts of violence on a wide scale. They broke up Republican meetings and attacked scalawags, who were considered traitors to their race. But blacks were their favorite target, especially those who were considered "impudent" toward whites, were well-educated, or had achieved any kind of economic or political success—in other words, blacks who didn't "know their place." However, no black could feel safe, because these organizations often attacked randomly. In a "Negro chase" held in 1870 in Laurens County, South Carolina, white vigilantes sent 150 freedmen fleeing from their homes; 13 were hunted down and killed. One of the worst attacks occurred during 1873 in Colfax, Louisiana, where armed blacks held off white vigilantes for 3 days; when the blacks were finally overwhelmed, the whites massacred about 50 even though they had raised a white flag. Blacks often received whippings from the terrorists, a particularly degrading form of punishment because of its association with slavery days. Sometimes the targets were black institutions, especially schools. The racist groups were especially active at election time, using violence and intimidation to stop blacks from voting. With their help, the Democrats in 1870 won the elections in North Carolina, Alabama (where the Republicans regained power in 1872), and Georgia.

The states raised mostly black militias to quell the violence, but the governors did not use them. For one thing, they did not believe that armed ex-slaves would be a match for trained Confederate veterans (which many of the terrorists were), and for another they feared that using mostly black forces might trigger a general race war. After several years of violence, the federal government acted. In May 1870, Congress passed a Force Act making it a federal crime to try to stop people from voting and authorizing the president to use federal troops to stop violence. Another Force Act in February 1871 strengthened the previous measure. The Ku Klux Klan Act (later known as the Civil Rights Act) of April 1871 treated the armed groups as treasonous conspiracies, and in their case suspended some of the legal protections normally granted to criminal suspects. Under this legislation, the administration of President Ulysses S. Grant began prosecuting many hundreds of suspected terrorists in 1871. Many others fled to escape prosecution. The racist vigilante groups collapsed, and the violence subsided—for the time being.

## Dwindling White Support

From around 1870 on, Northern support for Radical Reconstruction declined, and the federal government became increasingly reluctant to intervene in the South. The North was in the midst of an economic revolution, with large capitalist enterprises replacing the small shops that had accounted for most manufacturing production before the Civil War. This development raised new issues that turned Northern attention away from Reconstruction. When the panic of 1873 ushered in a major five-year economic depression, concern for the freedpeople declined still further. The depression also weakened the Republicans politically, so that the Democrats captured the House of Representatives in the 1874 elections. Also, Northern financiers and industrialists were investing in the South and to a great extent had taken economic control of the region away from the local planters. These Northerners believed that their investments would not be safe without political stability. More and more these businessmen, who had great influence within the Republican Party, became convinced that the Reconstruction governments could not maintain order.

In 1872 Congress pardoned almost all Confederate supporters who had been prohibited from holding office under the Fourteenth Amendment. In the *Slaughterhouse Cases* (1873) and *United States v. Cruikshank* (1876), the Supreme Court reduced the federal government's power to defend civil and political rights, giving most enforcement authority to the states. Congress did pass the Civil Rights Act of

1875, guaranteeing equal access to hotels, public transport, theaters, and "other places of amusement," but it was never seriously enforced, and the Supreme Court ruled it unconstitutional in the *Civil Rights Cases* (1883). Founded in 1865, the Freedman's Savings and Trust Company failed in 1874. Many thousands of freed people had placed their small savings in this bank. The federal government's failure to give them significant relief demonstrated the North's lack of interest in aiding the freedpeople by the mid-1870s.

Within the Southern states, the Republican governments lost much of their white support in the early and mid-1870s. Those governments expanded social services and gave heavy subsidies to railroads in the hope of developing the Southern economy. As a result, state debt mounted and taxes had to be raised. These hikes had little impact on blacks because most were too poor to pay much in taxes, but many white landowners were angered by them. Also, the Republican governments were discredited because of widespread corruption. The enlargement of the public treasury tempted some politicians to steal funds. The growth in government services and spending gave political leaders more favors to dispense— for example, railroad subsidies or contracts to provide textbooks for the new Southern schools—in exchange for bribes and other favors. The same thing was happening in the North, but most Southern whites blamed blacks and their allies.

Under the radical governments, the Southern railroad system was extended into remote areas inhabited mostly by white small farmers. These farmers had been self-sufficient before the war, growing mostly food for their own use. When the railroads came, they began growing cotton for market. However, during the depression of the 1870s, cotton prices fell by 50 percent. Many of the whites lost their land and became sharecroppers and tenant farmers.

These problems helped the Democrats return to power during 1874 in Arkansas, Texas, and Alabama. (In Alabama, furthermore, planters reduced the black vote by threatening not to employ blacks who voted Republican. This seemed to support the view of Stevens and other Radicals that blacks would not be able to defend their rights without economic independence.) Then, inspired by the good showing of Democrats in the 1874 national elections, the Southern Democrats resumed their violent activities on a large scale. In the 1875 elections, Mississippi Democrats used what was called the "Mississippi Plan" or the "shotgun policy." Forming armed groups, they used tactics like those of the Ku Klux Klan a few years before, except that the Mississippians were so brazen that they did not even wear disguises. And so Mississippi was "redeemed," the term used by Southern Democrats when they won a state election and ended Radical Reconstruction.

In 1871 the federal government had intervened in the South against the Klan and other violent groups. But with Washington, D.C.'s support for Southern Republicans declining in the 1870s, the Grant administration did nothing in 1875 about the situation in Mississippi. Neither did it respond to Democratic violence the following year in Louisiana, organized by the White Leagues, and in South Carolina, led by Wade Hampton's Red Shirts. In the 1876 presidential campaign, Republican candidate Rutherford B. Hayes promised to bring the South "the blessings of honest and capable local self-government," a polite way of saying he would end Radical Reconstruction. The election results were disputed, but the Democrats agreed to accept Hayes as president when he agreed to end the use of federal troops in the South and to provide federal aid for various Southern economic development projects. While federal troops remained in their barracks, the last three Republican governments in the South—in South Carolina, Louisiana, and Florida—were toppled in 1877.

Some gains of the Reconstruction era were preserved in the South. The worst provisions of the Black Codes, such as those restricting the movement of the freedmen, were not restored after Reconstruction. Nor were the most extreme attempts to exploit black labor, such as the apprenticeship laws. Blacks maintained some of their educational gains. And eventually, nearly a century later, the civil rights legislation and constitutional amendments of Reconstruction were implemented. But for the time being, the triumph of the Democratic "Redeemers" meant a grave setback for racial equality.

## THE NORTH DURING RECONSTRUCTION

Northern as well as Southern blacks gained new rights during the Reconstruction era. The Civil Rights Act of 1866 and the Fourteenth Amendment voided some of the pre–Civil War legislation in the North that discriminated against blacks. Northern states could no longer prohibit blacks from entering their borders, nor could they any longer prevent blacks from testifying against whites. Also, the Fourteenth Amendment was used successfully to sue against discrimination in public transport. In the late 1860s and early 1870s, for example, blacks in Ohio won damages against railroad companies that excluded them from first-class compartments. In 1873 a black woman went to court after being excluded from a dining car on a Mississippi steamboat. The Iowa supreme court ruled in her favor, declaring that the Civil Rights Act and the Fourteenth Amendment required integrated railroads. Most state courts ruled that the Fourteenth Amendment required equal, not integrated, public transport facilities; that is, if whites-only first-class compartments or dining cars were established, equivalent facilities would have to be created for blacks. But by the late 1870s, most transportation in the North was integrated. Pennsylvania, for example, in 1867 barred the exclusion or segregation of blacks on streetcars and railroads.

Some states passed laws to integrate public accommodations. The first to do so was Massachusetts, in an 1865 law that banned licensed inns, places of amusement, and public meetings from excluding blacks. In 1873 New York also passed a pioneering law eliminating segregation in public accommodations. Whites, however, put up greater resistance to the integration of public accommodations such as inns, hotels, restaurants, and theaters than to the integration of public transport. To whites it seemed that sharing public accommodations with blacks was a step toward social equality between the races, which the overwhelming majority of whites strongly opposed. Blacks argued that social equality was not the issue because their goal was not to socialize with whites, but merely to receive equal service in facilities opened to the general public.

Yet only a few blacks were prepared to challenge segregation in public accommodations. Most did not want to face the abuse and insults they would almost certainly receive. Besides, many blacks could not afford to go to white hotels, theaters, or restaurants. Also, because of the strength of white opposition, black leaders usually chose not to seek the integration of such facilities for fear that attempts to do so would endanger gains in other areas. And so, except in areas such as northern Ohio and parts of Massachusetts, where white prejudice was comparatively mild, segregated public accommodations remained the rule.

Sometimes the small number of well-to-do blacks—most of whom won white favor by adopting white styles of dress, speech, and manners—gained access where ordinary blacks were refused. But another category of blacks—those with relatively light skin—did not generally receive special favor from whites, although they usually formed the elite within the black community. A theater owner in Columbus, Ohio, found this out in 1873, when he began allowing light-skinned blacks to sit on the main floor with whites while dark-skinned blacks continued to sit in the balcony. He discontinued the new policy because, he said, "so many people spoke about it, and their tone was so unfavorable." In Latin American countries, the population was divided into many racial categories based on skin tone. But for most whites in the United States, there were just two categories— black and white.

The integration of public schools, like that of public accommodations, was a very controversial matter; many white parents did not want their children to attend schools with blacks. Indianapolis, San Francisco, and Cincinnati were among the cities where schools were segregated. The supreme courts of Nevada (1872), California (1874), and Indiana (1874) ruled that blacks could be sent to separate schools. In 1867 the Michigan legislature mandated school integration. Whites put up fierce resistance in Detroit, where the Democratic-controlled school board fought off desegregation until court action by blacks forced it to yield in 1871. Even then, at great expense, it replaced the schools' double desks with single ones to make sure that blacks and whites did not sit too close to each other! Other places in Michigan, such as Ypsilanti, resisted into the twentieth century.

Some blacks, too, resisted school integration. Suspicious of whites, they were concerned about how their children would be treated in integrated schools. Also, many preferred to have their children taught by black teachers, which would be more likely in black schools. And black teachers, who had a vested economic interest in separate schools, resisted integration. But despite opposition from both sides, school integration spread during the Reconstruction era. Chicago, Boston, Cleveland, and Milwaukee operated mixed schools. Columbus, Ohio, integrated its high schools in 1872 and its primary schools 10 years later. In 1875 the Iowa supreme court ruled that separate schooling violated the Fourteenth Amendment.

The Fifteenth Amendment, ratified in 1870, gave Northern as well as Southern blacks the right to vote. Black Republicans won election to the state legislatures in Massachusetts and Illinois and to local offices in a number of states. But in 1880 blacks made up less than 2 percent of the northern population; therefore, black voters had a limited impact and most black politicians had no chance of winning elections.

In addition to the Civil Rights Act of 1866 and the Fourteenth and Fifteenth Amendments, Radical Republicans in the North were sometimes willing to go out on a limb for black rights. This could mean a loss of votes for the Republican Party, since the black votes gained might be outweighed by the loss of white votes, especially with the Democrats constantly telling white voters that the Republicans were the party of blacks. Therefore, blacks made their greatest civil rights gains in states where Republicans had a majority large enough to survive such Democratic attacks. Where the parties were more evenly matched, Republicans were more cautious and progress for blacks was slower.

# CHAPTER 6

# The Triumph of White Racism: 1878 –1915

## LOSING THE RIGHT TO VOTE

The end of Reconstruction meant that the Republican-controlled White House had agreed to let the white planters and businesspeople of the South—the "Redeemers"—control the politics of their region through the Democratic Party. Black hopes for legal and political equality in the South lay in ruins. The decline of blacks' status in the South occurred gradually, not suddenly; when the process ended, blacks found themselves in a South more rigidly racist than ever.

The 1880s were years of transition between Reconstruction and the new, extreme forms of racism that emerged in the 1890s and early 1900s. Most eligible black men in the South continued to vote for about 15 years after the end of Reconstruction. Blacks also continued to hold office. Black representatives sat in the Virginia Assembly until 1891. Between the late 1870s and the early 1890s, more than 50 blacks won election to North Carolina's legislature and almost 50 to South Carolina's. At least one black congressman from the South sat in the U.S. House of Representatives until 1901. In many southern states, blacks continued to receive political appointments, although to minor posts. In some areas of the Upper South, including eastern Virginia and eastern North Carolina, the Republican Party remained strong. There, the black vote determined election outcomes.

Steps were being taken, however, to make sure that blacks would no longer be a powerful political force, especially in the Deep South. Some states passed laws giving the governor or legislature the power to appoint people to many local positions that previously had been elective offices. One purpose of such measures was to prevent blacks from being elected to important local posts in areas where most voters were black. Under the new arrangement, blacks sometimes received appointments. But now they were beholden to white politicians, not black voters; therefore, they did not act as independent spokespersons for black interests. In contrast to the situation during Reconstruction, few blacks now held law enforcement posts and few sat on juries. State legislatures drew congressional districts in ways that weakened the impact of the black vote. In Mississippi most black voters were concentrated in one congressional district, leaving the other five mostly white. Alabama took the opposite approach; it divided the black vote among the state's six congressional districts so that none had a black majority.

Legislation was passed to reduce the size of the black vote. Poll tax laws, for example, required voters to bring proof of having paid the tax when they came to vote. Since poor and uneducated people were unaccustomed to saving written documents, such laws kept some blacks from voting. For the same reason, some blacks lost their vote because of laws requiring citizens to register several months before the election and then to present their registration certificates on election day. Other laws made the voting process itself difficult, especially for the uneducated. South Carolina passed the Eight-Box Ballot Act in 1882, and Florida followed in the late 1880s. A separate ballot box was displayed for each elected office. The voter had to deposit the right ballot in each box. This could be difficult for illiterate voters, many of whom were black. If some uneducated whites also lost their vote because of these various laws, that was fine with the Redeemers, who represented the better-off, more conservative whites.

Unethical and illegal procedures also cut down the black vote. Under the Eight-Box Ballot Act, when a black presented himself to vote, the election officials might move the boxes around to make it even more difficult to find the right box for each ballot. Election officials set up polling places in areas that were inconvenient for blacks. In some cases, whites resorted to bribery, threats, and violence against blacks, although less often than during Reconstruction.

## White Competition for Black Votes

If the Redeemers took all these steps to disfranchise blacks, why did they still allow many to vote in the 1880s? The reason is that the Redeemers often could benefit from the black vote. They generally represented the wealthier southern whites: the large landowners, or planters; the merchants; and the growing number of local industrialists. They favored conservative policies that protected the interests of those groups. They lived mostly in the plantation areas of the South, called the black belt in the Gulf states from Florida to Texas because of the color of the rich soil; most southern blacks also lived in the black belt counties, where more often than not they were a majority.

Outside the black belt were the so-called white counties. Here the soil was poorer; the whites were poorer; and blacks were few, because the plantation system had never been established there. Also, in the white counties many farmers had declining incomes because farm prices had begun to fall sharply in the 1870s. Therefore, during the 1880s whites from these counties began running their own, more radical candidates against those of the Redeemer, or conservative, Democrats; the radicals advocated such policies as railroad regulation to reduce rates, higher corporate taxes, and cheap credit.

If the poorer whites were much more numerous than the well-off ones, how could the Redeemers hope to win elections? Part of the answer was that more often than not, the Redeemers could control the black vote. They often worked with local black leaders to achieve this control. Black politicians campaigned in the black community for the Redeemer candidates. In return, the blacks were rewarded with a certain number of state jobs to distribute among their followers. The Redeemers also used their influence in Washington, D.C., to get federal jobs for black leaders. Sometimes simple intimidation was used to get blacks to vote the "right" way. Often the pressure came from the wealthy planters, on whom black sharecroppers and laborers depended for their livelihood.

But these methods were not always enough to beat the white-county radicals. Despite all the pressures, black voters sometimes broke with the conservatives to join the poorer whites. That happened in Virginia in 1879. Blacks from the eastern plantation counties joined with voters in the western white counties to give candidates of the Readjuster movement a majority in both houses of the state legislature. The Readjusters, a Democratic faction led by William Mahone, then enacted laws that increased aid for education, eliminated the poll tax, increased corporate taxes while reducing taxes on small farmers, and protected the civil and political rights of blacks.

With economic conditions continuing to deteriorate for many small farmers in the 1880s and 1890s, radical white challenges to the Redeemers became more common; as a result, competition between white factions for the black vote became more intense. Therefore, neither side felt sure that it could control the black vote, which goes far toward explaining why the competing white factions eventually came together to take the vote away from blacks.

In 1890 Mississippi became the first state to disfranchise blacks. There, the dominant Redeemer Democrats had used the black vote against their more radical opponents in the 1880s. But in 1889 they decided that the black vote represented a threat. The preceding year, the Republicans had captured the White House and both houses of Congress for the first time since the early 1870s. The state's Redeemers worried that the Republicans would now pass federal voting rights legislation to assure blacks the right to vote as they wished, free from pressure and intimidation. In 1890 Republican U.S. senator Henry Cabot Lodge introduced a Force bill to do just that. (It was eventually defeated.) At a constitutional convention that year, the Redeemers supported black disfranchisement. Representatives from the white counties were glad to accept it, since the black vote had usually worked against their radical candidates.

The conservative Democratic delegates from the black belt counties would have been glad to simply impose property, educational, and literacy tests upon potential voters; these would have excluded not only the great majority of blacks but many poor whites, who usually voted for the radical Democrats. But the white-county delegates opposed such tests. And so the convention had to find ways to disfranchise voters on a racial basis while pretending to be color-blind. Several constitutional provisions were adopted. A two-year residency requirement was imposed, because young blacks tended to move frequently. Men convicted of types of crimes that whites associated with blacks, such as arson, bigamy, and petty theft, lost their vote permanently. (Men convicted of murder, rape, and grand larceny, on the other hand, were not disqualified forever!) The most dishonest provision was the "understanding clause." A would-be voter had to either read a section of the Constitution or explain a section when it was read to him. This gave voting officials a great deal of leeway to make their own judgments. They could and did disqualify uneducated blacks (and sometimes even highly educated ones) while putting poorly educated whites on the voting rolls.

South Carolina acted next, at the initiative of the radical Democratic faction. With the backing of small farmers from the white counties, Benjamin R. Tillman defeated the Charleston-based Redeemer wing of the Democratic Party and became governor in 1890. But four years later the conservatives used black votes in an effort to defeat Tillman's own chosen successor. Tillman concluded that his faction could not be sure of staying in power until all blacks were deprived of the vote. Using the rhetoric of white supremacy to hide his partisan purpose, he argued that South Carolina's Eight-Box Ballot Act of 1882 did not disfranchise enough blacks and that more must be done if white rule was to survive. The result was South Carolina's constitutional convention of 1895. Copying what Mississippi had done, the delegates adopted residence and poll tax requirements while passing an understanding clause to keep lower-class whites on the rolls.

## The Populist Party and Disfranchisement

Elsewhere in the South, conservative and radical whites fought harder than ever for the black vote during the early and mid-1890s as worsening economic conditions strengthened the opposition among small white farmers to the conservative Redeemers. At the beginning of the 1890s these farmers, organized into the National Farmers' Alliance and Cooperative Union, helped establish a new national political party: the People's Party, also called the Populist Party. It represented small and middle-size farmers in the West and South. The party urged the federal government to reclaim part of the public land that had been virtually given away to giant corporations, to expand the money supply to reduce the value of the dollar and thus help debtors pay their obligations, to establish a cheaper system of credit for farmers, and to seize control of the railroads. Conservative southern Democrats (and conservatives throughout the country) considered the Populists to be dangerous radicals.

In the South, white Populist leaders wanted to form a political coalition with blacks. In organizing the party there, they asked for and received the help of the Colored Farmers' Alliance and Cooperative Union, formed in 1886 and claiming over 1 million members. Tom Watson, the Populist Party's leader in Georgia, was a particularly outspoken supporter of an interracial alliance. He proclaimed that "the accident of color can make no difference in the interest of farmers, croppers, and laborers" and that "you [blacks and whites] are kept apart that you may be separately fleeced of your earnings."

In general the Populists were unsuccessful in the South, despite a major national economic depression that began in 1893. Many blacks voted for Populist candidates. But the Redeemer Democrats generally won by manipulating and intimidating many other blacks in the usual ways. An exception was North Carolina, where a Populist-Republican coalition captured the state legislature in 1894 with the help of black votes. New legislation set limits on interest rates, raised taxes on business, and increased spending on schools and charitable institutions. Also, the coalition repealed earlier laws making voting harder for blacks, which resulted in the election of about 300 black judges. Blacks also won positions as deputy sheriffs and policemen and received federal patronage jobs. But then, in the 1898 election, the Democrats regained power through a campaign using racist rhetoric to alarm whites. Guns were brought into the state by a group called the Red Shirts, which used scare tactics and violence against blacks. The vicious campaign climaxed with a race riot in Wilmington in which 11 blacks were killed and 25 wounded.

After 1896 the Populist Party virtually disappeared. Many former Populists, bitter over the use of black votes against them, turned rabidly racist and became advocates of black disfranchisement. Many conservatives, despite their triumph, wanted the same thing: they feared that their opponents might eventually succeed in using black votes to create a "second Reconstruction," as in North Carolina. Also, whites in general wanted to end the fraud and violence that usually accompanied competition for the black vote. The result was a wave of black disfranchisement campaigns beginning in 1898, accompanied by savage and inflammatory white supremacist rhetoric.

In 1898 Louisiana called a constitutional convention, which imposed the usual literacy and property requirements for voting. It also approved a new method to protect poor whites, called the grandfather clause; it stated that persons who had voted before 1867 (before blacks got the vote), or whose fathers and grandfathers had done so, did not have to meet the new requirements. Similar approaches were taken in North Carolina (1900), Alabama (1901), Virginia (1902), Georgia (1908), and Oklahoma (1910). Some states adopted still another method for getting otherwise unqualified whites on the voting rolls; registrars could waive the usual requirements simply by declaring them eligible to vote on the basis of "good character." All 11 states of the old Confederacy adopted poll taxes. These measures, taken together, proved highly effective. In Louisiana the number of registered black voters declined 99 percent, from 130,000 in 1896 to 1,300 in 1904. Alabama had 181,000 registered black voters in 1900 and only 3,000 in 1902.

The southern states took one additional step to remove blacks from politics. With the defeat of the Populist Party, most of the South became a one-party, Democratic region: the candidate who won the Democratic primary almost always won the general election. The Democratic parties of the southern states excluded blacks from their primaries, which became known as white primaries. South Carolina adopted the white primary first in 1896, and by the end of 1915 all southern states had done so. Keeping blacks out of the Democratic primaries in effect excluded them from southern politics.

## National Responsibility for Disfranchisement

The entire nation, not just the South, was responsible for disfranchisement, for white southerners received encouragement from the federal government and from a growing number of northerners. In *Williams v. Mississippi* (1898), the U.S. Supreme Court gave a green light to disfranchisement by declaring that the poll tax and literacy requirements for voting were constitutional. Also, at the turn of the century, public opinion was being influenced by new "scientific" racial doctrines that proclaimed blacks to be inferior by nature and therefore unchangeable. These doctrines influenced the work of sociologists, journalists, and novelists around the country. With the public exposed to a constant stream of racist opinion, it is no wonder that an Alabama advocate of black disfranchisement could state in 1900 that "we now have the sympathy of thoughtful men in the North to an extent that never before existed."

Racial discrimination was also promoted by America's foreign expansion during the 1890s. In 1898 the United States, under Republican president William McKinley, fought and won the Spanish-American War, which was sparked by Spanish efforts to suppress a rebellion in Cuba. As a result of the conflict, the nation gained political power over millions of dark-skinned people in the former Spanish possessions of the Philippines, Puerto Rico, and Cuba. In separate developments the United States annexed Hawaii in 1898 and a number of other Pacific islands in the same period, all homes to nonwhite peoples.

These acquisitions strengthened racism throughout the country. The *Atlantic Monthly* magazine commented, "If the stronger and cleverer race is free to impose its will upon 'new-caught, sullen people' on the other side of the globe, why not in South Carolina and Mississippi?" John W. Burgess, a political scientist at Columbia University, stated that "the Republican party, in its work of imposing the sovereignty of the United States upon 8 millions of Asiatics, has changed its views in regard to the political relations of races and has at last virtually accepted the ideas of the South upon that subject." As if to confirm this, President McKinley made a triumphant tour of the South after the war to signal that Republicans had completely abandoned their former policy of protecting the rights of southern blacks. All of this, of course, encouraged southerners to strip away black rights not just in voting but in all matters.

## SEGREGATION AND LYNCH LAW

Segregation of the races dated back to at least the early nineteenth century, and by the Civil War it was commonplace in the South. And despite Reconstruction-era legislation, separation continued in many places, including schools, libraries, museums, hospitals, parks, poorhouses, churches, orphanages, county courthouses, and cemeteries. In some cases Jim Crow was required by law, in most it was a matter of custom.

As the Redeemer era began, however, there was still some flexibility in the South. Up to the mid-1880s, no state required segregation on the railways. Blacks were often asked to leave first-class railroad cars and were sometimes violently removed, but in other cases they were allowed to ride unmolested. In 1885 T. McCants Stewart, a black lawyer and journalist, took a train down the East Coast to test the existence of segregation. When the train departed Washington, D.C., for the South, he said, "I put a chip on my shoulder, and inwardly dared any man to knock it off." But he found to his surprise that "along the Atlantic seaboard from Canada to the Gulf of Mexico . . . a first-class ticket is good in a first-class coach." Also, in public accommodations such as hotels and restaurants, Jim Crow often but not always prevailed. On urban streetcars it was the exception, not the rule.

In the three decades after Reconstruction, Jim Crow followed a pattern similar to that of black disfranchisement: at first it spread slowly; but then, beginning in the late 1890s, it was extended rapidly to almost every point of contact between blacks and whites. As soon as the Redeemers overthrew Reconstruction, they passed legislation segregating the schools. This was not especially significant, since the region's schools were already segregated in practice. Legislation segregating railroad cars was more important, since railway segregation was not always practiced. Florida led the way in 1887, requiring separate first-class compartments for whites and blacks. Mississippi followed in 1888, and by 1901 nine southern states had passed such laws.

Until the late 1890s, railroad car segregation was the only form of racial separation required by law in a majority of southern states. But at that time, a flood of Jim Crow laws were passed. As with black disfranchisement, it happened with the encouragement of the U.S. Supreme Court. In 1896 the Court ruled in *Plessy v. Ferguson* that Louisiana's railroad segregation law was constitutional. The Court based its ruling on a "separate but equal" doctrine, which held that segregation was constitutional if equal facilities were provided for blacks. This was one of the Supreme Court's most important decisions, because it gave the green light to Jim Crow in all its forms. Intensified racism around the country also helped clear the path for southern segregation, as it did for the disfranchisement of blacks.

Until 1899 just three southern states had established separate waiting rooms for blacks at railroad stations. But within the next 10 years, all of the other southern states created them. Up to 1901, only Georgia required separation of black and white passengers on streetcars. But then North Carolina (1901), Virginia (1901), Louisiana (1902), Arkansas (1903), South Carolina (1903), Tennessee (1903), Mississippi (1904), Maryland (1904), Florida (1905), and Oklahoma (1907) followed suit. In 1906 the city of Montgomery went still farther by requiring separate streetcars. Blacks boycotted streetcars with separate seating in Savannah, Jacksonville, and other cities after 1900, but to no avail. Steamboats and ferries also became segregated after 1900. From 1911 to 1914 Louisville, Baltimore, Richmond, Roanoke, Ashland, Winston-Salem, Greensboro, Greenville, Augusta, and Atlanta became the first cities to require housing segregation. A few towns excluded blacks completely. In many places where Jim Crow had long been practiced by custom—such as prisons, hospitals, orphanages, hotels, and restaurants—segregation was now required by law.

The first years of the twentieth century witnessed attempts to carry segregation even farther so that it would reach into every cranny of southern life, no matter how small. Legislation required segregated ticket lines and even specified just how far apart the lines had to be. North Carolina and Florida insisted that the textbooks used by black and white students be stored separately during the summer. South Carolina passed a law with detailed instructions for segregating factory workers so the races would never work in the same room or use the same staircases, doorways, and exits. Separate water fountains and swimming pools and separate Bibles for taking oaths in court were required. Oklahoma insisted that telephone companies provide separate booths for whites and blacks. This was the era when WHITES ONLY and COLORED ONLY signs went up everywhere to mark off these separate facilities.

These measures introduced a new era in race relations. Previously, segregation had often been a matter of custom that was sometimes put aside—for middle-class blacks of accomplishment, for example, or for individual blacks held in esteem or affection. Now Jim Crow was being written into laws that were strictly enforced against all blacks and stretched to include even the briefest and most insignificant contacts between black and white (such as at water fountains). These changes emerged from a doctrine of white racial supremacy more extreme than the country had yet known. The general superiority of whites over blacks had, of course, been proclaimed by whites since the seventeenth century. But the new racial doctrine was more thoroughgoing and rigid, insisting that even the worst white was better than the best black.

The deepening of racism led to the rise of southern demagogues who degraded American political life with the language of vicious race hatred. Benjamin Tillman, governor and then U.S. senator from South Carolina, described blacks as "akin to monkeys" and an "ignorant and debased race." James K. Vardaman, the governor of Mississippi, advised a crowd that "the way to control the nigger is to whip him when he does not obey without it, and another is never to pay him more wages than is actually necessary to buy food and clothing." No wonder that in 1903, black novelist Charles W. Chestnutt observed that "the rights of the Negroes are at a lower ebb than at any time during the thirty-five years of their freedom, and the race prejudice more intense and uncompromising."

## Racial Violence

In the climate of racism and hatred, violence against blacks was common. We have already noted the 1898 Wilmington riot in connection with a race-baiting Democratic political campaign in North Carolina. New Orleans witnessed a three-day race riot in 1900, with white mobs ranging over the city to terrorize blacks. In 1906 Hoke Smith called for black disfranchisement in his campaign for the Democratic nomination for governor of Georgia. The campaign unleashed viciously antiblack feelings. The press in Atlanta—by the turn of the century the most important city of the South—carried wild reports about black crime and scare stories claiming that black rapists, murderers, and other criminals were moving from rural areas into the city. Atlanta's press also ran calls for lynchings and the reestablishment of the Ku Klux Klan. A month after the campaign, rumors that black rapists had attacked white women started a race riot. Whites rampaged through Atlanta, attacking blacks at random. When blacks began to defend themselves on the third day, the police sided with the white assailants. When the violence finally ended, around 25 blacks and 1 or 2 whites had been killed, and many more had been injured.

But the most common form of racial violence in this era was lynching. Lynching was the murder—outside of the judicial system, without due process, and usually by mobs—of persons suspected of violating laws or unofficial codes of behavior. Commonly the victims were hung from trees, and often they were castrated. Blacks had been victimized by lynchings since the pre–Civil War era, but in the 1880s the number of these murders increased sharply. From 1889 to 1899, about 104 blacks were lynched per year in the South (and 23 per year in the

A black man and a white man drink from separate water fountains. Jim Crow laws adopted in the South during the late nineteenth and early twentieth centuries established strict segregation of the races.

North). From 1900 to 1909, the average declined to about 84 per year in the South (and 8 per year in the North).

How did white southerners justify lynching in general? The need to protect white women from black rapists—long an obsession of white southerners—was the usual defense. South Carolina politician Benjamin Tillman gained a sort of fame by saying that if the lynching of rapists violated the U.S. Constitution, then "to hell with the Constitution." But examination of individual lynchings shows that they were prompted by charges of murder more often than anything else, and that suspicion of robbery was another frequent trigger for mob action. Often the supposed crime was not a crime at all; trying to vote, testifying in court, or accepting a federal patronage job could result in the murder of a black person. A lynching might even follow a small, perhaps accidental, violation of the southern code of racial behavior. Blacks were supposed to be subservient to whites at all times. Failing to say "mister" to a white man; looking directly into the eye of a white man—or worse, a white woman; or speaking to a white in a disrespectful (or simply nonsubmissive) way could mean death. Whenever they were in the presence of whites, blacks had to be very careful of their behavior, down to the smallest details.

Where were lynchings most likely to occur? They happened most often in rural areas where the population was very scattered, where the black population was increasing, and where many of the blacks were new residents. The growing number of blacks and the scattered nature of the population increased whites' sense of insecurity. The new black residents, not well known to their white neighbors, were more likely to be feared than longtime residents. The absence of close neighbors made it difficult for the victims to obtain help from fellow blacks.

## BLACKS IN THE ECONOMY OF THE NEW SOUTH

In the late 1870s, the South entered a period of significant economic growth. Political stability was restored with the overthrow of Reconstruction, and the depression of the 1870s ended in 1879. Northern and English capitalists, as well as southerners, saw investment opportunities in the region's industry. Southern manufacturing began to expand rapidly in the 1880s, although not nearly as fast as northern manufacturing.

The number of railroad miles in the South grew from 16,600 in 1880 to 39,100 in 1890. The value of the timber in the Gulf states of Texas, Louisiana, Mississippi, Alabama, and Florida soared from $13.1 million in 1880 to $73.1 million a decade later. The iron industry grew in Birmingham, Alabama, and in various towns of Tennessee and Virginia; between 1876 and 1901, pig iron production expanded by 17 times. Before the Civil War, almost all southern cotton had been processed elsewhere; in the 1880s a large-scale cotton textile industry emerged, especially in North Carolina, South Carolina, Georgia, and Alabama. From 1880 to 1900, the number of southern cotton mills increased from 161 to 400.

What role did blacks have in this New South, as it was called? The cotton mills provided employment—although at very low wages—for the many white small farmers who lost their land because of declining cotton prices. By agreement between planters and cotton mill owners (who were often planters themselves), blacks were kept entirely out of the mills to assure the planters of continued control of their black labor supply. Had large numbers of blacks left the plantations to do factory work, those remaining behind would have been in a better bargaining position.

Industrialists, however, were happy to hire blacks for railroad construction and in mines, iron foundries, and tobacco factories. With black and white workers pitted against each other, it was easier to keep wages down. When white workers went on strike, blacks were sometimes used as strikebreakers. Often, whites went on strike when employers hired blacks for the more skilled, higher-paying craft jobs; employers were thus discouraged from doing so. As a consequence, while many blacks had done skilled work as slaves, the proportion of blacks employed in the crafts declined sharply between 1865 and 1890.

Yet in some cases the two races acted together, especially in the Knights of Labor, an early trade union established in 1878. The Knights tried to unite all workers regardless of color or skill level. By 1886 it had organized over 30,000 black workers in the South. In the 1880s the union carried out strikes involving blacks and whites, including railroad strikes in Texas and Arkansas and coal miners' walkouts in Alabama and Tennessee. The Knights faded after 1886, and the group was replaced as the major trade union association by the American Federation of Labor (AFL), an umbrella group for craft unions headed by Samuel Gompers. In 1890 Gompers took a practical and rational view of organizing black workers:

> [White] wage-workers like many others may not care to socially meet colored people, but as working men we are not justified in refusing them the right of the opportunity to organize for their common protection. Then again, if [labor] organizations do [refuse them that right], we will only make enemies of them, and of necessity they will be antagonistic to our interests.

Four years later, AFL-affiliated unions in New Orleans led black and white workers out on a general strike to demand a 10-hour day, overtime pay, and closed shops (meaning that only union members could be hired).

As in many other areas of American life, however, racism gained ground within the AFL around the turn of the century. By 1900 the federation was admitting unions that openly restricted membership to whites; the justification was that otherwise these unions would not join the federation at all. By the early 1900s, Gompers's views were clearly racist. Previously, he had said that blacks became strikebreakers when they were excluded from unions. Now he blamed strikebreaking on the supposed inability of the nonwhite races to work cooperatively for the common benefit. Gompers described black strikebreakers in a 1904 Chicago labor dispute as "hordes of ignorant blacks" and as "huge, strapping fellows, ignorant and vicious, whose predominating trait was animalism." In 1905 he proclaimed that "caucasians are not going to let their standard of living be destroyed by negroes, Chinamen, Japs, or any others." The hostility of the AFL cost blacks jobs. So did the spread of segregation around 1900. Also, the growing number of white women leaving their homes to take jobs sometimes displaced blacks.

Meanwhile, though, the growing number of black college graduates helped to swell the ranks of the black professional class. The black business class also grew as the spread of segregated housing, especially in the newer southern cities, created all-black neighborhoods. But the overwhelming majority of urban blacks were stuck in personal service or unskilled jobs.

## The Exploitation of Sharecroppers and Laborers

Despite its industrial growth, the New South did not become a modern, industrialized society like the North. Going into the twentieth century, it remained a mostly rural region in which the great majority of blacks still worked the land. As we have seen, blacks on the plantations did not want to work for wages, because wage laborers worked in groups supervised by whites, as during slavery. They preferred to farm a piece of the planter's land on their own for a share of the crop. By 1880 less than half of the South's rural blacks worked for wages, and by 1900 the figure was less than 25 percent.

But although rural blacks managed to escape intensive white supervision of their labor, they were far from free of white control. They became victims of a cycle of debt that was almost impossible to escape and that trapped many white as well as black sharecroppers. At the beginning of every crop cycle, each sharecropper signed a contract with a local merchant. Under its terms, the farmer received supplies from the merchant as a loan; in exchange the merchant received what was called a lien on the crop, meaning that the merchant would control the marketing of the crop and take repayment of the loan from sale of the crop later on. The merchant charged a high price for the supplies (the credit price, as opposed to the lower cash price) and added a high interest rate. Then, after the harvest, the merchant sold the crop and credited the sharecropper with what was known as the "inside price," which was lower than the market price that the merchant had actually received. Not surprisingly, at the end of the agricultural year the farmer's debt to the merchant was greater than his income from the crop; in other words, the sharecropper owed the merchant money. The contract provided that in such a case, the farmer had to once again give the merchant a lien on the crop. This often continued for a lifetime, with the debt always increasing and the sharecropper completely dependent on the merchant for survival. (The farmer could not get supplies from other merchants because his crop was already pledged, and he usually had nothing else that would be accepted as security.) This system, called debt peonage, was outlawed by the U.S. Supreme Court in *Bailey v. Alabama* (1911), but in reality it survived for decades.

Those working for wages were no better off. In 1880 rural laborers, white and black, were lucky to earn $10 a month in many parts of the South. Planters preferred to hire black workers; because blacks had fewer opportunities to purchase land or get city jobs, they were willing to work harder for less. An Alabama planter commented in 1888 that only a black laborer "would be as cheerful, or so contented on four pounds of meat and a peck of meal a week, in a little log cabin 14 × 16 feet, with cracks in it large enough to afford free passage to a large sized cat."

Even for the few blacks who could afford to buy land, becoming an independent farmer was difficult. Some whites were willing to sell blacks inferior land, but not the fertile land of the black belt. In 1891 F. M. Gilmore, an Arkansas black man, wrote:

> Land Lords has got us Bound To Do Just as They Say or git off of his Land, and we air Compeled to Do so . . . and they say it is not entend [intended] from the begaining for a Dam negro to have . . . [his or her own land except for] a small peace of Land in the South, an it is only 6 feet by 4 wide [by] 4 ft deep [a grave].

By 1900 blacks owned a smaller share of the land than they had at the end of Reconstruction.

After the Redeemers took power, they quickly passed laws making it easier to exploit black farmers and laborers. (Often, they were simply reviving laws repealed during Radical Reconstruction.) To force blacks to sign work contracts, vagrancy laws were written broadly to make it possible to arrest almost any unemployed person. Laws also barred wage workers, sharecroppers, or tenants already under contract from accepting a better offer from another planter. Because of the Fourteenth Amendment's guarantee of equal protection of the laws, the legislatures could not apply these measures only to blacks. But many were written to cover only those counties with heavy black majorities. The elimination of blacks from law enforcement positions after Reconstruction further assured that these laws were rarely enforced against whites.

Another type of law excused planters from paying wages to their laborers until they (the planters) received their share of the crop from sharecroppers. This transferred the risks of farming from the planter to the wage earner—if the crop failed, the wage workers did not get paid. In addition, laws barred persons from grazing their animals on the open range; this made it impossible for the landless to own livestock. Hunting rights were also restricted by law.

New criminal laws provided extremely long jail sentences for petty crimes against property. Mississippi declared any theft of livestock to be grand larceny punishable by five years in prison. South Carolina sent burglars to prison for life. The main purpose of such laws was to protect white property against black crime. As a result, a great number of blacks were sent to prisons—many more than the prisons could hold. An outgrowth of this situation was the convict-lease system, a bonanza for corporations and individual employers. Under this system many black prisoners were hired out as cheap labor to planters, railroad companies, timber enterprises, and other firms. Often, they were hired as strikebreakers. The leasing fee was very small, but large enough to encourage county and state officials to arrest blacks as a way to bring in government revenue and keep taxes low. Officials often pocketed part of the fee, which made false arrests of blacks even more tempting.

Those who hired convicts had little motivation to treat the prisoners well, since the latter were not free to leave. State laws imposed no or few restrictions on the number of work hours or the kinds of labor that could be imposed. The laborers' health was neglected, they were sometimes brutally whipped, often they were virtually starved, and their clothes sometimes consisted of just a few badly torn garments (and no shoes). In the Mississippi prison system, the death rate for blacks from 1880 to 1885 was 11 percent per year—an astounding rate, especially considering that most prisoners were relatively young. For whites the rate was also very high, but only half as great as for blacks.

## THE NORTH: INDUSTRIAL GROWTH
## AND THE BEGINNINGS OF THE GHETTO

Just as racial progress had been made in both North and South during Reconstruction, deterioration of race relations occurred in both sections afterward. In the North, the years between 1880 and 1915 witnessed growing housing segregation, eventually resulting in black ghettos. Meanwhile, the rise of large-scale factory production meant a declining economic status for blacks.

Although blacks had always lived in the worst neighborhoods of northern cities, poor whites could also be found there. A few blocks in a row might be exclusively black, but not large neighborhoods. This began to change after 1880. One reason was the rise of large-scale industry. Rapid industrial growth was the major reason the nation's urban population skyrocketed from 6 million in 1860 to 42 million in 1910. As cities grew large, people could no longer simply walk to their destinations. Therefore, new types of transportation emerged, including electric streetcars, buses, elevated trains, and subways. This made for quicker travel, which meant that the population could spread out into separate ethnic, class, and racial neighborhoods. Also, the growth of urban industry brought new zoning regulations that separated business districts from residential areas (previously, businesses and residences had been jumbled together); this further encouraged the spreading and sorting out of the population. Housing segregation, then, grew fastest in cities like New York, Philadelphia, and Chicago, which were expanding and industrializing most rapidly. In cities where population and industry were expanding more slowly—medium-size Midwestern cities like Omaha, Indianapolis, and Minneapolis; western cities like Los Angeles; and southern cities—residential segregation took longer.

But this alone does not explain the ghetto's rise. After all, whites still had choices of neighborhoods. White ethnic neighborhoods were not strictly limited to one group—ethnic mixing still existed to a degree. Also, whites could move into better neighborhoods as their incomes went up. But blacks became increasingly hemmed in as racism deepened throughout the country at the end of the nineteenth century. A growing number of realtors refused to sell homes to blacks in areas where whites lived; also, restrictive covenants barring homeowners from selling to blacks became more and more common in property deeds.

The racism behind such restrictive practices was strengthened by an increase in the flow of rural black migrants to northern and western cities. From 1870 to 1890, only about 80,000 blacks moved from the South to the North and West. But from 1890 to 1910, the number grew to some 200,000. The black population of Chicago increased from just under 15,000 in 1890 to about 44,000 in 1910. During those years New York City's black population expanded from 36,000 to 92,000. Migration may have increased because the first generation of southern blacks born after slavery came of age between 1890 and 1910; never having experienced bondage, they may have been less willing than their parents to accept the oppressive conditions of the South. Whatever the reason, their northward migration heightened white northerners' fear of blacks and their determination to segregate them.

The mostly black neighborhoods that emerged included the Tenderloin and San Juan Hill sections on Manhattan's West Side and, later, Harlem in upper Manhattan, the Central Avenue area in Cleveland, Chicago's South Side, and the Heights area in Detroit. These neighborhoods did not become virtually all black until after 1915, when the stream of black migrants from the South became a flood. But before then, they were already well on their way to becoming ghettos.

As blacks were forced into these areas, they became the most crowded sections of the city. Since blacks had less choice of housing than whites, landlords could force them to pay higher rents. Early in 1912, a Chicago real estate operator took out two ads for the same apartment. One read "seven rooms, $25"; the other read "seven rooms for colored people, $37.50." Blacks' lack of choice also made it easier for landlords to avoid making needed repairs, so housing deteriorated. Meanwhile, vice districts with gambling establishments and houses of prostitution began to appear in the emerging ghettos. One reason is that the police prevented such districts from developing in white areas but did not bother to take action in mostly black communities.

As ghettos began forming, the growth of industry reduced employment opportunities for blacks. Before massive industrialization, a significant minority of blacks had labored in the skilled trades, often working for themselves. But the new manufacturing plants could produce goods more cheaply and so forced many of these craftspersons out of business. Furthermore, few of them could find jobs in the new plants. Many white employers believed—out of pure prejudice—that blacks were suited only for agricultural work. Another major obstacle to black industrial employment was the trade union movement. We have seen how southern blacks were increasingly excluded from labor unions in the late 1890s and early 1900s; the same thing happened to northern black workers. Record-level European immigration was another reason for black economic decline; white employers could more easily act out their racial prejudices when an abundant supply of white labor from the Old World was available. And so blacks were hired in industry only for the lowest-paying, lowest-skilled jobs.

The statistics show that blacks rapidly lost economic ground in the late nineteenth and early twentieth centuries. In Cleveland, 32 percent of black men worked at skilled trades in 1870; over the next 40 years, the figure dropped to 11 percent. Blacks fared even worse in cities with more industry and more immigrants than Cleveland; in New York, for instance, the 1910 figure was below 5 percent. With fewer black men able to support their families adequately, more black women left the home to work, mostly as servants and maids; in New York at the turn of the twentieth century, 59 percent of all black women worked, compared to about 25 percent of white women.

Skilled tradespeople were not the only blacks to suffer economically. Blacks in service employment also felt the impact of growing racism, housing segregation, and industrialization. In the mid–nineteenth century, blacks worked as waiters in a number of fashionable downtown restaurants where all or almost all the patrons were white. Some black businessmen—especially black barbers, tailors, and caterers—had well-to-do white clienteles. These blacks, many of them mulattoes with white relatives, were even allowed limited access to white social circles and sometimes lived in the same neighborhoods as their white clients. This changed in the late nineteenth century. Upper-class whites, taking advantage of the new forms of urban transportation, moved to the outskirts of cities or to the suburbs as blacks became confined to a few segregated neighborhoods. That mobility, plus intensifying white racism, broke the ties between these blacks and their white customers and destroyed the livelihoods of the former.

Blacks were now faced with dwindling economic prospects and forced to live in increasingly segregated neighborhoods that symbolized most whites' contempt for them. Some blacks simply gave up in despair and dropped out of mainstream society. They abandoned all efforts to find jobs, spent their time standing idly on the streets, gambled, drank heavily, had loose sexual morals, and often engaged in crime. Such people, later known as the underclass, became a permanent part of the ghetto.

On the other hand, the rise of ghettos created a new class of black entrepreneurs to serve a mostly black clientele. These businesspeople included real estate operators, undertakers, theater owners, insurance agents, bankers, doctors, and lawyers. Some entrepreneurs provided "race products"; Madame C. J. Walker, for example, made a fortune after inventing a hair-straightening process. But most people in the emerging black communities were poor, which limited both the size of black businesses and the number of black businesspeople who could succeed.

Some southern migrants may have improved their lot, because even low-wage jobs in northern cities were preferable to the grinding poverty of the rural South. But the economic fortunes of most northern blacks—low in the best of times— were in decline.

## SURVIVING SOUTHERN REPRESSION:
## THE ERA OF BOOKER T. WASHINGTON

In the South and North, the hopes inspired by the Emancipation Proclamation and Radical Reconstruction lay shattered. Blacks faced growing obstacles not only to a decent life but even to basic survival. Against all odds, they tried to forge strategies that might make possible a better life in America.

In the South, black political activity survived for more than two decades after the Redeemers took power. Even during the first decade of the twentieth century, blacks still engaged in political activities such as boycotting newly segregated streetcars, boycotting newspapers that were especially abusive (for example, referring to black children as "coons"), and campaigning against efforts to disfranchise them. But once the ballot was lost, open protest became extremely dangerous. Not until after World War II would the region's blacks be able once again to fight back politically.

As racial oppression grew, one option was simply to leave the South. Immediately after Reconstruction, many blacks became interested in moving westward. Just after Alabama's Democrats won control of the state from the Radical Republicans in 1874, a black convention in Montgomery declared that, like the Israelites, blacks have to "seek new homes . . . beyond the reign and rule of Pharaoh." Southern crop failures in 1878 sparked further interest, and early in 1879 black conventions in New Orleans, Vicksburg, and Nashville sought to promote westward migration. The movement was led by Benjamin "Pap" Singleton and Henry Adams, both former slaves, who encouraged blacks to resettle in Kansas. By August 1879, some 7,000 had taken their advice (while thousands of others moved elsewhere in the West).

Some black leaders, such as Richard T. Greener, dean of the Howard University Law School, approved of this development. But Frederick Douglass and others saw migration as a surrender to racism; he believed that blacks must fight bigotry wherever they were.

The westward migration collapsed following a hostile welcome from local whites and a harsh winter in 1879–80. In the early 1890s, migration to the Oklahoma Territory began; the migrants established over two dozen all-black towns, beginning with Langston in 1891. Because the settlers separated themselves from whites, their towns were allowed to survive; however, the residents lived in severe poverty.

Some blacks seeking to escape rural poverty went to southern cities to find work. But southern industrial growth was limited, and blacks faced discrimination. Mostly for economic reasons, a small but growing stream of blacks began moving toward northern cities around 1890, but the flow remained limited until World War I.

Some black leaders tried to revive separatism. In the late nineteenth century, Bishop Henry McNeal Turner of the African Methodist Episcopal church urged blacks to return to Africa while Bishop Lucius H. Holsey of the Colored Methodist

Booker T. Washington, president of Tuskegee Institute, was the most powerful black man in America from the mid-1890s to his death in 1915. He urged blacks to put aside civil rights issues and concentrate on building up their economic power.

Episcopal church called on the federal government to create a state for blacks in the West. Few blacks found either proposal attractive.

Neither political action, migration within the country, nor emigration out of America offered much hope; therefore, blacks turned increasingly toward self-advancement through the development of their own communities. One approach was through education, and educational progress was in fact one of the few bright spots in the lives of southern blacks after Reconstruction. Black illiteracy declined from over 90 percent in 1865 to about 30 percent in 1913 (although in 1917 only 2,132 blacks were in college). In 1900 over 1.5 million black schoolchildren were being taught by 29,000 black teachers. This achievement is especially impressive considering that the Redeemer governments discriminated against black schools. While state legislatures used tax revenues to lengthen the school year, increase teachers' salaries, and reduce class size for white schools, they sharply cut funds for black schools. Florida in 1898 spent $5.92 per white student and $2.27 per black student; South Carolina in 1915 spent $13.98 for each white student and only $2.57 for each black student.

To compensate, the major black religious denominations all worked to establish and improve black schools. By 1900, for example, black Baptist churches were supporting 80 elementary and high schools. The denominations also speeded up the process, begun during Reconstruction, of creating black colleges. The African Methodist Episcopal church founded six colleges between 1870 and 1886, and the Colored Methodist Episcopal church founded four between 1878 and 1902. In 1900 there were 34 such institutions.

Blacks could not have established secondary schools and colleges without financial help from the white religious denominations. Assistance came from the American Missionary Association, an arm of the Congregational church. Additional aid came from the Baptists' Home Mission Society and the Methodist Episcopal church's Freedmen's Aid Society.

Also crucial to the development of black schools were wealthy white capitalists who had made their fortunes in the late-nineteenth-century industrial boom, including oil millionaire John D. Rockefeller, railroad magnate Collis F. Huntington, and steel baron Andrew Carnegie. One motive for their financial contributions was certainly humanitarian: they felt an obligation to help the less fortunate. But northern capitalists also hoped to benefit from their generosity. After the Civil War, they became major investors in the South, and they knew that improved education would make their southern workforces more productive. They were especially interested in giving money to industrial schools that taught practical craft and mechanical skills, rather than to liberal arts institutions.

Much of the white funding for industrial education went to Booker T. Washington, the South's foremost black educator. The slave son of a black mother and a white father, he attended Hampton Institute, a Virginia vocational school, in the 1870s. In 1881 Washington organized an industrial school in Tuskegee, Alabama. At Tuskegee Institute men learned to become better farmers as well as carpenters, painters, plumbers, blacksmiths, bricklayers, and other types of skilled workers. Women at Tuskegee learned such "female" skills as nursing, cooking, and sewing. By 1890 Washington had developed a good reputation among southern white leaders, and when he began going North in the early 1890s to raise funds for his school, the educator expanded his circle of powerful white friends.

## The Strategy of Self-Development

Then, in 1895, Washington gave a speech that suddenly turned him into one of America's major leaders, regardless of race; it made him a highly influential figure among whites and the dominant figure in black America until his death in 1915. Invited to give an address at the Atlanta Cotton States and International Exhibition, he used the opportunity to present his philosophy of race relations and his views on black advancement. Washington stated that blacks should abandon the political struggle against discrimination and assured his mostly white audience that "the wisest among my race understand that the agitation of questions of social equality is the extremest folly." Blacks would carve out their place in American society, he believed, not by political activity but by being thrifty, working hard, and acquiring trade, farming, and business skills—that is, by education and economic self-advancement.

Whites, Washington told his audience, should encourage such efforts at advancement and make blacks partners in building the southern economy. He noted that in the past blacks "have, without strikes and labor wars, tilled your fields, cleared your forests, builded your railroads and cities, and brought forth treasures from the bowels of the earth." If given the encouragement, Washington continued,

> you will find that they will buy your surplus land, make blossom the waste places in your fields, and run your factories. While doing this, you can be sure in the future, as in the past, that you and your families will be surrounded by the most patient, faithful, law-abiding, and unresentful people that the world has seen.

He was saying, in other words, that southern blacks had been and could continue to be a source of cheap labor that did not cause trouble.

The sentence that came closest to summing up the address was Washington's assurance that "in all things that are purely social we can be as separate as the fingers, yet one as the hand in all things essential to mutual progress." Essentially Washington was offering whites a deal that became known as the Atlanta Compromise: blacks would abandon the political struggle for equality in exchange for a role—and a subordinate one at that—in the economy. This was just what southern whites wanted to hear from a black man. And so to many whites, Washington was a savior who had found a solution to the race problem based essentially on white terms.

The reaction to his address was swift. After he had finished talking, whites walked up to shake his hand, a violation of the southern racial code, which decreed that blacks must never be treated as equals. The next day he was flooded with telegrams praising the speech. Soon after, a speakers' bureau offered Washington $50,000—an enormous amount of money then—to make a series of addresses. President Grover Cleveland thanked him "with great enthusiasm" for making the speech. The *Charleston News and Courier* praised him, but in a way that insulted blacks in general: "His skin is colored, but his head is sound and his heart is in the right place." The *Atlanta Constitution* described the speech as "the most remarkable address delivered by a colored man in America."

Washington became a man of great power. Wealthy white capitalists in the North sought his advice before contributing to black colleges; he urged them to give to industrial schools that taught trade skills rather than to liberal arts colleges offering a broader education in the arts and humanities. This control over contributions gave him great influence over black educators. When Republicans controlled the White House, they gave low-level federal jobs to blacks. After 1900, Presidents Theodore Roosevelt and William Howard Taft turned to Booker T. Washington for advice about which blacks should receive them, and they usually followed his recommendations. Roosevelt even invited Washington to dine at the White House in October 1901, partly to discuss black appointments. His influence over federal patronage was another source of Washington's power within the black community.

Washington's great influence with powerful whites enabled him to develop a huge circle of black allies—known as the Tuskegee Machine—that became the dominant political force throughout black America. Black politicians and educators could not afford to cross him because of his control over political patronage and school aid. Black newspaper editors were afraid of his power to retaliate against them; thus, not much criticism of the Tuskegee president appeared in print.

Some have argued that Washington became the chief black leader in the country only because powerful whites allowed him to. Certainly, this accusation contains a great deal of truth; Washington could not have risen as he did without the support of leading whites. Yet at the same time, most blacks in both the North and the South admired him as their foremost leader. One group in the black community in particular agreed with Washington's philosophy. As we have seen, the growth of housing segregation in both northern and southern cities led to the development of a new, expanding class of black professionals and businesspersons serving mostly black neighborhoods. These blacks owed their success to patience, hard work, thrift, and education rather than to political battles against discrimination. Also, their roots were in the emerging black ghettos that provided them with almost all of their customers. The preceding generation of black businesspeople had had white customers and aspired to equality with whites. But the new generation had little if any white clientele, rarely associated with whites, and had little interest in doing so. The members of the new black bourgeoisie identified with Booker T. Washington's approach of self-reliance and noninvolvement in politics, and they formed the core of his black support. Washington sought to advance the fortunes of that class—and also to strengthen his power—by creating in 1900 the National Negro Business League, of which he became president.

## Was Washington an Uncle Tom?

Booker T. Washington has been accused of being merely an Uncle Tom, a tool of powerful whites for controlling blacks. It is true that Washington often sounded as if he were speaking for whites as he urged blacks to create their own opportunities by hard work instead of demanding that whites eliminate discrimination through legal and political concessions. "I fear that the Negro race lays too much stress on its grievances and not enough on its opportunities," he said. In a speech at Fisk University, he advised blacks to react to discrimination and mob violence with "patience, forbearance, and self-control" and asked them "to suffer in silence."

But if whites believed that Washington favored black subordination forever, they were mistaken. As a black southerner, Washington was trying to develop a strategy for black progress in an extremely hostile environment. By the time of his Atlanta speech in 1895, the racial advances of Reconstruction were turning into a nightmare of retreat. The opportunities for effective black political activity were dwindling. Discrimination seemed a fact of life for the immediate future. Under these conditions, Washington concluded that the only thing blacks could do was improve the economic fortunes of themselves and their communities by self-help. As their importance in the U.S. economy increased, he believed, blacks would eventually achieve legal and political equality.

If whites had listened more carefully to the Atlanta speech, they might have understood this when he said: "No race that has anything to contribute to the markets of the world is long in any degree ignored. It is important and right that all privileges of the law be ours." Washington worked quietly behind the scenes against black disfranchisement, segregation, and exclusion of blacks from juries. But considering the overwhelming prejudice against blacks, he thought that public protest would only cause an angry white backlash. He may or may not have been right, but his position was understandable. Some have credited him with sowing the seeds of black nationalism by urging black self-reliance and the building up of the black community. Indeed, the ghetto-based black entrepreneurs who enthusiastically backed him would be among the leading supporters of future nationalist organizations; also, future nationalist leaders such as Marcus Garvey would hail Washington as one of the inspirations for their movements.

But even if Washington cannot fairly be condemned as an Uncle Tom, the effectiveness of his strategy can be questioned. He urged blacks to acquire craft skills and establish small businesses just at a time when the new, giant industrial corporations were wiping out craft jobs and swallowing up small businesses. Also, it is difficult to separate economic and political issues, as Washington tried to do. So long as blacks faced severe discrimination, most would face restricted economic opportunities and would remain poor. And although the segregation of blacks into ghettos might create opportunities for black professionals and businesspeople, the average black consumer had little money to spend, and this sharply limited the growth of the black middle class. Furthermore, black businesspersons faced discrimination in obtaining the credit they needed to maintain and expand their businesses. The National Negro Business League reported that black enterprises doubled in number from 20,000 to 40,000 between 1910 and 1914. But they still represented the efforts of just a small minority within a black population of about 10 million.

Washington has also been accused of promoting racial discrimination and violence by encouraging whites to believe that blacks would not resist oppression. It is impossible to know for certain whether there is any truth to this charge. We can say, however, that he certainly did not reduce the severity of racism and discrimination. In fact, the situation deteriorated after his Atlanta address: disfranchisement and segregation spread in the South in the years after his speech, as did housing segregation and employment discrimination in the North. For these and other reasons, northern blacks and white liberals began to form organizations that broke with Washington's approach to racial issues.

## RESISTING OPPRESSION: VOICES FROM THE NORTH

From the beginning, Booker T. Washington had black critics. One was John Hope, president of Atlanta University and later of Morehouse College. He commented on Washington's Atlanta Exposition address in February 1896, five months after it was made:

> I regard it as cowardly and dishonest for any of our colored men to tell white people and colored people that we are not struggling for equality. . . . If equality, political, economic, and social, is the boon of other men in this great country of ours, then equality, political, economic, and social, is what we demand.

But most supporters of the civil rights struggle came from the North, where blacks were freer to express themselves. On October 6, 1895—less than three weeks after Washington's address—the *Detroit Tribune* commented sarcastically that the "latest Tennessee lynching should be exhibited at the Atlanta Exposition as a fine specimen of one of the staple products of the South." In 1900 T. Thomas Fortune—editor of the *New York Age* and founder in 1890 of the short-lived Afro-American League, a civil rights organization—expressed a very different view from Washington's, stating: "It took tons of blood to put the Fifteenth Amendment into the Constitution and it will take tons to put it out. You want to organize and keep your powder dry."

Harry C. Smith, editor of the *Cleveland Gazette* since the 1880s, attacked all forms of discrimination and was a strong supporter of integrated schools, believing that they were the key to ending racial prejudice. In 1890 Smith was a cofounder of the Afro-American League with T. Thomas Fortune, and subsequently he became a critic of Washington. In 1901 William Monroe Trotter and George Forbes founded the *Boston Guardian* specifically to oppose Washington. Driven by an intense dislike of the Tuskegee educator's views, Trotter in 1903 attended the national convention of the Washington-controlled Afro-American Council. He tried to present anti-Washington resolutions but was not recognized. Just a few weeks later, on July 30, 1903, Trotter was in the audience for a speech by Washington at the AME Zion Church in Boston. Trotter shouted out hostile questions at Washington, and the commotion that followed became known as the Boston Riot. Trotter served a month in jail for his disruption.

Ida Wells-Barnett took a very different approach than Washington. Editor of the *Memphis Free Speech* in Tennessee, in 1892 she denounced in her newspaper the lynching of three of her friends. Two months later, she wrote another antilynching editorial. Soon afterward, when Wells-Barnett was out of town, a white mob burned down the newspaper's offices in retaliation, and she was warned never to return to Memphis. Wells-Barnett moved to the North, where she wrote antilynching articles for the *New York Age* and went on antilynching lecture tours. Believing that pressure from abroad could help blacks, she visited Britain in 1893 and 1894. Her trips inspired the formation of several British antilynching and antisegregation organizations.

Black women's clubs that sprang up in the 1890s were by no means anti-Washington, and their primary prupose was not to promote equal rights. Rather, they were self-help groups that established such programs as nurseries and kinder-gartens for the children of black working women, girls' homes, and evening schools for adults. Yet the clubs did have a political dimension. The major organization of black women's clubs—the National Association of Colored Women (NACW), founded in 1896 and headed by Mary Church Terrell—supported the white-led women's suffrage movement and urged it to back the right of black as well as white women to vote. The NACW also spoke out on issues such as lynching and Jim Crow.

## W. E. B. Du Bois and the Niagara Movement

In 1903 a collection of essays called *The Souls of Black Folk* appeared. Its author was W. E. B. Du Bois, a northerner teaching history at Atlanta University and the first black American to receive a doctor of philosophy degree. A landmark in black history, the volume included a thoughtful and eloquent criticism of Booker T. Washington. Du Bois acknowledged that Washington's Atlanta address had made him "the most distinguished Southerner since Jefferson Davis." But he went on to speak on behalf of those "educated and thoughtful colored men in all parts of the land . . . [who feel] deep regret, sorrow, and apprehension at the wide currency and ascendancy which some of Mr. Washington's theories have gained." Du Bois attacked the two major elements of Washington's thinking: his emphasis on industrial education over higher learning (such as literature, history, and science), and his belief that the black struggle for legal and political equality should be abandoned, at least for the foreseeable future.

Du Bois believed that blacks, like any other group, could not advance them-selves without the leadership of highly educated individuals, whom he called the Talented Tenth. Mere industrial education, he argued, could not create such a leadership group. Du Bois also believed that without legal and political rights, blacks' chances for advancement were small. He asked,

> Is it possible and probable, that nine millions of men can make effective progress in economic lines if they are deprived of political rights, made a servile caste, and allowed only the most meagre chance for developing their

exceptional men? If history and reason give any answer to these questions, it is an emphatic *NO.*

Furthermore, Du Bois felt that black dignity was more important than economic well-being and that Washington's philosophy was especially harmful on that score. He asserted that accepting legalized discrimination, as Washington urged, "is bound to sap the manhood of any race in the long run." Furthermore, Du Bois contended that by advocating industrial education and money making to the exclusion of almost anything else, Washington was preaching a "Gospel of Work and Money to such an extent as apparently almost completely to overshadow the higher aims of life." Du Bois argued that Washington "practically accepts the alleged inferiority of the Negro race" and stated that "Negroes must insist continually, in season and out of season, that voting is necessary to modern manhood, that color discrimination is barbarism, and that black boys need education as well as white boys."

Those blacks who wished to continue the fight for civil rights realized that the days when they could count on the Republicans for help were gone. During the first two years of his presidency, Theodore Roosevelt took several actions that encouraged blacks. For example, he invited Booker T. Washington to the White House in 1901 (an act that enraged southern whites) and appointed a black customs collector in Charleston, South Carolina, in 1903. But later on he showed almost complete indifference to black needs. In particular, blacks resented his reaction to a riot in Brownsville, Texas. Responding to racial insults, parts of three companies in the black 25th Infantry participated in the riot. The 25th had served valiantly in the Spanish-American War. But when some of its men refused to identify the guilty soldiers, Roosevelt discharged the 3 companies—167 men and officers—without honor. Blacks had long taken pride in the achievements of their soldiers, and they remembered this incident with bitterness for decades. President William Howard Taft, elected in 1908, was too interested in building southern white support for the Republican Party to take any interest in black needs.

With no hope of government support, blacks seeking full equality had to take the initiative. In 1905 Du Bois followed up his words with action when he called a meeting of educated blacks who shared his views. In July 1905, 29 blacks gathered at Niagara Falls, Canada. More would have attended, but pressure from Washington and his allies had frightened some people away. The gathering formed the Niagara Movement and chose Du Bois as its leader. This founding conference published a platform that demanded for blacks "every single right that belongs to a freeborn American, political, civil, and social." More specifically, the document called for manhood suffrage regardless of race, the elimination of all caste distinctions founded on color, and equal employment opportunities. (Employers and unions both were denounced as responsible for employment discrimination.) The platform also advocated constant protest to achieve these goals.

By the end of 1905, Du Bois claimed that 17 states had active branches of the Niagara Movement. In 1906 the Illinois branch helped secure the appointment of

W. E. B. Du Bois was an outstanding black scholar and civil rights leader. He criticized
Booker T. Washington for telling blacks not to fight for equal rights.

a black to the New Chicago Charter Committee, which reportedly was considering a proposal for segregated schools. The Illinois branch also fought the spread of
racist ideas at a time when, as we have seen, they were becoming more common in
the various arts. In 1906 a stage play called *The Clansman*—based on a novel by
Thomas Dixon—opened in Chicago. It portrayed blacks of the Reconstruction
era as ignorant, corrupt, and determined to have sexual relations with white
women, by rape if necessary. With the help of Jane Addams, a white social worker
in Chicago, the chapter persuaded local critics not to review the play. Meanwhile,
the Massachusetts chapter fought a bill in the state legislature to legalize segregated railroad cars. In 1907 the national organization urged all northern branches
to fight for civil rights legislation and southern branches to fight discrimination in
railroad accommodations. Chapters also were asked to seek new trials for blacks
convicted on doubtful evidence by juries from which blacks had been excluded.

But the Niagara Movement did not accomplish very much. Du Bois sought
recruits only from what he called "the very best class" of blacks—the Talented
Tenth—and membership was probably never more than a few hundred. The gap
between Du Bois's Talented Tenth and the great majority of blacks was so large
that the movement never had much influence among ordinary people. Also, the
Niagara Movement did not have enough money; pressure from Washington
discouraged wealthy, sympathetic whites from contributing. Finally, conflict between Du Bois and William Monroe Trotter weakened the organization. Only 19
members attended the group's fourth annual meeting in 1908.

## The NAACP and the National Urban League

During that year, however, an event occurred that inspired the creation of a more
successful civil rights movement. In August 1908 a race riot broke out in Springfield, Illinois, just one-half mile from the home of Abraham Lincoln. A white
woman stated that she had been assaulted and then raped by a black man. Soon
afterward she changed her story and blamed a white man. But it was too late.
White mobs went on a spree of lynching, flogging, and property destruction. Some
5,000 state militia had to be called in.

The violence shocked not only blacks but a growing group of liberal whites—
mostly from professional groups including social workers and college professors—
especially because it occurred in Lincoln's hometown and just months before the
100th anniversary of his birth. A group of whites and blacks signed a call that
appeared in the *New York Evening Post* in February 1909; it asked interested
citizens to attend a meeting for the "discussion of present evils, the voicing of
protests, and the renewal of the struggle for civil and political liberty." White
signers included social worker Mary White Ovington; Oswald Garrison Villard,
editor of the *Evening Post* and grandson of abolitionist William Lloyd Garrison;
William English Walling, a writer and socialist; social worker Jane Addams;
philanthropist J. G. Phelps Stokes; Mary E. Wooley, president of Mount Holyoke
College; Rabbi Stephen S. Wise; and John Dewey, professor of philosophy at
Columbia University. Among the black signers were Du Bois; black minister

Francis J. Grimké; Bishop Alexander Walters of the African Methodist Episcopal Zion church; Ida B. Wells-Barnett, a journalist and antilynching crusader; and Mary Church Terrell, a leader of the National Association of Colored Women.

Responding to the call, about 300 people gathered in New York City on May 31 and June 1, 1909. They agreed on the need for a new organization to fight for racial equality. But many of the whites opposed an open break with Booker T. Washington and favored the adoption of moderate resolutions. The more militant of the black participants, including Wells-Barnett, newspaper editor William Monroe Trotter, and the Reverend J. Milton Waldron, were suspicious about the motives of the whites, opposed to any dealing with Washington, and in favor of more radical resolutions. After a great deal of debate, the group decided not to invite Washington. Other differences were smoothed over. A Committee of Forty was chosen to make plans for a permanent organization.

May 12–14, 1910, a second meeting in New York City established the National Association for the Advancement of Colored People (NAACP). The gathering chose Moorfield Storey, a constitutional lawyer from Boston, as president, and William English Walling as chairman of the executive committee. A year later a board of directors was established with Villard as chairman. In June 1910 the executive committee chose Du Bois as director of publicity and research. He was the only black to hold a high-level position in the organization's first years.

In its charter of incorporation of January 1911, the organization stated its goals as follows:

> To promote equality of rights and eradicate caste or race prejudice among the citizens of the United States; to advance the interest of colored citizens; to secure for them impartial suffrage; and to increase their opportunities for securing justice in the courts, education for their children, employment according to their ability, and complete equality before the law.

The NAACP grew significantly in its first years. Members of the executive committee immediately created branches in the major cities of the North and the Upper South; by the end of 1912 there were 11 chapters. The number of chapters then doubled each year until World War I, thanks partly to the organizing efforts of Joel Spingarn, a Columbia University professor who succeeded Villard as chairman of the board of directors in 1914. In November 1910, Du Bois produced the first issue of a monthly magazine called *The Crisis*, the NAACP's official publication. It contained news about race issues around the globe, provided accounts of racial injustice in the United States, offered editorial viewpoints, reported on NAACP activities, featured prominent blacks in a "Men of the Month" column, and reviewed books. *The Crisis* was popular from the beginning; it had 31,000 subscribers by 1914 and 100,000 by 1918. Its success increased the NAACP's credibilty and drew in new members and financial contributors.

The NAACP scored some early successes. In 1911 a black lawyer, William H. Lewis, was elected to the previously all-white American Bar Association. Soon after, though, he was excluded when members discovered his race. NAACP president Moorfield Storey protested, and Lewis's membership was restored in

1912. In 1915 the NAACP's branches fought the showing of a movie, *The Birth of a Nation*, by filmmaker D. W. Griffith. Based on Thomas Dixon's novel, *The Clansman*, the movie was just as racist as the stage version of the book a decade before. It depicted Reconstruction as an attempt by barbaric blacks to take over the South and have their way with white women; Ku Klux Klansmen were shown as heroes for saving the South from this fate. The NAACP condemned the film, saying it would promote racial hatred and mob violence. Local chapters organized protest meetings and set up picket lines at movie theaters where it was being shown. In Boston and elsewhere, these actions led to the withdrawal of the film.

The NAACP fought major battles in Washington, D.C., during the presidency of Woodrow Wilson. During the campaign of 1912, Democratic candidate Wilson stated: "I want to assure them [black Americans] that should I become President of the United States, they may count upon me for absolute fair dealing for everything by which I could assist in advancing the interests of their race in the United States." Encouraged by this message, more blacks voted for him than had voted for previous Democratic candidates. But southern Democrats were influential in Wilson's administration, and in 1913 black federal workers found themselves being segregated within government agencies, especially the Post Office and the Treasury Department. Office space, lunchrooms, and bathrooms were separated into white and black areas. Also, many blacks in the Post Office and Treasury were demoted.

The NAACP led the protests. *The Crisis* condemned the spread of Jim Crow into the nation's government. The NAACP organized mass protests in the North. It obtained 20,000 black and white petition signatures, which were brought to the White House in November 1913. These efforts had an impact. In 1914 the Treasury Department began to reverse its Jim Crow policies, and advocates of segregation within the federal government lost much of their influence in the Wilson administration.

The Democrats gained control of Congress as well as the White House in the 1912 elections. During the first two years of Wilson's presidency, Congress—egged on by southern Democrats—considered many new bills to promote racial discrimination. They included measures to establish railroad and streetcar segregation in the nation's capital, bar blacks from serving as officers in the army and navy, ban marriages across racial lines, segregate black and white federal employees, and block all African immigrants from entering the country. The NAACP began a lobbying effort, as its leaders met with both administration officials and members of Congress. Due in part to this pressure, Congress adjourned in March 1915 without passing any of the racist bills.

From its beginning, the NAACP was active in the fight against lynching. Its first action was sparked by an incident at Livermore, Kentucky, during April 1911. A black man accused of murdering a white was brought to the town opera house and tied down on the stage. Tickets then were sold to those wishing to watch the lynching. Reacting to this incident, the NAACP adopted an antilynching resolution. A copy was sent to President Taft, who said he could not act because

# THE CRISIS

## A RECORD OF THE DARKER RACES

Volume One                    NOVEMBER, 1910                    Number One

Edited by W. E. BURGHARDT DU BOIS, with the co-operation of Oswald Garrison Villard, J. Max Barber, Charles Edward Russell, Kelly Miller, W. S. Braithwaite and M. D. Maclean.

### CONTENTS

PUBLISHED MONTHLY BY THE

### National Association for the Advancement of Colored People

AT TWENTY VESEY STREET                                    NEW YORK CITY

ONE DOLLAR A YEAR                                    TEN CENTS A COPY

The front cover of the first issue of *The Crisis*, the magazine of the National Association for the Advancement of Colored People. The high quality of the publication, edited by W. E. B. Du Bois, helped the NAACP win supporters.

lynching was not a federal offense. (In later years the NAACP would work for federal antilynching legislation.) Also in 1911, the organization hired a detective agency to investigate a lynching in Coatesville, Pennsylvania. But the investigators could not dig up enough evidence to charge anyone with the crime.

The NAACP's most important work involved attacking discrimination in the courts. Denial of the right to vote was regarded as one of the most harmful forms of discrimination. The NAACP, and especially Arthur Spingarn, the chairman of its legal committee, convinced the federal government to challenge Oklahoma's grandfather clause. Moorfield Storey argued the case before the U.S. Supreme Court, which in Guinn v. United States (1915) struck down the grandfather clauses of both Oklahoma and Maryland as violations of the Fifteenth Amendment. This was probably the most important victory for the NAACP in its first five years.

In 1905 blacks and whites in New York City founded two organizations to advance the economic and social well-being of black Americans. The Committee for Improving Industrial Conditions of Negroes tried to expand job opportunities for blacks. The National League for the Protection of Colored Women helped young black women coming North for domestic work to adjust to city life. Under the leadership of George Haynes, a black graduate student of social work at Columbia University, the two organizations in 1910 formed a third group—the Committee on Urban Conditions—to promote the education and training of young black men and women as social workers. In 1911 the three groups united to form the National Urban League, which continued the work of each. Operated by social workers of both races, the league delivered services to blacks in a more professional and effective way than had the older charity organizations.

The creation of the NAACP and the National Urban League represented a turning point in the history of black Americans. For decades after Reconstruction, racism and racial discrimination had intensified in all areas of the country. Meanwhile, many blacks had given up on the struggle for equality. But these new organizations signified a new beginning in the struggle by blacks and their white allies for equal rights and a decent life for all Americans.

# CHAPTER 7

•••••••••

# World War I through the Great Depression: 1914 –1941

## THE FIGHT TO SERVE IN BATTLE

In 1914 war broke out in Europe between the Allies (Britain, France, and associated countries) and the Central Powers (Germany, the Austro-Hungarian Empire, and other states). In April 1917 the United States entered what would become known as World War I, on the side of the Allies. Most blacks shared the patriotic feelings of other Americans and backed what President Wilson called a crusade "to make the world safe for democracy." In 1917 and 1918, blacks bought over $250 million of war bonds and stamps. Both W. E. B. Du Bois and Robert R. Moton, successor to the late Booker T. Washington at the Tuskegee Institute, backed the war. So did most black organizations and most of the black press.

There were some dissenters. In November 1917 the *Messenger*, a publication edited by black socialists A. Philip Randolph and Chandler Owen, stated that if black leaders supported the war, then they should "volunteer to go to France to make the world safe for democracy. We would rather fight to make Georgia safe for the Negro." Washington, D.C., clergyman Francis Grimké and some others agreed. But they were only a small minority.

Many young black men were eager to fight in France against the German enemy, but the Wilson administration had other ideas. At the very beginning of American involvement, the government decided that the four regular black army regiments—the 9th and 10th Cavalry and the 24th and 25th Infantry Regiments—would be stationed in the United States. And when the draft was established in May 1917, the government had no plans to accept blacks. After the NAACP protested to Secretary of War Newton Baker and both houses of Congress, however, the policy was reversed.

But the army intended to use blacks as laborers rather than combat soldiers. NAACP pressure forced Secretary Baker to promise in December 1917 to use a significant number of blacks in combat, although they would serve only in segregated units. Eventually, over 30,000 fought in two black divisions, the 92nd and 93rd, made up of black National Guard units and black draftees. But many more blacks served as laborers; they made up one-third of all army labor troops, although only a little more than one-eighth of all draftees were black. Meanwhile, blacks were allowed to serve in the navy only as cooks, as mess men, and in other low-level, noncombat posts (and they were excluded completely from the marines). Despite Baker's promise, only about 20 percent of black troops ever saw combat.

As in previous wars, racial discrimination was widespread. Draft boards more often excused whites from service than blacks. In the South, blacks who owned their own land were more likely to be drafted than those who worked for white landowners as laborers, sharecroppers, or tenants. In army camps, blacks had to cope with inferior conditions. Their tents often lacked the flooring found in white soldiers' tents. In a camp near Baltimore, 300 black soldiers lived in a single barracks, while only 38 whites lived in one the same size. Their clothing was inferior, and often they lacked winter garments. Since many white officers believed that blacks faked illness, blacks needing medical treatment often got none. At some locations there was no mess for blacks; they had to eat outside. Some service organizations, including the YMCA—which was the largest one—did little to provide black soldiers with recreational or social activities. Hostess Houses, where women visiting the soldiers could find lodging, were not open to black women until April 1918, and then conditions for them were so bad that few came.

As for the training itself, blacks were often shortchanged. To keep blacks under control, the army decided that no more than one-third of the soldiers in any camp should be black. This meant that many southern blacks had to be sent North, where weather conditions cut down on training time. Also, many northern blacks who would otherwise have been trained in the South had to remain in the North. As for those who did train in the southern states, some had their instruction cut short to avoid racial incidents. The men of the black 15th Infantry, New York National Guard (later part of the 93rd Division), were sent to Spartanburg, South Carolina, in the fall of 1917. Some were thrown off streetcars and sidewalks. Many felt the sting of racial insults. One was beaten. Therefore, the unit was shipped off to France after only 12 days of training.

Discrimination also occurred in officer training. Soon after the United States declared war, 14 officer training camps were established, none open to blacks. Secretary of War Baker made it clear that if blacks wanted officer training, they would have to get it in a segregated camp. Some black leaders opposed such a compromise with segregation. But most agreed with NAACP president Joel Spingarn, who said that if black officers proved their effectiveness, a segregated camp would in the long run be a blow against segregation.

To prove that blacks were interested in an officer training program, students from Howard University and other black colleges went around the country urging young men of their race to apply for training. In late April 1917, Spingarn brought hundreds of applications to a meeting with Secretary Baker. A few days later, the NAACP was told that an officer training camp for blacks would be established. It opened in July 1917 at Des Moines, Iowa, with 1,250 candidates. In October 1917, 639 received their commissions. Other commissioned officers of the 92nd and 93rd Divisions were drawn from the four regular black regiments.

The army was basically hostile to the idea of black officers. It signaled this attitude in 1917 by forcing the resignation of Colonel Charles Young, a highly able regular officer in the 10th Cavalry Regiment. Black officers could not serve in white units. In black units, no black officer was to outrank, or even to equal in rank, any white officer. Furthermore, military authorities believed that black soldiers had more respect for white officers than for black. So black units were generally led by white officers—and often by southern whites who were openly hostile to blacks. Of the eight regiments in the two black divisions, only the 370th Regiment, 93rd Division was officered by blacks all the way from colonel downward, and some of these officers were later replaced in France. In the 92nd Division, no blacks ranked higher than captain. In the black labor units, all of the commissioned officers and almost all of the noncommissioned ones were white.

Amid all of the racism and discrimination, the federal government did take a significant step forward in racial policy. In October 1917 Emmett J. Scott, former secretary to Booker T. Washington, was appointed a special assistant to the secretary of war on matters concerning blacks. He received thousands of complaints about mistreatment and investigated as many as he could. He also tried to publicize the achievements of black soldiers. And although he did not have the power to accomplish a great deal, many black leaders applauded his appointment. No black had ever been in such a visible position in the executive branch before, and Professor Kelly Miller of Howard University commented, "I regard the appointment of Mr. Scott . . . as the most significant appointment that has yet come to the colored race."

## SERVING IN FRANCE

Black laborers in Europe were organized into 46 engineer service battalions, 44 labor battalions, 15 pioneer infantry regiments, and two infantry companies. Along the French coast, black stevedores won the admiration of observers by unloading up to 5,000 tons of cargo at one port in a single day. Others built warehouses and supply dumps at ports and railroad facilities, cut wood, erected barracks, quarried stone, constructed or repaired railroads, and built roads. Some had the unpleasant task of finding and burying the dead.

Both in the United States and in France, the laborers were sometimes treated more like animals than men. To punish them for poor work, their officers sometimes had them handcuffed with cowbells attached. The officers often kicked and punched them for supposed offenses. Their food, housing, and clothing were bad, and they hardly ever received passes.

As in earlier wars, most black combat soldiers overcame the obstacles placed in their way by white prejudice and fought well. The 369th Regiment of the 93rd Division (formerly the 15th New York National Guard) became the best known of the black regiments and was later called the Fighting 369th. Like all regiments of the 93rd Division, it was assigned to the French army. In September 1918, the 369th was in the front line of a major Allied offensive, taking heavy losses as it moved forward against strong German resistance. The regiment saw action for 191 days, more than any other American regiment, although it had received less combat training than any other. The French gave the entire regiment the croix de guerre medal, and about 170 of the officers and men received it as individuals.

The 370th Regiment, 93rd Division, (formerly the 85th Illinois National Guard) participated in an Allied drive in August, seizing almost 1,900 prisoners and 200 machine guns. From September onward, the regiment was part of an offensive that drove the Germans from France into Belgium. On September 30 the regiment failed to take a German position due to confusion in the unit; inadequate training and the replacement of popular black officers help to account for this failure. Nevertheless, 71 men received the French croix de guerre and 21 were given the Distinguished Service Cross by the U.S. Army.

The 371st Regiment, unlike the three others in the 93rd Division, consisted not of National Guardsmen but of draftees. Nonetheless, its performance compared favorably with the others. Taking part in the Allies' September 1918 offensive, the regiment fought its way forward despite fierce enemy attacks that used infantry, artillery, mortar, gas, and airplanes. It received the croix de guerre with palm, the highest French decoration for a regiment. Sixty officers and 124 men won either the croix de guerre or the Distinguished Service Cross, making the 371st the most decorated regiment in the 93rd Division.

The 372nd Regiment, 93rd Division (organized from six National Guard units) also saw action in the offensive of late September 1918. According to a white officer, the regiment's First and Third Battalions suffered very heavy casualties because they would not retreat under heavy attack. The regiment received the croix de guerre with palm despite the unit's mediocre white leadership.

The 92nd Division consisted entirely of black draftees. It fought under General Robert Bullard, commander of the American Second Army, who hated blacks and had a personal grudge against the white commander of the 92nd. Bullard did what he could to discredit the division's black soldiers. Yet the 92nd performed reasonably well, for the most part. In August 1918, it moved to the front near the German border. The regiment beat back a number of German attacks from August to mid-September. It then took part in the American offensive in the Argonne Forest. But the Division's 368th Regiment fell into confusion from the beginning of the attack on September 26 until it was relieved on September 30.

Not surprisingly, the army did not evaluate fairly the performance of its black soldiers. The entire 92nd Division was blamed for the failure of the 368th

Regiment, for example. Similar failures of white units were often minimized. But this one collapse was used for many years to label all blacks as incompetent soldiers.

Still, the black soldiers gained a great deal of confidence from the knowledge that they had served their country well. And they gained additional confidence because French officers treated them with respect and French civilians, men and women, socialized with them on an equal basis in cafés and even in private homes. American officers were alarmed and told the French that this kind of treatment would lead to trouble back in America—and they were right. The black soldiers learned in France that subordination of black to white was not practiced everywhere. This knowledge made many of them determined to resist racial discrimination when they came home. W. E. B. Du Bois caught their spirit in his article "Returning Soldier," which appeared in *The Crisis* of November 1918: "We return. We return from fighting. We return fighting."

## WORLD WAR I AND THE GREAT MIGRATION

As soon as World War I began in Europe in 1914, the heavy flow of immigrants from there to the United States decreased sharply. Without the benefit of immigrant labor, factories—especially in the North and West—were short of workers. Until then, blacks had been used mostly as strikebreakers; when hired as regular workers they were given only the most menial jobs. Now they were needed in the tens of thousands to keep the industrial economy running. So in the spring of 1915, northern and western companies—especially the steel mills and railroads— began sending labor agents down South to recruit blacks, offering free transportation. Using the usual methods of intimidation, southern whites at first tried to stop blacks from leaving the region, but that proved impossible. The migration to northern cities became much heavier in 1916, spurred on by floods and the destruction of cotton crops by boll weevils. The migration peaked in 1917, though it continued at a declining rate until the end of the war, late in 1918.

All together, the South lost about 400,000 blacks to the rest of the country during the Great Migration. From 1910 to 1920, the black population in the South grew by less than 2 percent, while the number of blacks in the other sections increased by almost 44 percent, from 1.08 million to 1.55 million. The proportion of blacks living outside the South was still only 15 percent in 1920 (up from 11 percent in 1910). But foreign immigration was restricted in the early 1920s, and from 1920 to 1930, the South lost another 749,000 black migrants; from 1930 to 1940, another 349,000 departed. By 1940, 25 percent of all blacks lived outside the South.

Why did so many southern blacks leave their native region? The most important reason was the higher wages of the North and West. Most male migrants had been rural laborers in the South, earning less than $2.00 a day. In the North and West they did much better, even though 90 percent of them did unskilled work. In the factories of Pittsburgh during World War I, for example, 62 percent of them received between $2.00 and $3.00 a day, 28 percent were paid between $3.00 and $3.60, and 5 percent received more than $3.60, while only 5 percent earned less than $2.00 a day. In the war plants of Newark, New Jersey, they received $2.60 a day, and in the factories and foundries of Hartford, Connecticut, they earned $4.00 a day. Black women also increased their income by leaving the South, although they received less pay than black men, just as they had back home. A woman working for Swift's Packing Company in Chicago was pleased to write home that "We get $1.50 a day and we pack so many sausages we dont have much time to play, but it is a matter of the dollar with me, and I feel that God made the path and I am walking therein."

Money was not the only reason blacks migrated. They also wanted to escape the South's racial oppression and make more of their lives than they ever could in their native region. The combination of monetary and nonmonetary motives was expressed by a black in Newbern, Alabama, who hoped to find work up North: "many places here . . . the only thing the black man gets is a peck of meal and from three to four lbs. of bacon per week, and he is treated as a slave." In November 1917 a migrant working in Chicago wrote a letter to a friend back home in Hattiesburg, Mississippi, that shows how migrants benefited both materially and psychologically:

> I was promoted on the first of the month I was made assistant to the head carpenter when he is out of the place I take everything in charge and was raised to $95 a month. . . . I should have been here 20 years ago. I just begin to feel like a man.

Other reasons for migrating, according to a survey taken by W. E. B. Du Bois, were the desire for better schools, the pursuit of better living conditions generally, and the wish to vote.

Still, the migrants faced serious problems after they left the South. Migration led to increased racial friction in the North, especially where migrants were used as strikebreakers. In 1917 a number of race riots occurred. When white workers went out on strike in a Philadelphia sugar refinery, black replacements were brought in. The strikers attacked them, which led to a race riot. Other riots, not directly connected with economic competition, took place in New York; Newark, New Jersey; and Chester, Pennsylvania.

The worst racial clash during the war broke out in East St. Louis, Illinois. The city was a major industrial center with a great wartime demand for unskilled labor. But its black population almost tripled from 6,000 to 16,000, more than the number of jobs available. The result was competition between the races for work. Tensions grew in 1916 when blacks, who were excluded from the labor unions there, were hired as strikebreakers.

The riot began on July 1, 1917, when white joyriders shot randomly into black homes, and armed blacks retaliated by killing two of the riders. A four-day riot followed, in which white mobs stormed through the city randomly attacking black men, women, and children. When it was over, half of the black population had fled town. More than 100 blacks were shot, mutilated, and beaten. Eight whites were killed, some by shots seemingly intended for blacks. The National Guard stood by, while the city police attacked reporters photographing the white mobs and destroyed their film. Although whites committed the vast majority of the violence, 11 blacks got long prison sentences for killing 4 whites, while only 8 whites were given lengthy terms for the deaths of 39 blacks.

Because of the Great Migration, the black population of most major northern and western cities climbed rapidly between 1910 and 1920: in New York from 92,000 to 153,000, up 67 percent; in Chicago from 44,000 to 109,000, up 150 percent; in Philadelphia from 84,000 to 134,000, up 59 percent; in Detroit from 6,000 to 42,000, up 600 percent; in Kansas City, Kansas, from 9,000 to 14,000, up 55 percent.

As the new arrivals poured into the cities during the war, black neighborhoods grew into ghettos, large enough so that people could spend most of their lives there without leaving. This growth frightened whites, who took ever stronger steps, including violence, to limit the expansion of the black communities. Consequently, the black population grew faster than the areas to which it was restricted. That meant a worsening of living conditions. One problem was overcrowding. In Pittsburgh, about half of all migrant families lived in one-room dwellings; in Chicago, many one-family houses became two-family homes. A second problem was run-down housing; in Newark, housing that had long been shut down as undesirable, and which had no kitchen ranges, baths, or toilets, was reopened. A third problem of ghettos was high rent. Black migrants in Cleveland, for example, paid rents that were from 50 percent to 75 percent higher than those paid by whites.

The National Urban League worked hard on behalf of the migrants. Bringing together professional social workers and black community leaders, it tried to provide employment, job training, and decent housing. The League also taught the migrants about the sanitary practices essential for living in cities (how to dispose of garbage, for example). But although it helped many of the migrants, the League could make only a small dent in their huge problems.

## THE POSTWAR RACIAL CLIMATE

During World War I and in the years just after, a new racial climate began to emerge. Blacks seemed more willing to express their opposition to racial oppression and to act against it. One reason was that the Great Migration increased the number of blacks in the North and West, where they were free to protest and to vote. Changes in employment also had an impact. In their traditional service jobs (servants, waiters, barbers), blacks served individual whites on a personal basis and therefore could not escape close white supervision. But now blacks were moving into factories with thousands of workers, where their relationship to white employers was much less personal. Under these conditions, blacks may have felt less controlled and freer to express themselves. Similarly, as black neighborhoods grew into ghettos, blacks had less contact with whites. For all the evils of the ghettos, they did create an environment in which black pride and self-expression could emerge. Also, many returning black soldiers were ready to claim their rights after having fought in what had supposedly been, after all, a war to make the world safe for democracy.

During the war there were already signs that blacks would be quicker than before to take offense at racial abuse. The NAACP's struggle against discrimination in the army was one signal. Another was a silent parade organized on Fifth Avenue in New York City by the NAACP to protest the East St. Louis riot. Held on July 28, 1917, it drew 5,000 marchers and 20,000 spectators. A sign in the parade reading, "Mr. President, why not make America safe for Democracy?" showed that the war was making blacks more aware of their rights. During the same month, the Third Battalion of the black 24th Infantry was sent to Houston. There, the soldiers refused to sit in the black sections of theaters and streetcars; they also took down Jim Crow signs. In retaliation, the city police beat black soldiers. This led to a racial clash in which 17 whites and 2 soldiers were killed; 13 of the soldiers were later executed for murder. Soon afterward, the black Eighth Regiment of the Illinois National Guard was sent to Houston for training. On the way down, the soldiers defied Jim Crow signs at train stations in Arkansas and Texas. After being refused service at a store, they looted it.

After the war, the signs of defiance multiplied. In St. Joseph, Missouri, black soldiers refused to march in the victory parade when they were assigned to the very end, behind even the civic organizations. Some black soldiers from the South refused to obey the region's racial code when they returned home. For example, a veteran in Pine Bluff, Arkansas, refused to get off the sidewalk when told to do so by a white woman. Also, blacks were more likely to meet violence with violence. A good example is the 1919 riots in Washington, D.C., Chicago (see page 148), and elsewhere in which blacks retaliated with force against whites who tried to invade black neighborhoods.

Growth in NAACP membership also expressed the new mood. James Weldon Johnson, editor of the black *New York Age*, became NAACP field secretary in 1916 and began organizing branches throughout the South. In April 1918 the organization had 9,900 members and 85 branches. After an organizing drive, its membership at the end of 1918 was 44,000 in 165 branches. Blacks also enlarged their role within the organization. In 1919 Mary Ovington White, one of the group's founders, reacted by commenting that "the National Association for the Advancement of Colored People, started by whites, [is] being organized all over the United States by Negroes." In 1920 Johnson—an outstanding songwriter, poet, and writer of fiction—became NAACP executive secretary, the first black to hold an executive office in the organization.

After the war a group of black tenant farmers and sharecroppers in Arkansas, weary of being in constant debt to their landlords, organized the Progressive Farmers and Household Union of America. Nothing better demonstrated black determination, since the odds were stacked so heavily against the organization:

the members were completely dependent upon their white landlords for their livelihoods, and the local authorities were entirely controlled by those landowners. Not surprisingly, when the members gathered for a meeting in October 1919 at Hot Spur, Arkansas, they were shot at. When they dared to fire back, armed white mobs went on a rampage in the area, killing more than 200 blacks.

As blacks became more outspoken, whites intensified their attacks. Southern whites were fearful that black soldiers might have picked up "wrong" ideas about equality in Europe. To make it clear that nothing had changed back home, whites sometimes met the returning soldiers at railroad stations and took away their uniforms. At towns in Texas, Mississippi, Alabama, South Carolina, and Kentucky, recently returned black veterans were assaulted and forced to leave. The number of lynching victims increased from 58 blacks in 1918 to 77 the following year. At least 10 of those lynched were black veterans.

But the worst violence in 1919 took the form of race riots around the country during the summer, which James Weldon Johnson called the "Red Summer." Racial tensions were inflamed by a postwar economic recession that made whites more fearful of black competition for jobs. Riots broke out in New York City; Charleston; Knoxville; Longview, Texas; Omaha, Nebraska; and elsewhere. Generally, they followed a pattern of white attack followed by black retaliation.

Chicago had the worst riot of all. The beaches along Lake Michigan were unofficially segregated. On Sunday, July 27, a black accidentally swam into an area reserved for whites. Whites began throwing stones at him, and he drowned. When police refused to make arrests, some blacks began assaulting whites. The news spread quickly through the city, and whites began striking back. Late Monday afternoon, white gangs attacked black workers as they left the stockyards and pulled black riders from streetcars. Black mobs retaliated, assaulting whites who worked in the black community. On Monday night, white mobs invaded black neighborhoods, and police often sided with the whites. The rioting spread on Tuesday, when blacks were attacked in the downtown Loop, and did not taper off until Wednesday.

Blacks resisted the white violence more effectively than they had in earlier years. In the Washington, D.C., riot that began on July 19, 1919, four whites died compared to just two blacks. But as a rule, most of the victims were black. Whites normally began the violence and invaded black neighborhoods, while blacks defended themselves but did not try to take the fighting to white areas. In Chicago, 23 blacks died compared to 15 whites, and 342 blacks compared to 178 whites suffered injuries. Blacks were almost bound to be the biggest losers in race riots. For one thing, in most parts of the country they were a minority. Another and even more important reason was that almost everywhere, unsympathetic whites controlled the government and law enforcement agencies.

Perhaps even more threatening to blacks than the race riots was the rise of a new Ku Klux Klan (KKK). Revived in 1915, it began to grow rapidly in the South after the war, when it led many of the attacks on returning black veterans. During the 1920s the second KKK spread throughout the country, reaching a peak membership of around 5 million in 1925. It was very strong not only in the South but in the Midwest as well. Politicians in those regions often had to join the Klan to win public office, and the KKK dominated the state governments of Texas and Oklahoma. The new Klan bullied and intimidated not only blacks but also immigrants, Jews, Catholics, and Asians—all of whom, the Klan believed, threatened to destroy the "superior" civilization of white Anglo-Saxon America. Riding at night in white hoods, especially in the Deep South, Klansmen committed murder, beatings, tarring and featherings, brandings, and other atrocities.

Yet, during the 1920s and 1930s northern blacks made significant political gains. Their major weapon was the ballot, which gave them a growing share of political power at the local, state, and federal levels. The black migration from the South made this possible, because once blacks left the region they could vote. With the number of northern black voters increasing quickly, politicians had to heed black opinion. Migration also expanded the number of capable black leaders, because blacks outside the South received a better education than those who remained. Migration was one reason black illiteracy fell from 61 percent in 1890 to 15 percent in 1940.

## BLACK POLITICS, PROTEST, AND PRIDE

Until the turn of the century, individual black politicians in the North supported the local white Republican organizations in exchange for small political favors. When they ran for office, they needed white votes to win, which is why few were elected. But as black neighborhoods grew into ghettos, black voters became a majority of the electorate in some areas of northern cities. This made possible the emergence of local black political machines within the Republican Party (and occasionally within the Democratic Party). True, the black leaders of these machines simply took orders from the white party bosses, and often they had no interest in fighting racism and poverty. But they did use their control of a growing black vote to obtain benefits for themselves and for the black community. These gains usually did not help the majority of blacks; nevertheless, they represented a clear advance over the previous era.

Black machines first appeared around the turn of the century; they became stronger during and after the war, as the black population grew and full-fledged ghettos made their appearance. The Chicago and New York City organizations were the most important. On Chicago's South Side, a black Republican organization appeared in the first decade of the twentieth century. Led by Ed Wright and Oscar De Priest, it elected two blacks to the state legislature in 1914. The following year De Priest won election as a city alderman. In 1928 the South Side elected De Priest to the U.S. House of Representatives, the first black to sit in Congress since 1901 and the first ever to be sent to Congress from the North.

As the black population expanded, Chicago's white politicians had to pay more attention to black concerns: the growing black vote was often needed to defeat the Democrats. The Republican candidate for governor of Illinois in 1916 threatened to move his campaign headquarters from a downtown Chicago hotel unless it stopped discriminating against blacks. Republican mayor William Hale ("Big Bill") Thompson, first elected in 1915, appointed a significant number of blacks to city government jobs. Black machine leader Ed Wright, who helped Thompson win reelection in 1919, became a South Side ward leader the next year. Thompson denounced racist remarks made by opposing politicians and tried to ensure that the police treated blacks fairly. Meanwhile, at the state level a 1917 law banned books, movies, and plays that provoked racial or religious prejudice. Two years afterward the Illinois legislature expanded the state's civil rights law to bar landlords and many types of businesses from indicating racial preferences in their advertising. After World War I, blacks had more political influence in Chicago than anywhere else.

In Harlem a black Republican machine was born in the century's first decade. Its leader was Charles W. Anderson, the first important black political leader in the history of New York state. Before the war, he secured higher-level and better-paying patronage jobs than blacks had ever received; the posts included customs inspectors, immigration inspectors, and assistant superintendents in the post office. In 1911 Anderson helped the first black city policeman obtain his job. His influence blocked the promotion of a judge who had refused to convict bartenders who violated state law by declining to serve blacks.

Black political influence grew in the 1920s as Harlem's black population shot up from around 73,000 to about 160,000 and its white population declined by 119,000. (Confined before 1920 to the area between 145th and 130th Streets, Harlem expanded southward in that decade to 110th Street.) Another reason for increasing black influence was the emergence of a black Democratic machine, led after 1915 by Ferdinand Q. Morton. Harlem remained loyal to the Republicans at the national level, but it became the first black ghetto to give the Democrats a significant number of votes in local elections; in 1921 the Democratic candidate for mayor got more than 70 percent of Harlem's black vote. Because neither party could take black support for granted, both had to make concessions to blacks.

In 1917 the Republicans nominated a black to run from Harlem's 19th Assembly District, and he became the first of his race to sit in the state legislature. During the 1920s five more blacks (four Republicans and a Democrat) entered the state legislature from the 19th and 21st Assembly Districts in Harlem. The first black city alderman was elected in 1919, and others followed over the next decade. In 1930 white politicians agreed to change the boundaries of municipal court districts so that the first two black municipal judges could be elected. Harlem was in the mostly white 21st Congressional District, so no black was elected to Congress until the boundaries were changed in 1944, enabling Adam Clayton Powell, Jr., to win a House seat.

In 1918 the state legislature expanded earlier civil rights legislation so that almost any type of public accommodation—including skating rinks, bowling alleys, and ice cream parlors—would be open to all races. A Harlem assemblyman successfully introduced a state housing bill that barred unfair evictions of tenants and unreasonable rent increases. Also, black city aldermen secured the construction of playgrounds and parks in Harlem during the 1920s. By 1930 black supervisors had been appointed in both the police and fire departments.

Blacks also had greater political clout at the national level after the war than before. In 1919 the NAACP called an antilynching conference. Because the southern states did not punish the lynching of blacks, the gathering called for legislation making lynching a federal crime. Three antilynching bills had been introduced in Congress in 1918. The NAACP decided to support the one presented by Rep. L. C. Dyer of Missouri. In 1922 the House passed it by a vote of 230 to 119. Twenty-four governors and 39 mayors urged the Senate to pass the Dyer bill. But it was killed by southern Democrats through a tactic known as the filibuster, which enabled a minority to prevent a vote on a bill by engaging in endless debate. (A two-thirds vote was required to stop debate.) Still, just a few years earlier it would have been impossible for an antilynching bill to get nearly as far as it did in 1922.

In 1930 President Herbert Hoover nominated Judge John J. Parker of North Carolina for a seat on the U.S. Supreme Court. Because Parker had in the past backed the literacy test, the poll tax, and the grandfather clause, the NAACP fought against his confirmation in the Senate. Thanks in large part to black pressure, the nomination was rejected. Furthermore, black voters helped to defeat U.S. senators from Kansas, Ohio, and California who had voted for Parker.

During and after World War I, the NAACP scored some important successes in its legal battle for racial equality. In *Buchanan v. Warley* (1917), the Supreme Court upheld the NAACP view that city ordinances restricting blacks to certain neighborhoods violated the Fourteenth Amendment's due process clause. But in *Corrigan v. Buckley* (1926), the Court rejected an NAACP appeal to strike down restrictive covenants in property deeds. The Court argued that while the government could not place limits on where any race could live, agreements between private persons about the control and use of property were not covered by the Constitution. The Court's decision in *Moore v. Dempsey* (1923) overturned the murder convictions of six Arkansas blacks who had tried to organize a farmers' union; the panel ruled that because the jury was all white and the trial was conducted in an atmosphere of mob intimidation, the defendants had been denied a fair trial. The NAACP also won two cases—*Nixon v. Herndon* (1927) and *Nixon v. Condon* (1932)—that barred the all-white primary in certain situations. Final victory would come in *Smith v. Allwright* (1944), when the Supreme Court ruled that all whites-only primaries violated the Fifteenth Amendment.

Black struggle was not limited to the arena of politics and government. It also included grassroots protest and organizing activity. In the 1920s blacks began organizing rent strikes against landlords who did not make repairs. In 1929 the *Chicago Whip*, a militant black newspaper, promoted a "Don't Buy Where You Can't Work" boycott campaign. The boycott idea spread in the 1930s; attorney William H. Hastie led one in Washington, D.C., in the early 1930s, and Adam Clayton Powell, Jr., led a Harlem campaign in the mid-1930s in which blacks picketed white-owned stores that refused to hire blacks. Blacks from the British West Indies, who began immigrating in large numbers in the 1920s, were especially active in such efforts; they had not in their homelands been subjected to the kind of racial discrimination that existed in the United States, and many of them were unwilling to tolerate it without a fight.

The growth of racial and cultural awareness and pride was another indication that blacks would no longer accept oppression. In 1915 black historian Carter Woodson organized the Association for the Study of Negro Life and History, which began publishing the *Journal of Negro History* the following year. In 1926 Woodson began Negro History Week, which eventually became Black History Month. In February 1919 a Pan-African Congress organized by W. E. B. Du Bois met in Paris. The gathering, consisting of 57 delegates from 16 countries and colonies, discussed plans for uniting Africa and called for an end to its exploitation. The Congress met again in 1921, 1923, and 1927. On a more popular level, Marcus Garvey organized a mass movement calling for a return to Africa (see the following section).

## NATIONALISTS AND RADICALS

At the suggestion of W. E. B. Du Bois, black leaders gathered at Amenia, New York, in August 1916, a year after Booker T. Washington's death. Everyone at the conference, including Washington's supporters, agreed that blacks must pursue legal and political equality. Du Bois and Washington had strongly disagreed over this a decade before. But now a consensus was developing as to the importance of the political struggle for equal rights.

Some blacks, however, remained outside this accord; they did not believe that protests against racial injustice could accomplish much. America, they felt, was so oppressive and fundamentally racist that blacks could not flourish unless they left and built their own nation. The outstanding spokesperson for this extreme nationalist viewpoint was Marcus Garvey, the most successful back-to-Africa advocate in American history. A native of the island of Jamaica, he moved to Harlem in 1916. Two years later he formed there a branch of his Universal Negro Improvement Association (UNIA), which he had founded back home in 1914. From his New York base, he urged blacks to leave the United States and establish their own country in Africa. Turning white racism on its head, he glorified everything black and denounced everything white. In his African Orthodox church, for example, the angels were black and Satan was white. Light-skinned blacks had long formed the elite in black communities. Garvey tried to turn the tables by scorning light-skinned blacks as not being real blacks.

His nationalism appealed to many black entrepreneurs, since their success was tied to the emergence of all-black ghettos. Garvey also was very effective in appealing to the black masses, particularly the recent migrants who had left their southern roots and were looking for a new identity. His UNIA began growing rapidly in 1919, and two years later its membership peaked at half a million. It had chapters in the Caribbean and Central America as well as the United States. In addition to the UNIA's claims of black superiority, ordinary blacks found very appealing the organization's elaborate rituals, colorful uniforms, parades, and titles of nobility. Most black leaders denounced him as a fraud; Garvey responded by calling them traitors to their race.

Garvey established many businesses, usually without success. The largest was the Black Star shipping firm, on which he spent over $1 million to buy and outfit ships. After four years in operation, it had lost $500,000. In 1923 Garvey was tried in federal court for engaging in mail fraud to raise money for the shipping line. The court sentenced him to a five-year prison term, which he began serving in 1925. President Calvin Coolidge gave him a pardon two years later and had him deported as an undesirable alien. Garvey tried unsuccessfully to reestablish his movement from Jamaica and London.

Garvey's plan to resettle blacks in Africa was impractical. Most blacks did not want to return there. Even if they had, the enormous costs would have made it impossible. Still, Garvey's efforts were significant. By creating the first mass black movement in U.S. history, Garvey showed that many blacks were skeptical about the possibility of ever attaining equality in America. Also, before Garvey came along, the great majority of blacks had accepted the white view of Africa as backward and uncivilized. But as a result of Garvey's work, many blacks began taking a more positive view of their ancestral homeland.

Radical black intellectuals formed another, very different source of dissent. They included A. Philip Randolph and Chandler Owen, editors of the *Messenger*; W. A. Domingo, editor of the *Emancipator*; Cyril V. Briggs, editor of the *Crusader*; and Joe Bibb, William Linton, and A. C. MacNeal, editors of the *Chicago Whip*. Unlike the NAACP and other mainstream organizations fighting for racial equality, they did not believe that racism could be eliminated primarily by protesting against discrimination or by going to the courts. They argued that black problems had economic roots; the source of racial bigotry, they felt, lay in the capitalist economic system. The capitalist class, the radicals argued, encouraged racial prejudice to divide workers and so to keep wages down. The only way to achieve racial equality was for black and white workers to unite within the trade union movement so that their bosses would not be able to play one group off against the other. Final victory would be achieved when all workers joined the socialist political movement to replace capitalism with an economic system that gave control of the economy to the workers.

In 1920 the Socialist Party in New York ran Randolph for state controller and Owen for the state assembly from Harlem's 21st District. The party, however, gained few supporters in Harlem or other black communities. Some black radicals joined the Communist Party, the branch of the socialist movement that supported the Russia's Bolshevik Revolution of 1917. But at the end of the 1920s, it had only a few dozen black members. Most ordinary blacks were practical. They were much more interested in concrete reforms that would benefit them immediately than in abstract ideas about capitalism, socialism, or communism. Also, the great influence of the church in black communities was a barrier against the spread of radical ideas. Anyway, most unions had little interest in uniting blacks and whites. On the contrary, most of them wanted to keep blacks out.

## THE NEW DEAL

The Great Depression—the worst economic crisis in American history—began with the stock market crash of 1929. It deepened in the early 1930s with massive business failures and unemployment that reached 25 percent in 1933. Blacks felt the worst of this terrible crisis. As always in hard times, they were the first to be laid off. Also, black workers were concentrated in some of the hardest-hit industries, such as construction and mining. Many blacks, including household domestics and chauffeurs, performed personal services that were considered luxuries, not necessities, and so were laid off when bad times came. In addition, so many whites were unemployed that they began competing for menial jobs usually reserved for blacks, such as hospital attendant, delivery boy, and janitor. Especially but not only in the South, whites formed groups that pressured employers to fire blacks and hire unemployed whites in their place, and their intimidation tactics often worked.

Statistics showed the results. A National Urban League study of more than 100 cities in the early 1930s revealed that black unemployment was 30–60 percent higher than the rate for whites. More than 50 percent of blacks were unemployed in some of the major industrial cities. In October 1933 nearly 18 percent of blacks were on relief, almost twice the figure for whites. In the cities almost 27 percent of blacks received relief, close to three times the proportion of whites.

In previous economic crises, the federal government had largely stayed on the sidelines. But Franklin D. Roosevelt, elected president in 1932 on the Democratic ticket, followed a different approach. Almost immediately after taking office, Roosevelt made it clear that through a series of programs known as the New Deal, he would make a major effort to promote national recovery and help those in need. Since blacks were much poorer than whites, these programs should have been especially helpful to them. But Roosevelt had no plan to fight racial bias in the distribution of government benefits. For blacks, then, the question became: How much would they share in government programs developed to help the poor and revive the economy?

The answer to this question is mixed. Because Roosevelt did not have an equal rights policy for blacks, much depended on the attitude of those who ran each particular federal program. In some cases the administrators had little interest in preventing discrimination and hired no black advisers to help them do so. Programs run by these agencies did blacks little good and often hurt them.

The Agricultural Adjustment Administration (AAA) was created in 1933 under Secretary of Agriculture Henry A. Wallace. The AAA administered a government program to raise agricultural prices by paying farmers to cut production. In the South, the landowners received the payments for reducing cotton production but were supposed to give part of the money to their tenants and sharecroppers. Many landlords did not do so, however, especially with blacks. In the South, not one black sat on any of the local boards that enforced the law; blacks were not allowed to participate in selecting the candidates for the board, although they could vote once the candidates were picked. Besides, it was very dangerous for individual blacks to accuse their landlords of withholding money; in the South, it would have been considered subversive for a black to accuse a white of dishonesty. Finally, AAA headquarters in Washington, D.C., showed no interest in helping blacks on this matter. Another problem for blacks was that because production was being cut, less farm labor was needed, and many blacks were evicted. From 1930 to 1940, the number of black tenants and sharecroppers declined by over 190,000, and much of the decrease was due to the AAA program.

Blacks criticized the National Recovery Administration (NRA), established in 1933 under General Hugh Johnson, more than any other New Deal agency. The goal of the NRA was to increase consumer purchasing power. One method was by establishing minimum wages. But the NRA set these minimums in ways that hurt blacks. Very low minimums were set in the NRA codes for the South, where most blacks still lived—and especially in the southern industries where blacks were heavily employed. Also, enforcement of the minimum wage was often ineffective, especially for blacks, who rarely sat on local compliance boards. Many employers who did adopt the minimum wage fired their black employees and hired whites instead; since they could no longer pay blacks less, they preferred to have white employees. To increase workers' wages still more, the law creating the NRA guaranteed the right of workers to form unions and bargain collectively with their employers. But the law did not prohibit unions from discriminating against blacks, so the spread of unions sometimes resulted in the firing of black employees.

The higher wages resulting from the NRA meant higher prices for all consumers. But black workers often did not receive higher wages. So in the black community, prices went up while income frequently did not. Since no one within the NRA was charged with protecting black interests, nothing was done to remedy this situation. Roy Wilkins, assistant secretary of the NAACP, stated that "the harm which NRA has done black workers . . . far outweighs the good." Other blacks commented that NRA stood for "Negroes Ruined Again" or "Negro Rights Assassinated."

## Black Gains

Other programs, though, gave substantial help to blacks. The Public Works Administration (PWA) was established in 1933 to spark economic recovery through various construction programs that created jobs and helped neighborhoods. It was managed by Secretary of the Interior Harold Ickes, a white who had headed the Chicago NAACP in the early 1920s. Some blacks criticized him for appointing Clarke Foreman, a white southerner, as a special adviser on racial matters. But Foreman proved that he had a genuine interest in helping blacks.

Furthermore, Ickes appointed Robert Weaver, a black Ph.D. in economics from Harvard, as Foreman's assistant. The national PWA office pressured local committees in charge of PWA programs to include blacks and to avoid discrimination.

PWA projects that benefited blacks included schools and hospitals in black neighborhoods. Even more important, the agency constructed low-cost housing. Of the PWA Housing Division's 46 projects, 14 were exclusively for blacks and 17 others were for both blacks and whites. Blacks made up 24 percent of the tenants in PWA housing. Some black leaders were concerned about the federal government's involvement in segregated housing. But according to a 1931 study of President Herbert Hoover's Committee on Negro Housing, more than half of all residences occupied by blacks were below modern housing standards, and so, not surprisingly, most blacks were pleased with the PWA's housing program.

Many blacks found work in the construction of PWA housing. At first contractors hired few blacks. But then the PWA declared that the percentage of the payroll going to blacks had to be at least half of the black percentage of the area's workforce. So if 30 percent of a city's skilled workforce was black, at least 15 percent of the pay for skilled workers had to go to blacks.

The Works Progress Administration (WPA) was established in 1935 under Harry Hopkins, a white New York social worker. It was one of the most important agencies of the New Deal, providing both relief and a wide variety of work in areas ranging from construction to the arts. Hopkins and Aubrey Williams, a white Alabaman who was one of his top aides, wanted to help blacks; as a result, WPA's headquarters in Washington, D.C., pressured local authorities not to discriminate. In some places, the proportion of WPA jobs held by blacks exceeded the black proportion of the population. Black leaders observed that discrimination against blacks existed anyway, since the proportion of blacks needing such jobs was so much higher than the proportion of whites needing them; had there been no discrimination, more jobs would have gone to blacks. In addition, it was especially hard for southern black women to get WPA jobs. Under the southern racial code, black and white men could work together on outdoor construction projects. But indoors—where women usually worked—the mixing of whites and blacks was unacceptable. Also, many southern whites depended on black women as domestic help and so opposed their use in WPA employment. Still, great numbers of blacks worked for the WPA—some 400,000 in 1938; 300,000 in 1939; and 250,000 in 1940.

The National Youth Administration (NYA), a branch of the WPA headed by Aubrey Williams, provided work and skills training for young people in and out of school. A black woman, Mary McLeod Bethune, was appointed the NYA's director of Negro affairs. The founder of Bethune-Cookman College and of the National Council of Negro Women, Bethune saw to it that blacks sat on every southern state's NYA advisory board. With her help, the NYA gained an excellent reputation for racial fairness and admitted 64,000 black youths into its student work program. The Civilian Conservation Corps (CCC) was another program to help the young; its work camps were segregated, but some 200,000 black male youths and young men were admitted to them.

Mary McLeod Bethune, center, founded Bethune-Cookman College and served as director of Negro affairs in the National Youth Administration during the 1930s. She also headed the unofficial Black Cabinet, made up of black New Deal officials. At the right is Eleanor Roosevelt, wife of President Franklin D. Roosevelt, who gave her support to many black causes.

Unlike the Agricultural Adjustment Administration, the Farm Security Administration (FSA), created in 1937, assisted many black farmers. That success was due to the strong efforts of its leader, white southerner Will Alexander, to prevent racial discrimination. The FSA loan program to enable southern tenants and sharecroppers to buy their own land was small in scope. Fewer than 10,000 loans were granted, and blacks received 21 percent of them. As with other New Deal programs, this can be looked at in two ways. The 21 percent share was close to the 23.8 percent black share of the southern population; but on the other hand, blacks made up 40 percent of the region's nonlandholding families, so their share of loans should have been around that figure. The FSA also distributed rehabilitation loans to penniless farmers so they could buy farm equipment and supplies. Black farm families received 23 percent of the 854,000 loans of this type in the mid- and late 1930s.

Despite discrimination, blacks for the first time since Reconstruction received a significant amount of federal assistance. And for the first time in *all* of American history, a significant numbers of blacks in the federal government had some influence—if not in making policy, then at least in carrying it out. We have already noted the presence of Robert Weaver in the PWA and Mary McLeod

Bethune in the NYA. Other black advisers on race issues included Forrest B. Washington, dean of the Atlanta University of Social Work, in the Federal Emergency Relief Administration; attorney William H. Hastie in the Interior Department; social worker Lawrence Oxley in the Department of Labor; Edgar Brown in the CCC; and Eugene Kinckle Jones, who left his post as the National Urban League's executive secretary to work as an adviser in the Commerce Department. They had only limited influence. White federal officials were not accustomed to seeing black government employees above the level of janitor, and many of them did not want to work with their new black colleagues. Also, the advisers could not do much unless the top officials of their agencies opposed racial discrimination. Still, in some agencies they were able to reduce discrimination by calling attention to biased practices.

These black federal advisers tried to increase their influence by banding together as the Interdepartmental Group on the Special Problems of the Negro. Founded in February 1934 at the suggestion of Interior Secretary Ickes, the group did not last beyond the following January, partly because the members could not agree on a strategy. Two years later they formed an unofficial Black Cabinet, a network for sharing information, resources, and strategies. Chaired by Mary McLeod Bethune, the Black Cabinet did not have any apparent impact on policy. Its real value was as a symbol of the growing black presence in Washington, D.C. Mrs. Bethune was an especially powerful symbol of that presence. A strong, outspoken leader with access to President Roosevelt, she did not hesitate to speak her mind to the chief executive about the suffering of blacks. Blacks had long been on the outside looking in; now it seemed they were finally working their way inside and becoming a recognized part of America.

## High-Level Allies

Although President Roosevelt developed programs that helped blacks, he did not throw his support behind measures specifically aimed against racial discrimination. In private, the president explained that because powerful southern Democrats controlled key committees in Congress, he could not afford to antagonize them by attacking racial discrimination, or else "they will block every bill I ask Congress to pass to keep America from collapsing. I just can't take that risk." Nevertheless, black leaders were disappointed at the president's refusal to support the struggle for federal antilynching legislation during the 1930s. They also failed to obtain White House support for proposals in Congress to prohibit racial discrimination by unions. Roosevelt also refused to endorse drives against the white primary and the poll tax. Nor did the White House back an attempt by the NAACP and the National Urban League to include agricultural and domestic workers in the federal pension plan created by the Social Security Act (1935); as a result, a high proportion of black workers were not entitled to social security pensions.

Yet some individuals high in the administration did go out of their way to extend a hand to blacks—in particular, the president's wife, Eleanor Roosevelt, and Interior Secretary Harold Ickes. Their impact on policy was limited. Mrs. Roosevelt unsuccessfully encouraged her husband to endorse antilynching legislation. Ickes wanted to speak out publicly in support of such legislation, but he was barred by the White House from doing so. However, they found other ways to show their support for racial equality. Mrs. Roosevelt wrote to administrators of government programs to protest against racial discrimination; she also urged them to support projects of special interest to blacks. She endorsed NAACP membership drives; visited black churches, schools, and PWA housing projects; attended interracial meetings; and invited blacks to White House receptions. In 1937 Ickes convinced the president to appoint William H. Hastie as district judge for the Virgin Islands, the first black federal judge. Both Mrs. Roosevelt and Ickes addressed NAACP gatherings.

Mrs. Roosevelt and Secretary Ickes made their best-known gesture to blacks in 1939, after the Daughters of the American Revolution (DAR) denied famous black opera singer Marian Anderson permission to perform in Constitution Hall in Washington, D.C. Mrs. Roosevelt resigned from the DAR in protest. After Anderson was also barred from singing in the school auditorium of a white Washington, D.C., school, Ickes invited her to sing from the steps of the Lincoln Memorial, and on Easter Sunday 1939 she gave an outdoor concert there before an unsegregated audience of some 75,000 blacks and whites. The gathering included federal judges, cabinet members, and members of Congress as well as ordinary Americans. This event had tremendous symbolic value for blacks; the concert was remembered for many years because it showed so vividly that at last blacks had friends in high office, and even in the White House.

## New Voting Patterns

The New Deal brought a revolution in black voting patterns. For all of its shortcomings, the Roosevelt administration gave many blacks vital assistance in a time of great need; appointed far more blacks than previous administrations; and showed in various symbolic ways that it was concerned about the nation's black citizens. Many blacks idolized President Roosevelt and Mrs. Roosevelt. When the president ran again in 1936, they broke their tradition—dating back to Reconstruction—of supporting Republicans and gave about two-thirds of their votes to Roosevelt. Also, black voter registration and turnout increased under Roosevelt because of enthusiasm for the New Deal.

Because of the New Deal's popularity, blacks began voting more often for Democratic candidates for all offices and at all levels of government. In 1934 Arthur W. Mitchell became the first black Democrat sent to Congress when he defeated the reelection bid of black Republican Oscar De Priest in Chicago. Black Democratic political machines grew in northern and western cities. Republicans had long taken the black vote for granted, but they could no longer do so. As the

Democrats began running more black candidates, Republicans did the same. The result was a modest increase in the number of black officeholders at both state and local levels; for example, between 1925 and 1929, 27 black state legislators were elected, and between 1932 and 1936, 38 were chosen. But although Democrats did receive more black votes at the local and state levels than before, they did significantly better at the national level. Only when the Democrats became identified with civil rights legislation after World War II did the great majority of blacks begin voting Democratic across the board.

## THE BLACK FIGHT FOR JUSTICE IN THE 1930s

The New Deal represented a big step forward for blacks, but it did not include a civil rights policy. All black leaders agreed that racial progress would require continued struggle by blacks. But the Great Depression sparked fresh debate over the best strategy for achieving justice, and much of the debate occurred within the NAACP.

The NAACP's major strategy was to fight in the courtroom and in the legislatures for equal legal rights. Sometimes, as when the NAACP fought job discrimination, its struggles for legal equality also brought economic benefits to blacks. But most of its civil rights activities had no direct economic impact. In the 1930s, many younger members believed that at a time of massive unemployment and poverty, greater emphasis should be placed on economic issues than on legal rights. Although not all of these young mavericks were socialists, they agreed with the black radicals of the 1920s who had argued for an emphasis on working-class unity. Howard University political scientist Ralph Bunche and economist Abram Harris were among this group. Charles Houston, an older member of the organization and its legal counsel, felt the same way. They believed that the NAACP should work for a labor movement that would bring together skilled and unskilled workers regardless of race. However, it was not clear how this could be done so long as whites did not want integrated unions.

During the 1930s the NAACP did focus some of its attention on economic issues. In the early 1930s, the federal government hired workers to build flood-control levees along the Mississippi River. The NAACP learned that blacks were receiving less pay than whites and were being compelled to work 12 hours a day, every day of the week, with no holidays or overtime pay. In 1933 the NAACP successfully pressed Congress to investigate the situation. As a result of the probe, wages and working conditions were improved for all flood-control workers. The NAACP also gave legal and financial help to the Southern Tenant Farmers Union (STFU). Founded in July 1934 in Tyronza, Arkansas, it brought together white and black tenants and sharecroppers to negotiate with landlords for fair contracts. By 1936 it had over 30,000 members, about one-third of them black. But by year's end, the STFU was dying out because of fierce landlord resistance.

The NAACP's major mission remained the promotion of legal equality. Perhaps its most famous courtroom case of the 1930s involved nine young black men

Demonstrators stage a vivid antilynching protest in Washington, D.C., in 1934. At the time, passage of a federal antilynching law was the top goal of the National Association for the Advancement of Colored People.

known as the Scottsboro boys. In 1931 they were accused at Scottsboro, Alabama, of raping two white women on a freight train. The evidence against the young men was doubtful, and the NAACP agreed to handle their legal defense. Soon, though, the International Labor Defense, a Communist group, convinced the defendants to turn the case over to them. In the mid-1930s the NAACP was asked to take over the case again. Although the Scottsboro boys were convicted and sentenced to terms as long as 99 years, by 1950 they had all won release with the NAACP's help.

Walter White investigated lynchings during the 1920s and published a book on the subject called *Rope and Faggot: A Biography of Judge Lynch* (1929). As the NAACP's executive secretary beginning in 1931, White devoted more of the organization's time to working for federal antilynching legislation than to anything else during the 1930s. At the NAACP's urging, Senators Robert Wagner of New York and Edward P. Costigan of Colorado introduced an antilynching bill. Support for federal legislation had grown since the 1920s, and many state legislatures, city councils, and civic organizations passed resolutions endorsing it. But like the Dyer bill in 1922, Wagner and Costigan's proposal was filibustered to death in May 1935 by a Senate minority headed by southern Democrats. President Roosevelt's refusal to support it was a key element in its defeat. Similar legislation passed the House in 1937 by a vote of 277 to 120, but again southerners filibustered it in the Senate. Further efforts in 1939 and 1940 also failed; with the number of lynchings declining by then, public support waned.

While the NAACP focused on lynching, other groups stressed economic issues. Some young NAACP militants, having failed to change the direction of that organization, formed the National Negro Congress in 1935 at Howard University under the leadership of black attorney John P. Davis, veteran black labor leader A. Philip Randolph, and Ralph Bunche. In 1936 its first national assembly elected Randolph president and Davis executive secretary. Although the congress took positions on many issues, one of its main interests was improving the economic status of blacks through the organization of integrated trade unions.

At first it looked as if the National Negro Congress might become a rival of the NAACP. But by 1940 the Communist Party had become a major force in the organization. It used the congress to promote the interests of the Soviet Union, although they had no connection to the needs of blacks. For example, after the Soviet Union formed its short-lived alliance with Nazi Germany in 1939, Communists and their sympathizers within the congress introduced resolutions opposing any U.S. assistance to those fighting the Nazis. Randolph, an opponent of the Communists, refused to run for reelection in 1940, calling the Soviet Union "The death prison where democracy and liberty have walked their 'last mile.'" Few blacks supported the Communist Party, even though it ran a black man, James W. Ford, as its vice-presidential candidate in 1932, 1936, and 1940. Therefore, the National Negro Congress declined rapidly after 1940.

Meanwhile, Randolph became involved in an important struggle for black jobs. In 1939 war broke out in Europe. The United States did not enter the conflict until the end of 1941. But in the meantime, the U.S. government began to strengthen America's military forces. In 1940 the War Department began placing large contracts with defense plants. These contracts sparked economic production and created many jobs, bringing about the end of the Great Depression. But military contractors practiced blatant racial discrimination in their hiring practices and also segregated workers by race. In January 1941 Randolph announced that unless the government assured blacks of an equal opportunity to obtain defense plant jobs, he would lead a march on Washington, D.C., by tens of thousands of blacks. He expected that the ten-thousand-strong Brotherhood of Sleeping Car Porters, which he had organized in the 1920s and 1930s (see the following section), would provide many of the marchers. His strategy was effective; on June 25, 1941, President Roosevelt, alarmed by the possibility of the march, signed Executive Order 8802. It barred racial discrimination by employers that held government contracts and also prohibited discrimination in federal training programs for defense production. The order also established a Fair Employment Practices Commission (FEPC) to promote compliance with the order.

This was the first time that Roosevelt took clear action on an important civil rights issue. True, the FEPC was a temporary agency and did not have the power to force contractors to hire blacks. Nevertheless, it represented a beginning that could be built upon later. Also, Randolph's success showed that black protest would become much more effective as blacks joined mass organizations such as Randolph's brotherhood. Had that union not existed, Randolph's threat to bring thousands of blacks into the streets might not have been taken seriously.

## THE TRADE UNION MOVEMENT

As we have seen, during World War I blacks entered the nation's factories in large numbers for the first time. When the postwar recession of 1919–1920 hit, employers often fired blacks before whites. (This led blacks to use the expression "Last to be hired, first to be fired.") But when the economy picked up again, blacks were rehired. And so, although blacks worked mostly in unskilled jobs and were more likely than whites to be laid off in bad times, they finally became a permanent part of the industrial economy. By 1930, 36 percent of black workers had industry-related jobs, compared to just 14 percent in 1890.

Despite the growing black presence in the factories, the majority of unions in the American Federation of Labor (AFL) did not want to organize blacks. At any rate, most AFL unions were organized by craft and were interested primarily in organizing skilled craft workers. Since most blacks were unskilled workers, they had little hope of joining these AFL unions. The few exceptions included the United Mine Workers, the International Ladies' Garment Workers' Union, and the Amalgamated Clothing Workers' Union, which were organizing on an industrywide rather than a craft basis; to be effective, they had to organize all workers, whatever their race.

Because black workers were not welcome in most unions, some of the radical blacks discussed above (see "Nationalists and Radicals," page 152) tried to organize black trade unions and associations. Between 1917 and 1923, A. Philip Randolph and Chandler Owen formed some half-dozen labor organizations. But by 1925, all of these groups had failed.

Randolph fared much better with the Brotherhood of Sleeping Car Porters, which he founded in 1925. The porters, almost all black, had a reputation for very high-quality work. Passengers knew them as consistently efficient, dependable, and courteous. Whites often referred to them as the "better type" of black. In the black community, the porters were considered an elite because they had steady jobs; met wealthy and powerful people; and traveled widely, bringing home news from around the country. But on the job, they received very low pay for very long hours; their basic work month was 400 hours or 11,000 miles, whichever came first, and their starting pay was less than $100 a month.

The Pullman Company used every method it could to fight the brotherhood. It encouraged porters to spy on their pro-union fellow workers and bring back information to management; organized a company union; fired union members; and when all else failed, hired violent thugs. Still, Randolph and the porters carried on their struggle for years, gaining the support of the NAACP, the Urban League, and even the AFL, which admitted the brotherhood into its ranks. In 1935 the porters voted overwhelmingly to be represented by the brotherhood; the company then recognized the union. Two years later the union and management agreed on a contract; it contained significant wage increases and a reduction of the work month from 400 to 240 hours.

But a fundamental change in the American labor movement had to occur before black workers could be organized in large numbers. In 1930, according to the NAACP, only about 50,000 blacks belonged to national unions. Even after the Great Depression began, the AFL did not seriously try to organize blacks. In the early 1930s, the federation chartered several unions to organize workers on an industrywide basis, but the drive failed because the AFL did not give these unions adequate support. Blacks picketed the AFL's 1934 convention. Inside, Randolph called for the expulsion from the AFL of all unions that had discriminatory policies, but the delegates rejected the proposal.

The National Industrial Recovery Act of 1933 gave workers the right to form unions, but that law was declared unconstitutional by the Supreme Court in 1935. That year, however, the National Labor Relations Act, also known as the Wagner Act, recognized the workers' right to organize. Since neither act banned racial discrimination by unions, black leaders feared that, as in the past, the union movement would grow at the expense of black jobs. But this time, blacks benefited from unionization. Late in 1935, the few industrial unions in the AFL formed the Committee for Industrial Organization, whose goal was to unionize all workers in every industry. Soon the committee broke with the AFL and changed its name to the Congress of Industrial Organizations (CIO). In 1936 and 1937, the CIO began organizing steel and automobile workers on a nonracial basis. In the late 1930s, the CIO's Textile Workers Organizing Committee organized black as well as white workers in the Deep South, over the objections of the Ku Klux Klan. The Packinghouse Workers Organizing Committee appointed Henry Johnson, a black, as its assistant director in 1939.

CIO unions included blacks because they knew that mass-production industries could not be organized successfully unless all workers—skilled, semiskilled, and unskilled—were included. Seeing the success of the CIO, the AFL began making more serious attempts to organize industrial unions (although its craft unions continued their discriminatory policies). Since blacks were the lowest-paid workers, they had the most to gain from unionization. Therefore, most blacks eagerly joined (and by doing so, destroyed a long-standing myth that black workers could not be unionized because of an inability to cooperate). In 1940, around 600,000 blacks belonged to trade unions—about 12 times more than in 1930. By 1945 the figure had doubled to 1.25 million.

The CIO unions helped blacks in three ways. First, they improved the wages of black workers because of their bargaining power with employers and  their insistence that workers receive equal pay for the same work, regardless of race. Second, they created a new arena in which blacks usually had equal rights, at least outside the South. Within their unions, blacks could vote for their leaders and vote in favor of or against proposed contracts, just as white members did. And third, the CIO with its millions of members became a powerful political force for the interests of poor and working people, categories that included most blacks. In later years it would be an important force in favor of civil rights legislation.

# CHAPTER 8

# World War II and the Postwar Years: 1941–1960

### FIGHTING RACISM ABROAD AND AT HOME IN WORLD WAR II

In September 1939, Germany capped a series of aggressive actions in Europe by invading Poland. Britain and France then declared war on Germany as World War II began. Within a year Germany had overrun most of western Europe, including France, and was threatening an invasion of Britain. Meanwhile, tensions between the United States and Japan increased as the expansionist Japanese government committed aggression against China and other areas of Asia. On December 7, 1941, Japanese warplanes attacked the U.S. naval base at Pearl Harbor in the Hawaiian Islands. Soon the United States was fighting alongside Britain, the Soviet Union, and lesser Allied countries against the Axis nations led by Germany, Italy, and Japan.

The great majority of blacks were enthusiastic about U.S. involvement in World War II. Germany, the most powerful Axis country, was ruled by the racist Nazi Party. Though the Nazis saved most of their hatred for Jews, they believed in black inferiority. That is why blacks recalled with pride the 1936 Olympic games in Berlin, Germany, where black American runner Jesse Owens reportedly angered Germany's Nazi chancellor, Adolf Hitler, by winning four gold medals. That also is why blacks were upset in 1936 when "Brown Bomber" Joe Louis lost a boxing match to German Max Schmeling and why they were overjoyed when Louis defeated Schmeling in a 1938 rematch. As for Germany's ally Italy, blacks recalled its bloody 1937 conquest of Ethiopia, until then the only independent black nation in Africa.

In 1940 the United States began building up its war industry and armed forces. Blacks wanted to enlist, but as in past wars, the armed services at first discouraged them. However, a draft law passed in September 1940 contained an antidiscrimination clause, thanks partly to pressure from the Committee on Participation of Negroes in National Defense, organized in 1938 at the initiative of Robert Vann's *Pittsburgh Courier*. During the war more than a million black men and women entered the various services; about 500,000 of them served abroad in Europe, North Africa, the Pacific, and Asia.

## Discrimination and Progress

Once in the service, blacks discovered that discrimination still ran rampant, especially during the early years of the war. As in previous wars, blacks received inferior, segregated training and served in segregated units. More often than whites, black troops were assigned to service units or menial work. The navy accepted blacks only as mess attendants, or stewards, who performed tasks like making the beds and shining the shoes of the officers; the army air corps at first used blacks only as maintenance personnel. Initially the marines did not accept blacks at all. During the war, less than 1 percent of black soldiers became commissioned officers, compared to 11 percent of whites. The few who received commissions were allowed to command only blacks. They became targets of abuse and were excluded from officers' clubs.

Perhaps the most absurd example of World War II racism was the Red Cross's decision to segregate the blood of blacks and whites in the blood banks established for soldiers. This seemed especially ridiculous because Dr. Charles Drew, medical director of the Red Cross blood program, whose research in blood preservation had made blood banks possible, was black. (He resigned over the policy of segregating blood.)

In 1943 rage against segregation and discrimination in the armed forces erupted into violence both overseas and at home. That year the number of deaths among white officers in black outfits increased sharply. The best explanation is that black soldiers, fed up with poor treatment, were killing white officers during combat, when the blame could be placed on the enemy. Black troops fought back against white soldiers at U.S. military installations in Britain, Australia, and the South Pacific during the summer of 1943. The anger of black civilians at the treatment of black soldiers was one reason for the occurrence of violence in black ghettos at about the same time. The worst race riot during World War II happened in Detroit. There, on June 20 and 21, 1943, fights between the races resulted in the deaths of 25 blacks and 9 whites. On August 1 and 2, 1943, a riot raged in Harlem over a rumor that a black soldier had been killed by a white policeman. Around midyear, major racial disturbances also occurred in Beaumont, Texas, and Los Angeles.

Black pressure, along with manpower shortages, forced some limited concessions. At first the army air corps seemed to have no plan to utilize blacks except as maintenance workers: none were being trained as pilots. But in January 1941 the NAACP filed a lawsuit on behalf of Howard University graduate Yancey Williams, who wanted to enter the corps as a flight cadet. Just after the suit was filed, the

War Department announced the establishment of a training center for black flyers at Tuskegee, Alabama. In January 1943 William H. Hastie, a black aide to the secretary of war, resigned because of the air corps's failure to train blacks in technical specialties. His resignation convinced military authorities to give blacks some opportunities for training in engineering, communications, and other technical fields.

In April 1942 the navy announced that blacks would be admitted for general service rather than just as mess attendants. However, at war's end 90 percent of black sailors were still mess men. Furthermore, the black general service recruits were trained separately and were rarely promoted—only 52 of the 165,000 blacks who served in the navy during the war received officers' commissions. Few blacks received assignments to combat ships, although late in the war that began to change. The great majority of the black general service recruits were construction workers, laborers, or longshoremen; again, though, toward the end of the war a growing number of them worked as radio operators, carpenters, shipfitters, and in other skilled positions. In June 1942 the marines opened recruitment to blacks for the first time ever, and by the war's end 17,000 black marines had served. But organized into separate units, they saw only limited action. There were no black marine officers during World War II.

Of the 1 million blacks who served in the war, about 700,000 were in the army, where little progress was made toward ending discrimination. In 1944 the War Department issued an order to integrate the post exchanges, theaters, and buses on army bases. However, it went largely unenforced. The order's major purpose may have been to win black votes for President Roosevelt in the 1944 election. The black Second Cavalry received two years of combat training and then was sent to North Africa early in 1944. Once there, however, it was suddenly turned into a service unit to do common labor. When Secretary of War Henry Stimson explained that blacks did not have enough education to use modern weapons, the black community reacted with indignation. This response forced the general staff to send the black 92nd and 93rd Infantry Divisions into battle soon after. Because of heavy American casualties in the Battle of the Bulge (December 1944) in Belgium, the last major German offensive of the war, black volunteer infantrymen were sought. All-black platoons were added to previously all-white companies, and the two races fought side by side across Germany in the war's last months. This was the closest to desegregation that the army had ever come. But when the fighting ended, the black platoons were returned to all-black service units.

The women's service corps discriminated, too. The WAVEs (navy) and SPARs (coast guard) at first did not accept blacks. The black Alpha Kappa Alpha sorority protested this exclusion just before the 1944 presidential election, and both corps were opened to blacks in October 1944. The Marine Women's Reserve, or Marinettes, never accepted blacks during the war. The WACs (army) admitted black women from the start of the conflict, but they usually did menial work while whites received technical training for more skilled tasks. In March 1945, about 100 black WACs at the Lowell General Hospital at Fort Devens, Massachusetts, went on a sit-down strike after the hospital's commanding officer reportedly said that the blacks should do all the "dirty work." Only one black WAC unit went overseas, just a few months before the war's end.

## Military Contributions

Despite the usual discrimination, black Americans once again made major contributions to their country's war efforts. Hailed as symbols of black heroism were the two most important black air units: the 99th Pursuit Squadron (later known as the 99th Fighter Squadron) and the 332nd Fighter Group. The 99th went into combat in June 1943 and in July helped to cover the Allied invasion of Sicily; the black pilots performed dive-bombing, strafing, patrolling, and armed reconnaissance. Soon afterward the squadron supported British troops in eastern Italy. The success of the 99th led to the creation of the 332nd, which also operated in the European theater. These units, along with the black 447th Bombardment Group, flew more than 15,000 sorties, shooting down 111 planes in the air and destroying 150 on the ground. Black pilots earned 88 Distinguished Flying Crosses and about 800 Air Medals.

The army's black 92nd Infantry Division was unable to overcome the obstacles that most black units faced, including inferior training and hostile white officers. In Italy in 1944, the men often fled in the face of enemy pressure and fired their weapons recklessly. Other black combat troops fought valiantly, however. In the European theater, black infantrymen fought bravely in the Battle of the Bulge late in 1944 and during the march across Germany in 1945. Black field artillery, antiaircraft, tank, and tank destroyer batallions in Europe often received citations for outstanding service.

In the Pacific theater, the 24th Infantry Regiment participated in the taking of the New Georgia Islands from the Japanese in May 1942. In June 1944 the regiment fought effectively along with black marines in the battle of Saipan in the Mariana Islands. In April 1944 the 93rd Infantry Division got its first taste of combat when it helped to capture Bougainville Island in the Solomons. Later in the year the division fought in the Treasury Islands, at Moratai Island in the Dutch East Indies, and finally in the recapture of the Philippines from Japan.

Black service and supply units provided important assistance to combat forces. After the Allied invasion of Nazi-occupied France in June 1944, truck drivers ferried supplies from the French coast toward the battlefront along various routes. The drivers on one of the routes, two-thirds of whom were black, became famous as the Red Ball Express. Working in 36-hour shifts without sleep, they delivered about 6,000 tons of supplies a day. Black chemical warfare units in Europe created smoke to cover Allied troop movements and operations. In December 1944 the 161st Chemical Smoke Generator Company created an artificial fog in the Saar River valley of northeastern France; one of the largest human-made fogs ever created, it hid the movement of the entire 90th Division.

Beginning in December 1942 some 15,000 American soldiers—about 60 percent of them black—built the Ledo Road through South Asian jungle under threat of Japanese attack. The road was used to bring supplies to the anti-Japanese forces in China. Black engineering, chemical warfare, and other units were praised by General Douglas MacArthur for their bravery in the successful effort to drive the Japanese from Papua New Guinea, in January 1943. In China and elsewhere in Asia, black engineers built runways and landing strips for Allied planes.

## THE POSTWAR CLIMATE

For many reasons, favorable conditions for combating racism and discrimination existed in the years after the war. The fight against Nazi racism made many white Americans question U.S. racial practices. White Americans became still more aware of the evils of racism at the end of the war, during which the Nazis exterminated 6 million Jews and millions more belonging to other "inferior" groups.

After the war many nonwhite, Third World colonies of Europe began to win their independence. At the same time relations between the United States and the Soviet Union, which had been wartime allies, worsened as cold war tensions grew. With the two countries competing for favor in the new nonwhite nations, the Soviets used American racism as a propaganda weapon against the United States. Stopping the spread of Soviet Communism became the nation's major foreign policy goal in the late 1940s, and so the U.S. government had an important reason—aside from simple justice—to tackle racial discrimination.

We have seen that around the turn of the twentieth century, "scientific" theories of black inferiority influenced the educated class; at that time, those writing about racial problems believed that they stemmed from the innate inferiority of blacks to whites. But race prejudice among the educated started to ease after 1920 as Franz Boas, Otto Klineberg, and other anthropologists began disproving racist theories; a growing number of informed whites now believed that the roots of racial conflict lay in white prejudice, not black inferiority. Many books on race published in America during the 1940s expressed this viewpoint. In his pioneering *An American Dilemma* (1944), Swedish sociologist Gunnar Myrdal stated that racial problems stemmed from the failure of white Americans to live up to their country's ideals. Books sharing this opinion included *ABCs of Scapegoating* (1948), by social psychologist Gordon Allport, and *Brothers under the Skin* (1942), by journalist Carey McWilliams. White southern liberals spoke out, among them Georgia sociologist Howard Odum in *Race and Rumors of Race* (1943) and South Carolina journalist W. J. Cash in *The Mind of the South* (1941). The new attitude toward race relations began to appear in school textbooks and in professional and liberal publications.

Liberal, mostly white organizations began to form coalitions with black-led civil rights groups to fight prejudice and discrimination. They included Jewish groups such as the American Jewish Congress, the American Jewish Committee, and the Anti-Defamation League of B'nai B'rith; Catholic clergy and organizations such as the National Catholic Welfare Conference; the American Civil Liberties Union; and Americans for Democratic Action. The two labor federations, the AFL and

CIO, the latter with many black members, were important parts of the coalition. Blacks began working with Mexican American organizations in the West and with Puerto Rican groups in the Northeast. In 1948 the Leadership Conference on Civil Rights brought liberal organizations together for joint lobbying efforts in Washington, D.C.

Meanwhile, blacks became both more determined and more capable than ever of advancing their interests. Many blacks significantly improved their economic well-being during the prosperous 1940s and 1950s. The number of blacks with white-collar jobs increased greatly; this helps explain why black income jumped from 41 percent of white income in 1939, to 51 percent in 1947, and to 57 percent in 1952, and why by 1953 blacks owned almost a third of the homes in which they lived. Blacks were determined to keep and expand these gains. Partly as a consequence, and partly because of growing white support for civil rights, NAACP membership soared from 51,000 in 1940 to 351,000 in 1945; this made it possible for the organization to expand its activities. Because of both rising black income and the efforts of the United Negro College Fund, founded in 1943, the number of blacks in college rose from 23,000 in 1940 to 114,000 in 1950, giving blacks a much broader base for their future leadership.

Black political power grew in the 1940s as migration out of the South skyrocketed. Migration increased for two reasons. First, the prosperity of the industrial North during the 1940s attracted southern black farmers trying to escape poverty. Second, white southern farmers began to replace human labor with machinery during that decade; as a consequence, many black sharecroppers and tenant farmers were thrown off the land, and many agricultural wage laborers could not get work. The South lost about 1.6 million blacks to the North and West between 1940 and 1950. Because blacks could vote once outside the South, white politicians in the North and West had to pay greater heed to the rapidly expanding black electorate.

## Small Inroads against Bias

For all these reasons, some limited progress against discrimination was possible in the 1940s and early 1950s. Important symbolic victories came with the integration of professional sports. Professional baseball had begun excluding blacks entirely in the late 1880s, which led to creation of the Negro Leagues in the early twentieth century. But in 1947 Branch Rickey, general manager of the Brooklyn Dodgers, broke the color barrier by bringing Jackie Robinson to the major leagues; enduring the vicious taunts of many players and fans, Robinson quickly became a star. By the mid-1950s, many of major league baseball's best players were black. The National Football League accepted its first black players in 1946. Other professional sports soon followed suit.

Blacks made many small advances on the civil rights front at the state and local levels. In the 6 years following the riots of 1943, 33 cities formed human relations commissions to ease racial tensions and discrimination. The work of black and white churches and other organizations helped to nearly eradicate lynchings by the early 1950s—in 1952 there were none, for the first time since lynchings were first recorded in the early 1880s. The biracial Southern Regional Council was formed in Atlanta in 1944. Made up of clergy and professionals, it cautiously promoted the slow elimination of Jim Crow. A one-week black boycott of the bus system in Baton Rouge, Louisiana, in 1953, ended the system of segregated seating that forced blacks to ride at the back of the bus.

In the North, the Fellowship of Reconciliation, an organization dedicated to nonviolent social change, established the biracial Congress of Racial Equality (CORE) on a national basis in 1942. In 1946 the Supreme Court barred segregated seating on interstate buses in *Morgan v. Virginia*. With the Court on its side, a group of black and white CORE members, including black pacifist Bayard Rustin, tried to integrate buses in the Upper South in 1947. For sitting black next to white, Rustin and others in the group went to jail and he served on a chain gang. But except for the black press their efforts were ignored, and they did not achieve any concrete results. They did, however, establish a pattern for future action.

In the mid-1940s black schoolteachers demanded and won equal pay in many southern cities. Some voluntary integration occurred in the South in the late 1940s and early 1950s. More than 40 private colleges opened their doors to blacks, and several southern cities started admitting the two races to parks, museums, and public libraries without discrimination. The Supreme Court's *Smith v. Allwright* (1944) decision banned the white primary system that excluded blacks from voting in Democratic primaries. Also, a number of southern states eliminated the poll tax; the requirement to pay the tax in order to vote had kept some blacks from casting ballots. These developments made it possible for southern blacks to vote in larger numbers. In 1940 only 250,000 southern blacks, or 5 percent of the voting-age southern black population, were registered to vote; in 1952 the number was 1 million, or 20 percent. Almost all of the gains occurred in the Upper South. As the black vote grew, a handful of blacks were elected to city councils in several Upper South cities and some were appointed to minor local positions. Starting in 1939, the Supreme Court began requiring new trials for convicted southern blacks because of the exclusion of blacks from juries. As a result, blacks for the first time in decades began to appear on juries in some parts of the South. By 1955, six southern states had passed laws to restrict the Ku Klux Klan.

Discrimination came under attack in many northern and western states and localities. Between 1945 and 1953, 12 states and 30 cities passed fair employment laws, thanks in large degree to pressure from black and Jewish groups as well as some Protestant and Catholic organizations. By 1949, 18 states had banned segregation in public transportation vehicles, restaurants, hotels, educational institutions, parks, libraries, and places of amusement. With the black electorate growing rapidly outside the South, two new blacks joined William Dawson of Chicago in the House of Representatives: Adam Clayton Powell, Jr., from Harlem in 1944, and Charles C. Diggs, Jr., from Detroit in 1954, both Democrats like Dawson. On the national level, the Red Cross stopped labeling its blood by race in the late 1940s. Around the same time many medical, legal, and other professional associations opened their doors to blacks.

Significant as postwar progress may have been, it only scratched the surface of racial discrimination. Though the black middle class grew, most blacks remained poor. Despite some gains, the great majority of southern blacks still could not vote, primarily because of intimidation and discriminatory use of literacy tests. That was especially true in the Lower South; in Mississippi, for example, less than 2 percent of voting-age blacks were on the registration rolls in 1955. By the mid-1950s barely a dent had been made in segregation and other forms of discrimination in the Lower South. In the North, whatever segregation existed was in decline. But northern states and cities that had banned employment discrimination did not have the resources to carry out strong enforcement programs. Furthermore, very few states and cities took action against housing discrimination. A truly effective war against racial bias and its consequences would require leadership from the federal government.

## THE TRUMAN ADMINISTRATION

After the war, civil rights groups and their allies promoted an aggressive legislative program at the federal level. With lynchings in sharp decline, antilynching legislation was no longer the top civil rights priority. Now the major goal was the establishment by Congress of a permanent Fair Employment Practices Commission (FEPC) with the power to enforce a ban on employment discrimination in both the private sector and the federal government. Under pressure from A. Philip Randolph, Roosevelt had established an FEPC by executive order in 1941. But the order was only a temporary wartime measure; it covered only government contractors, not the private sector in general; and it gave the commission authority to investigate discrimination but not to force employers to end it. To fix these shortcomings Randolph created the Committee for a Permanent FEPC in 1943, and the NAACP, too, began pressing for a permanent and stronger commission.

Civil rights advocates, led by the NAACP and backed by many liberal and labor groups, also pushed for other types of antidiscrimination laws. These included legislation prohibiting poll taxes, which in some states were still used as a qualification for voting; banning discrimination in the sale and rental of housing; implementing the Supreme Court's *Morgan v. Virginia* (1946) decision prohibiting segregated seating on interstate buses; giving home rule to Washington, D.C., which was 35 percent black in 1950 (since 1878 it had been ruled by a three-person board appointed by the president); and prohibiting federal aid to all government and private agencies that discriminated by race.

Until the postwar period, black leaders avoided attacks on segregation, fearing that the subject was too controversial. For example, blacks had long been arguing that the southern states should spend as much for black schools as for white—but they did not claim that segregating students by race was itself discriminatory. At the end of World War II, however, civil rights organizations felt stronger and more confident than ever because of their increasing membership and the improving racial climate. Therefore, black leaders like NAACP executive secretary Walter White, NAACP attorneys Charles Houston and Thurgood Marshall, and labor leader A. Philip Randolph began to denounce separation of the races in 1947. Soon they and others began political and legal attacks upon segregation, particularly in the armed forces and in the schools.

## The Politics of Civil Rights

Vice President Harry Truman became president when Franklin D. Roosevelt died in April 1945, just a few months before the end of World War II. We have seen that although Roosevelt created social welfare programs that helped many blacks, on civil rights matters he remained silent. But Truman found himself in a different political situation. As we have noted, a growing number of whites expressed liberal racial views after the war. Also, when the cold war began in the late 1940s, many feared that racism would hurt the United States in its rivalry with the Soviet Union. Last but certainly not least, the rapid growth of the northern black population meant a major increase in the size of the black vote. Faced with these political realities, President Truman became a vocal advocate of civil rights progress.

As early as 1945, President Truman began urging Congress to pass FEPC and anti–poll tax legislation. In August 1946 he endorsed an antilynching law, something the NAACP had long but unsuccessfully tried to get Roosevelt to do. In June 1947 Truman spoke at the NAACP's annual conference. He asserted that because the democratic nations must convince the world of their superiority to Communist dictatorships, "we can no longer afford the luxury of a leisurely attack upon prejudice and discrimination." And to strengthen the attack on racial bias, he stated "we cannot, any longer, await the growth of a will to action in the slowest state or the most backward community. Our national government must show the way."

The President's Committee on Civil Rights, appointed by Truman in December 1946, issued its report in October 1947. Called *To Secure These Rights*, it endorsed many of the civil rights coalition's demands, including desegregation of the armed forces. But would President Truman give full support to the entire report, including its controversial opposition to military segregation? Political pressures from various sources shaped the president's decision.

In December 1947, former cabinet member Henry Wallace announced that he would run for president in 1948 as the candidate of the left-wing Progressive Citizens of America, a group heavily influenced by Communists. Wallace and the Progressives strongly supported civil rights. Only a few prominent blacks, including W. E. B. Du Bois, actor Canada Lee, and singer and actor Paul Robeson endorsed Wallace. But Truman feared that many black voters might defect to the Progressives. He also worried that others might support the Republicans' likely nominee, Thomas E. Dewey, whom many black leaders believed had forged a good civil rights record as governor of New York.

Not surprisingly, then, Truman gave strong general support to the proposals of the Committee on Civil Rights in his January 1948 State of the Union Address. The following month he delivered a special civil rights message to Congress, the first ever sent by a president to Capitol Hill on that subject. In it he advocated a variety of antidiscrimination proposals but largely avoided the issue of segregation. Further political pressures, however, would force Truman to take a stand on the segregation issue a few months later.

Protestors outside the Democratic National Convention demonstrate against military segregation in July 1948. Carrying a picket sign at the left is A. Philip Randolph, president of the Brotherhood of Sleeping Car Porters and leader of the movement against Jim Crow in the armed forces. Note that one sign calls for a boycott of the draft.

In November 1947, A. Philip Randolph and Grant Reynolds founded the Committee against Jim Crow in Military Service and Training, which won enthusiastic support among ordinary blacks. (Early in 1948 it became the League for Nonviolent Civil Disobedience to the Draft.) Testifying before the Senate Armed Services Committee in March 1948, Randolph declared, "This time Negroes will not take a Jim Crow draft lying down." Unless segregation and discrimination were banned, he warned, "I personally will advise Negroes to refuse to fight as slaves for a democracy they cannot possess and cannot enjoy."

In addition to black opinion, Truman also felt pressure from within his own Democratic Party. At the Democratic National Convention in mid-July 1948, northern liberal and big-city delegates, led by Minneapolis mayor Hubert H. Humphrey, passed a civil rights resolution stronger than any the party had ever endorsed. It included a call for the end of discrimination in the military and for action against discriminatory employment practices. Under pressure from both white liberals and blacks, Truman issued two executive orders on July 26: Executive Order 9980 against employment discrimination in the federal government, and Executive Order 9981, requiring "equality of treatment and opportunity" in the armed forces. When asked at a press conference whether "equality of treatment" meant integration, Truman answered with a simple "yes"; the chairman of the Democratic National Committee gave Randolph a similar assurance.

Truman's pro–civil rights stance paid off in the November 1948 presidential election, which he narrowly won. In protest against the Democratic Convention's liberal civil rights plank in July, many southern delegates walked out. This led to the formation of the anti–civil rights States' Rights Party. But its candidate for president, Senator Strom Thurmond of South Carolina, captured only 4 Deep South states with 38 electoral votes. On the other hand, Truman won almost 70 percent of the black vote, without which he would have lost California, Ohio, and Illinois, for a total of 78 electoral votes.

## The Truman Record

Truman clearly benefited from black support; but what concrete gains did blacks make as a result of his policies? The most important advance resulted from the president's executive order integrating the military. In September 1948 Truman appointed a seven-member panel, known as the Fahy Committee, to implement the order. The panel required each armed service to develop a desegregation plan. All of them, especially the army, resisted. But the committee kept the pressure on, and by the time the Korean War broke out in 1950, all had taken some steps toward desegregation. During the war, shortages of white manpower speeded up the process of integration. Desegregation accelerated further when officers discovered that it improved black morale without causing the racial friction that some had feared. In the years just after the Truman administration, desegregation of all U.S. armed forces was basically completed.

In the area of housing, progress was limited. By 1952 federal agencies had integrated 210 public housing projects. But there was little change in the private housing market during the postwar years. There, restrictive covenants remained common, even after the Supreme Court banned them in *Shelley v. Kraemer* (1948). Furthermore, federal housing agencies did not challenge segregated housing in the private sector. Both before and after World War II, the Federal Housing Administration (FHA) even had a policy of refusing to insure housing loans that might promote racially mixed housing. Truman proposed a housing bill that contained antidiscrimination provisions, but Congress removed them before passing the legislation in 1949.

Blacks benefited from Truman's social welfare legislation; increases in the minimum wage and the expansion of Social Security to include agricultural workers helped many blacks. But although Truman's housing bill contained provisions for low-income housing and slum clearance, Congress eliminated them.

After the 1948 election, President Truman acknowledged the black community's role in his victory by selecting blacks for significant posts. In October 1949 he selected William H. Hastie for the Third Circuit Court of Appeals, the most important judgeship ever held by a black. The following summer he selected Anthony J. Howard to sit on the Washington, D.C., municipal court. Thanks to these and other judicial appointments by Truman, black judges were no longer such a rare sight in federal courtrooms. Other black appointees included Ambrose Caliver, as assistant commissioner in the Office of Education; Howard University professor Robert P. Barnes to the board of the National Science Foundation; and Edith Sampson as alternate U.S. delegate to the United Nations. Truman's appointees occupied higher levels of authority than blacks had previously reached.

President Truman's Justice Department broke new ground by supporting NAACP positions in several important legal cases. In the Supreme Court, the department successfully argued in *Shelley v. Kraemer* that restrictive covenants were unconstitutional. The Justice Department and the NAACP also argued successfully before the Court against state laws requiring segregation in interstate travel and in higher education. In December 1952, Attorney General James P. McGranery filed a brief against public school segregation in *Brown v. Board of Education of Topeka* (1954), a momentous case decided by the Supreme Court during the Eisenhower administration (see the following section).

Despite these gains, the Truman administration's civil rights record fell far short of the hopes of blacks and their allies. That was because Congress rejected virtually all of the civil rights legislation proposed by the president. It refused to pass his proposals to create an FEPC, to abolish the poll tax, to bar segregated terminals in interstate transportation, to make lynching a federal crime, to ban housing discrimination, and to give home rule to Washington, D.C. Southern Democrats in the Senate often staged filibusters—endless debates—to prevent the full Senate from voting on civil rights bills. Senate rules required a two-thirds majority for "cloture," or a cutoff of debate. Southern Democrats, combined with conservative midwestern and western Republicans, usually could muster enough votes to prevent cloture.

But not all administration defeats can be blamed on filibusters. Truman's Democratic Party included both racist whites from the South and blacks and liberals from the North and West. Trapped within this contradiction, Truman tried to support civil rights without offending the white South. This meant that while he backed civil rights measures with rhetoric, he often did not press Congress very vigorously to pass them. Furthermore, although public opinion was becoming more liberal on racial issues, it still was not ready for great changes. Consequently, the important gains made under Truman represented only a small beginning in the national battle against racial discrimination. It would take a massive, grassroots civil rights movement to generate the political pressure needed to make major strides against racial injustice.

## THE EISENHOWER ADMINISTRATION

Dwight D. Eisenhower, elected president in 1952 and 1956 on the Republican ticket, was less committed than Truman to civil rights progress. Not surprisingly, then, blacks gave Eisenhower's opponent, Democratic candidate Adlai E. Stevenson, almost 75 percent of their votes in 1952 and between 60 and 65 percent in 1956. Also, Eisenhower was the first Republican presidential candidate since 1928 to carry any southern states. Therefore, the new president owed a greater political debt to opponents of civil rights than to blacks.

As a conservative, Eisenhower did not believe that the government should promote rapid social change. Attempts to quickly transform society often led to an unacceptable amount of violence, in his view. He was also skeptical about whether federal laws or force could alter deeply rooted practices such as segregation; he felt that changes of attitude were also required, and that they occurred only gradually. Finally, Eisenhower believed that the federal government should have carefully limited powers and should act only in matters clearly beyond the authority of the states.

Eisenhower was most likely to act when he had unquestionable authority, and when discrimination was highly visible and so could be used by the Soviet Union as cold war propaganda against the United States. His authority was clear in Washington, D.C., a federal district. Furthermore, because official representatives and private citizens from nonwhite countries visited the nation's capital, the existence of segregation there was often an embarrassment to the nation. Therefore, Eisenhower acted against it. Beginning in 1953 he worked with considerable success to root out segregation from the District's schools, government, public accommodations, businesses, and transportation. Segregation in the armed forces was another form of very visible discrimination that clearly came within the authority of the president as commander in chief. Eisenhower acted to complete the military integration process begun by Truman. Blacks continued to face discrimination in the armed services for decades—in assignments and promotions, for example. But by the mid-1950s segregation had just about ended. Eisenhower also integrated southern navy yards and many veterans' hospitals.

In other areas the president was much less vigorous. Believing that the right to vote gave individuals the power to guard all their other rights, Eisenhower sent bills to Congress to protect black voting rights. On the other hand, the shortcomings of those bills showed the president's reluctance to use the full force of federal power. When giving literacy tests to those applying to vote, southern registrars often asked whites easy questions and blacks impossible ones, such as "How many bubbles are in a bar of soap?" The Civil Rights Act of 1957 allowed the Justice Department to sue registrars who discriminated in this and other ways. But the maximum penalty was just a $300 fine or 45 days in jail. The law also allowed the U.S. attorney general to go to court on behalf of individuals being discriminated against. Here lay the bill's basic weakness: it called for attacking the problem in court one case at a time, instead of sending in federal registrars to register voters.

The law also raised the Justice Department's civil rights section to the status of a division, with its own assistant attorney general. Additionally, it created the U.S. Civil Rights Commission to probe charges of racial discrimination of all types and to make reports to the president and Congress.

The administration's Civil Rights Act of 1960 authorized the appointment of referees to help blacks to register and vote. But the process was complicated and slow, involving a series of stages. This led NAACP executive secretary Roy Wilkins to comment that "The Negro has to pass more check points and more officials than he would if he were trying to get the United States gold reserve in Fort Knox. It's a fraud." Not only were these laws weak, but Eisenhower's Justice Department made little effort to use them. It filed only 10 lawsuits under these acts, and referees were employed only twice. As the first civil rights acts since Reconstruction, the laws had symbolic meaning, but not much more.

The president did little else to advance racial equality. For example, he took no important steps against housing discrimination and did not support antidiscrimination amendments to the 1955 housing bill proposed by black New York representative Adam Clayton Powell, Jr. Also, Eisenhower opposed legislation against employment discrimination in the private sector. Instead, he tried to convince individual businesspeople to hire more blacks, with predictably meager results. He also weakened a panel established by Truman to prevent employment discrimination in the federal government.

## *Brown v. Board of Education* and Southern Backlash

But Eisenhower's biggest civil rights failure came in connection with public school integration. Starting in the 1930s, the NAACP won a series of Supreme Court decisions requiring that qualified blacks receive equal (but not necessarily integrated) college educations in state-supported schools. During the late 1940s, the NAACP decided to oppose segregation itself. In 1950 the Supreme Court, in cases known as *Sweatt v. Painter* and *McLaurin v. Oklahoma State Regents*, virtually banned racial separation in state colleges as violating the Fourteenth Amendment's guarantee of equal protection of the laws.

The issue now was whether the Court would apply this principle to public elementary and high schools. In 1952, five cases challenging segregation at the public school level were combined into *Brown v. Board of Education of Topeka*. The southern states, anticipating that school segregation would be challenged, had for years been increasing their spending on black schools. But in the *Brown* case, Thurgood Marshall of the NAACP argued that segregated schools were by their nature unequal. Aside from making legal arguments, Marshall used evidence gathered by black psychologist Kenneth Clark from interviews with southern black schoolchildren. The interviews, Marshall stated, showed that simply by being segregated, these children were made to feel inferior to whites.

In its unanimous May 1954 ruling, written by Chief Justice Earl Warren, the Supreme Court agreed with Marshall. *Brown v. Board of Education* declared that "separate educational facilities are inherently unequal" and therefore violated the Fourteenth Amendment's guarantee of "equal protection of the laws." This reversed the Court's *Plessy v. Ferguson* (1896) decision, which had upheld segregation. The historic *Brown* decision, the most important civil rights ruling of the century, signaled the inevitable death of Jim Crow. In May 1955 the Court issued instructions for carrying out the decision. It placed enforcement in the hands of the federal district courts, which were asked to be flexible and take local conditions into account while moving forward reasonably quickly. ("With all deliberate speed" was the ambiguous phrase used by the Court.)

Eisenhower believed that the *Brown* decision was wrong; it represented exactly the kind of federal interference with long-established customs that he opposed. The president often stated that the ruling was the law of the land and must be obeyed, but he refused to endorse it and was very reluctant to enforce it. In 1956 he declined to support an amendment offered by Representative Powell that would have denied federal loans and grants for building segregated schools. Eisenhower did nothing in February 1956 when the University of Alabama blocked Autherine Lucy from integrating that school, even though the Supreme Court had ruled against segregation at the college level four years before *Brown*. In August 1956 he did not act when Governor Allan Shivers of Texas defied a court order to desegregate a high school in Mansfield, Texas. Finally, in Little Rock, Arkansas, the president took action. There, Governor Orval Faubus's defiance of a court order blocked the integration of Central High School in the autumn 1957 term. Furthermore, his lawlessness encouraged mob violence against the nine black schoolchildren seeking admittance. With great reluctance Eisenhower sent in federal troops, and the school was desegregated.

Eisenhower's hands-off policy encouraged fierce opposition to school desegregation. When Virginia senator Harry S. Byrd called for "massive resistance" to integration, the white South responded. In 1956 Virginia, Alabama, Georgia, Mississippi, South Carolina, and Louisiana declared the *Brown* decision void; North Carolina, Georgia, Mississippi, and Louisiana established penalties for obeying *Brown*; and Virginia, South Carolina, Georgia, Alabama, Mississippi, and Louisiana passed new school segregation laws. In March 1956, 101 of the 128 southerners in Congress signed the Southern Manifesto, in which they vowed to resist school desegregation by all available legal methods.

Some reactions to *Brown* were more extreme. In a direct response to the decision, a White Citizens Council was formed in Mississippi during the summer of 1954. Over the next five years, branches sprang up in nearly every southern city. Sometimes called "Klansmen in suits" by their opponents, the members were mostly middle-class or well-to-do business and professional people. Among other things, they often saw to it that civil rights supporters, black and white, lost their jobs and were denied credit. Meanwhile various Ku Klux Klan organizations sprang up, recruiting members from among the lower and lower-middle classes. Much of the southern violence during the middle and late 1950s was the work of these groups. The Mississippi lynchings of 14-year-old Emmett Till in 1955 and of

Mack Parker in 1959 were signs of the time. The president of the Belzoni, Mississippi, chapter of the NAACP was shot dead on the courthouse steps. Other black leaders were harassed, threatened, and shot at. In 1958 alone, the South experienced 50 bombings of churches, synagogues, and schools.

Southern white backlash, and Eisenhower's failure to respond seriously to it, brought civil rights progress to a crawl. In 1960 only 6.4 percent of southern black schoolchildren went to integrated schools, and in the Deep South the figure was only 0.2 percent (just 1 in 500 children). After *Brown*, the small number of blacks who voted in the Deep South became even smaller as threats and acts of violence became more common.

## Civil Rights Protest

Any southern blacks who wanted to protest injustice faced long odds. They had to deal not only with local hostility and White House inaction, but also with a national political climate unfavorable to any social protest against the status quo. Beginning in the late 1940s, Americans began to worry not just about Soviet Communism but also about real or imagined Communist subversives in the United States itself. Starting in 1950 Senator Joseph R. McCarthy, a Republican from Wisconsin, launched a reckless crusade against supposed Communist subversives at home. In the atmosphere of intimidation created by him and his supporters, critics of any aspect of American society were often suspected of being Communists. As a result, almost all liberal protest groups, including civil rights organizations, lost much of their support.

Yet only a year after the *Brown v. Board of Education* ruling, blacks in Montgomery, Alabama, staged a direct action protest that rocked the South and the nation. On December 1, 1955, Rosa Parks, a black seamstress and an NAACP and community activist, refused to give up her seat to a white man on a Montgomery city bus. Four days later blacks began an organized boycott of the bus system, forming car pools or walking to and from work instead of using public transportation. The leader of the boycott was the 26-year-old Martin Luther King, Jr., pastor of the Dexter Avenue Baptist Church, an Atlanta native who had moved to Montgomery not long before. During the boycott, which lasted just over a year, King displayed extraordinary leadership, aided by the spiritual and moral power of his soaring rhetoric, his strong commitment to social justice, his courage in the face of danger, and the strength that enabled him to rise above petty personal squabbles and to help his followers do the same. Before the boycott he had begun studying the nonviolent philosophy of East Indian independence leader Mohandas K. Gandhi. During the boycott, his understanding of and commitment to nonviolent social action deepened with both his own experience and the guidance of black pacifist Bayard Rustin.

On November 13, 1956, the Supreme Court ordered the desegregation of Montgomery's buses. Seating was to be on a first come, first served basis. This important victory inspired boycotts in Tallahassee and Birmingham. Early in 1957

King and other black ministers formed the Southern Christian Leadership Conference (SCLC) to promote civil rights. Between 1957 and 1960 there were over a dozen sit-ins at segregated southern facilities. Meanwhile, a civil rights protest movement emerged in the North with the revival of CORE in the late 1950s. But direct (as opposed to legal) action did not have enough support in the conservative 1950s to make a great mark on national policy. A May 17, 1957, Prayer Pilgrimage for Freedom in Washington, D.C., illustrated that weakness. King's speech on the theme "Give us the vote" won him national attention, and the 15,000 to 25,000 participants made the rally the largest civil rights demonstration to that time. But the turnout was less than half of that expected and did not impress either Congress or the White House. Major progress would be made only when protests became widespread and continuous, and when friendlier presidents occupied the White House.

# CHAPTER 9

# The Civil Rights Revolution, Black Power, and White Backlash: 1960 –1968

## DIRECT ACTION AND THE NATIONAL CONSCIENCE

On February 1, 1960, four students from North Carolina Agricultural and Technical College, a black school, began a new era in civil rights history when they sat down at a whites-only lunch counter in Greensboro. Refused service, they remained in their seats until closing time. Their simple demand for lunch-counter service sparked a direct action movement against discrimination that brought the civil rights struggle from the courthouses to the streets and revolutionized American race relations.

After Greensboro, a sit-in movement led by black college students spread like wildfire. By the end of February it had reached seven southern states. In April longtime civil rights activist Ella Baker brought the sit-in leaders together in Raleigh, North Carolina. She urged them to form their own grassroots, democratic organization independent of the established civil rights groups, which she felt were too centralized and too dependent on a single leader. The result was the formation of the Student Nonviolent Coordinating Committee (SNCC), a decentralized organization favoring group decision making and encouraging the development of leadership in local black communities. The philosophy of SNCC (pronounced "snick") was based upon the principles of racial equality, integration, and nonviolence. Soon the northern-based CORE, guided by the same beliefs, joined the direct action struggle. Martin Luther King, Jr.'s SCLC helped with financial assistance. The NAACP Legal Defense Fund, which had become a separate

On February 10, 1960, two student demonstrators from St. Augustine College stage a sit-in at a whites-only lunch counter in Raleigh, North Carolina. The white waitresses ignore them.

organization from the NAACP in 1939, provided the demonstrators with legal assistance, while the NAACP lobbied Congress for civil rights legislation.

After 18 months, sit-ins had taken place in all of the southern states and a few northern ones. Participants, who soon included some northern whites, targeted just about any kind of segregated facility, including theaters, churches, swimming pools, retail stores of all types, shopping centers, and drive-in movies. Often the nonviolent demonstrators became targets of white violence; but with the support of economic boycotts, they frequently managed to desegregate their targets.

In the meantime, the 1960 election sent to the White House Democratic senator John F. Kennedy of Massachusetts, who was much more open to black appeals for justice than President Eisenhower had been. During the campaign, Kennedy reached out to blacks in a number of ways. When Martin Luther King, Jr., was jailed in Atlanta in connection with civil rights demonstrations, Kennedy telephoned his wife, Coretta Scott King, to express his concern. Kennedy's brother and adviser, Robert Kennedy, called the judge who had jailed King; the next day the civil rights leader was freed. John Kennedy also visited King's father, a powerful clergyman in Atlanta's black community; expressed support for the sit-ins; and promised to issue an executive order against discrimination in housing built with federal assistance.

The views of the Republican presidential candidate, Vice President Richard M. Nixon, were not much different than Eisenhower's. Not surprisingly, then, about 70 percent of black voters backed Kennedy. Without black support, Kennedy would have lost the states of Michigan, South Carolina, Texas, Pennsylvania, Illinois, and New Jersey, worth 137 electoral votes. Kennedy beat Nixon by only

84 electoral votes and 125,000 popular votes; therefore blacks obviously formed an important part of Kennedy's winning coalition. Yet because his margin was so narrow, Kennedy owed debts to many interests and had to be careful not to offend any of them. Besides, Kennedy's major concern was fighting the cold war against Communism in Berlin, Laos, Vietnam, Cuba, and other world trouble spots. Heavy pressure from the civil rights movement would be needed before the new president would take strong steps against racial discrimination.

Fortunately for the cause of racial equality, the movement was able to keep up its pressure after the election, moving from sit-ins to new forms of direct action. The Supreme Court in *Boynton v. Virginia* (1960) extended earlier rulings against segregation in interstate transportation, declaring that the ban on Jim Crow applied to stations and terminals as well as vehicles. In 1961 CORE decided to make the ruling a reality. It launched a series of "freedom rides," the first of which headed South from Washington, D.C., on May 4, 1961, with seven blacks and six whites aboard two buses. In Rock Hill, South Carolina, black activist John Lewis—later the head of SNCC and eventually a U.S. representative—was badly beaten while attempting to use the bus terminal's whites-only bathroom. At the terminal in Anniston, Alabama, a white mob attacked one of the buses. In Birmingham, Alabama, a Klan-organized crowd assaulted riders with sticks, metal pipes, and fists when they got off the bus; Police Commissioner Eugene "Bull" Connor had agreed in advance to give the Klan 15 minutes to do its dirty work without police interference.

On May 14, 1961, this Greyhound bus carrying freedom riders arrived in Anniston, Alabama. There, a group of whites met the bus and set it afire. Some of the freedom riders, members of the Congress of Racial Equality, wait outside the bus.

To President Kennedy and his brother Robert, the U.S. attorney general, the freedom rides came as an unwelcome distraction from foreign policy matters. But whether they liked it or not, the freedom riders became front-page news around the world after Birmingham. Following another attack on them at the Montgomery, Alabama, bus terminal, Robert Kennedy ordered about 600 federal marshals to that city. Other groups, including SNCC and King's SCLC, began conducting freedom rides; they received better federal protection than had the first riders. Finally, in September 1961 Robert Kennedy asked the Interstate Commerce Commission to begin carrying out the Court's 1960 ruling against segregated facilities in interstate transportation. During the following months, the Justice Department had all Jim Crow bus terminal signs taken down, and by the end of 1962 segregation in interstate transportation had just about disappeared.

The wave of civil rights activities continued to sweep the South through the early and mid-1960s, forcing the federal government to stay involved in the struggle for equality. In 1962 James Meredith won a court order permitting him to become the first black student at the University of Mississippi at Oxford. But on September 20, 1962, Governor Ross Barnett personally blocked Meredith from entering the school. Ten days later hundreds of federal marshals protected Meredith when he moved into a campus dormitory. That sparked rioting by white students and outsiders, forcing President Kennedy to federalize the Mississippi National Guard and send in thousands of army troops for what became a two-day battle with the mob. He also went on television to urge Mississippians to obey the law. Soon peace was restored at the now-integrated university.

Under growing pressure from the civil rights movement and its allies, the president in November 1962 finally carried out his campaign promise to issue an executive order banning discrimination in the sale or rental of federally financed housing. But because the order did not include privately financed housing, it covered less than 20 percent of all residences.

## Martin Luther King, Jr., Leads the Struggle

By the start of the 1960s, Martin Luther King, Jr., was the generally acknowledged leader of the nonviolent, direct action campaign for civil rights. Building upon grassroots organizing work done by SNCC activists, and assisted by other southern black ministers in the SCLC—including Ralph Abernathy, Wyatt Tee Walker, Andrew Young, James Bevel, C. T. Vivian, Fred Shuttlesworth, and Jesse Jackson—he conducted nonviolent campaigns throughout the Lower South aimed primarily at segregation. King and other advocates of nonviolent protest had a basically optimistic view of humankind. They believed that the sight of racists beating people who did not fight back would arouse the conscience of the nation. It would, they felt, make Americans painfully aware of the hatred and violence that lay at the heart of racism. Then, having becoming aware, the nation would demand change.

One of King's early campaigns took place in Albany, Georgia, beginning in December 1961, when he and the SCLC were invited by the local Albany

Movement. Laurie Pritchett, the sheriff in Albany, understood King's strategy. Avoiding all violence in public, he made mass arrests of demonstrators in the hope of exhausting the movement. Once in prison, demonstrators were mistreated and some were beaten, but this happened out of the view of reporters and cameras. When King himself went to jail, Pritchett prevented him from becoming a martyr by arranging for his release. By the end of 1962, the Albany struggle had ended in failure.

But King applied the lessons of Albany to his next target, which was Birmingham, Alabama. He chose that city for several reasons. Birmingham was a symbol of white racism at its most extreme. Many bombings against civil rights targets had occurred there since the late 1950s, and King called it the most segregated city in America. Also, because of the city's larger size, King could create a bigger confrontation there than in Albany; this would increase the chances of arousing northern opinion and forcing President Kennedy to act against discrimination. Finally, King knew that Bull Connor, Birmingham's hot-tempered police commissioner, had neither the intelligence nor the self-control of Sheriff Pritchett.

King's campaign began on April 3, 1963. Participants demanded desegregation and equal employment opportunity through marches, rallies, sit-ins, and boycotts. At first the police avoided violence, although they began making arrests after a court banned demonstrations. King, one of those arrested, wrote his famous "Letter from a Birmingham Jail." He did so in response to white moderates who sympathized with his goals but criticized his methods for often being illegal and for creating tension between the races. On the matter of legality, King said there was a higher moral law that required the use of nonviolent civil disobedience against the great evil of segregation. As for racial tension, he wrote:

> We who engage in nonviolent direct action are not the creators of tension. We merely bring to the surface the hidden tension that is already alive. We bring it out in the open, where it can be seen and dealt with. . . . Injustice must be exposed . . . to the light of human conscience and the air of national opinion before it can be cured.

Soon after his release from jail, King raised the stakes of confrontation by including children in the marches. A crisis finally came on May 3, when Connor ordered the police to use high-pressure fire hoses, nightsticks, and dogs against demonstrators—adults and youngsters alike. In retaliation, young men from poor black neighborhoods came downtown to throw objects at the police. Birmingham's white leaders were frightened. On May 10, white businesspeople agreed to desegregate their premises.

The agreement itself represented a limited advance, but the Birmingham movement had a much deeper impact. Television film of the police brutality shocked most white Americans outside of the South—and some white southerners as well—just as King had hoped. As a result, public support for major civil rights legislation soared. Other forms of southern resistance to change further strengthened that support. In his inaugural address early in 1963, Governor George Wallace of Alabama declared "Segregation now! Segregation tomorrow! Segregation forever!" Then, on June 11, just a month after the Birmingham violence, Wallace symbolically "stood in the schoolhouse door" at the University of Alabama at Tuscaloosa to stop two blacks from registering. President Kennedy used Wallace's action as the opportunity to make a major television address to the nation. He denounced racial discrimination and stated that the era of mere token concessions to blacks was over; federal, state, and local authorities, he argued, must act. On June 19 he sent to Congress the strongest civil rights legislation since Reconstruction. It attacked segregation, employment discrimination, and discrimination in programs receiving federal support.

Like Wallace's schoolhouse stand, acts of southern violence increased northern support for civil rights. On the same night that Kennedy went on television, the nation was startled to hear that the NAACP's field secretary in Mississippi, Medgar Evers, had been shot in the back and killed on the front lawn of his home in Jackson, the state capital. Arousing even more disgust was the bombing of the Sixteenth Street Baptist Church in Birmingham on September 15, which killed four black girls.

## The March on Washington, D.C.

In the meantime, civil rights supporters from around the country gathered in Washington, D.C., on August 28, 1963, for a monumental demonstration called the March on Washington for Jobs and Freedom. It was initiated by A. Philip Randolph and organized by Bayard Rustin. Randolph's roots were in the labor movement, so the march was originally intended to be a demonstration for a massive federal job-creation program as much as for civil rights. To maximize support, however, the planners increasingly focused on racial equality, and in particular on Kennedy's civil rights bill. Much of the nation was now in sympathy with the cause of racial justice, and backing poured in from labor, civic, ethnic, and other groups. The White House, which had originally opposed the march for fear of violence, reversed itself after march organizers dropped early plans for civil disobedience and made other changes. Over 200,000 blacks, whites, and Hispanics gathered on August 28 at the Washington Monument and marched to the Lincoln Memorial for the largest rally held in the nation's capital to that time.

Except for James Farmer of CORE, who was in a Louisiana jail, the top civil rights leaders all spoke: Randolph, leader of the Brotherhood of Sleeping Car Porters and an AFL-CIO vice president; King of the SCLC; Wilkins of the NAACP; Whitney Young of the National Urban League; and John Lewis of SNCC. (Lewis reluctantly modified his original fiery speech to keep Washington, D.C., Catholic archbishop Patrick O'Boyle on the program.) So did Walter Reuther, president of the United Auto Workers, and other white speakers.

King's address became one of the most famous orations in American history. Using the words "I have a dream" as a theme, King eloquently described his vision of a prejudice-free nation and then ended the speech with the cry of a black spiritual: "Free at last! Free at last! Thank God almighty, we are free at last!"

Whether or not the speech or the rally swayed any members of Congress in favor of Kennedy's civil rights bill is not known. But the gathering was perhaps the most inspiring day of the civil rights movement.

## CIVIL RIGHTS GAINS AND SOCIAL WELFARE LEGISLATION

Inspiration gave way to deep concern when President Kennedy was assassinated less than three months later, on November 22, 1963. Vice President Lyndon B. Johnson of Texas succeeded him. As Senate majority leader in the 1950s, Johnson had worked successfully to defeat or water down civil rights legislation. Would he now kill Kennedy's civil rights bill from the White House? This fear proved unwarranted: Johnson had changed with the times and was fully committed to the measure. Instead of weakening it, he got it strengthened. His superb persuasive skills, along with pressure from the now-powerful civil rights lobby in Washington, D.C., led by the NAACP's Clarence Mitchell, secured passage of the bill on July 2, 1964.

The Civil Rights Act of 1964 was the broadest and strongest civil rights legislation since Reconstruction. The act prohibited segregation and other forms of discrimination in public accommodations such as restaurants, lunch counters, hotels and motels, theaters and movie houses, sports arenas, and concert halls. The law also barred segregation in state and locally owned facilities and gave the attorney general new powers to end school desegregation—most importantly, the power to withhold federal funds from segregated school systems. Despite strong southern resistance, progress in desegregation was much faster after the act than before. The law also outlawed job discrimination by employers, labor unions, and employment agencies and created the Equal Employment Opportunity Commission (EEOC) to investigate charges of discrimination. (This section of the act protected women as well as minorities.) Another key and very controversial provision of the law required a cutoff of all federal aid to any program or activity that practiced discrimination.

### Voting Rights

Also, the Civil Rights Act of 1964 promoted voting rights by requiring that literacy tests be conducted in writing and declaring that a sixth-grade education was adequate proof of literacy. But civil rights groups wanted stronger action, specifically the dispatch of federal registrars to the South to enroll black voters. Because advocates of equality believed that the right to vote was the foundation for other rights, attempts to register black voters in the South became a key part of the direct-action campaigns of the early 1960s.

In 1961 SNCC's field staff, led by a black mathematics student at Harvard named Bob Moses, began doing civil rights work in the most dangerous areas of the rural Deep South. Soon SNCC's major goal was enrolling black voters—by April 1962, it had joined with CORE, SCLC, the NAACP, and the Urban League in the Voter Education Project. The most difficult challenge was rural Mississippi; there the civil rights groups worked together as the Council of Federated Organizations (COFO). But because of intimidation and violence, only about 4,000 blacks had been added to Mississippi's voting rolls by the summer of 1964. To speed things up, Moses organized the Mississippi Freedom Summer project in 1964, which brought hundreds of northern white and black college students to the state to help blacks register. SNCC leaders wanted the students to participate not just because they needed more fieldworkers; they also believed, correctly, that attacks against middle-class northern whites by local racists would attract more national attention than assaults against blacks.

As they often did, the racists soon obliged with mindless violence. On June 21, 1964, three civil rights workers disappeared near Philadelphia, Mississippi: James Chaney, a black from Mississippi, and Michael Schwerner and Andrew Goodman, whites from New York. Almost immediately, national and worldwide attention focused on the state. On August 4, FBI agents found the bodies of the three close

The Reverend Martin Luther King, Jr., addresses CORE and SNCC workers outside the Democratic National Convention in Atlantic City, New Jersey, on August 24, 1964. Behind him are posters of the three civil rights workers recently murdered in Philadelphia, Mississippi. From left to right, Andrew Goodman of New York, James Chaney of Mississippi, and Michael Schwerner of New York.

to Philadelphia. Although Neshoba County deputy sheriff Cecil Price was clearly involved, no convictions were possible from local all-white juries.

The killings shocked most of the nation. But further developments would be necessary before Congress enacted new and stronger voting rights legislation. One thing that helped was President Johnson's overwhelming victory in the November 1964 election. Against conservative Republican senator Barry M. Goldwater, who had voted against the Civil Rights Act of 1964, Johnson received a record 61 percent of the total vote, including more than 95 percent of black ballots. Goldwater carried only the Deep South states of Louisiana, Mississippi, Alabama, Georgia, and South Carolina, plus his home state of Arizona. The results showed that the Deep South was out of touch with the national political mood and gave Johnson a mandate to move forward in civil rights matters.

Martin Luther King, Jr., provided the final political push needed to pass new voting rights legislation. In 1963 SNCC began a voter registration campaign in Selma, Alabama, where blacks made up over half the population but only about 2 percent of the registered voters. In January 1965—one month after receiving the Nobel Peace Prize—King became involved in the Selma campaign. As in Birmingham, he hoped for a large-scale confrontation that would arouse the nation's conscience. Just as Bull Connor's brutality had helped King to expose the ugliness of racism in Birmingham, Sheriff Jim Clark of Dallas County unintentionally helped King in Selma. On January 22 he personally beat a black woman who was trying to register to vote. Arrests and beatings of voters and peaceful demonstrators occurred during the weeks that followed.

On March 7, 1965, the authorities made their biggest mistake. Demonstrators gathered on the Selma side of the Edmund Pettus Bridge to begin a 50-mile voting rights march to Montgomery, the capital of Alabama. Colonel Al Lingo's Alabama state troopers were on the other side to block their way. The marchers started crossing the bridge; when ordered to go back to town, they stopped but refused to turn around. Suddenly, the troopers charged forward, beating and trampling the protestors, who now began running back toward Selma. An outraged nation saw all of the events of "Bloody Sunday" on television. A second march took demonstrators to the Edmund Pettus Bridge again. But this time King had arranged with the authorities to turn the marchers back after they reached the bridge, which he did over the protests of militant young SNCC activists. Finally, and with federal protection, the Selma-to-Montgomery march was held from March 21 through March 25. By the end, some 50,000 political leaders, celebrities, and ordinary Americans from around the country had joined in.

President Johnson had not planned to introduce any additional civil rights legislation until 1966. But the events in Selma changed the political climate and made immediate action possible. On March 15 the president went before Congress, urging it to pass a voting rights bill. To show his commitment to racial justice, Johnson at the end of his speech said, "We shall overcome." Many supporters of racial justice, watching the speech on television, wept as the president spoke these words, which were from the anthem of the civil rights movement.

Congress passed the Voting Rights Act of 1965 on August 4. The law met the major demand of civil rights supporters by authorizing the use of federal voting examiners in the South. Their job was to determine who was eligible to vote in elections at all levels and in party primaries. After doing this, the examiners could require state or local officials to enroll all those found qualified. Examiners could be sent wherever literacy tests were used as a voting qualification and less than 50 percent of eligible voters were registered. This meant that they could be used in Alabama, Virginia, South Carolina, Georgia, Mississippi, Louisiana, and 26 counties of North Carolina. (In the 1970s the law was rewritten to include some parts of the North, but its coverage was still mostly in the South.) Also, the federal government could send observers to the polling places in these states to see if discrimination was occurring. Furthermore, literacy and similar tests were suspended in those states and counties—a sixth-grade education was a valid substitute for such tests. In addition, no voting or election laws passed in those states and counties would go into effect until approved by the U.S. attorney general. In addition, the law directed the attorney general to challenge in federal court the use of poll taxes as a voting qualification in state and local elections. (In 1964 the states had ratified the Twenty-fourth Amendment to the Constitution, which banned payment of a poll tax as a requirement for voting in federal elections but did not apply to state or local voting.)

## Desegregation, Voter Registration, and Public Officeholding

The civil rights legislation passed under President Johnson tore down some of the major barriers to racial equality. The Civil Rights Act of 1964 led to the death of Jim Crow. The threat of losing federal aid under the act forced the South to desegregate its schools. In 1964 only 2 percent of the black students in the 11 states of the old Confederacy went to integrated schools. By 1968 the figure was 20 percent. Two years later over 90 percent of all southern school systems were desegregated, although many schools had only a handful of blacks or whites and strong resistance continued. The desegregation of public accommodations such as stores, hotels, restaurants, and transportation vehicles proceeded quickly over these years.

The Voting Rights Act of 1965 created a political revolution. From 1964 to 1969 the proportion of eligible blacks registered to vote increased from 27 percent to 60 percent in Georgia, from 19 percent to 61 percent in Alabama, from 7 percent to 67 percent in Mississippi, and from 32 percent to 61 percent in Louisiana. In the South overall, more than two-thirds of eligible blacks were on the voting rolls by 1970. Southern candidates now had to court black as well as white voters to win elections.

Blacks were also gaining greater influence in northern politics. As southern farmers replaced black labor with machinery, over a million blacks moved to northern cities during the 1950s and again during the 1960s. Because of this, and

Black plantation workers in a field at Ita Bena, Mississippi, in June 1966.
In the background a group of civil rights marchers walks by, encouraging blacks
to register and vote under the Voting Rights Act of 1965.

also because whites were moving from the cities to the suburbs, blacks were becoming a majority or near majority in many urban centers. In addition, the civil rights movement inspired an increase in black voter turnout. The movement could also take credit for a decline in white prejudice, which meant that some whites became more willing to vote for black candidates.

After the 1968 election, a record nine blacks sat in the House of Representatives, eight from the North and one from Missouri, a border state. In 1968 Shirley Chisholm of Brooklyn became the first black woman ever elected to the House. Two years earlier Republican Edward Brooke had become the first black elected to the U.S. Senate since Reconstruction; he was elected from Massachusetts, where blacks made up just 3 percent of the population. In 1967 Carl B. Stokes of Cleveland and Richard B. Hatcher of Gary, Indiana, became the first two blacks elected as mayors of major cities. In both North and South, the number of elected black officeholders skyrocketed. In 1964 about 100 blacks held elective office around the nation; in 1970, the figure was nearly 1,500.

Presidents Kennedy and Johnson appointed more blacks to federal posts than had any previous chief executive, some of them at the highest levels ever. Kennedy made Thurgood Marshall the first black to sit on New York's Second Circuit Court, the most influential of the federal appeals courts. Kennedy also chose six black judges for various district courts. Robert Weaver became head of the Housing and Home Finance Agency, George Weaver was picked as assistant secretary of labor, and Carl T. Rowan was appointed deputy assistant secretary of state. Blacks were chosen as ambassadors to Finland and Norway.

President Johnson chose Marshall as solicitor general in 1965 and in 1967 as the first black to sit on the Supreme Court. Constance Baker Motley became the first black woman to serve as a federal judge. Johnson selected Robert Weaver as the first secretary of the new Department of Housing and Urban Development in 1966, making Weaver the first black cabinet member. Rowan became director of the U.S. Information Agency. Andrew F. Brimmer became the first black to serve as a governor of the Federal Reserve Board, and Hobart Taylor was the first black on the board of the Export-Import Bank.

## Help for the Poor

President Johnson steered many liberal social spending programs through Congress—far more than any president since Franklin D. Roosevelt. Like Roosevelt's New Deal programs, they mostly benefited Americans earning below-average incomes and so were of special help to blacks. As part of his Great Society program, as he called it, Johnson secured passage of Medicare in 1965 and Medicaid in 1966; they provided health benefits for the elderly and poor, respectively. Starting with the Elementary and Secondary Education Act of 1965, Johnson increased federal aid to education, especially to schools attended by children of the poor. His Model Cities program, enacted in 1966, tried to improve the general well-being of poor people living in slums.

In January 1964 Johnson declared "an unconditional war on poverty"; in August, Congress passed his Economic Opportunity Act, the centerpiece of his War on Poverty. The act created many of Johnson's key antipoverty progams as well as the Office of Economic Opportunity (OEO) to manage them. The Job Corps offered vocational training for poor youngsters. The Neighborhood Youth Corps gave poor youths part-time work so they could stay in school. Johnson greatly expanded a food stamp program begun in 1961 to help poor people buy the basic necessities of life. In the late 1960s, Head Start provided preschool education for more than 2 million children from disadvantaged homes. A Legal Services program made lawyers available to the poor. Community Action Programs encouraged the poor to mobilize politically at the local level.

President Johnson's Great Society and War on Poverty programs, the equal employment provision of the Civil Rights Act of 1964, and the general prosperity of the decade helped many blacks to improve their economic standing. In 1960, 57 percent of all blacks lived below the poverty line; by the end of the 1960s, the proportion was down to 33 percent. Black income increased faster than white income.

## OBSTACLES TO PROGRESS

Starting in the mid-1960s, a growing number of blacks began to reject the goal of integration and the strategy of nonviolence. New, angry black leaders appeared on the scene, denouncing white Americans, including liberals, as incurable racists with no intention of ever accepting blacks as equals. They believed that the pursuit of integration would require blacks to abandon their own identity to enter an American mainstream that did not really want them. Instead, the new voices asserted, blacks should work together to build their self-pride, their own economy, and their own communities. Finally, they believed blacks must go beyond the two major strategies being used to attack racism: seeking legal redress in the courts and engaging in nonviolent direct action. The legal strategy assumed that the nation's judicial system was basically fair; the direct action strategy assumed that the consciences of whites could be moved. But the new black voices rejected both assumptions, and so many of them—although not all—argued that blacks must "use any means necessary," including violence, to defeat racism.

Many Americans, and especially white liberals, were shocked as a growing number of blacks (although a minority) voiced these views. How, they asked, could blacks express such anger toward American society just when they were making major progress? Wasn't the civil rights movement tearing down the walls of legalized discrimination? Weren't blacks finding greater acceptance in white society? Wasn't the average black improving his or her economic well-being?

There were many reasons for the seeming contradiction between growing progress and growing anger. The same pattern has occurred often in modern history. When long-oppressed groups finally start to win their rights, they often expect to win total victory very quickly; this is known as the "revolution of rising expectations." But when they realize that complete victory will not come immediately, frustration and bitterness set in. Another reason is that many blacks had long believed that the fight for freedom had two parts: the struggle for legal equality, which was fought by the NAACP and the other civil rights organizations; and the struggle to develop self-pride, cultural identity, and black institutions, as expressed by Booker T. Washington and Marcus Garvey. Once major progress had been achieved in the fight for legal equality, it was natural that many blacks would turn to the task of defining and developing themselves. There are many other explanations as well, a large number of them linked to the problems of northern blacks in particular.

### Northern Bias

The North was a breeding ground for black nationalism. The victories of the civil rights movement did not greatly change the lives of northern blacks. Jim Crow had never been as strong in the North as in the South; anyway, it had been on the decline in the northern states since the end of World War II. Furthermore, northern blacks had long been free to vote.

But the problems that northern blacks *did* have—including poverty, unemployment, and poor housing—required a far larger commitment of resources than the War on Poverty provided, and so proved much more difficult to eliminate than Jim Crow and voting discrimination. This caused northern blacks great frustration, leading many of them to question the willingness of even liberal whites to help them. With regard to housing, the federal government sponsored many urban renewal projects after World War II that replaced dilapidated slums with better housing. But often the poor blacks who had lived in the demolished or renovated slum buildings could not afford to live in the new housing. Another urban renewal practice replaced slums with office buildings or other public structures (such as Lincoln Center for the Performing Arts in New York City, which displaced many thousands of slum dwellers). Blacks often commented that "urban renewal equals Negro removal."

In the decades after the war, millions of southern blacks flocked to northern cities. At the same time, millions of middle- and working-class whites left those cities for suburban towns that kept blacks out. Between 1960 and 1970, for example, the black population of the 34 largest U.S. cities increased by 2.9 million, while their white population went down by 1.9 million. And during the same decade, the white population of the suburbs surrounding those 34 cities increased by 12.5 million; in the same suburbs, racial discrimination kept the increase in black population down to 800,000. Many whites moved to the suburbs simply because postwar prosperity made it possible for them to afford their own homes for the first time. But many others were anxious to leave the cities because blacks were moving in. This pattern was known as "white flight." Because the disappearing whites included liberals as well as conservatives, supporters of civil rights as well as opponents, some blacks claimed that their white allies were hypocrites who talked one way but lived another.

Restrictive covenants were on the decline by the 1960s, but there were many other ways to separate black and white housing. Real estate brokers practiced racial steering, showing blacks housing only in black or in "changing" neighborhoods. This was perhaps the most common discriminatory practice. The brokers also engaged in blockbusting. First they moved a black person or family into an all-white neighborhood. Then they spread rumors that more blacks were moving in. Whites, fearing a sharp decline in the value of their homes, sold to the brokers at a low price. The brokers then sold to blacks at a high price; middle-class blacks paid it because discrimination made finding homes difficult. Soon, the neighborhood was all black. Many states and cities had exclusionary zoning regulations that limited low-income housing to poor neighborhoods. Also, banks often used a practice called redlining, which limited housing loans to certain geographic areas and made it difficult for people in black neighborhoods to obtain mortgages.

Some states and cities outlawed housing discrimination. But they did not have enough personnel and other resources for effective enforcement. In 1968 the Johnson administration pushed through the Fair Housing Act. Unlike President Kennedy's executive order of 1962, it banned discrimination by private lending institutions, such as the real estate industry and banks, as well as by government agencies. Therefore, it covered 80 percent of all housing instead of the 20 percent covered by Kennedy's order. Still, it was a weak measure. It failed to define clearly just what practices were illegal. Also, it did not authorize the Department of Housing and Urban Development to order an end to discriminatory practices. Instead, the act required either the individuals claiming discrimination or the Justice Department to file lawsuits in federal court. This was a much more difficult and time-consuming process. Overall, the act simply was not up to the hard task of combating housing bias.

The North's response to school integration strengthened the feeling of many blacks that northern whites were hypocrites on racial matters. A strong majority of northern whites favored the integration of southern schools. But northern schools were another matter. When talk began in the mid-1960s about busing northern schoolchildren outside their neighborhoods to achieve integration, the great majority of whites were opposed. They argued that in the South, separate schools for the races had been intentionally created by law, whereas in the North, school segregation resulted from segregated housing patterns. Some whites believed that this distinction was significant; others simply did not want their young children to be transported by bus or did not want their children to go anywhere but to familiar neighborhood schools. But still others did not want their children to attend schools with large numbers of blacks, especially poor blacks. Whites argued that schools should be organized on a community basis; they said that integration would occur naturally once housing discrimination ended. But an end to housing discrimination was nowhere in sight, and blacks rejected that argument. The busing issue would heat up more when the Supreme Court in 1968 specifically authorized busing as a way of speeding up school integration.

## Unemployment and Black Households

Despite the economic progress made by some blacks during the 1960s, blacks overall lagged far behind whites. In 1969 blacks still earned well under two-thirds of white income. Black unemployment declined but remained nearly double the white rate. Besides, the number of permanently unemployed blacks was growing. As we have seen, many whites left the northern cities as southern blacks poured into them. A large number of companies followed whites into the new suburbs, from which blacks often were unofficially barred. In 1945 nearly 70 percent of all industrial jobs were in the cities; in 1970 the figure was down to 40 percent. As a result, many poor urban blacks could not reach manufacturing jobs. Furthermore, industrial automation—replacing workers with machines—was eliminating many of those jobs. It also created new jobs, but those required more skills than the jobs that were wiped out—skills that poor, uneducated blacks did not have. The consequences were felt mostly by young blacks—the unemployment rate for young nonwhites grew from less than 25 percent in 1960 to 29 percent in 1970. But even worse, a growing number of young blacks—especially those without much education—now had little hope of *ever* finding work.

Black men with little chance of employment often left their families, encouraged by rules that made women and their children ineligible for welfare when a husband or boyfriend lived at home. Many of these unemployed men never got married, because they could not support a family; this left many poor black women without marriage partners. As a consequence, the proportion of nonwhite families headed by a female grew from around 18 percent in 1950 to about 28 percent in 1970. Female-headed households were more likely to be poor than male-headed households—in 1967 the average full-time female black worker earned $63 a week, compared to $90 a week for the typical black male. Therefore, many black families, especially those headed by women, were trapped in poverty with almost no chance to escape. This growing group of blacks would later become known as the inner-city black underclass. This development further dashed the hopes aroused among northern blacks by the civil rights movement—for many of them, things seemed to be getting worse, not better.

## Antipoverty Cutbacks and the Vietnam War

President Johnson's Great Society and War on Poverty programs gave valuable assistance to poor blacks. But not enough funding was provided to make a great difference for most of them. The Office of Economic Opportunity—which ran most antipoverty programs—spent an average of only $70 a year on each poor person. Funding was highest in 1964, the first year of the antipoverty effort. Cutbacks began in 1965, largely because of an increasingly expensive U.S. military effort to prevent a Communist takeover of South Vietnam.

As the war in Southeast Asia escalated, U.S. military presence in Vietnam grew, reaching 500,000 by 1968. Segregation had been eliminated in the armed services, but discrimination continued—in 1967, for example, blacks made up more than 13 percent of the army's enlisted men but only 3.4 percent of its officers. Also, for many reasons blacks were more likely than whites to serve. A major one was that most blacks had no chance to go to college and so were not eligible for the student draft deferments obtained by many whites. As a consequence, blacks were more likely than whites to end up in Vietnam. When they got there, they were more likely than whites to be assigned to combat—20 percent of the draftees in combat were black. Part of the reason was that blacks, who had fewer educational opportunities than whites, scored lower on army tests. That prevented them from getting assigned to desk jobs. But even comparing blacks and whites who scored the same on the tests, blacks were more likely to end up in combat—therefore, racism seems to have been a factor in assigning draftees. For these reasons, more than 22 percent of the army's dead and injured were black as of late 1966. This fueled yet more resentment among blacks.

## BLACK POWER

Black anger and disillusionment with American society was bound to make itself felt at the political level. Some of the first symptoms appeared in the South. In

1964 black activists in Mississippi formed the biracial Mississippi Freedom Democratic Party (MFDP) to challenge white racists for control of the regular Mississippi Democratic organization. Led by NAACP state chairman Aaron Henry, grassroots activist Fannie Lou Hamer, white minister Ed King, and others, an MFDP delegation challenged the state's white racist delegates to the Democratic National Convention in August 1964. But President Johnson did not want to offend southern whites in an election year. Backed by most white liberal leaders in the Democratic Party, he agreed to seat only two of the MFDP delegates—and they would be at-large delegates, not members of the Mississippi delegation. The MFDP rejected this arrangement.

President Johnson, Vice President Hubert Humphrey, a long-time civil rights supporter, and other liberal leaders said that to win elections and accomplish anything in politics, compromises were necessary. But many black civil rights activists were angry and began to question the sincerity of their white allies in the civil rights coalition. These liberals, it seemed to them, were more interested in keeping the support of southern white racists than in sticking with civil rights principles. Therefore, some blacks asked, Why not scrap political alliances with these false friends? Why not, instead, force whites to deal seriously with blacks by building up black power outside of the mainstream political system? Since blacks were only 11 percent of the national population and a minority in every state, it was not clear how far this approach could take them. But in March 1966 Stokely Carmichael and other SNCC leaders began an all-black political party in Alabama, officially called the Lowndes County Freedom Organization but also known as the Black Panther Party because of its symbol. It ran an all-black slate of candidates in the county, which was 80 percent black. (They lost as a result of election fraud.)

In May 1966 Carmichael defeated John Lewis for the leadership of SNCC. For some time, Carmichael had been questioning the value of white alliances, and he had already rejected nonviolence. The following month during a civil rights march in Mississippi, he began using the slogan "black power." This quickly became headline news, because everyone sensed that the slogan reflected a new attitude among some blacks. "Black power" was a vague term. Some of its supporters said it simply meant that blacks would now build up their own communities and institutions and then seek alliances with whites on better terms. But many black power advocates went farther, often describing themselves as black nationalists. They felt that white America could not rid itself of racism, and that therefore blacks should live as much as possible apart from whites, instead of trying to integrate into white society. They advocated self-determination and self-development through the creation of black political, economic, and cultural institutions. The most extreme black power advocates were black separatists, who favored the formation of a black nation. Some black power supporters advocated violence, others did not. But most rejected integration, and so also rejected the civil rights coalition of blacks and white liberals. Not surprisingly, SNCC expelled its last white members in December 1966.

## The Spread of Black Discontent

Although born in the Deep South, the cry of black power got its warmest welcome in the northern ghettos, where despair and anger were strongest. Years before Carmichael was born, a Chicago-based black organization called the Nation of Islam was preaching an unorthodox brand of Islam and calling for the creation of a separate black nation. The Nation of Islam was founded in Detroit around 1930 by an Arab merchant, Wadi Farrad. After Farrad died in 1934, Elijah Muhammad—originally named Elijah Poole—became its leader. Muhammad regarded whites as "blue-eyed devils" who had enslaved blacks, the superior race. He claimed that whites had invented Christianity to keep blacks under control by making them meek, obedient, and nonviolent.

The Nation of Islam, Muhammad claimed, would teach blacks to follow the true religion of Allah; to take pride in their superiority over whites; to defend themselves from white violence by striking back if necessary; to build black businesses and strengthen black communities through discipline and hard work; and eventually to carve out a nation from the United States. The Nation of Islam's approach attracted some middle-class blacks; they could imagine themselves as leaders of the new black nation. But the Black Muslims appealed most to the poorest, least educated, and often angriest blacks—those who felt they had no hope of achieving any kind of success and self-respect in a white-dominated world. Those least hopeful about their future were black convicts, and it was in the prisons where the Muslims had their greatest recruiting success.

The most famous prison convert was Malcolm Little, a pimp, thief, and drug dealer who became Malcolm X after his conversion. (The "X" that Malcolm and other Black Muslims used represented their unknown African family names.) Elijah Muhammad regarded Malcolm as his most brilliant follower and appointed him the leader of Harlem's Mosque Number 7 in the early 1950s. A decade later Malcolm brought national attention to the Muslims with his attacks on the southern civil rights movement. He claimed that any blacks who believed whites would accept them as equals were "insane," and he scorned civil rights activists for being nonviolent in a country where violence was the rule.

Malcolm and Elijah Muhammad had a falling out in 1963. After a pilgrimage to Mecca and conversion to orthodox Islam, Malcolm abandoned his sweeping damnation of all whites and formed his own black nationalist organization, the Organization for Afro-American Unity, in March 1964. A man of deep yet controlled and dignified anger, Malcolm was a mesmerizing speaker who expressed the rage of northern blacks better than anyone of his era. Although he was assassinated in 1965 at age 39, apparently on the orders of the Nation of Islam leadership, his *Autobiography of Malcolm X* (1964) would become the bible of most supporters of black power and black nationalism.

Black rage spread far beyond the ranks of the Black Muslims during the middle and late 1960s. The growing dissatisfaction of northern blacks was expressed in various ways. In every year from 1964 through 1968, many northern cities and towns experienced major black riots. These were different from the old race riots in which whites attacked blacks. The riots of the 1960s were begun by blacks and occurred in black neighborhoods. The violence was directed especially at white-owned property and symbols of white authority, such as police personnel and firefighters. As the riots spread through the North, civil rights expressions like "We shall overcome" and "Black and white together" gave way to shouts of "Burn, baby, burn" and "Kill Whitey."

The worst riot of 1964 occurred in Harlem. But that disturbance would seem small compared to the enormous riot in August 1965—a few days after President Johnson signed the Voting Rights Act—in the Watts section of Los Angeles. Over six days, 34 were killed and more than 1,000 injured. Property damage came to $35 million. Some 14,000 National Guardsmen were needed to stop the violence. In 1966 smaller outbreaks erupted in Cleveland, Chicago, Atlanta, and 35 other cities and towns. The summer of 1967 was marked by two huge riots. The worst violence since Watts occurred in Newark, with 23 killed during six days in July 1967. A little more than a week later Detroit erupted. After a week of rioting, 43 were dead and more than 2,000 injured in the largest race riot since the New York City Draft Riots of 1863. Eleven were killed in a Cleveland riot in 1968. In many of the riots, careless gunfire from police and National Guardsmen contributed to the bloodshed.

In the early and mid-1960s, equal rights advocates had felt great optimism over the gains they were making. But partly because of the riots, much of that optimism had changed to anxiety about race relations by the late 1960s. The National Advisory Commission on Civil Disorders, known as the Kerner Commission, investigated the riots. In its 1968 report, the panel found that white racism was their major cause and concluded that America was "moving toward two societies, one black, one white—separate and unequal."

## Political and Cultural Nationalism

Declining faith in America meant the spread of black nationalism. The northern-based CORE shifted its approach from integration to black "self-determination" after Floyd McKissick replaced James Farmer as its national director in January 1966. That year the organization officially declared that it was no longer committed to integration or nonviolence, and McKissick called nonviolence a "dying philosophy." McKissick did not exclude the possibility of alliances with whites, but the organization removed its remaining white members in 1967. In 1968 Roy Innis, even more committed to a nationalist approach than McKissick, became CORE's leader. Beginning in the late 1960s, blacks held a number of national black power conferences. The first was the July 1967 Black Power Conference in Newark, New Jersey, with more than 1,000 in attendance. It called for division of the United States into two nations, one white and one black.

The black power movement also expressed itself through community-based groups that sought black control of ghetto institutions. In 1968 black playwright and poet Imamu Amiri Baraka (formerly named LeRoi Jones) founded the Black Community Development and Defense organization in Newark. Among other things, it tried to increase black political power in Newark by electing black candidates (although Baraka's ultimate goal was violent revolution against white America). In 1970 Baraka played an important role in electing Kenneth Gibson as the city's first black mayor.

In the spring of 1967 an experimental community school board was created in the mostly poor and black Ocean Hill–Brownsville section of Brooklyn. For the next year and a half, it battled the United Federation of Teachers over the hiring and dismissal of teachers. Some board members, influenced by black nationalism, considered the white, middle-class teachers in the community's schools as outsiders forced upon them by white authorities who cared nothing about the welfare of blacks. It is true that often the ghettos did not get the best teachers: some were inexperienced, and others were sent to the ghettos after failing elsewhere in the city. But the board violated the right of due process in May 1968, when it dismissed 13 white teachers and 7 white administrators without any hearings. Other white teachers were threatened and harassed. After a teachers' strike in the fall of 1968, the teachers were rehired and the school board was suspended. Because the union's membership was mostly Jewish, the nationally publicized conflict weakened the black-Jewish alliance that was central to the civil rights coalition.

Some small nationalist groups advocated violent revolution. Founded in 1963, the Revolutionary Action Movement attempted to build a black liberation army, but massive arrests in 1967 put it out of commission. The Republic of New Africa, created in the late 1960s, called for a black nation in the Deep South states; its armed wing was the Black Legion.

But the largest and best-known armed black organization of the late 1960s and 1970s was the Black Panther Party for Self-Defense. It was founded in Oakland, California, in October 1966 by black college students Huey Newton and Bobby Seale to fight police brutality. The Panthers openly carried weapons on the streets. When a group of them entered the California state legislature in 1967 carrying automatic weapons in protest against a gun control bill, the Panthers became national celebrities. The party soon spread across the country, opening chapters in many ghettos (although it had only a few thousand members). Eldridge Cleaver, an ex-convict and author of *Soul on Ice* (1968), a book about the effect of racism on young black men, became its most articulate spokesperson.

The party combined black nationalism with Marxism, calling for black self-determination while praising North Korean Communist leader Kim Il Sung as an outstanding revolutionary and selling copies of *Quotations from Chairman Mao Tse-tung* (also known as the Little Red Book). The Panthers were not antiwhite and in fact welcomed white support. They won a great deal of sympathy from the white student radical movement of late 1960s, which had emerged out of anti–Vietnam War activity on college campuses. This support may have misled the Panthers into believing that many whites endorsed their program. Actually, the campus radicals spoke for only a very small (although very visible) part of the white population.

Local police departments and the Federal Bureau of Investigation (FBI) considered the Black Panthers to be extremely dangerous. These agencies were not fussy about the methods they used against the party, which included infiltrating it with informers and conducting raids; in a Chicago raid, Panther leaders Fred Hampton and Mark Clark were killed, although they had offered no resistance. The police also started shootouts that killed a number of Panthers. Other confrontations with police, however, were apparently begun by the Panthers—not surprisingly for a group that popularized the slogan, "Off the pigs" (kill the police). But whoever was to blame for the violence, one thing was clear: the authorities had much more firepower and many more personnel than did the Panthers. By end of the 1970s, the Panthers had been largely defeated.

Other black groups avoided politics and promoted what was known as cultural nationalism. The best known of the cultural nationalists was Ron Karenga, who founded the San Francisco-based organization US to make blacks aware of their African heritage. To advance this educational process, he invented the supposedly African holiday of Kwanza and dated it close to Christmas, when people would be more likely to observe it. Although Kwanza was a creation of Karenga's, he based it on actual African practices, and so in that sense it was African. A growing number of blacks celebrated it in the last decades of the twentieth century.

Black nationalism advanced black pride, especially among young people. They took pride in their dark skins, insisting that they be called "black" rather than "Negro" or "colored"—"Black is beautiful" became their watchword. They also promoted the term Afro-American (or, later, African American) as an expression of pride in their roots. Black Americans had become increasingly interested in Africa since 1957, when Ghana became the first black nation on the continent to win independence from its European colonial rulers. As black nationalism spread in the late 1960s, many young blacks began to wear African styles of dress and express interest in everything African. Black high school and college students demanded black studies programs, including courses in African and African American history.

Some young blacks identified with the nonwhite Third World generally, and especially with Third World liberation movements and revolutionary leaders. Many were influenced by *The Wretched of the Earth* (1963), written in Algeria by psychiatrist and philosopher Frantz Fanon. Fanon's book glorified violence in the battle against oppression. In 1967 the leaders of SNCC and CORE began to support the Palestinians in their conflict with Israel, which caused great concern among Jewish supporters of civil rights.

## WHITE BACKLASH AND THE CIVIL RIGHTS MOVEMENT

Black power and black nationalism were sharply attacked by civil rights leaders such as Martin Luther King, Jr., of the SCLC, Roy Wilkins of the NAACP,

Whitney Young of the National Urban League, and Bayard Rustin of the A. Philip Randolph Institute. On the moral level, they condemned the movement for rejecting the idea of a common humanity in favor of an outlook that divided humankind into hostile races. Furthermore, supporters of integration argued that black separatism could not possibly work. Where, they asked, would blacks get the resources to establish a separate economy capable of employing all blacks? And how could black separatists possibly win a military conflict with the U.S. government? Some separatists hoped for assistance from the Third World in their armed struggle. But it was difficult to see how countries struggling to get on their own feet, and in many cases hoping for U.S. aid, could help.

Some supporters of integration acknowledged that by praising blackness, nationalists might create a sense of pride for some. But they claimed that in the long run, pride had to be based on accomplishment, not racial identity. Furthermore, they warned that pride would not solve the political, social, and economic problems faced by blacks. A real solution would require a strong government commitment—much stronger than the War on Poverty—to marshal the country's vast resources for the benefit of the less fortunate. Blacks constituted just a little more than 10 percent of the population, and they would need political allies in the struggle to win such a commitment from Washington, D.C. Nationalism, the integrationists contended, would drive away many northern liberal friends and isolate blacks politically.

Blacks did, in fact, lose political allies as a result of "white backlash." Some of the backlash came in the early 1960s, before black power had made its mark, and was directed against the civil rights movement itself. In the spring of 1964, segregationist Alabama governor George Wallace successfully exploited this backlash and ran well in the Democratic presidential primaries of Wisconsin, where he took 34 percent of the vote, and Indiana, where he captured 30 percent. But on the whole, the civil rights struggle increased the amount of white support for racial equality. Most of the white backlash came later—in the mid- to late 1960s—in reaction to black power rhetoric and the ghetto riots. This phase of white backlash involved white moderates and liberals as well as conservatives. In 1964, 50 percent of whites felt that blacks were moving too fast. In the autumn of 1966—just months after the cry of black power was first heard, and following a summer of 38 riots—the figure was up to 75 percent.

Congress responded to the new mood. In September 1966 the Senate defeated a fair housing bill that would have allowed the secretary of housing and urban development to order the end of discriminatory practices after an investigation. (The Fair Housing Act passed two years later required a finding of discrimination by federal courts; see "Obstacles to Progress," page 195.) The same month Congress imposed new restrictions on the use of antipoverty funds. In the November 1966 elections, the Republicans gained 47 seats in the House and 3 in the Senate. Most of those defeated were Democratic liberals who had supported the civil rights agenda. In California, former movie actor Ronald Reagan was elected governor.

Voters seemed to be rewarding him for his opposition to the Civil Rights Act of 1964 and his severe condemnation of the Watts riot in 1965. In 1967 Congress expressed the new mood when it turned down money for rat control in the ghettos. Clearly, the era of legislative action to promote civil rights and assist the poor had passed its peak.

## The Radicalization of Martin Luther King, Jr.

Martin Luther King, Jr., continued his struggle for justice against this conservative tide. After Congress tore down the legal foundations of Jim Crow by passing the civil rights legislation of 1964 and 1965, King decided to go North to fight the ills of the ghettos there. He chose Chicago as his first target. King went there in January 1966 to seek better housing conditions for blacks through rallies and demonstrations against housing discrimination.

But King discovered that the North was in many ways a different—and tougher—target than the South. Chicago mayor Richard Daley was no Bull Connor or Jim Clark. The powerful boss of the city's Democratic machine, Daley was—like most northern big-city mayors—a shrewd, moderately liberal politician. Although he saw King as a threat to his power, Daley welcomed him and his followers to Chicago instead of sending the police up against them. Daley said he agreed with King's goals and promised to replace all slum housing by 1967, even though he knew that was impossible. In short, the Chicago mayor was much too intelligent to create martyrs the way Connor, Clark, and others had done in the Deep South. There was no national outpouring of support for King's campaign, as there had been after the violence in Birmingham and Selma.

Furthermore, King underestimated the amount of bigotry and white backlash in the North. In July and August 1966, he led his supporters on a series of marches into an all-white neighborhood to demand integrated housing. Violent white crowds greeted the demonstrators with Confederate flags and Nazi swastikas and threw bottles, bricks, and rocks at the marchers. On August 5 King fell to one knee after a rock hit him on the temple. Later he would comment: "I've been in many demonstrations all across the South, but I can say that I have never seen—even in Mississippi and Alabama—mobs as hostile and hate-filled as I've seen in Chicago."

Also, King did not give enough attention to poverty as a cause of the housing problem. Most of the Chicago demonstrators could not afford the houses in the neighborhood where they marched, regardless of racial barriers. And poverty was more difficult to fight than Jim Crow practices—it would require a national commitment of many billions of dollars. Could an expensive federal commitment of this sort be won by demonstrations like those that had brought down Jim Crow in the South? Many black leaders, and particularly Bayard Rustin, did not think so. Rustin believed that it could be attained only through the political system, by using black voting power and forging coalitions with the labor movement and other allies.

Having failed, King reached a face-saving agreement with local real estate interests and the city government that did little either to create new housing or to desegregate existing housing. His lack of success in Chicago and the cutbacks in federal programs for the poor in 1966 and 1967 made King wonder whether America would be able to render justice to blacks.

In the meantime, King was becoming more and more disturbed by the nation's massive use of violence in Vietnam, as were others in the civil rights movement. SNCC condemned the war in January 1966. (Former SNCC activist Julian Bond, who had just been elected to the Georgia state assembly, expressed his approval of SNCC's position. Reacting in outrage, the assembly refused to seat him until ordered to do so by the U.S. Supreme Court.) King himself was concerned, not only because of his opposition to all violence, but also because he knew that cuts in antipoverty spending were linked to the increasing cost of the war. Like SNCC, he also was disturbed by the racial aspects of the war: the fact that the Vietnamese victims of U.S. violence were nonwhite and that blacks were doing more than their share of combat.

Roy Wilkins and Whitney Young avoided criticizing the war; they did not want to split the civil rights coalition and alienate President Johnson. But King concluded that he had to speak out against what he considered an immoral conflict. By mid-1966 he had become outspoken enough to anger President Johnson, who limited him to a minor role in the June 1966 White House Conference on Civil Rights. Early in 1967 King urged America's youth to refuse the draft, and in April 1967 he led a huge peace march and rally in New York City. Young and Wilkins criticized King. And as if fighting discrimination, poverty, war, and criticism from other black leaders was not enough of a burden, King was subjected to illegal electronic snooping and other forms of harassment by the FBI—all because its director, J. Edgar Hoover, believed without good evidence that King was a Communist.

Despite all these difficulties, King continued to support integration and non-violence, which to him were basic moral principles. But after the failure of his Chicago campaign, King became more radical. His Chicago experience convinced him that the cause of civil rights for blacks was just the beginning of a long, difficult struggle that must move on to a fight for economic justice. Now he supported government ownership of basic industries and heavy federal spending to assist the poor, including a guaranteed annual income. To win such a program, King believed, massive demonstrations by the poor would be necessary. In late 1967 King and his SNCC colleagues began organizing the first one: a Poor People's Campaign in Washington, D.C.

## King's Death and Nixon's Rise

While the planning was going on, King went to Memphis, Tennessee, in March 1968 to support striking black sanitation workers seeking a living wage—another sign of his growing attention to economic issues. Back in the city the next month to offer more help, King was shot dead on April 4 while standing on the balcony of a Memphis motel. Enraged blacks rioted in more than 100 cities. A suspect in the killing, James Earl Ray, was quickly captured and convicted. (Some blacks believed that Ray was just the enforcement arm of a white conspiracy, but this has never been proved.)

King's death was a hard blow to the already damaged civil rights coalition. King had been its most important leader, and the only one favoring integration who could communicate with black power advocates; they respected his opposition to the Vietnam War and his growing interest in radical change. Because of his eloquent criticism of black nationalism and violence, he was also the one black civil rights leader who could still inspire whites to work for racial equality. Now, King and his unifying power were gone.

The value of King's leadership soon became clear. A few weeks after his death, the SCLC under its new leader, Ralph Abernathy, carried out King's Poor People's Campaign in Washington, D.C. Caravans of the poor came to the nation's capital in early May. Until June 24 they lived in a shantytown called Resurrection City, built near the Lincoln Memorial. The campaign failed badly. One reason was the heavy rains that turned the campsite into a swamp. But more important was the absence of King. Without him, the SCLC leadership lacked the vision and strategy that might have focused the nation's attention on the plight of the poor. As a result, Resurrection City was largely ignored, and the morale of participants collapsed.

On June 5, 1968, the civil rights coalition suffered another major defeat. Former attorney general Robert Kennedy, brother of murdered former president John F. Kennedy, was assassinated during his race for the Democratic presidential nomination. Kennedy had become increasingly committed to the civil rights cause during the 1960s. In the late 1960s, he also supported striking migrant farmworkers led by Cesar Chavez, as well as the emerging movement for American Indian rights. By 1968 he was the only white political leader who could unite the less fortunate of all races, including blue-collar white workers, around a liberal program of racial equality and economic justice. The deaths of Kennedy and King left a huge leadership gap in the struggle for those goals.

Because of Kennedy's death, Vice President Hubert Humphrey had an easy time winning the Democratic presidential nomination in 1968. Humphrey had been a maverick civil rights supporter in the late 1940s and remained a firm advocate of racial equality afterward. Throughout his career, he was also a staunch backer of social welfare legislation to benefit the poor. But in the 1968 campaign, he moved toward the political center, stressing the limits upon what the federal government could accomplish.

Yet from the viewpoint of the movement for racial equality and economic justice, Humphrey was far superior to his two major opponents. Alabama's George Wallace, running as an independent, was a backlash candidate, pure and simple. Threatening to run over demonstrators with his car, he expressed the anger felt by many whites against both black ghetto militants and white campus radicals. He attacked President Johnson's Great Society and the supposedly incompetent "pointy-headed Washington bureaucrats" who ran it. And although Wallace did not sink to outright racist rhetoric, his record in Alabama left no doubt where he stood on civil rights.

Republican candidate Richard Nixon had never, during his long political career, been either a strong supporter or opponent of civil rights. In 1968 he knew which way the wind was blowing and followed it, trying to win backlash votes but in a much less crude way than Wallace. To win the support of southern whites who felt betrayed by the Democrats, he adopted a "Southern strategy" forged with the help of powerful South Carolina senator Strom Thurmond. In his speeches, Nixon stressed the need for "law and order." He opposed the fair housing legislation before Congress and the busing of schoolchildren to achieve racial balance in the public schools. His vice-presidential running mate, Governor Spiro Agnew of Maryland, was more frank than Nixon about his indifference to black concerns. When asked why he did not campaign in the nation's ghettos, he explained that "if you've seen one city slum, you've seen them all."

Nixon defeated Humphrey very narrowly, with 43.4 percent of the vote to the Democrat's 42.7; Wallace received 13.5 percent of the vote. For blacks the election's significance was not just the defeat of Humphrey, their preferred candidate; it was also the fact that the two backlash candidates—Nixon and Wallace—together received nearly 57 percent of all ballots and that just one-third of all white voters backed Humphrey, compared to 85 percent of blacks. These realities signaled the beginning of a more conservative political era; in the next quarter century, blacks more often than not would be out of tune with a mostly conservative white electorate.

# Progress and Setbacks in a Conservative Era: 1969 to the Present

## THE POLITICAL CLIMATE

Already faced with white backlash in the late 1960s, the civil rights cause continued to be troubled by declining white support after 1970. For one thing, the victories of blacks and their allies during the 1960s sparked the formation of new rights movements. This meant that advocates of black equality had to compete with new causes for public support. Among the most important was the feminist movement, which sought equality for women. Knowing that American society had systematically assaulted the dignity of black men for centuries, most black women were reluctant to participate in the women's movement. But many white liberal women (and some white men) joined it. A large number had been active supporters of the civil rights movement; now they focused more on their own concerns. Other new causes claiming a share of white liberal support included rights movements for Hispanics; American Indians, or Native Americans; homosexuals; the elderly; the disabled; and consumers. Also, the extremely popular environmental movement swept the country in the 1970s.

Economic trends posed another problem for the civil rights movement. The American economy expanded rapidly from the end of World War II until around 1970. Then other countries such as Japan and Germany began seriously to challenge American domination of world markets. Meanwhile, America became less competitive because of a slowdown in productivity growth (that is, a decline in the growth of output per work hour). This led to a slowdown in the expansion of the economy, which meant fewer new jobs were being created. In the 1970s, the average income of Americans stopped increasing. The economic pie no longer seemed to be enlarging, and many whites began to worry that a bigger slice for blacks would mean a smaller one for them. Therefore, they became more reluctant to support equal employment opportunities. Also, government budgets became tighter, and so public spending to aid the poor decreased.

Beginning around 1970, controversies over how to enforce the civil rights laws of the 1960s often put blacks and whites on opposite sides of the fence. By 1970 most whites probably accepted the principle of a color-blind policy under which everyone, regardless of race, would have an equal chance to vote, get a good education, get a decent job, and so on. But at about the same time, various federal agencies and the federal courts began going beyond the color-blind approach. Under pressure from the NAACP Legal Defense and Educational Fund and other rights groups, they began requiring positive steps to eliminate the consequences of past discrimination. For example, employers guilty of discriminating in the past had to do more than simply stop discriminating; they also had to raise the proportion of blacks in their workforces. Similarly, colleges that had once excluded blacks now had to take positive steps to attract black students to their campuses. This approach was used in most areas of civil rights enforcement.

These positive steps were known as affirmative action. Most blacks and some whites supported the concept. They argued that after systematically oppressing blacks for more than 300 years, whites could not fairly expect blacks to compete on an equal basis; blacks needed, and were owed, special consideration. Supporters also maintained that a color-blind approach would allow whites to continue discriminating while claiming not to, because in many cases it would be impossible to prove an intent to discriminate. Only by requiring specific hiring results, supporters believed, could major progress be made.

Many (perhaps most) whites and some blacks opposed affirmative action, however. They believed that American society should be based on the principle of equal rights for individuals, regardless of the racial, religious, ethnic, or other group to which they might belong. Affirmative action, its critics said, established the principle that members of certain groups had more rights than members of other groups. This, they claimed, represented reverse discrimination: just as whites had been given special rights in the past, now blacks were being given special rights.

The end of America's postwar economic boom and the controversy over affirmative action pulled white voters farther to the political right. As they had since the New Deal, blacks voted mostly for Democratic presidential candidates in the late twentieth century. But after having supported Lyndon Johnson in 1964, white voters from 1968 into the 1990s gave more of their ballots to Republican than to Democratic nominees. This meant not only that Republicans won most presidential elections, but also that Democratic candidates became more conservative in order to win back white voters. Whites also began voting Republican more often in elections below the presidential level, although that change came more slowly.

## Nixon, Ford, and Carter

As we saw in chapter 9, President Richard Nixon (1969–1974) won the 1968 election by appealing to white backlash, particularly in the South. His actions as president were a continuation of that strategy. In 1969 and 1970, Nixon nominated for the Supreme Court two southern judges, Clement Haynsworth and Robert Carswell. Their commitment to civil rights was questionable. Partly for that reason, the Senate rejected both nominations. Nixon also tried to stop affirmative action, to halt busing for the purpose of desegregating schools, and to weaken the Voting Rights Act of 1965 when it came up for renewal in 1970. In each case either the courts or Congress stopped him. He did, however, manage to slow down the implementation of civil rights laws by weakening the agencies that enforced them. Nixon also sought to limit assistance for the less fortunate. In 1970 he vetoed a bill creating public works jobs and then accepted a smaller-scale compromise measure in 1973. Also, Nixon managed to eliminate some War on Poverty programs.

Although generally opposed to affirmative action, Nixon launched a program known as the Philadelphia Plan, which required construction workers' unions involved in federal projects to hire a certain proportion of black apprentices. As a probusiness politician, he was more willing to put the burden of affirmative action on unions than on business. Nixon also tried to turn black nationalism in a conservative direction by promoting what he called black capitalism. To help minority businesses, his administration increased funding for the Minority Business Enterprise in the Commerce Department and for the Small Business Administration.

Vice President Gerald Ford became president in 1974 when Nixon resigned to avoid impeachment. Ford followed basically the same policies. Unlike Nixon, he did not seriously try to weaken the Voting Rights Act when it expired again in 1975. But Ford opposed affirmative action and sent antibusing proposals to Congress. He also vetoed just about every major bill passed by Congress to aid the poor, opposed federal bailouts for financially troubled cities, and cut back sharply on food stamps and other programs. He did, however, appoint the second black to serve in the cabinet: Secretary of Transportation William T. Coleman.

President Ford narrowly lost the 1976 presidential election to the Democratic candidate, former Georgia governor Jimmy Carter. Carter represented a new type of southern white politician who accepted and even endorsed the changes brought about by the civil rights movement. (The fact that they now needed the votes of newly enfranchised blacks, of course, helped bring about their conversion.) Blacks supported him enthusiastically, and not only because of his civil rights views. A Southern Baptist and a Sunday school teacher, Carter had strong religious beliefs, which he expressed in a way that struck a chord with blacks. Blacks gave him more than 90 percent of their votes, without which Carter could not have won.

Recognizing the crucial black contribution to his triumph, Carter appointed a number of blacks to high posts. Patricia Harris, the first black woman in the cabinet, became secretary of housing and urban development. Former congressman Andrew Young became the U.S. ambassador to the United Nations. Carter also selected Walter McCree as solicitor general in the Justice Department; Drew Days III as assistant attorney general for civil rights; Clifford Alexander, Jr., as secretary of the army; and Ernest Green as assistant secretary of labor. John Lewis became associate director of Volunteers for Action. Louis Martin joined the White House staff as a special assistant to the president.

But Carter did not always please the black community, mostly because he had to please an increasingly conservative white community. While not entirely against affirmative action, he was not wholly for it either. In particular he opposed strict affirmative action quotas, as opposed to more flexible goals. Politically, he could not support quotas; had he done so, many more whites would have left the Democratic Party. Many blacks also resented Andrew Young's forced resignation as ambassador to the UN. This happened in August 1979 after Young had an unauthorized meeting with representatives of the Palestine Liberation Organization, a group at war with Israel and which the United States did not recognize. Still, blacks acknowledged that Carter strengthened civil rights enforcement agencies, attempted to upgrade fair housing legislation, and vetoed an antibusing proposal.

Carter's spending policies were in tune with the more conservative times. He was more interested in balancing the budget than in promoting new spending programs for the poor. School lunch programs and financial aid to black students were cut to bring federal spending down. Carter also failed to give strong support to full employment and health care bills introduced by liberal Democrats in Congress.

## Reagan and Bush

Former California governor Ronald Reagan easily defeated President Carter and independent candidate John Anderson in 1980. Once again some 90 percent of black voters chose Carter. But in the three-way race, Reagan won 55 percent of the white vote and overall received just under 51 percent of the vote, to Carter's 41 percent. Reagan was a true, hard-line conservative, much more so than Nixon or Ford. Unlike those two, Reagan seemed to believe that racial discrimination had nearly disappeared and was no longer a problem of any real significance. His attacks on civil rights enforcement were broader and deeper than those of Nixon and Ford. Reagan sharply reduced the number of civil rights enforcement personnel. The Department of Justice filed far fewer antidiscrimination suits under Reagan than it had under Nixon, Ford, or Carter. In the mid-1980s William Bradford Reynolds, Reagan's assistant attorney general for civil rights, unsuccessfully tried to persuade the Supreme Court to outlaw affirmative action.

In the early 1980s, Reagan did not even back a bill to make Martin Luther King, Jr.'s birthday a national holiday. When a reporter asked Reagan if he believed the baseless charges that King had been a Communist, the president said: "We'll find out in 35 years," referring to when FBI files would be opened to the public. When the holiday measure passed Congress in 1983, however, Reagan signed it.

Reagan's appointments indicated his aggressive opposition to the views of civil rights advocates. Although it had no enforcement authority, the U.S. Civil Rights

Commission (CRC) issued reports critical of Reagan's policies. To stop these attacks, Reagan became the first president to try packing the CRC with members whose views mirrored his own. In 1981 Reagan fired the CRC's chairman, which no president had done before. He replaced the chairman with Clarence Pendleton, a conservative black Republican. After a battle with Congress in 1982, Reagan succeeded in creating a conservative majority on the CRC.

In 1981 Reagan selected a black man, William Bell, to head the Equal Employment Opportunity Commission (EEOC). Because Bell seemed to have no qualifications for the post, this choice sparked an outburst of protest from civil rights supporters. The following year Reagan replaced Bell with Clarence Thomas, another black conservative. Civil rights and liberal groups later charged that Thomas changed the commission's policy to bring it into line with his own opposition to affirmative action. Reagan selected another black Republican, Samuel Pierce, to the cabinet as head of the Department of Housing and Urban Development (HUD). When Reagan reversed Carter administration efforts to enforce fair housing policy, Pierce made no objection. In fact he rarely said anything in public, and so became known as "Silent Sam." Later revelations indicated that his main concern was funneling HUD contracts to loyal Republicans.

Reagan opposed the social welfare agenda backed by the great majority of civil rights advocates. He believed that large government programs for the poor destroyed individual initiative and kept the poor in poverty. Reagan imposed major reductions on many of these programs (see "Middle Class and Underclass," page 240). These economic initiatives were more successful than his civil rights policies, which the courts and Congress often blocked.

For blacks, the most disturbing thing about Reagan's policies may have been the strong public endorsement they received when he ran for reelection in 1984. Democrat Walter Mondale won the overwhelming majority of black votes. But Reagan, who got just 9 percent of black ballots, captured 66 percent of the white vote and 59 percent of all ballots. Mondale carried only his home state of Minnesota and the predominantly black District of Columbia. Clearly, most whites were walking down a different political path than the great majority of blacks.

This pattern continued in 1988, when Vice President George Bush defeated Democrat Michael Dukakis, governor of Massachusetts, by about 10 percentage points. Bush got only 11 percent of the black vote but about 60 percent of the white vote and 54 percent overall. Early in his campaign, Bush called for a "kinder, gentler America," which appeared to be a commitment to modify Reagan's policies. But his own campaign contradicted that promise. One of Bush's major television advertisements featured a black convict named Willie Horton, who had raped a white woman while on a parole granted by Governor Dukakis. Blacks condemned this ad for playing to centuries-old white fears of black male sexuality and violence.

Bush's record as president did not do much to improve his standing among blacks. One decision that they applauded was his appointment of Colin Powell in 1989 as the first black chairman of the military's Joint Chiefs of Staff. But Bush's other major black nominees were much more controversial. In 1989 he offered William Lucas, a black Republican from Michigan, as assistant attorney general for civil rights. A former sheriff and county executive, Lucas had no civil rights background. He also had no courtroom experience and admitted to the Senate Judiciary Committee that "I'm new to the law." The committee rejected his nomination.

In 1990 Bush picked black conservative Clarence Thomas to succeed the retiring Thurgood Marshall on the Supreme Court. Many liberals opposed him, criticizing his record as Reagan's EEOC chairman and his lack of significant experience as a judge. The nomination became a burning national controversy when Anita Hill, a black attorney and law professor at the University of Oklahoma, testified at his confirmation hearing. She stated that Thomas had made unwanted sexual advances toward her when she worked for him at the EEOC. Her testimony greatly increased the pressure on Congress from liberals—and especially feminists—to reject him. Blacks were divided. Some opposed Thomas because of his conservatism. But polls showed that most blacks backed him, apparently because they wanted a black judge on the nation's highest court. The National Urban League took no position. The NAACP hesitated to oppose him, although eventually it did. Division among blacks helped Thomas to win narrow Senate approval in October 1991.

On matters of civil rights policy, Bush followed the Reagan pattern. This is illustrated by his record on an important piece of civil rights legislation. In 1990 Congress passed a bill setting aside a series of Supreme Court decisions that seriously hampered civil rights enforcement (see "Fair Employment Policies," page 225). Bush vetoed it. In 1991 he signed a similar bill, but only for political reasons. During that year's Clarence Thomas hearings, Republicans under the guidance of the White House attacked the truthfulness of Anita Hill's charges against Thomas. Although this helped the administration win Senate approval of Thomas for the Supreme Court, it opened Republicans to the charge of not caring about sexual harassment of women. In the same year, racist and former Ku Klux Klan leader David Duke ran a strong campaign for governor of Louisiana on the Republican ticket. To rebound from this double civil rights embarrassment, Bush signed the Civil Rights Act of 1991, a measure little different from the one he had vetoed the year before.

Shortly before he signed, however, Bush was embarrassed again when a memo written by White House counsel C. Boyden Gray became public. The memo ordered the elimination of all government affirmative action programs and regulations adopted since the 1960s. Bush condemned the memo and claimed it had been written without his knowledge. But many civil rights supporters believed that the memo much better represented the president's views than did the Civil Rights Act he had reluctantly signed.

## The Clinton Administration

In 1992 Democratic presidential candidate Bill Clinton, the governor of Arkansas, defeated Bush's reelection bid. That put the majority of black voters on the winning side for the first time in 16 years, as blacks voted 83 percent for the Democrat in a three-candidate race. Clinton was helped by the fact that a large part of the white vote that normally went Republican this time switched to independent candidate Ross Perot. Clinton, like Jimmy Carter, was more middle-of-the-road and less of a traditional liberal than most Democratic candidates. Trying to win back whites who had abandoned the Democrats, he condemned a black rap artist for racist remarks during the campaign. Clinton's comments were meant as a signal that he would not automatically support the black agenda. One of his campaign slogans described him as "A different kind of Democrat," which was meant to give the impression that he was as much a moderate as a liberal. Yet Clinton was still basically a supporter of civil rights, and certainly far more so than Reagan and Bush.

Clinton's appointments pleased blacks. At the beginning of his administration, he appointed a record number of blacks to the cabinet: Ron Brown, chairman of the Democratic Party since 1989, as secretary of commerce; Representative Mike Espy of Mississippi as secretary of agriculture; Hazel O'Leary, a power company executive, as secretary of energy; and Jesse Brown, director of the Disabled Veterans of America, as secretary of veterans affairs. Some of Clinton's other black appointees were Joycelyn Elders as surgeon general, Drew Days III as solicitor general, and Clifton Wharton as deputy secretary of state.

Still, blacks had reservations about Clinton. True, he supported affirmative action and reversed the Reagan-Bush pattern of weakening civil rights enforcement. But many blacks were bothered by his tendency to retreat when attacked by conservatives on Capitol Hill and elsewhere. In April 1993 he nominated Lani Guinier, a black professor of law at the University of Pennsylvania, to be assistant attorney general for civil rights. But the president withdrew the nomination when conservatives condemned Guinier for her unconventional proposals for increasing the political power of minorities. During his 1992 campaign, Clinton promised a modest public works program to provide employment opportunities, but he quickly reversed himself after taking office. In 1994 he dropped his support of a crime bill provision to prevent racial bias in the use of the death penalty.

On the key issue of affirmative action, however, Clinton remained firm. Republicans gained control of both houses of Congress in the 1994 elections, and in 1995 they began preparing attacks on affirmative action. Early in February 1995 Clinton ordered a review of all federal affirmative action programs to see if all were still necessary. A few months later the review defended most of the programs, a conclusion that Clinton strongly backed.

Considering the late-twentieth-century shift to the right in American politics, a great deal of civil rights progress occurred in the 1970s, 1980s, and 1990s. An important reason was that although whites were becoming more conservative, they were also becoming less racist. Thanks to the civil rights movement, many whites—though far from all—shed their old racial stereotypes and became more willing to accept blacks into American life on an equal, or at least more nearly equal, basis. Also, despite strong attacks on affirmative action policies, the government continued to apply them in most areas of civil rights. The separation of powers in the federal government between the executive, legislative, and judicial branches helped make this possible. Opponents of affirmative action were not able to gain control of all the branches of the government at once. At any given time, civil rights advocates found enough allies in either Congress, the federal courts, or the White House to prevent a fundamental change in civil rights enforcement policy. On the other hand, conservatives were much more successful in reducing government aid to the poor.

In 1994 Republicans won control of both houses of Congress for the first time since 1933. The next year they began an aggressive campaign on Capitol Hill to curtail or eliminate affirmative action and to severely cut social programs for the poor. At the same time, the Supreme Court issued major rulings that could seriously limit affirmative action programs. Were blacks about to feel the full impact of the conservative political drift of the preceding 25 years? Much would depend on whether the Republicans captured the White House and kept control of Congress in 1996.

The amount of black progress in the 1970s, 1980s, and 1990s varied greatly from one aspect of life to another. The sections below examine in detail the advances and setbacks experienced by blacks in the various areas of civil rights, in the pursuit of political power, and in the struggle for economic well-being.

## PUBLIC SCHOOL DESEGREGATION

The Office of Civil Rights (OCR) had the major responsibility for enforcing primary and secondary school desegregation under the Civil Rights Act of 1964. The OCR was created in 1966 as part of the Department of Health, Education and Welfare and was transferred to the newly created Department of Education in 1979. The Civil Rights Act called for a cutoff of federal funds to organizations or programs practicing racial discrimination. During the Johnson administration, the OCR used fund cutoffs, and threats of cutoffs, to force southern school districts to desegregate. When OCR efforts failed, the Justice Department took school boards to court.

As a result of the Johnson administration's efforts, 90 percent of the South's schools had both black and white students in 1970. This represented a great accomplishment in a very short time. Yet many of these integrated schools had only a handful of blacks or whites—they were not truly integrated. Also, school segregation was widespread in the North. Not mandated by law, it resulted mainly from segregated housing patterns—although sometimes school boards drew district lines and located new schools in ways that avoided integration.

Clearly, much remained to be done throughout the country. In Green v. County School Board (1968), the Supreme Court ordered a speeding up of desegregation in the South. Back in 1955 the Court had called for desegregation "with all deliberate speed," which could be interpreted to mean either quickly or slowly; in *Green* it spoke much more clearly, calling for each school board to present a desegregation plan "that promises . . . to work *now*" (emphasis in original).

But President Nixon, elected in 1968 with the help of the white South, wanted to slow down school desegregation. In 1969 his Justice Department backed Mississippi's request for more time to desegregate, but the Supreme Court refused. Never had Johnson's Justice Department supported such a request. In 1970 OCR director Leon Panetta was fired because he supported federal fund cutoffs for schools that did not desegregate. Nixon succeeded in eliminating cutoffs as a tool for advancing public school integration. The presidents who followed him, Republicans and Democrats alike, also declined to use them on the grounds that they were too extreme.

In the 1970s, school busing became the leading civil rights issue. The busing of students to achieve school integration had been used in the 1960s. But federal courts began to order busing much more often after the Supreme Court gave its approval for this approach, first for the South in 1971 and then for the North in 1973. Busing had long been used to transport millions of students who did not live within walking distance of any school. But when used as a tool for achieving racial balance in the schools, it caused an uproar of opposition from many whites. In some places, including Boston in the mid-1970s, whites tried to stop it through violence.

Presidents Nixon and Ford both supported legislation to stop or sharply limit busing. Yet while Congress felt growing public pressure against busing during the 1970s, there were always just enough representatives or senators to defeat serious restrictions. In 1980 Congress finally passed legislation to end busing for the purpose of integration. But by that time Democrat Jimmy Carter was president, and he vetoed the bill.

By the mid-1970s, long strides had been taken toward desegregation. Until 1963, less than 1 percent of black public school pupils in the South went to school with whites. By 1976, the region had the most integrated schools in the country (which was still the case in the mid-1990s). In that year, 47 percent of the region's black pupils went to schools where most students were white, while only 12 percent went to virtually all-black schools. Some southern whites tried to escape integration by sending their children to all-white private schools, but only about 5 or 10 percent of white families could afford them. In the North only 40 percent of black students went to mostly white schools while 18 percent went to nearly all-black schools. Progress was slower there because before desegregation efforts could begin, the courts generally required proof of intent to discriminate; that was harder to show in the North—there, segregation had not, at least in recent history, been established by law.

The mid-1970s represented a high-water mark for public school desegregation. Starting then, the Supreme Court—influenced by Nixon's four conservative appointments to the nine-judge Court—began to place limits on busing. In

*Milliken v. Bradley* (1974), the justices strictly limited the conditions under which students could be transported between cities and their suburbs to achieve school desegregation. Because many whites were moving from the cities to the suburbs (often to escape school integration), this ruling seriously hampered desegregation efforts. In *Dayton Board of Education v. Brinkman* (1977), the Court said busing could not be ordered for an entire school system unless a school board's discriminatory policies had affected the whole system.

President Reagan sharply reduced efforts to desegregate the public schools. He cut OCR's staff, which numbered 1,314 in 1980 (the year before he became president) to 913 in 1983. Reagan's Department of Education was reluctant to take school boards to court; it preferred to negotiate with local authorities, even when this cooperative approach did not lead to significant desegregation. The Emergency School Aid Act of 1972 provided funds to help school systems desegregate, but the Reagan administration refused to use the money for that purpose; instead, it was combined with general education funds. The administration opposed busing, and William Bradford Reynolds, Reagan's assistant attorney general for civil rights, said it would be used "only as a last resort."

With whites leaving the cities in both North and South and federal desegregation efforts becoming weaker, urban resegregation occurred after the mid-1970s. In the 1991–1992 school year, only 34 percent of all black schoolchildren in the country went to mostly white schools, the lowest figure since 1968. Meanwhile, the Supreme Court in *Freeman v. Pitts* (1992) placed another obstacle in the way of integration by making it easier for segregated school districts to escape federal court supervision and go back to local control before desegregation had been completed. In *Missouri v. Jenkins* (1995), the Supreme Court undermined state funding of a "magnet school" in a black Kansas City neighborhood that offered special courses to attract suburban white children.

Another problem connected to school desegregation was "second-generation" discrimination. This referred to disguised forms of racial discrimination, used mostly in the South, to keep black and white children apart even after school integration had occurred. For example, some school districts with a single educational program switched to a two-program system after integration. The less-well-prepared black students ended up mostly in a vocational program, while most whites were placed in the college preparatory program. Many educators said that the tests used to separate the students merely showed past experience, not future potential. Black teachers and administrators often experienced discrimination when black and white school systems were merged in the South. Many black teachers were fired, while black administrators frequently were demoted. Also, blacks charged discrimination in hiring and promotions. The OCR began attacking second-generation discrimination in the 1970s. But because this type of bias could not easily be proved, it was harder to fight than old-fashioned segregation, which was clearly visible.

## DESEGREGATION IN HIGHER EDUCATION

All 17 southern and border states had legally segregated systems of public higher education at the time of *Brown v. Board of Education*; that is, each state created one system for blacks and one for whites. The federal government has attempted to integrate these systems through the Office of Civil Rights, the same agency responsible for desegregating elementary and high schools.

The state college systems had abandoned their official segregation policies by 1970. But that year the OCR ruled that even a color-blind admissions policy would be considered discriminatory if it did not result in significant integration. This "results test," which the federal government also applied to most other areas of civil rights, required affirmative action measures. The colleges would have to do more than stop discriminating; they would have to take affirmative steps to make their student bodies more racially balanced.

President Nixon managed to stop OCR enforcement efforts until 1973, when the NAACP Legal Defense and Educational Fund won a court ruling that permitted the OCR to resume its activities. Soon the OCR began requiring the 17 states to encourage students to go to public colleges where their race was a minority, using a number of methods: recruitment programs, scholarships, creation of new educational programs, and the hiring of black professors for the mostly white schools and of white professors for the largely black schools. The proportion of blacks at the previously segregated, all-white schools rose from 3 percent in 1970 to 7 percent in 1978. This amounted to a significant jump, especially considering that college students, unlike elementary and secondary school pupils, cannot be ordered to go to a particular school.

Several developments, however, limited further progress. In 1978 the Supreme Court ruled in *Regents of the University of California v. Bakke* that a state college could not reserve seats for blacks or other minorities any more than it could do so for whites. However, the decision allowed schools that had practiced past discrimination to consider race, along with other factors, in deciding which students to admit.

In the 1980s, President Reagan showed little interest in eliminating discrimination in either public or private colleges. In January 1982 his administration reversed the Internal Revenue Service's 12-year-old policy of denying tax-exempt status to private colleges that practiced racial discrimination. Among the colleges benefiting would be Bob Jones University, a Christian school in South Carolina that prohibited interracial dating. An uproar of protest forced Reagan to back off, and in 1983 the Supreme Court struck down the administration's new policy. But Reagan imposed a more lenient policy than President Carter's toward previously segregated public colleges. His Justice Department dropped lawsuits begun by the Carter administration against southern state colleges and settled them out of court. To accomplish this, the administration accepted smaller steps toward integration than Carter's OCR would have approved.

During the Reagan years, a Supreme Court ruling temporarily reduced the enforcement power of the OCR in higher education. The Court declared in *Grove City College v. Bell* (1984) that under the Civil Rights Act of 1964, if a college program practiced discrimination, only that program could be deprived of federal funds, not the entire college. The Reagan administration opposed attempts by Congress to overrule that decision. But in 1988 Congress passed, over Reagan's veto, the Civil Rights Restoration Act, which canceled out the *Grove City* ruling.

Despite progress, racial imbalances at public colleges remained in the 1990s, especially in the South. In 1992 the Supreme Court in *United States v. Fordice* required public colleges to apply affirmative action policies when seemingly race-neutral policies perpetuated past discrimination.

Even non-southern public colleges, although not legally segregated, had few black students until the late 1960s. The same was true of most private colleges. The reasons included unofficial discrimination, the inferior public school education available to blacks, and the lack of opportunities for blacks in occupations requiring a college education. Most of these schools tried to enroll more blacks beginning in the late 1960s. At that time, white college administrators on the nation's major campuses generally believed in integration. Also, political pressure from blacks and white liberals had a major impact. A third reason was simply that under the 1964 Civil Rights Act, discrimination could lead to a cutoff of federal money by the OCR.

Beginning in the late 1960s, schools often lowered admissions requirements to make up for the poor primary and secondary education usually received by blacks. The City University of New York, for example, adopted an "open admissions" policy that admitted all New York City high school graduates. Colleges also tried to meet black student needs by introducing new programs. Many created black studies courses or departments. A number of colleges offered special mentoring for blacks.

There was wide agreement on the necessity of these measures. But other innovations, such as separate black student centers, dormitories, and graduations caused controversy. Many whites and some blacks saw them as growing out of the black nationalist movement of the late 1960s and claimed that they were just a new form of segregation. How would racism ever be eliminated, they asked, if the races remained separate? But others said that a degree of black separatism was needed to foster black identity and pride, which American society had crushed for so long.

Controversy also surrounded the creation of scholarships exclusively for blacks and other minorities. By the early 1990s, about two-thirds of traditionally white colleges were providing this type of student aid. In 1995, about 5 percent of all blacks and other minority college students held such scholarships. Attempts were made, however, to limit or abolish them. In December 1991 Lamar Alexander, President Bush's secretary of education, announced that he would bar scholarships based exclusively on race. Before the new policy could be applied, however, President Bush was defeated for reelection. His successor, President Clinton, supported race-based scholarships and scrapped Bush's policy. But in 1994, a U.S. court of appeals ruled that for-blacks-only scholarships given by the University of Maryland were unconstitutional. The following year the Supreme Court let that ruling stand. The Court, however, did not issue an opinion explaining the grounds for its action. For the time being, then, the ban applied only to the states within the jurisdiction of the appeals court that made the ruling.

Despite the limits placed on the desegregation policies of the government and the colleges, on the whole they were effective. By 1993 the black presence in all traditionally white colleges (whether or not they had ever been legally segregated) had grown to about 8 percent of all students. By comparison, in 1968 blacks had made up only 6 percent of the students at *all* colleges—*including* traditionally black schools. Total black college enrollment grew from 522,000 in 1970 to nearly 1.4 million in 1990. Not all of this progress could be credited directly to desegregation policies. The growth of a black middle class that could afford college tuition helps explain these increases; but that, in turn, was partly a result of civil rights enforcement of fair employment policies (see "Fair Employment Policies," page 225).

The existence of traditionally black colleges created a dilemma that divided blacks. The NAACP Legal Defense and Educational Fund supported desegregation, arguing that any black institution was a potential target for discrimination. But others argued that only black colleges could be counted on to serve the needs of black students and to be reliable guardians of black scholarship, history, and culture. The OCR has sometimes taken one side, sometimes the other. More often it has followed a policy that both sides accepted: upgrading the historically underfunded black colleges. Blacks favoring integration felt that improving these colleges would make them more attractive to white students. Those opposed to integration approved because they saw the policy as a way to create better black colleges. The actual effect of the policy since the late 1960s has been to promote some white enrollment without loss of the schools' black identity. These colleges remained an important institution for blacks: in the 1989–90 school year, more than 25 percent of blacks receiving bachelor's degrees obtained them at traditionally black schools.

## VOTING RIGHTS

More progress toward equality has been made in voting rights than in any other area of civil rights. The Voting Rights Act of 1965, which covered those parts of the South with the worst history of voting discrimination, was the major enforcement tool. Under that law, the Justice Department could send federal examiners to make sure blacks were registered, and federal observers to find out whether they were actually being allowed to vote. By dispatching them, or threatening to, the federal government helped blacks make great advances very quickly. Blacks also helped themselves; progress could not have occurred without the local black leaders and civil rights workers who mobilized blacks to register and vote. In 1972,

64 percent of all eligible southern blacks were registered, compared to 69.8 percent of southern whites. This was a very small gap, considering how pervasive discrimination had been just a few years before.

But just as with public school desegregation, southern authorities practiced various forms of "second-generation," or disguised, discrimination against black voters. These were not attempts to stop blacks from voting, but efforts to reduce the impact of their votes. One method was called annexation. When it seemed that blacks might become a majority in a town, the town government absorbed mostly white suburban areas. As a result, white voters continued to dominate elections. White-majority towns and cities sometimes changed the way their councils were elected, switching from a district system to an at-large or multimember system. Under the district system, each council member was elected in a different part of the city. Once blacks won the right to vote, they were in a position to elect candidates of their choice—usually black candidates—from their own neighborhoods. To stop this from happening, the local authorities sometimes adopted an at-large system by which all council members were elected by the entire city. In this way, the white majority could outvote the black minority in every council race. Large, multimember state legislative districts were based on the same principle: two or more legislators were chosen by all of the district's voters. At-large and multimember systems were the most common form of second-generation discrimination. A third approach involved redrawing the district lines for state legislative and city council elections so that whites would be the majority in each district.

To prevent second-generation discrimination, the Department of Justice relied on the preclearance section of the Voting Rights Act. It declared that before putting new laws about electoral procedures into effect, the states and localities covered by the Voting Rights Act had to submit them to the Justice Department for approval. From 1969 to 1973, the Supreme Court issued rulings that interpreted "electoral procedures" broadly, to include not only laws directly concerned with the right to vote, but also those imposing second-generation discrimination. Although the Justice Department did not have a large enough staff to stop all discriminatory laws, the Court's decisions helped it to block many of them.

The results of the Voting Rights Act have been apparent in the growing number of blacks elected to office in the South. Until the mid-1960s, hardly any blacks won election there. But in 1970 there were 731 elected black officials, or 49.8 percent of the national total of 1,479 black officeholders. In 1992, 5,110 blacks held elective office in the South, or 68 percent of all black elected officers (even though southern blacks were only 53 percent of the total black population that year). Also, the six states with the greatest number of black elected officials in 1992 were in the South: Mississippi (716), Alabama (702), Georgia (513), South Carolina (413), Louisiana (579), and North Carolina (458), all covered by the Voting Rights Act.

Attempts to reduce the effectiveness of the Voting Rights Act generally failed. In 1970 the law expired and had to be renewed. To secure his support among white southerners, President Nixon tried to weaken the new version by dropping the preclearance section; Congress, however, turned him down. Nixon made another attempt to weaken the act in 1970. The 1965 legislation applied only to those areas of the South with the worst history of voting discrimination; Nixon wanted the law to apply to the whole country. Civil rights backers opposed this; they believed that spreading enforcement efforts out across the nation would weaken enforcement activities where they were most needed—in the South. Congress agreed with them and again turned Nixon down. In voting for a five-year extension, Congress left the 1965 law basically unchanged.

In 1975 Congress again renewed the act, this time for seven years, and expanded it to protect Hispanic, Indian, and Alaskan language minorities. In the House of Representatives, 69 out of 105 southern whites supported the law's extension; in the Senate 13 of 24 southerners—all white—backed the renewal. This was strong evidence of the growing strength of southern black voters. Until around 1970, southerners in Congress fought furiously against all civil rights bills, but afterward they had to take into account the wishes of black voters.

## Results Test versus Intent Test

In 1980 the Supreme Court made it harder to use the Voting Rights Act against second-generation discrimination. In *City of Mobile v. Bolden,* the Justice Department charged that the authorities in Mobile, Alabama, had replaced district elections with at-large contests to prevent black voters from choosing black officials. The fact that no blacks had been elected under the new system formed the basis of the department's complaint. But the justices stated that under the Voting Rights Act, the courts could not overturn at-large voting on the basis of the election results, since the Voting Rights Act was not meant to guarantee any particular result. Instead, those complaining of discrimination had to meet an "intent" test: they had to prove that the authorities who established the at-large system had actually *intended* to discriminate.

The issue of whether to use the "intent" test or the "results" test caused great controversy. Most, but not all, civil rights supporters argued for the results test. Intent, they believed, was simply too difficult to prove: those who seek to break the law, they noted, do not make a public announcement of their intention to do so. Many supporters of the results test also noted that redistricting had long been used to assure various groups of representation. If affirmative action could be taken on their behalf, then why not for blacks, especially since blacks had so often been the *victims* of racial redistricting? Anyway, they denied wanting to guarantee the election of black candidates, saying they simply wished blacks to have a fair chance to elect candidates of their choice.

But supporters of the intent test, who were mostly white, said the results test would lead to an affirmative action quota system for black elected officials. Under a results test, they said, discrimination could be charged, for example, if a state with a 40 percent black population had only 20 percent black officials. The state would then have to redraw district lines until 40 percent of elected officials were black. But the Voting Rights Act, they continued, was passed to ensure every individual's right to vote, not to assure any group a certain number of public offices.

Some opponents of the results test also argued that the creation of black-majority districts actually could *reduce* black political influence. They contended that if blacks, for example, made up 30 percent of the population in three contiguous (connected) districts, they would be in a good position to swing the election in all three and help elect pro–civil rights whites over anti–civil rights whites. But if district lines were redrawn to place most of the blacks in one black-majority district, they would determine the outcome only in that district. This would give them a black representative, but the other two districts would now have only a handful of black voters; those districts might now elect anti–civil rights candidates.

When the Voting Rights Act came up for renewal in 1982, Congress—angered by the Reagan administration's failure to enforce civil rights laws effectively—included a provision that set aside the *City of Mobile* decision and allowed the results test to be used. Reagan at first opposed this change. But when it became clear that the provision had broad support—all but four southern senators voted for it—the president signed the measure. In *Thornburg v. Gingles* (1986) the Supreme Court, applying the results test for the first time, threw out multimember state legislative districts in North Carolina on the ground that they reduced the chance of black voters to elect candidates of their choice.

This did not settle the issue, however. After the 1990 census—as after every census—the states had to redraw congressional district lines to account for shifts in population. Under the 1982 Voting Rights Act, the Justice Department ordered some of the southern states to increase the number of black-majority districts when they redrew the lines. Its orders were based on the results test, which allowed the department to assume discrimination because these states had few or no black U.S. representatives. The states obeyed the Justice Department orders, which is one reason the number of blacks in the House of Representatives increased in the 1992 elections from 25 to 39.

In 1993 and 1994, however, whites charging reverse discrimination challenged the constitutionality of the new black-majority districts in several states. The first case to be decided by the Supreme Court was *Miller v. Johnson* (1995), involving a black-majority congressional district in Georgia represented since 1992 by black Democrat Cynthia McKinney. The Court decided that the district was unconstitutional because race was the "predominant factor" in drawing the district's lines. But on the same day the Court upheld without explanation California's 1992 redistricting plan, which had created nine new black- and Hispanic-majority congressional districts. So until the Court ruled on other challenges to black-majority districts, it would remain unclear how many such districts would be wiped out under the "predominant factor" test.

# FAIR EMPLOYMENT POLICIES

In the 1960s, most white Americans finally accepted the principle that employers should not consider race in deciding whom to hire, promote, or fire. But in the 1970s the economy slowed down, which meant fewer new jobs. Therefore, hiring and promoting blacks, it seemed, was more likely to come at the expense of whites. At the same time, affirmative action became a tool of fair employment policy. This meant that companies guilty of intentionally discriminating not only had to take a color-blind approach, but also—if color-blind policies failed to change significantly the employee racial mix—had to give blacks priority in hiring and promotions. At a time when jobs were becoming harder to find, affirmative action became more controversial in the equal employment field than in any other area of civil rights.

The term *affirmative action* was first used in an executive order issued by President Johnson in 1965, which banned all federal contractors and subcontractors, as well as unions involved in federal work, from practicing employment discrimination. An Office of Federal Contract Compliance Programs (OFCCP) was established in the Labor Department to supervise this policy. In 1968 the OFCCP began issuing affirmative action guidelines requiring contractors to submit "specific goals and timetables" for hiring blacks. During the early 1970s it started requiring federal contractors to hire specific numbers of blacks for their workforces based on the proportion of blacks in the local workforce. This approach produced significant but limited results. The OFCCP did not have enough personnel to review the actions of most contractors. Therefore, in most cases it had to rely on voluntary compliance.

Ray Donovan, President Reagan's secretary of labor, tried to limit the OFCCP's authority by announcing new rules in 1982. The OFCCP supervised all contractors with more than 50 employees and federal contracts worth more than $50,000. Donovan wanted to raise the numbers to greater than 250 employees and $1 million in contracts, which would have freed 75 percent of all federal contractors from the OFCCP's affirmative action demands. But opposition came from civil rights organizations, women's groups, and businesses that had built their employment policies around the existing rules. This pressure prevented Donovan from ever using the new rules. President Reagan did, however, cut the OFCCP's budget. He also slashed its staff by 52 percent, a reduction from which it never fully recovered.

To prevent employment discrimination by private employers in general, the Civil Rights Act of 1964 established the five-member Equal Employment Opportunity Commission (EEOC). At first, the EEOC was authorized only to persuade businesses to stop discriminating. If negotiations failed, the agency turned the matter over to the Justice Department. Liberals wanted to permit the EEOC to issue cease-and-desist orders against discrimination, but President Nixon was opposed. A compromise was reached: the Equal Employment Opportunity Act of 1972 gave the EEOC the right to take employers to court, and it also declared that the Civil Rights Act of 1964 applied to private employers as much as to government agencies and to private companies doing government work. With its new power, the EEOC was able successfully to sue AT&T, Household Finance, United States Steel, other companies, and some unions to force them to adopt affirmative action plans.

Meanwhile, the Supreme Court strengthened the legal basis for affirmative action. In *Griggs v. Duke Power Company* (1971), the Court issued its first interpretation of Title VII, the section of the Civil Rights Act of 1964 that barred employment discrimination. The case involved hiring standards at the Duke Power Company. In the past, Duke had discriminated against blacks by reserving certain jobs for whites. At the time of the *Griggs* case, the company had dropped that policy, but it required applicants for those jobs to have a high school education and to pass a general intelligence test. Neither of these requirements was related to the skills needed for the jobs. The requirements, although they seemed to be race-neutral, had a "disparate" impact on blacks—that is, they disqualified a higher proportion of black job applicants than white.

The Court ruled against Duke's job requirements. The justices stated that at workplaces with a record of past discrimination, job requirements violated equal employment opportunity when they maintained the results of past discrimination so that blacks continued to be underrepresented in the workforce, and when they were unrelated to the skills needed for the job. The fact that those who created the requirements had no intent to discriminate did not matter—it was the results of the requirements that counted. Under this decision, employers who had once discriminated would—if successfully sued—have to take affirmative action measures until the racial balance of their workforce matched the proportion of blacks in the local workforce.

In *United Steelworkers v. Weber* (1979), the Court approved the use—in some cases—of the strictest type of affirmative action plan, the type that required companies to train, hire, or promote specific numbers (quotas) of blacks. Such requirements could, the justices ruled, be used in voluntary affirmative action plans drawn up by employers and unions to remedy past discrimination, so long as the quotas were temporary and did not limit the opportunities of whites unnecessarily. Quota plans were stricter than those setting goals or targets, which did not oblige employers to reach any exact number (although opponents of affirmative action claimed there was no real difference between quotas and goals).

The Supreme Court, though, also set limits to affirmative action. In *Teamsters v. United States* (1977), the government sought to apply affirmative action to union seniority systems. A seniority system was basically a "first hired, last fired" rule for layoffs to protect employees who had worked the longest at a particular place. The Justice Department argued in *Teamsters* that in a firm that had once discriminated, the seniority rule maintained the effects of past discrimination: in such firms most of the black employees would be relatively new, and so, under the seniority rule, they would be the first fired. Therefore, the argument went, black employees should be given extra seniority to undo the impact of past discrimination. But the Court rejected this type of affirmative action. The justices said it should be used only when the seniority system itself had discriminated against blacks by giving them less seniority than whites hired at the same time.

Although the OFCCP and the EEOC were the major federal fair employment agencies, there were 16 others during the 1970s. The result was inefficiency in the enforcement of fair employment practices. President Carter tried to improve enforcement with a plan, approved by Congress in 1978, that concentrated power in the EEOC. For example, responsibility for discrimination in federal employment was transferred to the EEOC from the Office of Personnel Management, which had been very ineffective.

## Reagan, Bush, and the Supreme Court

The Reagan administration, on the other hand, did not want to improve enforcement. President Reagan opposed all affirmative action plans, whether they set goals or quotas. He believed that relief for past discrimination should go only to individuals who could prove that they had been the victims of bias; he opposed efforts to change the racial balance of the workforce by giving special treatment to blacks as a group. Therefore, the EEOC under Reagan did not seek affirmative action remedies for past discrimination. Going farther, Reagan's Justice Department urged the Supreme Court in *Wygant v. Jackson Board of Supervisors* (1985) and in *Sheet Metal Workers v. EEOC* (1985) to reject affirmative action entirely. The Court, however, refused.

But in a series of 1989 decisions, the Supreme Court seriously weakened fair employment policy and affirmative action generally, with the three conservative justices appointed by Reagan providing the deciding votes. *Ward's Cove Packing Co. v. Atonio* (1989) was one of the most important of these rulings. Under the 1971 *Griggs* decision, personnel practices having a disparate impact on blacks had to be scrapped, even if there was no proof of intent to discriminate. The employer would then have to adopt an affirmative action plan so that the workforce would have a higher proportion of blacks. The only way out for the employer would be to prove that those practices were a "business necessity"—for example, that a test for a job actually tested the skills needed for the job. But in *Ward's Cove*, the Court changed the rules. Now the burden of proof was on the employees: before affirmative action could be applied, they would have to prove that the personnel practices did *not* have a legitimate business purpose.

Also, *Ward's Cove* made it more difficult to claim that personnel practices had a disparate impact on blacks. Previously, disparate impact meant that the proportion of blacks employed at a firm was less than the proportion of blacks in the local labor force. For example, if 10 percent of Firm X's employees were black, while blacks made up 30 percent of the local labor force, then the firm's personnel policies were having a disparate impact on blacks and affirmative action would be required. But in *Ward's Cove* the Court said that the comparison must be between the black proportion of Firm X's employees and the proportion of blacks among local workers *qualified for the specific jobs* at Firm X. So if blacks made up only 10 percent of the qualified local workers, then Firm X's hiring policies would be legal—it did not matter that blacks were 30 percent of the total local labor force.

In *Martin v. Wilks* (1989), the Supreme Court allowed white firefighters to challenge a voluntary affirmative action plan approved by a federal district court, even though many years had passed since the plan's adoption. Apparently, affirmative action plans were never safe from challenge. But in *Lorance v. AT&T Technologies* (1989), the Court decided that persons who sought to prove that a seniority system was discriminatory had to file their objections within 300 days after the adoption of the plan. In *Patterson v. McLean* (1989) the panel interpreted the Reconstruction-era Civil Rights Act of 1866 narrowly, so that blacks could not use it as the basis for lawsuits concerning racial harassment at the workplace. The Court said the law applied only to discrimination in hiring, not to workplace conditions.

These 1989 decisions raised an outcry in the civil rights community. Immediately, most Democrats and some Republicans on Capitol Hill began drawing up legislation to set them aside. In 1990 Congress passed such a bill, but President Bush vetoed it, claiming that it would promote quotas. But the next year Bush was under greater political pressure, and so he signed the Civil Rights Act of 1991 (see "The Political Climate," page 209).

In the early and mid-1990s, however, the Supreme Court remained a conservative body. In *St. Mary's Honor Center v. Hicks* (1993), the Court made it more difficult to prove intentional job discrimination. It was no longer enough to show that an employer had given a false reason for a hiring, promotion, or firing decision. Employees would also have to show that the real reason they were dismissed or denied a job or promotion was employer bias. The Court's decision in *Adarand Constructors v. Peña* (1995), which jeopardized affirmative action for minority federal contractors, also had the potential to limit affirmative action programs in employment (see "Minority Contractors and Broadcasters," page 232).

The employment status of many blacks improved significantly from the late 1960s to the early 1990s. Most jobs above the menial level had once been closed to blacks; now most were open, at least to a degree. A growing proportion of blacks worked in the professions, in technical jobs, and in managerial positions. Blacks also increased their share of the higher-paying jobs in the federal civil service. Part of this progress clearly stemmed from fair employment policies. (For more details on black economic well-being in the late twentieth century, see "Middle Class and Underclass," page 240.)

## FAIR HOUSING

Less progress was made in fair housing than in any other major civil rights area. The Fair Housing Act of 1968 barred racial discrimination in about 80 percent of all housing. And in *Jones v. Alfred H. Mayer Company* (1968), the Supreme Court expanded the act's coverage to all housing through its interpretation of the Reconstruction-era Civil Rights Act of 1866, which guaranteed all citizens the right to "inherit, purchase, lease, sell, or hold" property. But the Fair Housing Act was difficult to enforce. The law was too vague: it failed to define adequately such basic terms as "fair housing," an "unfair housing practice," or an "aggrieved person" (victim of bias). Furthermore, the act did not permit the Department of Housing and Urban Development (HUD) to issue orders against discriminatory practices; to enforce the act, either the person claiming bias or the Justice Department had to file a lawsuit in federal court, a much slower process. Also, HUD could not investigate discrimination until it received a complaint.

Even if the law had been stronger, equal access to housing would still have been the most difficult of all civil rights to enforce. One reason was that whites resisted equal housing opportunity more than other forms of equality, much more than voting rights and more than equal employment opportunity. Another was that housing discrimination usually occurred in private transactions between individuals, and so was difficult to prove. But stronger legislation would still have made a difference.

Presidents Nixon and Ford had little interest in fighting housing bias: they both depended on votes from the white suburbs that wanted to keep blacks out. Nor did the Supreme Court help. In a series of decisions in the 1970s, it upheld local exclusionary zoning practices against low-income housing. In a 1977 case, for example, the justices imposed the intent test for proving that these practices were discriminatory. It was not enough to show that they resulted in the exclusion of blacks—intent to discriminate had to be shown, which was nearly impossible. Not surprisingly, little or no progress was made in fair housing. A 1979 HUD study showed that blacks faced discrimination in 70 percent of all rental transactions and in 90 percent of housing purchases.

President Carter made a much more serious effort to enforce the Fair Housing Act than the Republicans before him. To make sure that its lawsuits had maximum impact, his Justice Department selected cases that involved widespread discriminatory practices. Also, his administration tried to make the Fair Housing Act more effective by clarifying what discrimination was and who could be sued under that vaguely written law. In 1979 and 1980 Carter also supported unsuccessful attempts in Congress to strengthen the law.

The enforcement of fair housing policy went into sharp reverse under President Reagan. His administration dropped Carter's effort to clarify the Fair Housing Act. HUD sent very few cases on to the Department of Justice for prosecution. Arguing inaccurately that housing discrimination had greatly declined, the Justice Department drastically cut the number of lawsuits against biased practices. Instead, the administration relied on voluntary compliance with the Fair Housing Act. But this approach could not possibly work: real estate brokers and lending institutions profited from their discriminatory practices and so had no motive to stop them.

In 1988 congressional backers of a strong antibias policy finally succeeded in strengthening the Fair Housing Act of 1968. New provisions empowered HUD itself to judge the merits of a discrimination complaint instead of taking the matter to court, which could speed up the processing of cases. But to satisfy the Reagan administration, the amendments also gave those accused of biased practices the alternative of demanding a full trial in federal court. Therefore, the provisions represented only a limited gain.

In the 1970s and 1980s, Congress passed several laws to stop redlining, which included various practices by banks and mortgage companies that discriminated against minority neighborhoods in the granting of home mortgage loans. Under the Home Mortgage Disclosure Act of 1975, mortgage lenders in urban areas had to reveal how much mortgage money they loaned in the different neighborhoods of the city. Under the Community Reinvestment Act of 1977, federal agencies had to consider whether the lending policies of financial institutions met the needs of their home areas before deciding whether to allow them to open new branches.

Congress seemed to be taking a step toward affirmative action in 1989, when it required mortgage lenders to reveal the race, gender, and income level of both loan applicants and recipients. This information could have been used as a results test for determining whether banks should be required to improve the racial balance of those obtaining loans. In fact, Congress in 1991 considered such an approach in debate over an amendment to a banking bill. The amendment would have forced banks to lend more to minorities where the records showed that minorities were less likely to obtain loans than whites. But the House rejected the proposal.

In the 1990s, housing segregation and discrimination seemed as firmly established as ever. A growing number of blacks moved to the suburbs during the 1970s, 1980s, and 1990s. But they found that although it had become easier to leave the cities, discrimination moved right along with them. Real estate brokers often steered then into all-black neighborhoods with inferior housing. When blacks succeeded in moving into previously all-white areas, the whites frequently fled to another neighborhood or town. Also, according to a 1991 Federal Reserve Bank report, blacks at every income level had only half as much chance as whites at the same income level to get a home mortgage.

## THE DISTRICT OF COLUMBIA AND HOME RULE

The District of Columbia, or Washington, D.C., was created in the late eighteenth century as the nation's capital. Under an 1878 law, the District was ruled by a board appointed by the president of the United States, while Congress provided funds for the District and passed any laws necessary for running it. Between the end of World War II and 1950, Washington's black population grew rapidly to 35 percent of the total. (It reached 54 percent in 1960 and 71 percent in 1970.) Therefore, in the late 1940s the movement for racial equality made home rule for the District a civil rights issue. Between 1949 and 1965 the Senate passed home rule bills six times. In each case, however, they were blocked in the House by the District of Columbia Committee, which was dominated by southern racists.

As the civil rights movement picked up steam, District residents gained some concessions. In 1961 the states ratified the Twenty-third Amendment, which allowed its residents to vote for president and vice president. But whatever the District's population, it could have no more electoral votes than the least populated state. In 1970 Congress authorized Washington, D.C., voters to elect a delegate to the House of Representatives. The delegate could vote on whatever committees he or she sat, but not on the floor of the House, where the final votes on all bills were taken. In 1971 the Reverend Walter Fauntroy, a black Democrat, was selected as the District's first nonvoting delegate.

The wheels for home rule were set in motion when Charles Diggs, a black congressman, became chairman of the House District Committee in 1973. By the end of the year, Congress had passed a bill that gave District residents some home rule powers. It allowed District residents to elect a 13-member city council and a mayor. Under the law, black candidate Walter Washington was elected mayor in 1974. But the 1973 law did not give the District full home rule. By a two-thirds vote, the city council could override a veto by the mayor, but the president of the United States could then reimpose the veto. The District still depended on Congress for funds. Congress continued to legislate for Washington, D.C., and could also veto measures passed by the D.C. council.

By 1995 the District faced a budget crisis and was about to run out of money. One reason was that the home rule plan restricted the District government's ability to tax. Furthermore, the high rate of poverty in the District meant that tax revenue was small and the need for social services was great. Also, during the 1980s Washington, D.C., mayor Marion Barry had greatly increased spending without considering whether the District could afford it. In the spring of 1995, Congress passed a bill to deal with the crisis. It restricted home rule by creating a financial control board that would have the final say on all matters relating to the budget. Under the law, the board would remain in existence for at least eight years.

In 1978 Congress passed and sent to the states a constitutional amendment allowing the District full representation in Congress: two senators and as many representatives as it was entitled to by population. The amendment also provided for repeal of the Twenty-third Amendment, so that the District's electoral votes for president would be determined on the same basis as for the states. But when the seven years allowed for ratification ended in 1985, only 16 states had approved. (Three-quarters of the 50 states, or 38 states, were required for ratification.) Race was one obstacle to passage. But party politics probably played a larger role. Almost certainly, the District's large black majority would have elected Democrats to Congress, so most Republicans opposed the amendment.

## MINORITY CONTRACTORS AND BROADCASTERS

In the 1970s the federal government began reserving a percentage of federal contracts for black and other minority businesspeople. These quotas were known as set-asides. In 1977, for example, Congress passed the Public Works Employment Act, which provided $4 billion in federal money for local public works projects; the law required that 10 percent of the money go to minority contractors. White contractors went to the federal courts, challenging set-asides as unconstitutional reverse discrimination. But in *Fullilove v. Klutznick* (1980), the Supreme Court allowed this use of quotas—the strongest and most controversial type of affirmative action—to make up for past discrimination against black businesses by the federal government.

But 10 years later in *City of Richmond v. J. A. Croson* (1989), the Court struck down a Richmond, Virginia, plan that set aside 30 percent of all city contracts for minorities. To justify the plan, the city showed that although Richmond's population was 50 percent black, less than 1 percent of the city's major construction projects had gone to blacks in the past. But the Supreme Court rejected this argument because there was no direct evidence that past city governments had intentionally discriminated by favoring whites over blacks.

Once again, the issue was whether a results test or an intent test should be used to decide whether discrimination existed. In *Fullilove* the Court had accepted a results test, which showed that the black share of federal contracts was well below the black proportion of the U.S. population. In *Richmond*, however, the Court imposed the stricter intent standard on states and localities.

Under Congress's set-aside system, the number of minority contractors used by federal agencies and departments increased significantly. But white contractors often used fraud to get around the set-asides, hiring minority front men or women to pose as owners of construction firms. As a result, minority businesspeople did not get the full benefit of the set-asides.

In *Adarand Constructors v. Peña* (1995), the Supreme Court issued a major ruling involving federal set-aside programs. The Court declared that race-conscious federal programs are assumed to be unconstitutional unless they are "narrowly tailored" to achieve a "compelling government interest." The Clinton administration responded by suspending set-aside programs in 1996. The *Adarand* decision could potentially affect all federal affirmative action programs, not just set-asides, since it set a stricter standard for determining the constitutionality of those programs.

Acting at the demand of Congress, the Federal Communications Commission (FCC) in 1978 set up programs to increase minority ownership of radio and television stations. The Reagan administration, opposed to all affirmative action, tried to end them during the 1980s. But Congress prevented this by prohibiting the FCC from using any funds to eliminate the programs. The programs passed a Supreme Court test in *Metro Broadcasting Inc. v. Federal Communications Commission* (1990). The Court accepted the argument used in support of the programs:

that they were needed to increase the diversity of programming on the airwaves. It was the first time the Court had approved an affirmative action program whose stated purpose was other than remedying past discrimination. Gains under the programs were measurable, but small. In 1990 minorities owned 3.5 percent of the 11,000 broadcasting licenses, compared to less than 1 percent in 1978. In 1995, however, the new Republican majorities in both houses of Congress launched an attack on the programs, leaving their future in doubt.

## BLACKS AND THE JUSTICE SYSTEM

Historically, blacks were excluded from juries, especially in the South. When southern blacks won the right to vote in 1965, part of the problem was solved, because jury pools were usually selected from the voting rolls. But sometimes names were taken from the rolls on a racial basis, so that blacks continued to be excluded.

To prevent this, Congress in 1968 required that names for federal jury pools be selected randomly from the voting rolls. Four years later, Congress took a different approach. First, names would be chosen randomly. Then those selected had to identify themselves by race on federal jurors' forms so that racially balanced pools could be selected. The difference between the two laws represented the shift that we have seen in many areas of civil rights: from a race-neutral approach requiring only an end to biased practices, to an affirmative action, race-conscious approach designed to create racial balance.

Another significant issue remained. At the beginning of a trial, a jury was selected from the pool of available jurors. Prosecutors and defense attorneys had the right to exclude a certain number of people by using peremptory challenges, which are challenges that require no explanation. Some attorneys used this right to exclude people by race—for example, prosecutors might exclude blacks in a case where the defendant was black and the victim was white. In *Batson v. Kentucky* (1986), the Supreme Court barred prosecutors from doing this. The ruling stated that if a prosecutor's peremptory challenges seemed to follow a racial pattern, the judge could demand that she or he provide a nonracial explanation for them. The Court applied the same rule to defendants' attorneys in *Georgia v. McCollum* (1992). In 1991 the Court ruled that the *Batson* decision should apply to attorneys for both plaintiffs and defendants in civil suits.

Civil rights activists tried to secure racial fairness in another area of the legal system: the death penalty. A 1972 Supreme Court decision suspended all executions; four years later the Court allowed them to resume if the states took steps to make use of capital punishment fairer and more evenhanded. But statistics showed that even under the new procedures, minority defendants accused of killing whites were those most likely to be sentenced to death and executed. In 1988 and 1989 Congress rejected legislation that would have allowed minority defendants to use those statistics in sentencing hearings. In 1994 the House adopted a crime bill with such a provision; this was made possible by the support of

President Clinton and by the fact that a record number of black representatives had been elected in 1992. But when the provision came under sharp attack from conservatives, Clinton and the Democratic leaders in Congress decided to drop it so that the overall bill could be passed.

## SEEKING POLITICAL OFFICE: THE LOCAL AND STATE LEVELS

The Voting Rights Act of 1965 made it possible for blacks to enter the mainstream of American politics. In the South, millions of blacks voted for the first time. Between 1970 and 1992, the number of elected black officials in that region shot up from 731 to 5,110. The figure for the North also jumped sharply during those years, from 748 to 2,407. One reason was that the southern civil rights movement encouraged many northern blacks to get involved in politics; another was the increasing number of whites willing to vote for blacks; a third was the growing black population of the northern cities.

In November 1967 Carl Stokes won election as mayor of Cleveland, Ohio, and Richard G. Hatcher won his contest for mayor of Gary, Indiana. They were the first two blacks to become mayors of major American cities. Some of the black mayors elected afterward were Kenneth Gibson of Newark, New Jersey (1970); Thomas Bradley of Los Angeles, a city that was only 15 percent black (1973); Maynard Jackson of Atlanta, the South's largest city (1973); Coleman Young of Detroit (1973); Ernest R. Morial of New Orleans (1977); Richard Arrington of Birmingham, Alabama, once considered the most racist city in the country (1979); Harold Washington of Chicago against the most powerful urban political machine in America (1983); Wilson Goode of Philadelphia (1983); Harvey Gantt of Charlotte, North Carolina (1983); and David Dinkins of New York City (1989). Thousands of other blacks were elected mayor in smaller urban centers. The National Conference of Black Mayors was formed in 1975. The following year Kenneth Gibson became the first black president of the U.S. Conference of Mayors. Many others were chosen to sit on town councils and county commissions or to serve in such posts as sheriff or county executive. In 1992 blacks held 4,557 elective posts at the city and county levels, compared to just 719 in 1970. (Yet the 1992 figure still represented less than 2 percent of all public offices.)

Blacks benefited from the election of mayors of their own race. In the more backward cities and towns, especially in the South, black neighborhoods had been denied such basic public services as paved streets, garbage collection, and modern water and sewage facilities; now they received those services. Recreational facilities and police protection for blacks were generally upgraded. Black-controlled local governments usually increased the share of city contracts and jobs that went to blacks. Similar gains came in many places where whites remained in control; with blacks participating in elections, white politicians had to pay more attention to their needs. But those blacks who expected a dramatic attack on poverty were disappointed: localities lacked the funds even to begin a serious campaign on behalf of the economically underprivileged.

Blacks gained at the state level, too. After the 1994 election, a record 511 blacks sat in state legislatures, a big jump from 169 in 1970. In 1980 members of the California legislature's lower house chose black representative Willie L. Brown as speaker of the assembly; in that post he gained a national reputation as one of the most skilled legislative leaders in the country. No state had a black-majority population, yet in some of them the voters chose blacks for statewide office. California, with about a 15 percent black population, elected Wilson Riles as superintendent of public instruction in 1970 and state senator Mervyn Dymally as lieutenant governor in 1974. Although less than 5 percent of its residents were black, Colorado voters selected black state senator George Brown as lieutenant governor that same year. In 1985 state senator L. Douglas Wilder became lieutenant governor of Virginia, with a black population below 20 percent. Four years later Virginians selected him as governor, the first black ever elected chief executive of any state. In 1994 Carl McCall won election for comptroller of New York state, which had a black population of less than 15 percent.

Blacks in statewide office could not always please the black community, because they needed white votes to win. But the fact that they could win many white votes showed an easing of racism. Race still counted, however; some whites simply would not vote for blacks. For example, Los Angeles mayor Thomas Bradley narrowly lost his 1982 bid for governor of California; polls showed that his defeat could be traced to the switch of some white Democrats to the Republican candidate for racial reasons. Also, the Deep South states had the largest proportion of blacks but elected no blacks to statewide office: whites apparently found blacks in power most threatening where the black population was greatest.

## SEEKING POLITICAL OFFICE: CONGRESS

At the national level, a growing number of blacks won seats in Congress after 1968. After the 1970 elections raised the total from 9 to 12 in the House of Representatives, they joined together to form the Congressional Black Caucus the following year. This enabled them to coordinate their efforts and lobby more effectively with the House leadership on matters of importance to black citizens. In recognition of the growing black presence at all levels of politics, a black political think tank called the Joint Center for Political Studies was established in Washington, D.C., in 1970.

After the 1980 election the Black Caucus grew to 17, and after the 1990 election to 25, all but one a Democrat. In 1968, Shirley Chisholm of New York became the first black woman elected to Congress. In 1972 Barbara Jordan of Texas and Andrew Young of Georgia, former aide to Martin Luther King, Jr., became the first blacks since 1901 to be elected from the South; Young won in a mostly white district of Atlanta. During the 1980s, William Gray of Pennsylvania became the most powerful black in the history of Congress. He rose to majority whip in 1989, the third-highest House Democratic leadership position after House speaker and Democratic majority leader.

The Congressional Black Caucus, 103rd Congress (1993–1995), at the U.S. Capitol. On the steps, upper left to lower right: Representatives Edolphus Towns (D-N.Y.), Julian C. Dixon (D-Calif.), Louis Stokes (D-Ohio), Eleanor Holmes Norton (D-D.C.), Major R. Owens (over Rep. Norton's shoulder) (D-N.Y.), Bennie G. Thompson (D-Miss.), Cynthia A. McKinney (D-Ga.), Donald M. Payne (D-N.J.), Carrie P. Meek (D-Fla.), James E. Clyburn (D-S.C.), Corrine Brown (D-Fla.), Robert C. Scott (D-Va.), Alcee L. Hastings (D-Fla.), Barbara-Rose Collins (D-Mich.), Maxine Waters (partly hidden) (D-Calif.), Cardiss Collins (D-Ill.), Alan Wheat (D-Mo.), Kweisi Mfume (D-Md., caucus chairman), Senator Carol Moseley-Braun (D-Ill.), and Representative Harold E. Ford (D-Tenn.). Above the steps, left to right: Representatives William J. Jefferson (partly hidden) (D-La.), Gary A. Franks (R-Conn.), Earl F. Hilliard (D-Ala.), Mel Reynolds (D-Ill.), Melvin L. Watt (D-N.C.), Cleo Fields (D-La.), Charles B. Rangel (D-N.Y.), Sanford D. Bishop, Jr. (D-Ga.), Albert R. Wynn (D-Md.), Ronald V. Dellums (D-Calif.), Floyd H. Flake (D-N.Y.), Eva M. Clayton (D-N.C.), John Lewis (D-Ga.), and Lucien E. Blackwell (D-Pa.). Not pictured are Representatives William Clay (D-Mo.), John Conyers, Jr. (D-Mich.), Eddie Bernice Johnson (D-Tex.), Bobby Rush (D-Ill.), Walter R. Tucker (D-Calif.), and Craig Washington (D-Tex.).

While blacks gained strength on Capitol Hill, the white members of Congress became increasingly conservative. Therefore, blacks and the declining number of white liberals on the Hill had to spend more time defending past gains than breaking new ground. The Black Caucus did, though, succeed in one important new initiative: imposing economic sanctions against South Africa. Congress passed sanctions legislation in 1986 and then overrode President Reagan's veto.

In 1992 blacks scored another first. Carol Moseley-Braun was elected to the U.S. Senate from Illinois, becoming the first black woman and the first black Democrat to sit in that body. Other gains, possibly even more important, came on the House side that year. At the order of the Justice Department, a number of southern states created additional black-majority districts after the 1990 census (see "Voting Rights," page 221). Mostly as a result of that, black representation in the House grew from 25 to 39 after the 1992 elections (38 Democrats, plus one Republican from a white-majority district). Blacks now made up 15 percent of the House's Democratic majority. They chaired three House committees: Armed Services, Government Operations, and Post Office and Civil Service. Blacks also headed up 17 subcommittees. Much stronger than ever, the Black Caucus began to influence bills not directly related to civil rights. It was, for example, a serious player in negotiations over President Clinton's 1993 budget bill and his 1994 crime bill.

In the 1994 election, the Black Caucus grew to a record 41 (40 representatives and one senator), all but two of them Democrats. But the Republicans captured both houses of Congress for the first time in more than 60 years, leaving the caucus's 38 House Democrats a minority within the minority party, without any committee or subcommittee chairs, and with far less influence than before.

## SEEKING POLITICAL OFFICE: JESSE JACKSON AND THE PRESIDENCY

In 1972 Representative Shirley Chisholm of New York ran for the Democratic presidential nomination. But neither the Black Caucus nor many individual black leaders backed her, and she did not get far. The first major race for president by a black did not come until 12 years later. The candidate was the Reverend Jesse Jackson.

Jackson, a Baptist minister, had been an aide to Martin Luther King, Jr., in the 1960s. He became head of the SCLC's Operation Breadbasket, which used boycotts and other forms of economic pressure to get white-owned businesses to hire blacks. Jackson split with the SCLC after King's death. To continue the work of Operation Breadbasket, in 1971 he formed Operation PUSH (People United to Save Humanity, later renamed People United to Serve Humanity). He scored a major success in 1981, when Coca-Cola signed an agreement with PUSH. Anheuser-Busch, Kentucky Fried Chicken, and other corporations also came around. Jackson was also active in Democratic Party politics, challenging the Daley machine in Chicago. He led voter registration campaigns in black commu-

At a Labor Day gathering in Cleveland, Ohio, on September 7, 1987, Jesse Jackson announces his intention to run for president a second time in 1988.

nities. In 1983 Jackson went to Syria and secured the release of Lieutenant Robert Goodman, a U.S. navigator whose plane had been shot down over that country. With these accomplishments, the national attention that he received for them, and his ability to rouse black audiences with his electrifying speeches, Jackson moved to the front row of black leadership.

Jackson's decision to run for the Democratic presidential nomination, announced in October 1983, had three basic justifications. First, he believed that black victories at the local level—and especially Harold Washington's election as mayor of Chicago in April 1983—meant that he could run a strong campaign. Second, he felt that the Democratic Party was concentrating too much on winning back white voters who, since the 1960s, had grown more conservative and become Republicans. Jackson felt that the party was forgetting its traditional agenda of civil rights and economic justice and wanted to lead the party back to it. Third, he saw his campaign as a way of adding blacks to the voting rolls.

With his fiery words of optimism, Jackson aroused black audiences to great enthusiasm. "From the slave ship to the championship, from welfare to our share, from the outhouse to the courthouse to the statehouse to the White House, our time has come!" was an example of Jackson's stirring rhetoric. But black political leaders looked at his candidacy from a practical point of view. Some backed him, but many did not. One reason was their belief that he had no chance to win the nomination; his campaign, they felt, would turn blacks away from the real task of defeating Ronald Reagan's reelection bid. Also, one of the two major white candidates, Walter Mondale, had built up a record of strong support for civil rights as a U.S. senator and as Jimmy Carter's vice president. Some elected blacks saw Jackson as a threat to their power within the Democratic Party. Also, NAACP executive director Benjamin Hooks and other black leaders opposed Jackson's effort as a sure way to put blacks on the losing side of the primary campaign. The shortage of black endorsements cut down on his black vote and also hampered fundraising efforts.

Jackson also had overwhelming problems with white voters. Polls indicated that about 20 percent of all whites simply would not vote for any black—a sign that white racism was alive and well. But a much larger share of whites felt that Jackson was too radical. They opposed racial discrimination but also opposed his strong support for affirmative action; they also opposed his proposal that government guarantee everyone a job, fearing that it would be too expensive and give government too much power. Many whites also disliked his friendly ties with militant Third World leaders. These included Yasir Arafat, head of the Palestine Liberation Organization, whom Jackson publicly embraced in 1979, and Fidel Castro, whose revolution he praised during a visit to Cuba in 1984.

Jews normally were the white group most likely to vote for black candidates; their votes, for example, helped Harold Washington win in Chicago. But the great majority of them rejected Jackson because of his sympathy with the Palestinian cause in the Middle East; his reluctance to break with Nation of Islam leader Louis Farrakhan, who called Judaism a "gutter religion" and made other antisemitic remarks; and his own description of New York City as "Hymietown." Jackson tried to form what he called a rainbow coalition. And while it attracted some white peace activists, feminists, environmentalists, and others on the left, these represented only a small minority of the white population; the dominant color in his rainbow was black.

Still, Jackson achieved some of his goals in 1984: almost 700,000 new black voters registered between 1980 and 1984, many of them so they could vote for Jackson. Also, Jackson won 77 percent of all black votes in the Democratic primaries. Jackson got only about 5 percent of the white vote, however. Running third behind Mondale and Colorado's U.S. senator Gary Hart, he received 3.3 million votes, representing more than 18 percent of all Democratic primary votes, and won nearly 400 convention delegates.

In 1988 Jackson made another, more powerful bid to become the Democratic choice for president. This time none of the white candidates had a significant record of support for civil rights. Therefore, almost all major black leaders backed Jackson. In his second race, he made a greater outreach effort to other minorities, especially Hispanics and Native Americans, and to whites. For one thing, he placed greater emphasis this time on issues that went beyond race. He spoke eloquently about the drug problem. He talked about the plant closings that were occurring around the country because of foreign economic competition; noting that they were costing hundreds of thousands of whites as well as blacks their jobs, Jackson called upon the government to stop the shutdowns. In addition, he distanced himself from Farrakhan and avoided slips like the "Hymietown" remark of 1984.

His numbers improved greatly over 1984. Jackson ran a fairly close second to Governor Michael Dukakis of Massachusetts, winning 6.8 million Democratic primary votes, or just over 29 percent of the total. He captured 92 percent of the black ballots, which made it possible for him to win the Alabama, Georgia, Louisiana, Mississippi, South Carolina, and Virginia primaries. He also carried New York City and other major cities. All together, Jackson won around 1,200 convention delegates, three times his 1984 total.

Jackson also more than doubled his showing among whites, winning 12 percent of their votes. He was especially successful in economically troubled states like Michigan, where many automobile plants had closed. But once again the great majority of whites did not vote for him. Part of the explanation was racism. But as in 1984, an even more important reason was the conservative views of most whites, who would not vote for liberal or left-wing candidates regardless of color. That is why after Jackson lost the 1984 and 1988 primaries, the white liberals who defeated him went on to lose badly to conservative Republicans Reagan and Bush. Perhaps a middle-of-the-road or conservative black could win the presidency. In the mid-1990s many whites said they would vote for four-star general Colin Powell, the black former head of the Joint Chiefs of Staff who had become a national hero during the Persian Gulf War of 1991. (To their disappointment, though, he declined to run in 1996.) But a black candidate with Jackson's views had very little chance.

Still, Jackson had paved the way for more moderate black presidential candidates by showing that a black could run a serious race and take a substantial portion of the vote. And whether electable or not, Jackson could influence Democratic officeholders because of his popularity among black voters. When President Clinton took actions that displeased blacks in 1994 and 1995, Jackson threatened to run for president in 1996. Such threats reminded Democrats that they needed black votes to have any chance of keeping the White House.

## MIDDLE CLASS AND UNDERCLASS

After the civil rights revolution of the 1960s, many blacks took advantage of desegregation and affirmative action to move up the ladder of economic success. For one thing, more blacks obtained the education needed for success. In 1970, just 4.4 percent of all blacks over 25 had four or more years of college; by 1992 the proportion had risen to 11.9 percent (still well below the white rate of 22.1

percent). Blacks held just 1.9 percent of all administrative and managerial jobs in 1970; in 1993 the figure was up to 6.2 percent. The black share of professional positions grew during the same time from 2.6 to 7.0 percent.

The proportion of black families with annual incomes of more than $35,000 rose from 22.7 percent in 1970 to 29.6 percent in 1991. The proportion with incomes higher than $50,000 rose in those years from 8.9 percent to 14.8 percent. Within the federal government, blacks gained a greater share of the higher-paying jobs. In 1967, blacks filled only about 3 percent of the jobs in the top two pay ranges; in 1991 they held around 10 percent of those jobs.

But other economic numbers told a very different story. Black income as a percentage of white income climbed from 55.1 percent in 1965 to 61.5 percent in 1975. But then progress stopped, and in 1980 the figure was down to about 58 percent, where it remained in 1992. Between 1966 and 1970, the proportion of blacks living in poverty fell from nearly 49 percent to less than 34 percent. But again progress stopped, and the proportion remained at around the one-third mark in 1991—about three times the white rate. The proportion of black children growing up in poverty increased from 41.5 percent in 1970 to 45.6 percent in 1991.

How could this happen while the black middle class was growing? It occurred because while an increasing percentage of black families were earning incomes over $35,000, the proportion making under $10,000 was also increasing, from 21.9 percent of black families in 1970 to 26.4 percent in 1991—and a growing proportion of these had no source of income. As the black middle and upper-middle class grew, so did the number of black poor.

It is not hard to understand why more blacks were living comfortably after the civil rights revolution, but it is difficult to explain the increase of blacks living in poverty. A 1990 study by The Urban Institute found that when equally qualified blacks and whites were sent job-hunting, the whites received about 15 percent more job offers. This showed that racism still played an important part in the economic fortunes of blacks. At the same time, the 15 percent figure would have been far higher before the civil rights revolution. If the impact of racism was declining, then the major reason for the growth of black poverty could not be discrimination.

The best explanation, according to black sociologist William Julius Wilson and others, lay in the nation's changing economy. We have seen that as a result of automation and the movement of industry from the cities to the suburbs, the 1960s witnessed a growing number of permanently unemployed black men, especially young black men. They had children out of wedlock, without taking the responsibility of fatherhood. This resulted in a growing number of poor, female-headed families (see "Obstacles to Progress," page 195).

After 1970, these trends not only continued but speeded up—all because of changes in the international economy. America had dominated markets around the globe for 25 years after the end of World War II. Then, it began facing increased competition. Other industrialized nations such as Japan and Germany began producing better-quality automobiles and electronic goods at lower cost. Meanwhile, developing countries with their low-wage labor forces were producing basic manufactured goods such as steel, aluminum, and rubber at lower cost than U.S. firms. As a result, millions of U.S. manufacturing jobs disappeared in what became known as the deindustrialization of America. The Northeast and the Midwest, America's major industrial centers, lost so many jobs that they became known as the Rust Belt. Once southern blacks had flocked northward seeking industrial jobs. In the 1970s the flood tapered off, and in the 1980s there was a small migration back to the South.

Many white industrial workers lost their jobs. But blacks felt the impact most. Because of historical racism, they had never received equal educational opportunities. Therefore, they depended more than whites on the very jobs that were disappearing by the millions: unskilled and semiskilled union jobs in industry that offered decent pay and benefits but did not require a high level of education. New, high-paying positions were opening up in the professions, financial services, real estate, information technology, and other areas. But these types of work required much more education than most blacks had. Many blacks who had once worked in plants and factories now had to settle for low-paying, low-benefits service jobs, such as employment in fast-food restaurants or as clerks, taxi drivers, and so on. Others simply fell into the ranks of the permanently unemployed.

In 1992, 50.8 percent of blacks were not working. They either were unemployed but seeking employment (14.1 percent) or had given up looking for work (36.7 percent). Young blacks were hardest hit. In 1992, 42 percent of black males ages 16–19 were unemployed (compared to 18.4 percent of white males in that age group), and 37.2 percent of black females ages 16–19 were jobless (compared to 15.7 percent of white females). For black males in the 20–24 age range, the unemployment rate was 24.5 percent (in comparison to 10.4 percent for white males), while the figure for black females in that age group was 23.1 percent (in comparison to 8.3 percent for white females). These huge numbers of unemployed black youths formed the heart of what became known in the 1970s as the inner-city underclass.

## Despair and Rage in the Ghettos

The most important thing about the members of the underclass was not their present poverty but their lack of future prospects. At a time when finding a good job required education and skills, they lacked both. This situation bred hopelessness, which led to a wide variety of social ills. Underclass youths often felt that they would never be able to support a family and so did not expect to marry. Therefore, they began having sex at very early ages instead of waiting for marriage. The result was a growing number of out-of-wedlock births: by 1990, 66 percent— nearly two-thirds—of black babies were being born outside of wedlock, up from 24 percent in 1965. Most of them were born to poor teenage girls and young women. A growing percentage of the mothers were under 18, lacking not only money, skills, and job prospects but also the personal maturity to raise children. Often, they and their children lived in permanent poverty, depending on welfare to survive.

Drug use increased sharply throughout American society from the late 1960s onward. But in the inner cities, where it provided an escape from despair, addiction became an epidemic—especially after crack, a cheap form of cocaine, appeared on the streets in the early 1980s. A growing number of black babies were born addicted to crack. Drug users often shared needles; that is a major reason why 30 percent of those who died from acquired immunodeficiency syndrome (AIDS) through 1992 were black. Unemployed youths formed armed gangs that participated in the highly profitable drug trade. Some of these youths supported their parents financially. A much greater number died young from drug overdoses or in the gang shootouts that plagued inner-city streets and trapped people in their homes. Crime in general increased in the ghettos; the black prison population almost tripled from 1978 to 1991 (while the number of white inmates doubled).

The policies of the Reagan administration made things still worse for the underclass. President Reagan believed that most federal assistance to the poor caused poverty instead of curing it; like other conservatives, he argued that such aid made the poor dependent on government and discouraged them from taking steps to advance themselves. His administration tightened eligibility requirements for food stamps; Aid to Families with Dependent Children (AFDC), the basic welfare program; and Medicaid, which provided health care for the poor. He cut funds for the Legal Services Corporation, which gave the poor legal advice and representation. He slashed federal housing programs by almost 90 percent, just when the number of homeless people was soaring. Reagan also eliminated the Comprehensive Employment and Training Agency (CETA) and the Public Service and Employment Program, while trimming other government employment and training programs. The number of student loans was reduced. The cutbacks in job training and education assistance seemed especially foolish to Reagan's critics. What was the sense, they asked, of making such reductions just when an underclass crippled by a lack of education and job skills was growing rapidly?

Reagan was much more successful in scaling down assistance to the poor than in blocking civil rights enforcement. His reductions in federal spending for the poor amounted to about $10 billion a year. Most important of all, Reagan made it difficult to reverse his cuts. By sharply lowering income taxes while increasing military spending, he sent budget deficits and the national debt skyrocketing. Faced with this debt, future presidents would find it difficult to meet the needs of the poor.

To heal the crisis of the inner cities, it seemed to many, government had to tackle both civil rights and employment issues. Greater efforts to stop discrimination in employment were needed. But even more important for members of the underclass would be race-neutral action to expand employment, because affirmative action most often helped the black middle class, not those who lacked the skills for decent jobs. In the short term, some believed, government had to provide public-sector jobs for all those in need of work. In the long term, it had to end the mismatch between the low level of job skills among inner-city residents and the high level of job skills needed for postindustrial jobs. This, it was argued, could be done by expanding access to education and by providing, or paying business firms to provide, job training programs. Also, some stated that the federal government needed to change its broad economic policies. For example, they said government should put greater stress on encouraging economic growth to create jobs, and less stress on policies that controlled inflation by slowing down economic growth. But in the political climate of the mid-1990s, comprehensive action on these fronts seemed less likely than at any time since 1970. Concentration on one area, perhaps education and job training, might produce the best results.

Despair in the inner cities promoted anger and violence. A major race riot broke out in a black section of Miami in August 1980, leaving 16 dead and hundreds injured. A riot broke out in the Crown Heights section of Brooklyn in August 1991 after a Hasidic Jewish driver ran over and killed a seven-year-old black boy (accidentally, according to investigators). In the nights of violence that followed, another Hasid was killed at random by a black mob. Rap music, emerging from the inner cities, often expressed rage against women, Jews, whites in general, and homosexuals. Sometimes the lyrics described acts of violence against the targets of rage, especially women.

Buildings burn during the Los Angeles riot of April 1992. About 3,700 buildings were destroyed by fire.

But the Los Angeles ghetto riot of 1992 was the most vivid expression of black anger and despair. Late one night in March 1991, a man stood on his balcony trying out a new video camera. By chance, he recorded a group of white Los Angeles police officers beating a black suspect, Rodney King, on the street. Many Americans, black and white, and millions of others around the world, were shocked when the videotape was played on television. In April 1992, however, the police officers were acquitted by a suburban jury that had no black members. The verdict ignited an enormous riot in Los Angeles's south-central ghetto. Buildings were burned and whites driving by were dragged out of their vehicles and beaten. Stores were looted, although some of the owners defended their property with gunfire. The Crips and Bloods, Los Angeles's top two black youth gangs, played a major role in the violence. Residents of some of the city's wealthier neighborhoods bought guns and blockaded their streets. When the violence stopped after a few days, 38 were dead, about 4,000 were under arrest, and approximately 3,700 buildings lay in burnt ruins.

For a short while, President Bush and other leaders spoke in general terms about the need to help inner-city communities, and polls showed that most whites favored such assistance. But in an era when whites lacked confidence in their own economic future and strongly opposed higher taxes, sympathy for the ghettos faded quickly.

## Racial Polarization

Black anger was not limited to the underclass. Many members of the growing black middle class felt that their hopes were being thwarted. Black managers working in American corporations provide a good example. Between 1982 and 1992, the number of black men holding management positions in the corporate world increased by more than 20 percent. Black women had historically faced even more employment discrimination than black men. But in the period from 1982 to 1992, their presence in corporate management grew by about 65 percent. And yet many of these men and women were frustrated. Some complained that they had "black jobs"—jobs that mainly involved improving the company's racial image. A large number of black managers also complained that they did not have any "signoff power," or power to make important decisions. In addition they spoke of a "glass ceiling"—based on unofficial, or invisible, discriminatory practices— that limited how far they could rise within the corporate world. By the mid-1990s, very few blacks had reached the top level of management, where the important decisions were made: almost all the members of this inner circle were still white men.

Middle-class blacks faced many other forms of discrimination. As we have seen, housing remained widely segregated, so even blacks who could afford first-rate homes often had to settle for second-rate dwellings. The United States had long claimed to be a country where hard work would be rewarded with a high standard of living. This promise was finally beginning to come true for many blacks, yet they found that even with good incomes, they could not always live as well as whites with the same earnings. Members of the black middle class, like poor blacks, were subject to racial harassment. For example, they were much more likely than whites of any class to be stopped by police as crime suspects, and perhaps then roughed up. Some whites in the general population treated all black men as if they were inner-city criminals. Violent white racist groups that emerged in the 1980s, including youth gangs known as skinheads, assaulted black lawyers and corporate managers as well as blacks in the underclass. Members of the black middle class, then, were frequently reminded that no matter how high their status, their blackness was still a badge of inferiority in the eyes of many whites.

And so despite great progress in civil rights, the arts, and employment, race relations in late-twentieth-century America were tense. Many blacks of all classes remained suspicious of whites. A sizable number believed that whites were con-spiring against blacks—one theory blamed the spread of drugs on an organized white conspiracy to commit genocide against African Americans. Because blacks still felt excluded from full participation in American citizenship, the ideas of the black power movement continued to carry weight in the African-American community after the 1960s. Feeling rejected by America, some blacks in turn rejected white society and stressed their black identity. For example, although many black babies did not have permanent homes, a significant number of blacks opposed letting white couples adopt them; they believed that the children would be deprived of their black identity. The National Association of Black Social Workers endorsed this view.

Bolstering racial pride was a primary method for strengthening black identity. In the 1980s a collection of ideas emerged that became known as Afrocentrism. This school of thought emphasized the importance of Africa in the development of world civilization. Afrocentrism had the desirable effect of focusing greater attention on African history and culture, which had been mostly ignored in the West. But most scholars disputed the claims of the more extreme Afrocentrists, who argued that the ancient Egyptians were black; that ancient Greece, generally regarded as the cradle of Western civilization, was based on African civilization; and that Jesus Christ was at least partly black.

For a small but perhaps growing minority of blacks, elevating blacks involved putting down others. Louis Farrakhan, who as head of the Nation of Islam frequently denounced Jews as wealthy, powerful, and evil, gained influence in the black community during the 1990s. In 1995 he initiated a "Million Man March" for black men only to Washington, D.C.; it drew more than 500,000 black men, at least twice as many as attended the March on Washington for Jobs and Freedom in 1963. Professor Leonard Jeffries, chairman of the African American Studies Department at the City College of New York, and others claimed that a high proportion of slave traders had been Jews, although this had no basis in fact. Such views found increasing support among black college students in the 1990s. Not surprisingly, the spread of these beliefs reduced white support for the civil rights agenda.

During 1995 the degree of racial polarization in America became dramatically apparent in public reaction to the murder trial of O.J. Simpson, a famous black former football star found not guilty of murdering his white wife and her white male friend. The alleged racist practices of the Los Angeles Police Department became the core of the defense's strategy, and the public displays of joy by many blacks and of dismay by many whites over the acquittal offered a vivid demonstration of continuing racial division.

As the twentieth century comes to an end, the prospects for improved race relations in the near future does not look strong. The election of Ronald Reagan and George Bush in the 1980s, and of a Republican Congress in 1994, represents a conservative trend against civil rights enforcement and social spending. In the absence of a strong national commitment to continue the fight against racial discrimination and poverty, racial injustice and the resentments that always accompany it will continue to be part of the fabric of American life.

# BIOGRAPHIES

· · · · · · · · ·

**Allen, Richard** (1760–1831). Allen was the founder and leader of the African Methodist Episcopal church, the first black religious denomination in the United States. He was born into a Philadelphia slave family that was sold to a Delaware farmer around 1767. While still a boy, Allen became interested in religion and joined the white-controlled Methodist Episcopal Church. Meanwhile, his master agreed to let Allen hire himself out. With his earnings, he bought his freedom in 1786 and moved to Philadelphia. Allen joined St. George's Episcopal church there and attracted blacks to the church. When church officials tried physically to force blacks into the upstairs gallery in April 1787, Allen led the blacks in a walkout. He and Absalom Jones then formed the Free African Society, which in 1794 built the Bethel African Methodist Church in Philadelphia. In 1816, 16 independent black Methodist churches in Pennsylvania, Delaware, New Jersey, and Maryland united to form the African Methodist Episcopal church. Allen was elected its bishop, a post he held until his death. An opponent of returning to Africa, Allen helped organize a January 1817 meeting of 3,000 blacks in Philadelphia to condemn the just-formed American Colonization Society.

**Baker, Ella Josephine** (1903–1986). Ella Baker was a community organizer and civil rights activist who promoted grassroots democracy and a nonviolent, direct mass action approach to social problems. Born in Norfolk, Virginia, Baker grew up in rural North Carolina. From her family, Baker inherited pride in her black heritage, an independent spirit, and a sense of community obligation. After graduating in 1927 from Shaw University in Raleigh, North Carolina, she moved to Harlem. In 1931 she cofounded the Young Negro Cooperative League, which organized consumer cooperatives that helped people reduce their living expenses during the Depression through mass purchasing. During the 1930s she also became involved with women's groups, including a union of domestic workers and the Harlem Housewives Cooperative. As assistant field secretary for the National Association for the Advancement of Colored People (NAACP) from 1938 to 1942, she traveled throughout the South to bring in new members and money. From 1942 to 1946, she was the NAACP's national field secretary and then its director of branches. Baker left the national NAACP organization in 1946 partly because she believed that its leadership was too centralized and undemocratic and put too much emphasis on the legal struggle against racial discrimination. However, she remained active in the NAACP's New York City branch and was its president from 1954 to 1956. During the Montgomery bus boycott of 1955–1956, Baker became an adviser to Martin Luther King, Jr. In 1958 she became the leader of the Crusade for Citizenship, a voting rights project of the newly formed Southern Christian Leadership Conference (SCLC). Not used to dealing with women in positions of authority, however, the black ministers who led the SCLC did not give Baker their full support. Also, Baker was disturbed at the organization's heavy reliance on its president, Martin Luther King, Jr., because she favored decentralized, grassroots leadership over a strong, single leader. In April 1960 Baker played a key role in bringing the black student sit-in leaders together and convincing them to form their own organization, independent of established civil rights groups. That organization, the Student Nonviolent Coordinating Committee (SNCC), embodied Baker's ideal of a grassroots, democratic organization committed to nonviolent direct action. She remained an unofficial adviser to SNCC. In 1964 Baker and leaders of SNCC created the biracial Mississippi Freedom Democratic Party. From the mid-1960s until her death, Baker advised community and human rights organizations not only throughout the country but around the world.

**Bethune, Mary McLeod** (1875–1955). Mary McLeod Bethune was an influential educator, civil rights leader, and public official. She was born in Mayesville, South Carolina, the fifteenth child of former slaves. After graduating from Chicago's Moody Bible Institute in 1895, she moved back to the South and became a teacher. In 1904 Bethune founded a school for women in Daytona Beach, Florida. In 1923 Bethune merged it with a men's school to form Bethune-Cookman College, of which she was president. In the 1920s, she became an adviser to the Coolidge and Hoover administrations on minority issues and was also active in the National Urban League and the NAACP. Under President Franklin D. Roosevelt, Bethune served as director of the Division of Negro Affairs of the National Youth Administration (NYA) from 1936 to 1943. Through her efforts, blacks sat on every southern state's NYA board and 64,000 black youths were admitted into the NYA's student work programs. With her forceful and magnetic personality, she became chair of the unofficial Black Cabinet of black New Deal officials. Bethune had access to the White House and advised President Roosevelt. She also became both an adviser to and a friend of the president's wife, Eleanor. In 1937 Bethune founded the National Council of Negro Women and served as its president.

**Brooke, Edward William, III** (1919– ). Edward Brooke was the first black to sit in the U.S. Senate after Reconstruction and the first to be chosen by popular vote. Born in Washington, D.C., Brooke graduated from Howard University in 1941 and from Boston University Law School in 1948. He ran unsuccessfully for the Massachusetts state legislature as a Republican in 1950 and 1952. In 1960 he narrowly lost his race for Massachusetts secretary of state. Appointed to head the Boston Finance Committee, Brooke gained much favorable attention for rooting out corruption in government. He then was elected state attorney general in 1962 and in 1964, winning the second time by one of the largest statewide Republican majorities ever, even though blacks were only 3 percent of the population. Brooke was elected to the U.S. Senate in 1966 and reelected in 1972. A liberal Republican, he voted for antipoverty legislation and civil rights bills but was independent of civil rights groups and opposed militant and illegal activity. Brooke worked to increase federal support for low-income housing. Many Republicans thought he was too liberal, while many liberals criticized him for supporting President Lyndon B. Johnson's Vietnam War policies. Black militants often called him an Uncle Tom. In 1978 he was investigated for financial misconduct. Although Brooke was never charged with crimes, he lost his reelection bid that year. Afterward, Brooke worked as an attorney and consultant.

**Brown, John** (1800–1859). A white opponent of slavery who was on the fringe of the abolitionist movement, Brown gained fame for his use of violence in the antislavery cause. Born in Torrington, Connecticut, Brown was an unsuccessful businessman. In 1849 he joined the abolitionist movement and two years later began working in the Underground Railroad. In 1855 Brown went to the Kansas Territory, where pro- and antislavery settlers were in a shooting war. The following year Brown and six others (four of them his sons) killed five proslavery settlers. Brown then planned a military action that he hoped would spark a slave revolt. On October 16, 1859, Brown led 21 men in an attack on the federal arsenal at Harper's Ferry, Virginia (now in West Virginia). Two days later U.S. Marines recaptured the arsenal. In less than two months, Brown was tried and hanged for murder, instigating a slave revolt, and treason against Virginia.

**Brown, Willie L., Jr.** (1934– ). As speaker of the California state assembly, Willie Brown became one of the most powerful black politicians in America. He was born into an extremely poor family in Mineola, Texas. Brown graduated from San Francisco State University in 1955, having paid his way by working as a janitor and doorman, and received his law degree from Hastings College Law School in 1958. He lost a 1962 bid for a state assembly seat but won two years later. Skilled at the art of making compromises and finding allies, Willie Brown became a powerful figure in the assembly. In 1972 and 1980 he co-chaired the California delegations to the Democratic National Convention. Brown was elected speaker of the assembly in 1980. A brilliant manipulator of the assembly's rules of procedure, he beat back many efforts to remove him from the speaker's chair. The second most powerful California politician after the governor, Brown pushed civil rights, health, auto safety, crime, environmental protection, and gay rights bills through the assembly. A 1992 California term limits bill would have barred Brown from running for reelection again in 1996. Therefore, he resigned from the legislature in 1995 and ran successfully for mayor of San Francisco that year.

**Bruce, Blanche Kelso** (1841–1898). Blanche K. Bruce was the first black to serve a full term in the U.S. Senate. Born a slave in Farmville, Prince Edward County, Virginia, he left his master during the Civil War. After studying at Oberlin College from 1866 to 1868, Bruce moved to Bolivar County, Mississippi, where he became a well-to-do planter. In 1871 he was appointed assessor of Bolivar County and in 1872 became its sheriff. In 1874 the Republican-controlled Mississippi state legislature elected Bruce to the U.S. Senate. In Washington, D.C., he condemned racist vigilante groups in Mississippi and called for full compensation for black depositors in the failed Freedman's Savings and Trust Company. Bruce opposed the movement to exclude Chinese immigrants and spoke out for fairer treatment of American Indians. The Mississippi senator also favored restoring full political rights to former rebels. The end of Reconstruction prevented him from winning reelection in 1880. Afterward, however, he received a series of federal appointments.

**Bunche, Ralph Johnson** (1904–1971). Ralph Bunche was an expert on European colonialism who won the Nobel Peace Prize for his work at the United Nations. Born in Detroit, Bunche graduated summa cum laude from the University of California at Los Angeles. At Harvard University, he received a Ph.D. in political science in 1934. A radical during the 1930s, Bunche urged the NAACP to seek unity among black and white workers as the best way to end the oppression of blacks. In 1935 Bunche helped found the National Negro Congress. From 1938 to 1940 he assisted Swedish sociologist Gunnar Myrdal in doing research for *An American Dilemma* (1944), Myrdal's pioneering book on American race relations. During World War II, Bunche worked at the State Department as an expert on colonial issues. In 1947 he became head of the UN's trusteeship division. Bunche negotiated an end to the 1948–1949 Arab-Israeli War. For that he was awarded the Nobel Peace Prize in 1950, becoming the first black to obtain it. In 1956 Bunche was put in charge of a UN peace force in the Sinai Desert between Israel and Egypt. In 1960 he led a UN peace force in the Congo (now Zaire). Bunche was UN undersecretary general from 1967 to 1971. He supported the civil rights revolution in the 1960s, participating in key marches and rallies.

**Carmichael, Stokely** (later known as Kwame Toure) (1941– ). Using the slogan "Black power!" Carmichael turned the Student Nonviolent Coordinating Committee (SNCC) toward black nationalism while chairman of the organization. Born in Port-of-Spain, Trinidad, he grew up there and in New York City. While at Howard University, he joined SNCC in 1960. After graduating in 1964, Carmichael helped direct the Mississippi Freedom Summer voter registration campaign that year. In 1965 he headed a voter registration project in Lowndes County, Alabama, and helped form an all-black political party there called the Lowndes County Freedom Organization. Meanwhile, Carmichael was moving away from the traditional nonviolent, pro-integration stance of SNCC. Elected SNCC chairman in May 1966, he introduced the slogan "Black power!" the following month during a march in Mississippi. The slogan became popular among many blacks, especially in northern ghettos. Carmichael rejected integration because, he said, it meant that blacks should reject what they are and become just like whites. Blacks, Carmichael believed, must take pride in themselves, define themselves by their own standards, and build their own institutions. After traveling in the Third World in 1967, he returned as an advocate of violent revolution against capitalism and racism. From 1968 to 1969 he was prime minister of the Black Panther Party. He left the country in 1968 and lived in Africa. He eventually returned with a new name, Kwame Toure, and a radical nationalist program that attracted very few followers.

**Chisholm, Shirley Anita St. Hill** (1924– ). Shirley Chisholm was the first black woman to win election to the U.S. House of Representatives and to run for president. Of West Indian descent, she was born in Brooklyn, New York. A community and Democratic Party activist in Brooklyn, Chisholm broke with the party machine because it often ignored the needs of blacks and rarely endorsed black candidates. In 1964 she won election to the New York state assembly, only the second black woman to sit in that body. There, Chisholm became a leading supporter of government-funded day care centers and unemployment insurance for domestic workers. In 1968 Chisholm won a seat in the U.S. House of Representatives from Brooklyn. During her seven terms in the House, she pressed for racial equality and worked for women's rights. Chisholm was a founder of the National Women's Political Caucus. In 1972 she ran for the Democratic presidential nomination but received little support from black leaders. Since retiring from Congress in 1983, Chisholm has lectured around the country.

**Cuffee, Paul** (1759–1817). Paul Cuffee was a prosperous merchant and shipbuilder who promoted the colonization of Africa by African Americans. The youngest child of a free black man and an American Indian woman, Cuffee was born in rural Massachusetts and spent his boyhood working on the farm that his father bought in Westport in 1766. Cuffee was largely self-taught, although a private tutor helped him study navigation. At the age of 16, he became a common seaman on both whaling and trading vessels. In 1779 he and his brother David built a small vessel for trading between Massachusetts and New York. Paul invested his profits in larger and larger ships and by 1800 was engaging in whaling and trading in Newfoundland, along the North American coast, and in the Caribbean. He became the first wealthy African American, but that did not exempt him from constant racial insults and discrimination. Cuffee coped with this bias by remaining respectful, even to whites who did not respect him—his only choice if he wished to be successful. Still, he found a way to protest racial injustice: beginning in the late 1770s, he and his brother John refused to pay taxes. In their petitions to state, county, and local authorities, they argued—

among other things—that since blacks could not vote, they could, like the American colonists, stand on the principle of "no taxation without representation." In December 1780 they were briefly arrested, and in June 1781 they paid their back taxes. Despite the racial injustice that he endured, Paul Cuffee accepted the values of the American society in which he was raised: he believed, along with whites, that Africa was a backward, primitive continent whose civilizations were far inferior to those of Europe and the United States. Beginning around 1810 he began promoting the idea of settling African Americans in Africa; there, Cuffee argued, they could redeem Africa by introducing Western practices and beliefs—in particular, Christianity. Later, Cuffee also came to the conclusion that African Americans would never be given a fair chance in the United States; therefore, he stated, they should settle in Africa for their own sakes as well as for the benefit of Africans. Pursuing his beliefs, Cuffee spent five months in Sierra Leone, on the West African coast, in 1811 and early 1812. Having concluded that an African American colony could succeed there, he sailed to Sierra Leone with 38 African American settlers in December 1815; they arrived at their destination in February 1816. When the American Colonization Society was formed by prominent whites late in 1816, Cuffee voiced his approval and advised its leaders for a short time before his death.

**De Priest, Oscar Stanton** (1871–1951). Oscar De Priest was a political leader from Chicago's South Side and the first northern black to sit in Congress. Born in Alabama, De Priest moved to Kansas in 1878 and to Chicago in 1889. While earning a living as a painter and decorator, he became a worker in Chicago's Republican political organization. As a reward, De Priest was selected to serve on the Cook County Board of Commissioners from 1904 to 1908. As migration from the South increased Chicago's black population, black politicians stood a greater chance to win elections. De Priest in 1915 captured a city council seat in a South Side ward. In 1928 he carried the South Side's Third Congressional District ticket to win a seat in the U.S. House of Representatives. He won reelection twice. De Priest often spoke out against racial discrimination, and in 1933 Congress passed his amendment to ban it in the Civilian Conservation Corps. But when the Great Depression came, De Priest joined his fellow Republicans in opposing direct federal aid to the poor. This was a major reason why he lost his 1934 reelection bid to a black Democrat. De Priest sat on the Chicago city council from 1943 to 1947.

**Delany, Martin Robinson** (1812–1885). Known as the father of black nationalism in the United States, Martin Delany also was the first black to hold the rank of major in the U.S. Army. He was born in Charles Town, Virginia (now Charleston, West Virginia), the son of a slave father and a free black mother. His mother moved with him to Chambersburg, Pennsylvania, in 1822. Relocating nine years later, he became a leader of the Pittsburgh Anti-Slavery Society and a worker in the Underground Railroad. From 1845 to 1847 he edited the *Mystery*, a Pittsburgh-based black abolitionist newspaper. From 1847 to 1849 he co-edited Frederick Douglass's *North Star* in Rochester, New York. Delany entered Harvard College in 1850 to study medicine. But because of student protests against his presence, he was not allowed to complete his courses. After the Fugitive Slave Act was passed in 1850, Delany wondered whether blacks should remain in the United States. His *Condition, Elevation, Emigration and Destiny of the Colored People of the United States, Politically Considered* (1852) was the first full-scale black nationalist manifesto written in the United States. In it he argued that blacks were a nation and must define their own destiny separately from white America. In 1854 Delany organized the first National Emigration Convention. He favored black settlement in the Caribbean, Central America, South America, or Africa. He went to West Africa in 1859 to explore the possibilities for black American settlements. After the Emancipation Proclamation of 1863, Delany recruited blacks for the Union Army. Two years later he became a major with the 104th U.S. Colored

Troops. After the war, Delany worked for the Freedmen's Bureau for three years and then held minor posts under the Radical Republican government in South Carolina. But in the 1876 state election Delany infuriated many blacks by supporting the Democrats, who won the campaign and then ended Radical Reconstruction.

**Douglass, Frederick** (1817–1895). Douglass was the leading black abolitionist as well as an orator, writer, journalist, and public officeholder. Born a slave in Tuckahoe, Maryland, he was sent to Baltimore in 1825 as a houseboy. There, Douglass learned to read and write with the help of his master's wife and by using his own wits. In 1833 he began working as a plantation field hand. Unhappy over his new and hard life, he made an unsuccessful escape attempt in 1836. Two years later he succeeded, settling in New Bedford, Massachusetts. In 1841 Douglass spoke at a meeting of the Massachusetts Anti-Slavery Society. Tall, with a strong build and an excellent speaking voice, Douglass impressed his listeners. The society hired him as an agent, and over the next four years he was a traveling antislavery lecturer, often risking mob attack. Douglass also fought racial discrimination in the North, sitting in whites-only first-class railroad compartments on Massachusetts trains. (For his efforts he was sometimes unceremoniously thrown off the train.) His 1845 autobiography, *Narrative of the Life of Frederick Douglass, an American Slave,* proved that he was an outstanding writer as well as speaker, and so struck a blow against race prejudice. Douglass spent two years in Great Britain and Ireland, where for the first time he was treated as an equal. Upon returning in 1847, he established his own newspaper, the *North Star* (later renamed *Frederick Douglass's Paper*) in Rochester, New York. Douglass had once been a loyal follower of William Lloyd Garrison, but after moving outside of Garrison's New England stronghold, he became more independent. Abandoning Garrison's strict opposition to violence, Douglass in 1849 said that he would welcome a slave uprising. Later he declared that violence was justified in resisting the Fugitive Slave Act of 1850. During the 1850s he became involved in political activity, another form of action opposed by Garrison. Like Garrison, however, he supported complete integration of the races, looking unfavorably upon every all-black organization, even the black church. Douglass refused to support John Brown's raid on Harper's Ferry, Virginia, in 1859. During the Civil War, Douglass helped recruit black soldiers. As the conflict neared its end, he became a vocal supporter of voting rights for blacks. Douglass agreed with U.S. Representative Thaddeus Stevens that unless the former slaves were given land, they would be economically dependent on the South's white planters and therefore unable to defend their right to vote. A loyal follower of the Republican Party, Douglass was rewarded with political appointments in the District of Columbia in the 1870s and 1880s. From 1889 to 1891 he served as U.S. ambassador to Haiti.

**Douglass, Sarah Mapps** (1806–1882). Sarah Douglass was an abolitionist, an opponent of segregation, and an educator. She was born in Philadelphia to parents who were prominent in the city's free black community. Her mother, a Quaker, helped to found the Philadelphia Female Anti-Slavery Society in 1833. Douglass was educated by a private tutor because the public schooling available for blacks was of poor quality; for more advanced education, she attended a school for black children cofounded by her mother. Douglass herself established a school for black children in Philadelphia during the 1820s. She served as corresponding secretary of the Philadelphia Female Anti-Slavery Society and was a member of its board of directors and its education committee. A Quaker like her mother, Douglass fought against segregated seating in Quaker meetinghouses. In 1838 Douglass, her mother, and other blacks attended a wedding of white abolitionists. Philadelphia newspapers denounced this breach of the color barrier; two days afterward a mob burned down the headquarters of the Pennsylvania Anti-Slavery Society and set ablaze the Shelter for Colored Orphans. In 1853 Douglass became head of the girls' primary department of the Institute of Colored Youth, which eventually became Cheney State College. After the Civil War, she became vice-chair of the Women's Pennsylvania Branch of the American Freedmen's Aid Commission.

**Du Bois, William Edward Burghardt** (1868–1963). W. E. B. Du Bois won national and international fame as a black historian and sociologist, as well as an outstanding writer, editor, civil rights activist, and advocate of Pan-Africanism. He was born and raised in Great Barrington, Massachusetts, a town that was racially tolerant by the standards of the day. In 1885 Du Bois entered Fisk University in Nashville, Tennessee, and was shocked by the harshness of the southern racial caste system. After graduating in 1888, he went to Harvard College, where he earned a bachelor's degree cum laude in 1890 and a master's degree in 1891. Four years later Du Bois became the first black American to receive a doctor of philosophy degree from Harvard. His first book, *Suppression of the African Slave Trade to the United States of America, 1638–1870*, was published in 1896. His sociological study, *The Philadelphia Negro*, appeared three years later. Du Bois joined the faculty of Atlanta University in 1897 and supervised the publication of a series of influential books about black issues. In his *Souls of Black Folk* (1903), a collection of essays, he criticized black educator Booker T. Washington for opposing the black struggle for equality and for encouraging blacks to obtain trade skills instead of a liberal arts education. In 1905 Du Bois organized the Niagara Movement, a small organization of educated blacks that fought for equal rights. The movement did not get very far, but in 1909–1910 Du Bois helped establish the far more successful National Association for the Advancement of Colored People (NAACP). In 1910 Du Bois became the NAACP's director of publicity and research and editor of *The Crisis*, its monthly journal. In 1934 Du Bois resigned as editor, partly because he had begun to advocate separate black economic development, which conflicted with the NAACP's pro-integration stance. An advocate of self-government for black Africa, Du Bois organized a series of Pan-African conferences in Europe from 1919 to 1927 and later became known as the "father of Pan-Africanism." His *Black Reconstruction in America* (1935) was one of the few books of its time to defend Radical Reconstruction. During the 1940s he evolved from an independent radical to a pro-Soviet Marxist. In 1951 he was indicted as an unregistered agent of the Soviet Union, but was then acquitted. Still, the State Department prohibited him from traveling abroad until 1958. In 1961 Du Bois left the United States for the African nation of Ghana. As a parting shot, he joined the American Communist Party. Du Bois wrote novels and poetry. He also wrote an autobiography, *Dusk of Dawn* (1940).

**Farmer, James Leonard** (1920– ). A prominent civil rights leader during the 1960s, James Farmer is best known for organizing freedom rides into the South. He was born in Marshall, Texas, the son of a minister. Farmer graduated from Wiley College in 1938. At Howard University to study religion, he learned about the principles of nonviolent direct action used by Mohandas K. Gandhi in India. Farmer decided to apply Gandhi's methods in the cause of racial equality. In 1941 Farmer became race relations director of the Fellowship of Reconciliation, a pacifist group committed to social change. In 1942 Farmer helped establish the Congress of Racial Equality (CORE), of which he became chairman. During the early 1940s CORE—with Farmer participating—staged the earliest sit-ins, which forced two Chicago restaurants to serve blacks. In 1947 he was involved in the first freedom rides, an attempt by CORE to integrate interstate buses. After working for various labor organizations, he became a program director for the NAACP in 1959. But his interest in direct action led Farmer to return to CORE as national director in February 1961. Farmer immediately organized freedom rides to integrate southern bus terminals serving interstate buses. In late May, Farmer spent 39 days in a Jackson, Mississippi, jail for trying to integrate a bus terminal waiting room. Two years later he was jailed again after leading civil rights demonstrations in Plaquemines, Louisiana. In 1965 he conducted demonstrations in Bogalusa, Louisiana, that achieved the integration of the town's restaurants and theaters. Farmer resigned as head of CORE in 1966. After his departure, black nationalists became the dominant force in CORE. Running on the Republican and Liberal tickets, he lost a 1968 race for Congress to

Democratic U.S. Representative Shirley Chisholm. In 1969–1970 Farmer promoted affirmative action hiring as an assistant secretary for health, education, and welfare in the Nixon administration. Since then he has spent most of his time as a lecturer and teacher.

**Forten, Charlotte L. (Grimké) (1837–1914).** Charlotte Forten was an antislavery teacher, writer, and poet. Born in Philadelphia, she was the granddaughter of free black businessman and abolitionist James Forten; her parents and many other relatives were also active abolitionists. Since her father would not send her to Philadelphia's segregated schools, Forten received her early education from tutors. In 1853 her parents sent her to Salem, Massachusetts, where the schools were integrated. From 1856 to 1858, Forten taught in Salem before returning to Philadelphia because of illness. In 1855 she joined the Female Anti-Slavery Society. During the late 1850s, Forten published poetry in antislavery newspapers, including *The Liberator* and the *National Anti-Slavery Standard*. From 1862 until 1864, she taught newly freed slaves on South Carolina's Sea Islands, which had been captured by Union troops early in the Civil War. Her work was part of an experiment in educating former slaves that had the fervent support of abolitionists. During the afternoon Forten taught nearly 100 children; at night she taught adults who worked on the islands' cotton plantations. From the late 1860s to 1871 Forten worked at the Freedmen's Union Commission, helping to secure and coordinate funding for teachers in the South who were educating former slaves. In 1871–1872 she herself taught at a Charleston school. Subsequently, she wrote frequently on the subject of racial oppression.

**Forten, James (1766–1842).** Forten was a businessman, abolitionist, and reformer. Born in Philadelphia, he was the son of free blacks. After briefly attending school, he began working at about the age of nine. During the Revolution, he served in the American navy as a powder boy. After the Revolution, he was apprenticed to a sail maker in Philadelphia. At age 20 Forten became foreman of the workforce, and in the late 1790s he purchased the business. In 1800 Congress refused to act on a petition, signed by Forten, calling for changes in the Fugitive Slave Act of 1793. This disappointment sparked Forten's resolve to work for the abolition of slavery. In 1813 Forten led the opposition to state legislation that would require free blacks to register with the authorities and end free black migration to Pennsylvania. In 1814 he raised about 2,500 free blacks to defend Philadelphia against a possible British invasion during the War of 1812. Forten, however, questioned whether there was a place in the United States for blacks. So when the American Colonization Society was established in 1816 to settle free blacks in Africa, Forten supported its goal (although in 1817 he chaired a Philadelphia gathering of 3,000 blacks that expressed opposition to the society). But by 1819 he had changed his mind, and from then on was one of the most outspoken critics of colonization. Having become a wealthy businessman by the 1830s, Forten was one of the largest financial contributors to the abolitionist movement. Forten also became involved with a variety of other reform causes, including temperance, peace, and women's rights.

**Fortune, Timothy Thomas (1856–1928).** The leading black journalist around the turn of the twentieth century, T. Thomas Fortune was also an outspoken civil rights leader. He was born in Florida, the son of slaves. Fortune studied at a Freedmen's Bureau school, and later he attended Howard University in Washington, D.C. He edited the *New York Globe* from 1881 to 1884. Fortune then founded the *New York Freeman*, which he owned and edited. In 1887 it became the *New York Age*. The *Age* became the most highly regarded black newspaper in the country. Fortune's editorials called for complete racial equality. In 1893 he founded the National Afro-American League, an early civil rights organization that failed within three years for lack of support. In 1898 he helped establish another rights organization, the National Afro-American Council. Despite Fortune's militant views, he often defended Booker T. Washington. After it became known in 1907 that Washington was a financial supporter of the *Age*, Fortune had a mental collapse. In his last years, he wrote editorials and opinion columns and worked as an editor.

**Garrison, William Lloyd** (1805–1879). The most famous white abolitionist leader in the United States, William Lloyd Garrison was born in Newburyport, Massachusetts. He received little formal schooling and in 1818 was sent out as a printer's apprentice. In 1826 he became a newspaper editor and in 1829 began publishing an antislavery weekly, the *Genius of Universal Emancipation*. On January 1, 1831, Garrison launched the *Liberator*, which became the best-known abolitionist periodical in America. A man of uncompromising views, Garrison was one of the first abolitionists to advocate immediate emancipation. He rejected both violence and political activity, arguing that moral persuasion should be the abolitionists' sole weapon. Expressing his views in the most extreme terms and lashing out against all his critics, Garrison made many enemies and aroused violent public reaction. In 1835 an anti-abolitionist mob placed a rope around his neck and dragged him through the streets of Boston. In 1831 Garrison organized the New England Anti-Slavery Society, which he dominated. Two years later he was a key founder of the American Anti-Slavery Society, in which he had the major influence. Garrison's clout declined somewhat starting around 1840, as some abolitionists began running their own candidates for public office; these so-called political abolitionists also formed their own antislavery movement. During the 1840s some black abolitionists broke with Garrison over the use of violence. During the 1840s and 1850s Garrison denounced the Constitution as a compromise with slavery and contended that the North should renounce it and break with the South. This position aroused much protest among abolitionists. Yet Garrison and the *Liberator* continued to play an important role in stoking antislavery opinion.

**Garvey, Marcus Moziah** (1887–1940). Born in St. Ann's Bay, Jamaica, Marcus Garvey became the most successful black nationalist and back-to-Africa advocate in U.S. history. From a poor family, he had to leave school and become a printer's apprentice at age 14. Working around the Caribbean, he became conscious of discrimination against blacks. Garvey went to London in 1912, where he was influenced by African nationalists living there. While in London he read Booker T. Washington's autobiographical *Up from Slavery* (1901), which convinced Garvey of the importance of black economic self-help as the basis for independence from white control. Returning to Jamaica in 1914, he formed the Universal Negro Improvement and Conservation Association and African Communities League (generally shortened to Universal Negro Improvement Association, or UNIA). Its goals were to promote black commercial activity, pride in blackness, worldwide black unity, and—more and more, as time went on—a return to Africa. Arriving in New York in 1916, he began organizing UNIA chapters across the United States the next year. In 1918 Garvey started publishing *Negro World*, the newspaper of his movement. Soon he was attracting many thousands of followers. Often they were recent migrants from the rural South to the urban North, groping for a sense of identity in their new environment. The many race riots that followed World War I also promoted the organization's growth. In 1920, about 25,000 delegates from 25 countries attended the first UNIA international convention in Harlem. The organization's membership probably peaked at around half a million in 1921. Garvey preached a reverse brand of racism, contending that dark-skinned people were superior to light-skinned ones. He promoted many business enterprises. The best known was the Black Star Line of steamships for linking blacks around the world to Africa. Many thousands of blacks invested in the enterprise before it (like most of Garvey's businesses) collapsed. Although Garvey was probably guilty of poor business practices rather than dishonesty, a jury convicted him of mail fraud. In 1925 he began serving a five-year prison term. President

Calvin Coolidge commuted his sentence in 1927. Deported to Jamaica, he received a hero's welcome. But after 1930 his public support diminished sharply. In 1935 Garvey returned to London, where he died in poverty.

**Gray, William Herbert, III** (1941– ). William Gray became the highest-ranking black member in the history of the U.S. House of Representatives. He was born in Baton Rouge, Louisiana, and raised in Philadelphia. Gray earned a divinity degree from Drew Theological Seminary in 1966 and a theology degree from Princeton Theological Seminary in 1970. Gray served as a pastor in Montclair, New Jersey, and in Philadelphia. Elected to the House as a Democrat from Pennsylvania in 1978, Gray became chair of the powerful Budget Committee in 1985. Soon after, he was elected chair of the House Democratic Caucus. In 1989 he was selected majority whip, the third-ranking leadership position among House Democrats. Gray fought against Reagan administration attempts to turn back the civil rights clock and cut social spending. During the mid-1980s he helped obtain House approval for sanctions against the apartheid regime in South Africa. In 1989 rumors of financial wrongdoing by Gray made the rounds, but he never faced charges. In June 1991 Gray announced his departure from the House. He went on to head the United Negro College Fund.

**Hall, Prince** (1735?–1807). Hall was one of the earliest black abolitionists and nonviolent protesters against racial oppression in the United States. It is not known for certain where he was born or who his parents were. By his mid-teens Hall was the slave of a Boston leather craftsman, a trade Hall followed after he was freed in 1770. During the 1770s, Hall helped organize the first black Masonic lodge in the United States. The lodge received final approval from the Masons' London headquarters in a document dated 1784 but not received in Boston until 1787. The document named Hall, Boston's leading free black, as the lodge's master. Over the next decade, he established black Masonic lodges in Philadelphia and in Providence, Rhode Island. It is not clear whether he served in the Revolution, but he did make leather drumheads for the American side. In 1777 he and eight other blacks signed a petition to the Massachusetts legislature calling for the abolition of slavery on the grounds that it was incompatible with the principles of the Revolution. In 1788 Hall signed a protest against the slave trade; later in the year the legislature acted against it. Apparently, Hall had become a supporter of black colonization by 1787, when he joined 72 others in requesting the legislature to help blacks obtain funds for settling in Africa. During the same year, Hall signed a petition protesting the exclusion of black children from Boston's free school system. Since the exclusion was not removed, Hall in 1796 was among those requesting a separate system for blacks. Boston's selectmen agreed but said they had no place to house such a school, so in 1800 he allowed his own home to be used.

**Hamer, Fannie Lou** (1917–1977). Hamer was a civil rights activist in Mississippi and a founder of the Mississippi Freedom Democratic Party. Born in Mississippi to sharecropper parents, she was the youngest of 20 children. Hamer began picking cotton at age six. She received little schooling: the school term ran only from December through March, when landowners did not need agricultural laborers. By the time she was 12, Hamer's parents had saved up enough money to rent land, but a jealous white neighbor poisoned their livestock, ruining the family's prospects. Inspired by a local meeting of the Student Nonviolent Coordinating Committee (SNCC) in 1962, she made an unsuccessful attempt to register to vote in Indianola. For her efforts she was jailed and beaten; she was also thrown off the cotton plantation where she worked. Despite all this—or because of it—she became a SNCC activist. On her way back from a civil rights workshop, she tried to eat at a segregated bus terminal in Winona, Mississippi. Hamer was jailed and then beaten by two black inmates at the order of prison authorities, suffering permanent injuries. Hamer helped organize the 1964 Mississippi Freedom Summer Project, a massive attempt to register black voters. During that year she helped to found the biracial Mississippi Freedom Democratic Party (MFDP), of which she became vice-chairwoman. She was a member of the MFDP delegation to the 1964 Democratic National Convention that sought to unseat the all-white regular Mississippi Democratic delegates. The effort failed, but Hamer received national attention when she testified before the convention's credentials committee about her beatings and other experiences. In the late 1960s and 1970s she helped organize a food cooperative and a cooperative farm, raised funds for low-income housing, and helped start a day care center.

**Harris, Patricia Roberts** (1924–1985). Patricia Harris was the first black woman to serve as a U.S. ambassador and as a member of the federal cabinet. While a student at Howard University in the early 1940s, she joined a student sit-in to integrate a cafeteria. Harris was program director for the YMCA in Chicago from 1946 to 1949 and then assistant director of the American Council on Human Rights in Washington, D.C., until 1953. She received a law degree from George Washington University in 1960 and was an assistant U.S. attorney in the Justice Department's Criminal Division in 1960–1961. Harris became ambassador to Luxembourg in 1965. In 1977 President Jimmy Carter chose Harris as secretary of housing and urban development. Carter shifted her to secretary of health, education, and welfare in 1979. Harris ran unsuccessfully for mayor of the District of Columbia in 1982.

**Houston, Charles Hamilton** (1895–1950). As an attorney for the National Association for the Advancement of Colored People (NAACP), Houston pioneered the legal battle against racial discrimination in publicly supported schools. Houston was born in Washington, D.C. He graduated from Amherst College in 1915 and earned a law degree in 1922 and an advanced law degree the next year from Harvard Law School. From 1929 to 1935 Houston was a vice dean at the Howard Law School. From 1935 to 1940, he served as a special counsel to the NAACP. In that post Houston tried to force southern schools to meet their obligation under *Plessy v. Ferguson* (1896) to provide equal, if separate, education for blacks. In *University of Maryland v. Murray* (1936), Houston and Thurgood Marshall convinced the U.S. Supreme Court that a black student should be admitted to the state-supported, all-white law school at the University of Maryland because the school for blacks was far inferior. In *Missouri ex rel Gaines v. Canada* (1938), Houston persuaded the Court that Missouri's policy of giving scholarships to blacks for legal study outside the state was inadequate; the Court declared that blacks must be offered an equal legal education within the state. These decisions set the Court on a path that eventually led to *Brown v. Board of Education of Topeka* in 1954. In 1935 and 1938 Houston got the Supreme Court to overturn the conviction of black defendants on the grounds that blacks had been intentionally excluded from the jury. He also helped to write the successful legal argument in *Shelley v. Kraemer* (1948), wherein the Supreme Court outlawed racially restrictive housing covenants.

**Jackson, Jesse Louis** (1941– ). A civil rights leader and social activist, Jesse Jackson became the first serious black candidate for president of the United States. He was born out of wedlock to a high school student (who married while he was a child) in Greenville, South Carolina. In 1959 Jackson entered the University of Illinois. Facing discrimination there, he transferred to the North Carolina Agricultural and Technical College, a black institution in Greensboro. While there, Jackson organized civil rights sit-ins and marches in Greensboro. After graduating in 1964, Jackson attended the Chicago Theological Seminary and was ordained a Baptist minister in 1968. Meanwhile, Jackson went to Selma, Alabama, in 1965 to assist in Martin Luther King, Jr.'s voting rights campaign. In 1966 Jackson was put in charge of the Chicago branch of Operation Breadbasket, formed by King's Southern Christian Leadership Conference (SCLC). In 1967 he became the national director of

Operation Breadbasket, which pressured white-owned businesses to hire blacks and to stock products made by black-owned companies. In 1971 Jackson left Operation Breadbasket because of disputes with SCLC leaders. He created a similar organization of his own, Operation PUSH (People United to Save Humanity, later changed to People United to Serve Humanity). During the 1970s Jackson broadened its mission to deal with inner-city problems, including teenage pregnancy, drug addiction, and crime. In the early 1980s, Jackson became an international figure, convincing Syria's ruler to free a downed American pilot and traveling to Cuba to secure the release of American prisoners. Based in Chicago, Jackson helped Harold Washington become that city's first black mayor in 1983. Washington's victory encouraged Jackson to enter the 1984 Democratic presidential primaries. A dynamic campaigner and outstanding speaker, he stirred up great enthusiasm among most black voters. However, many black political leaders did not endorse him, primarily because they did not think he could win. Jackson sought to form a "rainbow coalition" of all races, but 95 percent of white voters supported his opponents. Many declined to vote for him because of racism, but still more because they believed he was too radical. He offended Jewish voters—the whites who most often voted for black candidates—by his sympathy for the Palestine Liberation Organization, his reference to New York as "Hymietown," and his apparent reluctance to break with Nation of Islam leader Louis Farrakhan. Still, he received nearly 3 million primary votes and won about 400 convention delegates. Running again in 1988, Jackson tried to moderate his image. He also reached beyond the black community by dealing with the concerns of nonblack minorities and white workers. This time he got much more support from black leaders. But Jackson's views were still too far to the left for most voters. Yet he more than doubled his white support over 1984 while capturing almost 7 million votes and about 1,200 convention delegates. After 1988 Jackson moved to the District of Columbia, where he worked in behalf of the homeless. He also backed statehood for the District and was elected a symbolic U.S. senator by D.C. voters in 1990. Jackson encouraged inner-city blacks to fight social ills by strengthening community institutions. While dissatisfied with what he considered President Bill Clinton's inadequate commitment to the disadvantaged, Jackson did not follow up on threats to run in the 1996 presidential election.

**Jackson, Maynard Holbrook, Jr.** (1938– ). Maynard Jackson was the first black mayor of Atlanta, Georgia. Born in Dallas, Texas, he graduated from Morehouse College in Atlanta in 1956, earned a law degree in 1964, and set up practice in Atlanta. In the 1968 Democratic primary, Jackson lost a race for the U.S. Senate. The following year he won his campaign for vice-mayor of Atlanta. By 1973 blacks had become a majority of the city's population, and that year Jackson defeated Atlanta's incumbent mayor to become the first black mayor of any major southern city. Previously, blacks had received few city contracts. They had also been underrepresented in some parts of the city's workforce. But Jackson opened up a new era, sometimes using affirmative action. For example, he reserved for blacks a percentage of contracts for building Atlanta's new airport and also gave priority to blacks in hiring police officers. Jackson appointed blacks to high positions such as police chief and improved city services to black neighborhoods. But he also worked closely with white businesspeople to develop the city's economy, which led some social activists to accuse him of ignoring the poor. Jackson won reelection in 1977 with significant white support. The city charter prohibited him from serving more than two consecutive terms, but Jackson was elected again in 1989. In 1992 he had heart surgery and decided not to seek another term.

**Johnson, James Weldon** (1871–1938). A man of many talents, James Weldon Johnson was an author, lyricist, attorney, educator, diplomat, and civil rights leader. He graduated from Atlanta University in 1894 and returned to his native Jacksonville, Florida, to become a school principal. In 1898 he became the first black admitted to the Florida bar. Two years later Johnson composed the lyrics to "Lift Every Voice and Sing," which became known as the Negro national anthem. Moving to New York in 1902, Johnson became a successful composer of lyrics for Broadway show tunes. He was appointed U.S. consul at Puerto Cabello, Venezuela, in 1906, and at Corinto, Nicaragua, in 1909. Johnson's sole novel, *The Autobiography of an Ex-Colored Man*, was published anonymously in 1912. In 1917 *Fifty Years and Other Poems*, a collection of his verse, appeared in print. He became editor of the *New York Age* in 1914. Two years later Johnson became field secretary of the National Association for the Advancement of Colored People (NAACP) and organized branches throughout the South. From 1920 to 1930, he served as executive secretary of the NAACP, the first black in that post. He investigated the killing of Haitians by U.S. Marines in 1920 and worked for the Dyer antilynching bill in the early 1920s. Johnson published anthologies of black poetry and spirituals and wrote *Black Manhattan* (1930).

**Jordan, Barbara Charline** (1936–1996). Barbara Jordan was a U.S. representative highly regarded for her legal and oratorical skills. Born in Houston, Texas, she graduated from Texas Southern University in 1956 and earned a law degree at Boston University in 1959. After serving as administrative assistant to a Texas county judge, Jordan won election to the Texas state senate in 1966. She was the first black woman to sit in that body and the first black to sit there since 1883. In 1972 Jordan was elected to the U.S. House of Representatives from Houston. As a member of the House Judiciary Committee, she voted for articles of impeachment against President Richard M. Nixon in 1974. She was a leader of the successful 1975 effort to extend the Voting Rights Act of 1965 in expanded form. She retired from politics in 1976 and afterward taught law at the University of Texas in Austin. Jordan addressed the Democratic National Convention in 1976 and again in 1992.

**King, Martin Luther, Jr.** (1929–1968). King was the most important leader of the nonviolent, direct action civil rights movement of the 1950s and 1960s, a winner of the Nobel Peace Prize, a leader in the movement against the Vietnam War, and an advocate of economic justice for the poor. He was born and raised in Atlanta. His father was a leading pastor there and a pillar of Atlanta's black community. King entered Morehouse College at age 15 and graduated in 1948. In 1951 King received a bachelor of divinity degree from Crozer Theological Seminary, where he first studied the nonviolent social protest philosophy of India's Mohandas K. Gandhi. In 1955 King obtained a Ph.D. in theology at Boston University. Meanwhile, in 1954 he had become the pastor of the Dexter Avenue Baptist Church in Montgomery, Alabama. In December 1955 blacks there began a boycott against segregated seating on the city's buses, and King was drafted to lead it. Thanks to a November 1956 Supreme Court ruling, the boycott ended in victory. During the boycott King deepened his commitment to nonviolent social protest. In 1957 King and other black ministers formed the Southern Christian Leadership Conference (SCLC) to spread the campaign against racial discrimination throughout the South, and King was chosen president. Two months after black students began the sit-in movement in February 1960, King helped form the Student Nonviolent Coordinating Committee. In 1961–1962 King led a civil rights campaign in Albany, Georgia. It failed, however, because local authorities avoided unfavorable publicity by not using violence in public. But in Birmingham, Alabama, where King began a campaign early in 1963, the authorities used police dogs and fire hoses against peaceful black demonstrators, including children. Watching the events on television, northern whites were outraged. Their reaction gave President Kennedy the political support he needed to introduce a bill that eventually became the Civil Rights Act of 1964. While under arrest during the Birmingham demonstrations, King wrote his "Letter from a Birmingham Jail," in which he eloquently defended his nonviolent but confrontational strategy. A few months after the Birmingham struggle, King addressed the 200,000-strong March on Washington in August 1963. His "I Have a Dream" speech became known as one of the greatest orations in American history, and it strengthened King's reputation as a great social and moral leader. In 1964 King's stature increased still more when he won the Nobel Peace Prize. In 1965 King's voting rights campaign in Selma, Alabama, and his Selma-to-Montgomery march met with police violence. Public outrage helped pass the Voting Rights Act of 1965. In 1966 King brought his movement north to Chicago. But the protest strategy that had brought down southern segregation did not work against the economic and social problems of the northern black ghetto. Meanwhile, King condemned the new black power movement's rejection of nonviolence and integration. But influenced by his failure in Chicago, King began putting greater stress on the issue of poverty and came to believe that American society might have to be fundamentally changed to achieve economic justice. Also, in April 1967 he spoke out strongly against the Vietnam War and led a huge antiwar march and rally in New York City. By 1968 King had decided to lead a massive national campaign against poverty. As a first step, he began organizing a Poor People's Campaign in the nation's capital. But while in Memphis to support striking black sanitation workers, King was shot and killed while standing on the balcony of his motel room.

**Lewis, John R.** (1940– ). John Lewis was a civil rights leader in the 1960s and later a member of the U.S. House of Representatives. He was born in Troy, Alabama, and grew up on a small farm. A student at Fisk University in Nashville, Tennessee, Lewis organized sit-ins there early in 1960. In April 1960 he was a founder of the Student Nonviolent Coordinating Committee (SNCC). In 1961 Lewis participated in a freedom ride and was seriously injured when he tried to enter the whites-only bus terminal bathroom in Rock Hill, South Carolina. On another freedom ride shortly after, Lewis was beaten and arrested in Montgomery, Alabama. From 1963 to 1966, he was chairman of SNCC. At the March on Washington for Jobs and Freedom in August 1963, he reluctantly toned down his fiery speech at the request of more moderate civil rights leaders. Stokely Carmichael defeated Lewis for the SNCC chairmanship in 1966, after which the organization adopted a black power program. Lewis left the group and remained committed to nonviolence and integration. He was director of the Southern Regional Council's Voter Education Project from 1970 to 1977 and associate director of Volunteers for Action, a federal agency, from 1977 to 1980. Lewis was elected to the Atlanta city council in 1982. Four years later he won a race for the U.S. House of Representatives. To get there he defeated Julian Bond, an old colleague from SNCC, in a bitter Democratic primary. In Congress he continued to advocate racial harmony and condemn black separatism. He still held his seat in the mid-1990s.

**Lincoln, Abraham** (1809–1865). The sixteenth president of the United States, Abraham Lincoln during the Civil War issued the Emancipation Proclamation that led to the elimination of slavery. He was born into a poor frontier family in Kentucky. His family moved to Indiana in 1816 and to Illinois in 1830. Lincoln received very little formal education but read extensively. He was a captain in the Black Hawk War (1832) against the Sac and Fox Indians. Elected to the state legislature as a Whig in 1834, he served until 1841. Admitted to the bar in 1836, he built a successful legal practice in Springfield, Illinois. While a U.S. representative (1847–1849), he supported the Wilmot Proviso to exclude slavery from territories won in the Mexican War. Lincoln also offered a proposal to free the slaves of the District of Columbia, but on a gradual basis and with compensation to the slave owners. During the 1850s he became increasingly disturbed by what he believed was growing slave-state control of the federal government. He denounced the Kansas-Nebraska Act of 1854 and the *Dred Scott* decision of 1857. But unlike the abolitionists, he did not advocate complete repeal of fugitive slave legislation or oppose the admission of new slave states under all circumstances. In the mid-1850s, Lincoln joined the new Republican Party. It opposed the extension of slavery into the territories but acknowledged that the Constitution protected slavery in the states. Lincoln was elected president on the Republican ticket in 1860 and reelected in 1864. Shortly after the Civil War began in April 1861, he stated that he sought not to destroy slavery but to save the Union. When Union generals freed slaves in their districts, Lincoln reversed their decrees. In the first year of the war Lincoln encouraged gradual, compensated abolition in the slave states still in the Union, but none of them accepted his proposals. By mid-1862 Union forces had suffered serious defeats and heavy casualties. Public opinion was moving in favor of emancipating the slaves and then using them as soldiers to ease the burden on whites. So in September 1862 Lincoln announced his Emancipation Proclamation, to take effect on January 1, 1863. It freed only slaves in rebel-held territories and so did not immediately free anyone. But it encouraged slaves to flee Confederate-controlled areas to obtain their freedom. Furthermore, everyone understood that the proclamation spelled the end of slavery, provided the North won the war. Lincoln was by no means hostile to blacks, but he shared many of the racial prejudices of his day and did not believe that whites and blacks could live together. Therefore, as he moved toward emancipation, Lincoln began developing plans for the voluntary colonization of freedpersons in Latin America. Nothing, however, came of them. In December 1863 Lincoln offered a plan for reconstructing the Southern states. It required that 10 percent of a state's voters of 1860 pledge loyalty to the United States and elect a new government. It made no provision for black rights except the abolition of slavery. Congress refused to admit states organized along Lincoln's lines. Lincoln died at the hands of an assassin in 1865.

**Malcolm X** (also known by his religious name, El-Hajj Malik El-Shabazz) (1925–1965). A leader of the Nation of Islam, or Black Muslims, Malcolm X became an outspoken critic of the 1960s civil rights movement and a powerful advocate of black separatism and self-defense. Malcolm X was born Malcolm Little in Omaha, Nebraska. His father, a Baptist preacher and a supporter of Marcus Garvey, was murdered when Malcolm was six. Malcolm dropped out of school and ended up at a home for problem boys. In the early and mid-1940s Malcolm lived in Boston and Harlem, where he survived as a petty criminal known as "Detroit Red." Malcolm was convicted of burglary in 1946. In prison he joined the Nation of Islam, an unorthodox Muslim group. Its founder, Elijah Muhammad, preached that whites were a race of devils and that blacks should separate from white America and form their own nation. In jail Malcolm also began to educate himself with the help of the prison library. Upon leaving prison in 1952, Malcolm dropped his "slave name" and replaced it with an "X" that symbolized his unknown African name. In 1954 Malcolm was appointed minister of the Nation of Islam's Mosque Number 7 in Harlem. After the civil rights revolution began in 1960, Malcolm became a prominent national figure because of his harsh condemnation of it. He scorned integration, stating that blacks only degraded themselves by trying to go where they were not wanted. Malcolm also believed that nonviolence was cowardly and mocked Martin Luther King, Jr. Many blacks denounced Malcolm as an uninformed bigot. But Malcolm, a brilliant and powerful orator who spoke with dignified rage, won a following among many others, especially poor northern blacks who believed that the civil rights movement did not deal with their problems. By 1963 Elijah Muhammad felt that Malcolm was taking too much of the spotlight for himself and getting too deeply involved in politics. After the assassination of President John F. Kennedy in November 1963, Malcolm commented that the murder was a matter of America's "chickens coming home to roost." For that, Muhammad—who did not want to unnecessarily antagonize the American public—suspended Malcolm from the Nation of Islam. In March 1964 Malcolm quit the organization. He founded his own Harlem mosque and the Organization of Afro-American Unity (OAAU), a black nationalist group. In the spring of 1964 Malcolm went on a pilgrimage to Mecca. Upon returning, Malcolm reported that although he still believed that America was a deeply racist nation, he no longer felt that all whites were racists. Malcolm remained a black nationalist, although he stopped denouncing civil rights activists as Uncle Toms. On February 21, 1965, Malcolm was shot dead while addressing a meeting of the OAAU. Three Black Muslims were convicted of his murder. After his death, most blacks disregarded Malcolm's quarrels with other black leaders and saw him as a symbol of black self-respect and dignity. The *Autobiography of Malcolm X* (1965) became must reading for millions of admiring blacks. Many liberal whites came to admire Malcolm, too, despite debate over exactly how far his views had changed during his last year.

**Marshall, Thurgood** (1908–1993). Marshall was the most important legal advocate for racial equality in the twentieth century, eventually becoming the first black justice on the U.S. Supreme Court. Marshall was born in Baltimore and raised in a middle-class home. He graduated from Lincoln University in 1930 and received a law degree from the Howard University School of Law in 1933. In *University of Maryland v. Murray* (1936), Marshall and Charles Houston, his mentor at Howard, argued before the U.S. Supreme Court on behalf of a black man who sought to enter the all-white law school at the University of Maryland. They successfully argued that under the "separate but equal" principle of *Plessy v. Ferguson* (1896) their client should be admitted because Maryland had no law school for blacks equal in quality to the one for whites. Afterward, Marshall became assistant to Houston, who was a special counsel for the National Association for the Advancement of Colored People (NAACP). In 1938 Marshall, too, became a special NAACP counsel, and the next year he helped establish the NAACP Legal Defense and Education Fund, of which he served as director until 1961. In 1950 the Legal Defense and Education Fund, under his guidance, won a series of Supreme Court cases that virtually forced publicly supported, all-white colleges to accept black students on an equal basis. Then Marshall tackled the more controversial issue of segregated public elementary and high schools. In *Brown v. Board of Education* (1954), he challenged *Plessy* by arguing that separate schools were by their very nature unequal. The Supreme Court agreed and stated that public school segregation violated the Fourteenth Amendment. As director of the Legal Defense and Education Fund, Marshall traveled throughout the South investigating cases of racial discrimination and violence—often at risk to his own personal safety. During the Korean War he went to South Korea to check reports of discrimination against blacks in army courts-martial. In 1961 President John F. Kennedy selected Marshall for the U.S. Court of Appeals for the Second Circuit. In 1965 President Lyndon B. Johnson appointed him U.S. solicitor general, making him the first black to hold that job. Two years later President Johnson chose him for the U.S. Supreme Court. The first black to sit on the nation's highest judicial body, Marshall was known as a liberal. He not only supported civil rights, including affirmative action, but also backed the rights of criminal defendants, women's rights, and abortion rights while opposing the death penalty. In the late 1960s, Marshall condemned black militants who rejected the legal system. In 1987 he took the unusual step of criticizing President Ronald Reagan on television for his civil rights record. Marshall retired from the Court in 1991.

**Moseley-Braun, Carol** (1947– ). Moseley-Braun was the first black woman to become a U.S. senator. Born and raised in Chicago, she graduated from the University of Illinois in Chicago in 1969 and earned a degree from the University of Chicago Law School in 1972. The following year she became an assistant U.S. attorney. In 1978 Moseley-Braun was elected to the Illinois House of Representatives from Chicago. She served for nearly a decade, supporting assistance to women and minorities, universal health care, and gun control while opposing the death penalty. Moseley-Braun was the first woman to become assistant majority floor leader. In 1987 she was elected Cook County recorder of deeds, the first black to hold an executive post at the county level. In 1991 Moseley-Braun surprised observers by announcing that she would run for a U.S. Senate seat held by Alan Dixon, a fellow Democrat. A major reason for her long-shot effort, she said, stemmed from the Senate's confirmation of Clarence Thomas, a conservative black, as U.S. Supreme Court justice earlier in the year—despite charges of sexual harassment against him by Anita Hill, a former employee of Thomas's. To Moseley-Braun, this demonstrated that the Senate was a white men's club out of touch with the concerns of ordinary people. The fact that Dixon was one of the few northern Democrats who voted to confirm Thomas made him an obvious campaign target for Moseley-Braun. In March 1992 she scored an upset victory over Dixon in the Democratic primary. In November she beat her Republican opponent despite the revelation that she had failed to pay taxes on income of her elderly mother. In the Senate she led a 1993 fight against restrictions on Medicaid abortions. By threatening a filibuster, Moseley-Braun blocked efforts in 1993 to renew a patent for the insignia of the United Daughters of the Confederacy. In 1994 she was the chief sponsor of a bill to fund the preservation of historically significant buildings at traditionally black colleges. Although generally a liberal, Moseley-Braun in 1993 offered a proposal for trying teenagers down to age 13 as adults for federal crimes involving the use of firearms. In 1995 she angered many fellow Democrats by offering an amendment giving media mogul Rupert Murdoch a multimillion-dollar tax break.

**Newton, Huey P.** (1942–1989). Huey Newton was the cofounder and leader of the Black Panther Party, a paramilitary organization that merged Marxist-Leninist revolutionary doctrine with black nationalism. Newton was born in New Orleans, where his father was a sharecropper and Baptist preacher. He grew up in the black ghetto of Oakland, California. Newton graduated from Oakland's two-year Merritt College in 1965 and took courses at San Francisco Law School. Newton and fellow student Bobby Seale formed the Black Panther Party for Self-Defense in October 1966 in Oakland, with Newton as minister of defense and Seale as chairman. The party described itself as a revolutionary group following the ideas of China's Mao Tse-tung, North Korea's Kim Il Sung, Malcolm X, and others. But its immediate goal was to stop police brutality against blacks in Oakland. Party members patrolled the ghetto with visible weapons, which was legal under California law, and popularized the slogan "Off the pigs!" (kill the police). Clashes with the police were inevitable. After his October 1967 run-in with the Oakland police that left one officer dead, Newton was convicted of voluntary manslaughter. Nationwide protests by blacks and student radicals took place, with "Free Huey!" as a rallying cry. In 1970 his conviction was reversed and he was freed. At least 24 Panthers had been killed in shootouts with police between 1967 and 1969. So after Newton left prison he announced that the party would, at least temporarily, put aside violence and concentrate on providing social services. But by the early 1970s the organization was in decline, not only because of the deaths of members, but also as a result of harassment by the FBI and local police authorities. Newton earned a doctor of philosophy degree in 1980. But he had already begun sinking into a life of petty crime that led to his murder by a drug dealer.

**Powell, Adam Clayton, Jr.** (1908–1972). An outspoken, independent-minded U.S. representative, Adam Clayton Powell, Jr., was one of black America's most popular political leaders in the 1940s, 1950s, and 1960s. Powell was born in New Haven, Connecticut, the son of the pastor of Harlem's Abyssinian Baptist Church, one of the largest black churches in the United States. Two years after receiving a doctor of divinity degree from North Carolina's Shaw University in 1935, he succeeded his father as pastor. During the 1930s Powell led protests against white-owned stores in Harlem that did not hire blacks. In 1941 he became the first black to sit on the New York city council. Four years later Powell won his first term in the U.S. House of Representatives. Other black representatives at that time generally followed the orders of the white political bosses of their hometowns. But Powell was his own man. He forced the House to desegregate its restaurants and other facilities. During the 1950s he introduced resolutions to bar the use of federal funds in ways that promoted racial discrimination. In 1956, for example, Powell proposed an amendment to prohibit federal aid for the construction of segregated schools. Although a Democrat, he supported Republican president Dwight D. Eisenhower's 1956 reelection bid after the Democratic candidate refused to back his amendment. In 1961 Powell became chairman of the House Education and Labor Committee. But in the 1960s his frequent absenteeism, his arbitrary conduct as chairman, his legal problems, his flamboyant lifestyle, and his support of the black power movement alienated a growing number of representatives. In 1967 the House voted to expel him. Powell was reelected in 1968, however, and the following year the Supreme Court ruled that the House's 1967 action had been unconstitutional. But in 1970 he narrowly lost the Democratic congressional primary to Charles Rangel.

**Powell, Colin Luther** (1937– ). Colin Powell was the first black to be appointed chairman of the military's Joint Chiefs of Staff. The son of immigrants from Jamaica, Powell was born in Harlem and grew up in the South Bronx. At the City College of New York, he joined the Reserve Officers Training Program because a military career was one of the few paths open to blacks. After graduating in 1958, he entered the army as a second lieutenant. In 1962–1963 and 1968–1969 Powell served stints in Vietnam. After serving in 1972 as a special assistant in the Office of the President in the White House, Powell became commanding officer of an infantry battalion in South Korea and then commander of a brigade in the 101st Airborne Division at Fort Campbell, Kentucky. From 1983 to 1986, Powell was senior military assistant to Secretary of Defense Caspar W. Weinberger. In 1987 Powell served as deputy assistant to National Security Adviser Frank Carlucci. Powell opposed the U.S. invasion of Panama and spoke against large spending increases for the Strategic Defense Initiative (often called "star wars"). In 1989 President George Bush selected him to be chairman of the Pentagon's Joint Chiefs of Staff. Powell got high marks for his management of the 1991 Persian Gulf War. When President Bill Clinton tried to lift the ban on homosexuals in the military, Powell spoke out in favor of the prohibition in 1993. Later that year he resigned as chairman of the Joint Chiefs and returned to civilian life. A man of seemingly high moral standards, calm self-confidence, and moderate political views, many whites as well as blacks saw him as a possible future president. In 1995 Powell considered but decided against running for that office in 1996.

**Prosser, Gabriel** (1775?–1800). Prosser plotted a large slave uprising, known as Gabriel's Plot, in Virginia. A slave who worked as a blacksmith just outside Richmond, Virginia, he learned to read and write from his master's wife. In 1800 Prosser led a group of slaves in organizing a rebellion. Recruiting from as far as 75 miles away from Richmond, the conspirators convinced hundreds to participate. Under Prosser's guidance, they made weapons and ammunition. They planned to march into Richmond on the night of August 30, 1800, burn down part of the town, seize weapons from the arsenal, and kill whites in the hope of sparking a general slave rebellion. But on that night, heavy rains wiped out bridges and roads, making it impossible to march. Moreover, slave informers had already told the authorities about the plot, and troops were stationed in Richmond to deal with the rebels. Within 6 weeks, between 20 and 30 plotters had been tried and hanged. Prosser himself went into hiding but was seized in late September 1800, jailed on September 27, tried on October 3, and hanged on October 7.

**Purvis, Robert** (1810–1898). A black abolitionist, Purvis served as president of the Pennsylvania Anti-Slavery Society. He was a native of Charleston, South Carolina. His father was a white cotton broker and his mother was a free black. When he was nine, Purvis was sent to Philadelphia and attended school there. In 1833 Purvis was 1 of just 3 blacks among the 63 founding delegates of the American Anti-Slavery Society. Afterward he was 1 of 6 blacks on the organization's board of managers. From 1839 to 1844 and from 1852 to 1857, Purvis headed Philadelphia's Vigilance Committee, which helped fugitive slaves. Some fugitives used Purvis's house as a hiding place. From 1845 to 1850, Purvis served as president of the Pennsylvania Anti-Slavery Society. He opposed the 1838 Pennsylvania constitution that took the vote away from free blacks. As a supporter of William Lloyd Garrison, he opposed violence. But after the Fugitive Slave Act of 1850 became law, Purvis said he would use force to resist capture. Discouraged by the Dred Scott decision of 1857, Purvis said he would welcome a foreign invasion if it led to the freeing of the slaves. He welcomed the Civil War and encouraged black enlistments.

**Randolph, A[sa] Philip** (1889–1979). Founder and leader of the mostly black Brotherhood of Sleeping Car Porters, Randolph led the struggle against racial discrimination in the labor movement and was also a major civil rights figure. He was born in Crescent City, Florida, the son of a minister in the African Methodist Episcopal church. Randolph grew up in Jacksonville, Florida, and moved to Harlem in 1911. In 1917 Randolph and Chandler Owen founded the Messenger, a radical black newspaper. Because he opposed U.S. participation in World War I, Randolph was arrested in 1918 and spent several days in jail. In 1920 he ran as the Socialist Party candidate for controller of New York state. Between 1917 and 1923 Randolph organized a series of unsuccessful black labor organizations. Then, in 1925, he founded the Brotherhood of Sleeping Car Porters. The nearly all-black Pullman porters earned a starting pay of less than $100 for a 400-hour month. Although the Pullman Company fought the union viciously for many years, in 1935 the porters voted overwhelmingly to be represented by the Brotherhood. Two years later the union won a contract that sharply reduced hours and increased wages. Randolph used the Brotherhood as a power base to fight racial discrimination in the labor movement. At the 1934 convention of the American Federation of Labor, Randolph called for the expulsion of member unions that discriminated on the basis of color. In 1941 President Franklin D. Roosevelt banned racial discrimination in defense industries after Randolph threatened to organize a march on Washington, D.C., by 100,000 blacks. Late in 1947, Randolph and Grant Reynolds organized the Committee Against Jim Crow in Military Service and Training (changed the next year to the League for Nonviolent Civil Disobedience to the Draft). In March 1948 Randolph stated that he would urge black youths to refuse to fight in a segregated armed forces. Partly because of Randolph's pressure, President Harry Truman banned military segregation later that year. After the American Federation of Labor and the Congress of Industrial Organizations merged in 1955, Randolph was one of two blacks elected to the AFL-CIO's Executive Council. At the AFL-CIO's 1959 convention Randolph again called for the expulsion of member unions that discriminated. That year Randolph became president of the Negro-American Labor Council, formed to work for the end of discrimination in organized labor. Randolph initiated the 1963 March on Washington for Jobs and Freedom. In 1965 Randolph joined Bayard Rustin to form the A. Philip Randolph Institute, an organization of black trade unionists.

**Revels, Hiram Rhoades** (1822–1901). The first black to sit in the U.S. Senate, Hiram Revels was born of free parents in Fayetteville, North Carolina. He was ordained a minister in the African Methodist Episcopal church in 1845 and then served as pastor of a Baltimore church. In 1863 Revels moved to St. Louis, where he established a school for freedpersons. During the Civil War, he recruited three black regiments and in 1864 became chaplain of a black regiment in Mississippi. After the war Revels settled in Natchez, Mississippi. In 1869 he was elected to the Mississippi state senate. In 1870 the state's Reconstruction legislature elected Revels to complete the U.S. Senate term of Jefferson Davis, who had abandoned his seat in 1861. Trying to defend black rights without antagonizing Southern whites, he favored returning all political rights to former supporters of the Confederacy. After his term ended, Revels in 1871 became president of Alcorn University near Lorman, Mississippi, a recently established black school.

**Rustin, Bayard** (1910–1987). Rustin was possibly the most important strategist of the nonviolent struggle for racial justice in the 1950s and 1960s. Born out of wedlock in West Chester, Pennsylvania, he was raised by his grandparents. He moved to New York City in 1931. During the 1930s he was a folksinger in Greenwich Village. In 1936 Rustin joined the Young Communist League, believing the Communists had a program to end poverty and war. Eventually disillusioned, he quit in 1941. That year Rustin began a long association with black labor leader A. Philip Randolph, helping him to organize a threatened (but never carried out) march on Washington, D.C., against job discrimination in defense industries. In 1941 Rustin also joined the Fellowship of Reconciliation (FOR), a pacifist organization. Rustin was its director of race relations from 1942 to 1953. In 1942 he cofounded the Congress of Racial Equality (CORE), originally an arm of FOR. During World War II, Rustin spent more than two years in jail for refusing military service. Rustin helped plan CORE's 1947 Journey of Reconciliation, an effort to end segregated seating on interstate buses in the Upper South. For his participation he spent 22 days on a North Carolina chain gang. In 1947 and 1948 Rustin worked in Randolph's movement to end segregation in the armed forces. Rustin became executive secretary of the War Resisters League in 1953. Two years later he was a key behind-the-scenes organizer of Martin Luther King, Jr.'s Montgomery, Alabama, bus boycott, helping King understand the principles of nonviolent social protest. Afterward, Rustin was a frequent adviser to King. He helped organize King's Southern Christian Leadership Conference (SCLC) in 1957. In 1960 he planned civil rights demonstrations at both the Democratic and Republican national conventions. He was the chief organizer of Randolph's 1963 March on Washington for Jobs and Freedom. He also planned the 1964 New York City school boycott against racial imbalance. By that time Rustin believed that the major problem for blacks in the future would be in the field of employment, not racial discrimination; therefore, Rustin advocated a coalition of blacks and organized labor to secure full employment policies. He and Randolph formed the A. Philip Randolph Institute in 1964 to pursue that goal. Two years later he helped develop Randolph's Freedom Budget for full employment. Rustin opposed the black power movement in the late 1960s, continuing to support racial integration and liberal political values. In 1975 he formed the Black Americans in Support of Israel Committee.

**Smalls, Robert** (1839–1915). A Civil War hero and member of the U.S. House of Representatives, Smalls was born a slave in Beaufort, South Carolina. Before the Civil War, his master hired him out to work as a seaman. In 1861 the Confederate authorities impressed him into service on a dispatch ship, the *Planter*. On May 13, 1862, he smuggled his family onto the ship. Smalls then steered the vessel through the Confederate batteries in Charleston Harbor and brought it into Union lines, winning national fame and an appointment as a U.S. navy pilot. Smalls was elected to South Carolina's constitutional convention of 1868 and then served in the state's house of representatives (1868–1870) and state senate (1870–1874). A relatively moderate Republican who believed the federal government should return land seized from rebels during the war, he won election to the U.S. House of Representatives in 1874. In 1876 he was reelected despite a Democratic campaign of violence. Two years later, however, he was defeated in an election marked by threats and fraud. But Smalls won again in 1880 and 1884. A delegate to South Carolina's constitutional convention in 1895, he fought unsuccessfully against the disfranchisement of blacks. Smalls was customs collector at Beaufort from 1889 to 1893 and from 1897 to 1913.

**Stevens, Thaddeus** (1792–1868). A member of the U.S. House of Representatives, Stevens was a crucial driving force behind Radical Reconstruction. A native of Danville, Vermont,

Stevens graduated from Dartmouth College in 1814 and established a legal practice in Pennsylvania in 1816. Ten years later he became an iron manufacturer as well. Serving in the Pennsylvania legislature from 1833 to 1841, Stevens aggressively opposed discrimination based on class and race. In 1837 he opposed the state's proposed new constitution because it limited the vote to whites. As a Whig member of the U.S. House of Representatives from 1849 to 1853, he favored the complete, unconditional exclusion of slavery from the territories. He served in the House as a Republican from 1859 until his death. From almost the beginning of the Civil War, Stevens argued for confiscating the property of Confederate supporters and arming the slaves. In 1863 he opposed President Lincoln's plan for reconstructing the South as far too lenient, and two years later he denounced President Andrew Johnson's plan on the same ground. At Stevens's initiative, Congress in December 1865 created the Joint Committee on Reconstruction, of which he was the most powerful member. Under his leadership, the committee shaped the terms of Radical Reconstruction. In 1866 Stevens pushed the Civil Rights Act and Freedmen's Bureau Act through the House over President Johnson's veto. He also drove the Fourteenth Amendment through the House that year. Early in 1867 Stevens secured House passage of legislation establishing military rule in the former Confederate states to assure black suffrage. He also was an unsuccessful supporter of giving land to the former slaves. He drew up articles of impeachment against President Johnson in 1868, but the Senate declined to convict the president.

**Sumner, Charles** (1811–1874). A member of the U.S. Senate, Sumner was its most outspoken opponent of slavery and supporter of Radical Reconstruction. Born in Boston, he graduated from Harvard College in 1830 and from Harvard Law School in 1833. Sumner then established a private law practice. In 1848 he helped establish the Free Soil Party, which opposed the expansion of slavery into the territories. Two years later he was elected to the U.S. Senate. In 1852 he won national attention for his attempts to block enforcement of the Fugitive Slave Act of 1850. During the mid-1850s he was a founder of the Republican Party. Sumner opposed the Kansas-Nebraska Act of 1854, and in May 1856 he attacked in strong language both the law and specific southern senators. Two days later U.S. Representative Preston Smith of Mississippi assaulted Sumner on the Senate floor, severely injuring him. Just six months into the Civil War, Sumner became the first prominent political leader to call for the emancipation of the slaves. He opposed the lenient terms for readmitting the southern states to the Union proposed by Presidents Abraham Lincoln and Andrew Johnson. He supported the Radical Reconstruction laws and constitutional amendments passed by Congress in 1866–1870. From 1870 until his death Sumner worked for a bill to outlaw most types of segregation and to guarantee blacks an equal right to serve on juries. After his death, Congress passed the Civil Rights Act of 1875, which contained most of Sumner's proposals. But the U.S. Supreme Court ruled it unconstitutional in 1883.

**Terrell, Mary Church** (1863–1954). Terrell was a leader in the black women's club movement, the fight for women's suffrage, and the struggle against racial discrimination. She was born in Memphis, Tennessee, to former slaves; her father was a prosperous businessman. In 1884 she received her B.A. degree from Oberlin College in Ohio, an integrated school. Four years later, Terrell received her M.A. degree there. After teaching in Ohio and Washington, D.C., she traveled and studied in Europe from 1888 to 1890. Afterward, Terrell became a leader of the growing black women's club movement. In 1892 Terrell was chosen to lead a new Washington, D.C., group called the Colored Women's League. Four years later it merged with the Federation of Afro-American Women to form the National Association of Colored Women (NACW), of which she served as president from 1896 to 1901. Under her leadership, NACW established day nurseries and kindergartens to make it easier for black mothers to work and supported the women's suffrage movement. Terrell spoke before white women's suffrage organizations and urged them to support voting rights for black women as well as white. In 1909 she and Ida Wells-Barnett were the only black women to sign the call that led to the establishment of the National Association for the Advancement of Colored People (NAACP); she also became a leader of its Washington, D.C., chapter. Terrell served on the District of Columbia School Board in 1895–1901 and 1906–1911, one of the first black women in the country to hold such a post. During the early 1920s, she was second vice president of the International Council of Women of the Darker Races. She was an active Republican in the 1920s and 1930s. In 1946 Terrell began a fight to join the Washington, D.C., chapter of the American Association of University Women; after a three-year battle, its color barrier came down. Terrell was chosen in 1949 to chair the Coordinating Committee for the Enforcement of District of Columbia Anti-Discrimination Laws; it sought the enforcement of antibias laws for the District that had been passed by Congress during Reconstruction. An author and lecturer, she dealt with such matters as women's suffrage, racial bias, lynching, debt peonage, convict leasing, and black history and culture. Terrell's most important piece of writing was her autobiography, *A Colored Woman in a White World* (1940).

**Thomas, Clarence** (1948– ). Thomas is the second black to sit on the U.S. Supreme Court. Born in Pin Point, Georgia, he lived there in a one-room, dirt-floor house. After the house burned down, he was sent to his grandparents in Savannah. Thomas attended Catholic schools, including Holy Cross College, from which he graduated in 1971. He received a law degree from Yale University Law School in 1974. While at Holy Cross he expressed sympathy with the black militants of the late 1960s, but by the mid- to late 1970s, he had become a conservative Republican, opposed to affirmative action and other liberal pro-grams; Thomas felt that they made blacks dependent on government and discouraged individual initiative. Thomas worked on the staff of Missouri's Republican attorney general in 1974–1977. In 1979 he began working as a U.S. Senate staffer. During the Reagan administration, Thomas was assistant secretary for civil rights in the Department of Education (1981–1982). He then served as chairman of the Equal Employment Opportu-nity Commission (EEOC) from 1982 to 1990. In 1990 he was appointed to the U.S. Circuit Court of Appeals for the District of Columbia. After Thomas had served for just one year, President George Bush nominated him to succeed the retiring Thurgood Marshall on the U.S. Supreme Court. Because of his limited experience as a judge and his opposition to the mainstream civil rights agenda, Thomas's nomination caused great controversy. Most liberal and civil rights groups opposed him, but a majority of blacks favored Senate approval. At his confirmation hearings Anita Hill, a law professor at the University of Oklahoma, charged that Thomas had made unwelcome sexual advances to her when she worked for him at the EEOC. Thomas angrily denied the charges. Finally, the Senate gave Thomas its approval by a narrow 52–48 margin in late 1991. Thomas soon began compiling a highly conservative record on the Court. In 1992 he backed one decision that reduced the scope of the 1975 Voting Rights Act and another that barred labor organizers from company property in most cases. During the same year, Thomas wrote a dissenting opinion that argued that the Constitution's ban on "cruel and unusual punishment" did not apply to abuses against prisoners.

**Trotter, William Monroe** (1872–1934). Trotter was a civil rights leader and newspaper editor. Raised in a middle-class black family in an almost all-white Boston suburb, he earned bachelor's and master's degrees at Harvard College in the mid-1890s. In 1901 Trotter started the *Boston Guardian*, which he co-edited with George Forbes. Trotter made the newspaper a militant voice against Jim Crow and launched attack after attack against Booker T. Washington for opposing black efforts to secure equal rights. In July 1903 Trotter created a disturbance in Boston by interrupting a speech by Washington. In 1905 Trotter joined W. E. B. Du Bois and others to found the Niagara Movement, dedicated to full racial equality. But quarrels between Du Bois and Trotter seriously weakened the organization. Trotter left it and in 1908 formed the National Equal Rights League. He did not join the National Association for the Advancement of Colored People, founded in 1910, on the grounds that it was dominated by whites. In 1915 he led protests in Boston against the showing of *The Birth of a Nation,* a racist film.

**Truth, Sojourner** (1797?–1883). A former slave, Sojourner Truth gained renown as a traveling preacher and a powerful speaker against slavery and for women's rights. She was born a slave in Ulster County, New York. From an early age, Truth claimed to speak with God. She became free in 1827 under a New York emancipation act. Truth moved to New York City and worked as a house servant. In the early 1830s, she began speaking at religious meetings and lived for several years in a religious commune. In 1843 Truth heard God instruct her to leave the city and preach. Now calling herself Sojourner Truth, she went to Long Island and then to New England on her new mission. In Massachusetts she encountered the Northampton Association, a group of prominent social reformers. There Truth met abolitionists and women's rights advocates. Later in the 1840s she became an abolitionist lecturer. Truth's words exposed her lack of education, but she spoke with an eloquence that emerged from her spiritual strength. That and her quick wit; self-confidence; and powerful, six-foot physique gave her command over her audiences. In 1850 Truth attended her first women's rights conference. In her first feminist speech the following year, she tried to break down gender stereotypes by expanding the definition of "women" beyond respectable white ladies. Presenting herself as an ex-slave and former laborer of great physical strength, she then asked "and ain't I a woman?" During the Civil War she collected food and other items for black soldiers. In the early 1870s she urged the federal government to provide land for freedpersons in the West.

**Tubman, Harriet** (1820?–1913). Born a slave on Maryland's Eastern Shore, Tubman became the most famous activist on the Underground Railroad. Put to work as a field hand in her early teenage years, Tubman escaped to the North in 1849. She then worked as a "conductor" on the Underground Railroad, helping slaves escape to the free states. Tubman seemed unsuited for such work. She was short and thin and could not read or write. Besides, a childhood head injury caused her to fall into a deep sleep from time to time. But Tubman was extremely intelligent, resourceful, and determined, and she seemed to be completely fearless. Thanks to her work as a field hand, she was also very strong. She made at least 15 trips into the slave states and led about 300 bondpeople out of the South, including her aged parents. Tubman told the slaves under her care that if any of them tried to turn back, she would shoot them. This helps explain how Tubman was able to bring all of her charges to freedom. During the Civil War, she accompanied Union troops in South Carolina, serving as a scout and spy. She encouraged slaves to abandon their masters and brought back information about Confederate defenses. After the war Tubman helped establish schools for former slaves. Later, she lived in Auburn, New York, where she built a home for the aged. A supporter of equal rights for women, she was a longtime associate of feminist Susan B. Anthony.

**Turner, Henry McNeal** (1834–1915). Henry McNeal Turner was the leading nineteenth-century black supporter of an African American return to Africa. Born to free blacks near Abbeville, South Carolina, he became a traveling preacher for the white-controlled Methodist Episcopal church. But in 1858 Turner joined the African Methodist Episcopal (AME) church, and four years later he became an AME pastor in Washington, D.C. In 1863 he was appointed a chaplain in the Union Army, probably the first black to hold that position. After the war he worked for the Freedmen's Bureau in Georgia. Turner was elected to that state's constitutional convention in 1867 and to its legislature the following year. But the legislature, dominated by opponents of Radical Reconstruction, passed a law in 1868 barring blacks from holding public office. In 1869 white harassment forced him to quit as postmaster in Macon, Georgia. After experiences like these, Turner concluded that blacks could gain their rights and self-respect only by returning to Africa. Furthermore, Turner argued, black Americans had a mission to save Africa by Christianizing it. When Turner became the AME church's bishop in 1880, he used his position to promote colonization. He also called upon the U.S. government to give blacks reparations for their work as slaves, to be used to finance emigration. But despite his efforts, he could not convince many blacks to return to the land of their ancestors.

**Turner, Nat** (1800–1831). Turner led the bloodiest slave revolt in U.S. history. Born a slave in Southampton County, Virginia, he learned to read and write from a son of his first master. A slave preacher, he had a vision in 1828 that God had selected him to lead a slave rebellion. When an eclipse of the sun occurred in February 1831, Turner took it as a sign that the revolt should take place soon. He chose four subordinates and selected July 4, 1831, as the date. An illness forced Turner to postpone the uprising. When on August 13 the sun seemed to be a strange color, he took it as another sign and scheduled the revolt for August 21. Starting out just after midnight of that day, he had only seven poorly armed followers. First they killed the entire family of Turner's master. As they marched through Southampton County, their number grew to about 70 unruly followers who killed about 60 whites. Troops gathered and broke up the revolt by August 25. Turner fled but was captured on October 30, 1831. While in prison he answered questions asked by the attorney assigned to defend him. These responses were published as *The Confessions of Nat Turner* (1832). Turner was found guilty on November 5 and hanged on November 11.

**Vesey, Denmark** (1767?–1822). A free black, Vesey plotted a major slave insurrection in South Carolina. Probably born in Africa, Vesey was the slave of a Caribbean slave trader. In the 1780s his master settled in Charleston, South Carolina. In 1800 Vesey won $1,500 in the South Carolina lottery and bought his freedom for $600. He also used his money to begin a successful carpentry business. Married to several slave women, he was angered by the fact that his children were slaves because of their mothers' status. For years Vesey preached against slavery to bondpeople in and around Charleston. In 1821 he completed plans for a revolt in Charleston. Giving leadership roles to blacks who were widely respected in their community, Vesey was able to recruit as many as 9,000 blacks. He originally set the uprising for July 1822. But when an informer began talking to authorities in late May, Vesey moved the date up to June 16. By then, however, the government had taken precautionary measures, and the revolt did not occur. Vesey was captured on June 22. Convicted by a special court for blacks, he was hanged on July 2, 1822.

**Walker, David** (1785–1830). A black abolitionist, Walker wrote a pamphlet urging the slaves to free themselves by any means necessary. Born a free black in Wilmington, North Carolina, he moved to Boston in the mid-1820s. There, he opened a secondhand clothing store. After *Freedom's Journal*, America's first black newspaper, appeared in 1827, Walker wrote articles for it, urging a fight against slavery using legal methods. He then wrote a pamphlet known as *Walker's Appeal* (1829), which in fiery language urged slaves to employ all means, including violence, to break their chains. Walker issued a second and then a third, even more militant, edition in 1830. The pamphlet terrified many white southerners. The slave states made it a crime to circulate or own a copy; some put a price on Walker's head. In June 1830 he was found dead. The cause of death was never determined.

**Washington, Booker Taliaferro** (1856–1915). Born a slave, Booker T. Washington became not only the leading black educator in the United States but also the most famous and powerful black in the country. After emancipation, his family moved from his native

Virginia to Malden, West Virginia. At age nine Washington began working as a salt packer. Three years later he started working in a coal mine, and in 1871 he became a houseboy. The following year Washington entered Hampton Institute in Virginia, paying his expenses by working as a janitor. He then taught school back in West Virginia. In 1879 Washington returned to Hampton as a faculty member. In 1881, he was selected to head the new Tuskegee Institute for blacks in Alabama. There, young men were taught agricultural and trade skills, while young women learned housekeeping skills. In the 1880s and 1890s Washington became a highly regarded educator, and he had great success in raising funds from white philanthropists. From 1881 to Washington's death, the Tuskegee Institute grew from 40 to 1,500 students and from 1 run-down building to nearly 200 solid and well-equipped structures. In 1895 Washington gained national fame for an address he gave at the Atlanta Cotton States and International Exhibition. He told his audience that blacks should put aside the struggle for equality and instead learn practical skills to build themselves up economically. His address was enthusiastically applauded by whites, since Washington seemed to be saying just what they wanted to hear from a black man: that blacks should accept an inferior status in American society. Afterward, white philanthropists often let Washington decide to what black institutions they should contribute, and Republican leaders consulted him concerning which blacks should receive political appointments. When President Theodore Roosevelt invited Washington to the White House for lunch in 1901, political appointments were a topic of conversation. Washington's ability to direct the flow of white money and political patronage into the black community made him the most powerful member of his race. He often used his power to silence his black critics. Nevertheless, a number of black thinkers, particularly the historian W. E. B. Du Bois, criticized him for abandoning the fight for racial equality. Yet Washington had not really given up on equal rights. He believed that in an era of growing racism, the best blacks could do was to build up their economic power so that someday they could ask for their rights from a position of strength. Behind the scenes he fought against lynching and laws to disfranchise blacks. Of his many books, the most famous is *Up from Slavery* (1901), an autobiography.

**Weaver, Robert Clifton** (1907– ). Robert Weaver was the first black to hold a federal cabinet post. He was born into a middle-class family in Washington, D.C. He earned a Ph.D. in economics at Harvard University in 1934. Weaver was an adviser on racial matters in President Franklin D. Roosevelt's New Deal. He served in the Public Works Administration from 1933 to 1937 and in the U.S. Housing Authority from 1937 to 1940. During World War II he served on a number of government boards. From 1947 to 1951 Weaver taught at Northwestern, Columbia, and New York universities. A specialist on housing issues, he became New York State rent commissioner in 1955. In 1961–1966 Weaver was administrator of the federal Housing and Home Finance Agency. He helped draft President John F. Kennedy's omnibus housing bill in 1961. Weaver's lobbying helped push through Congress the Senior Citizens Housing Act in 1962 and President Lyndon B. Johnson's Housing Act in 1964. Two years later President Johnson created the Department of Housing and Urban Development and made Weaver its secretary, a cabinet-level position. In that post he managed the Model Cities program to revitalize poor neighborhoods as well as other new programs to stop urban blight. He strongly supported Johnson administration legislation to stop discrimination in housing. After 1968 Weaver returned to the academic world.

**Wells-Barnett, Ida Bell** (1862–1931). A journalist who fought for the rights of blacks and women, Wells-Barnett became best known for her antilynching crusade. Born a slave in Holly Springs, Mississippi, at age 14 she became a rural schoolteacher, first near home and later at schools near Memphis, Tennessee. Ejected in 1884 from a segregated first-class railway compartment, she sued the railroad but lost. In 1889 she purchased a one-third interest in the *Memphis Free Speech* and afterward became editor. In 1891 Wells-Barnett lost her teaching job after using the editorial page to condemn inadequate school funding. In March 1892 three of her friends were lynched in Memphis while awaiting trial. In her newspaper, Wells-Barnett condemned lynching and urged blacks to leave the city. In May a white mob burned the offices of the *Free Speech.* That year Wells-Barnett, having left the South, began working for T. Thomas Fortune's *New York Age,* in which she wrote extensively about lynching. With Fortune's help she went on antilynching lecture tours. In 1893 and 1894, Wells-Barnett toured Britain and Ireland, inspiring the formation of antilynching and antisegregation organizations there. She moved to Chicago in 1893 and that year founded the city's first black women's civic club. In 1909 Wells-Barnett and Mary Church Terrell were the two black women who signed the call leading to the creation of the National Association for the Advancement of Colored People. Four years afterward Wells-Barnett established the Alpha Suffrage Club in Chicago to fight for women's right to vote.

**White, Walter Francis** (1893–1955). Walter White was executive secretary of the National Association for the Advancement of Colored People (NAACP). Born to middle-class black parents in Atlanta, White graduated from Atlanta University in 1916. Light-skinned, blond, and blue-eyed, he could have passed for white but chose to retain his black identity. White became secretary of the Atlanta NAACP in 1916. Two years later he joined the NAACP's national staff in New York. Posing as a white reporter, he traveled through the South to investigate lynchings and race riots. He wrote a study of lynching called *Rope and Faggot: A Biography of Judge Lynch* (1929). In 1931, White became NAACP executive secretary. That year he led a successful campaign to block Senate confirmation of a U.S. Supreme Court nominee who had expressed support for black disfranchisement. During the Great Depression of the 1930s, some NAACP members wanted to give greater attention to economic issues. But White kept the NAACP focused on securing federal antilynching legislation, a goal he failed to achieve. During his stewardship the NAACP scored important legal successes against the white primary and discrimination in education. He remained executive secretary until his death, but in 1949 the NAACP's board reduced his powers.

**Wilder, Lawrence Douglas** (1931– ). L. Douglas Wilder became the first black state governor since Reconstruction. He was born in Richmond, Virginia, graduated from Virginia Union University in 1951, and received a law degree from the Howard University School of Law in 1959. In 1969 he won a seat in the Virginia state senate as a Democrat, becoming the first black to sit in that body in the twentieth century. A moderate rather than a militant, he became one of its most powerful members. In 1985 he was elected Virginia's lieutenant governor. Four years later Wilder won the election for governor, becoming the first black governor since Reconstruction, and the first selected by popular vote. Virginia was a conservative state with a black population of less than 20 percent. But Wilder was helped by his moderate record and his stand in favor of abortion rights. However, he won by far less than expected, suggesting that many whites still would not vote for a black candidate. As governor, Wilder pleased conservatives by sharply cutting the state's budget. He also favored stiff penalties for criminals, including the death penalty. On the other hand, he remained pro-choice and supported civil rights legislation. In 1991 Wilder announced that he would seek the Democratic presidential nomination, but he quit the race in January 1992. Not permitted to succeed himself under Virginia law, he entered the 1994 U.S. Senate race as an independent but again dropped out.

**Wilkins, Roy** (1901–1981). Wilkins was executive secretary (later changed to executive director) of the National Association for the Advancement of Colored People (NAACP) during the civil rights revolution. Born in St. Louis, Wilkins graduated from the University of Minnesota in 1923, having worked his way through school. Using his college newspaper experience, he was employed from 1923 to 1931 at a black newspaper, the *Kansas City Call,* first as a reporter and then as managing editor. Urging a large black voter turnout in 1930, Wilkins helped defeat a racist U.S. senator from Kansas. Because blacks were a small minority of the population, Wilkins decided early on that the best way for blacks to fight racism was by methods that did not alienate the white majority. Wilkins joined the national staff of the NAACP in 1931 as an assistant to executive secretary Walter White. In that post he investigated the exploitation of black workers and led antilynching demonstrations. In 1934 he became editor of *The Crisis*, the NAACP's monthly publication. He also helped establish new NAACP chapters and spoke around the country. Wilkins led the organization as executive secretary from 1955 to 1977. He was an effective, clear-headed strategist in the struggle for civil rights legislation in the late 1950s and 1960s. Wilkins was a bit wary of direct action protests by civil rights activists, especially when they overshadowed the work of the NAACP. But he participated in the March on Washington in 1963, the Selma-to-Montgomery march in 1965, and the completion of James Meredith's Mississippi march in 1966 after Meredith was shot. In the late 1960s Wilkins opposed linking the racial justice and anti–Vietnam War movements. He strongly opposed the black power movement and black nationalism, regarding them as forms of reverse racism.

**Young, Andrew Jackson, Jr.** (1932– ). Andrew Young served as a close aide to Martin Luther King, Jr., as a member of the U.S. House of Representatives, as the U.S. representative to the United Nations, and as mayor of Atlanta. Born and raised in New Orleans, Young graduated from Howard University in 1951 and from Hartford Theological Seminary in 1955. Ordained a minister of the United Church of Christ, Young ran its voter education program for southern blacks in 1961–1964. Meanwhile, he had become involved with the Southern Christian Leadership Conference (SCLC) led by Martin Luther King, Jr. Young served as his administrative assistant in 1962–1964 and as SCLC's executive director in 1964–1968 and executive vice president in 1968–1970. In 1970 he lost a race for a U.S. House seat from Georgia, but 2 years later won in an Atlanta district that was over 60 percent white. In Washington, D.C., Young defended affirmative action and criticized President Richard M. Nixon's civil rights policies. President Carter appointed him ambassador to the United Nations in 1977. Two years later Young violated U.S. policy by meeting with a representative of the Palestine Liberation Organization and was forced to resign. He was elected mayor of Atlanta in 1981. Young worked hard to win the support of the suspicious white business community and was reelected easily in 1985. Barred from a third consecutive term, Young ran in, but lost, the Democratic primary for governor in 1990. Afterward he headed the committee preparing for the 1996 Olympic Games in Atlanta.

**Young, Whitney Moore, Jr.** (1921–1971). Whitney Young was the leader of the National Urban League during the civil rights revolution of the 1960s. He was born in Lincoln Ridge, Kentucky, son of the president of a black preparatory school. Young graduated from Kentucky State College in 1941. He then studied engineering and enlisted in the World War II army. Having obtained a master's degree in social work from the University of Minnesota in 1947, Young spent the next six years working for the National Urban League in St. Paul, Minnesota, and Omaha, Nebraska. In 1954 Young became dean of the School of Social Work at Atlanta University. He became the executive national director of the National Urban League in 1961, a post he held until his death. Young was extremely successful in convincing corporate leaders to integrate their workforces and contribute to the League's job training programs. In 1963 Young convinced the League's reluctant board members to expand the organization's activities into civil rights. That year Young spoke at the March on Washington for Jobs and Freedom, and two years later he participated in the Selma-to-Montgomery march. In 1963 Young called for a $145-billion "domestic Marshall Plan" to fight black poverty, and the following year he helped President Lyndon B. Johnson develop and pass War on Poverty legislation. At first he was a sharp critic of the black power movement. But, beginning in 1968, he incorporated some elements of the black power approach into National Urban League programs. In particular, Young sought to encourage the development of black ghetto leadership, to help ghetto residents gain control of their communities, and to promote black business. Initially, he supported American policy in Vietnam. But in 1969 Young came out against the war there. The funds being poured into it, he asserted, would do far more good in the cities of America.

# CHRONOLOGY

• • • • • • • • •

| | |
|---|---|
| **1619** | A Dutch vessel arrives in Jamestown, Virginia, leaving behind 20 Africans, the first permanent black residents of what would become the United States. They apparently are sold as indentured servants. |
| **1641** | Massachusetts passes the first law in British North America to recognize slavery. |
| **1661** | The Virginia legislature passes the colony's first law recognizing slavery. |
| **1667** | A Virginia law states that masters do not have to free baptized slaves. |
| **1680** | A Virginia law requires slaves to obtain their masters' permission to leave their plantations. |
| **1688** | Quakers in Germantown, Pennsylvania, make the first known protest against slavery in British North America. |
| **1691** | Virginia requires freed slaves to leave the colony. |
| **1692** | Virginia bars intermarriage between whites and blacks, slave or free. |
| **1696** | Carolina creates special courts for slaves. |
| **1705** | Virginia bars blacks from testifying against whites. |
| **1712** | A slave revolt in New York City results in the deaths of nine whites. |
| **1715** | A North Carolina law requires emancipated slaves to leave the colony. |
| **1721** | South Carolina bars free blacks from voting or holding office. |
| **1722** | South Carolina requires freed slaves to leave the colony. |
| **1723** | Virginia requires slave owners to obtain permission from the colony's governor and council before freeing their slaves. |
| **1723** | Virginia prohibits free blacks from voting and limits their role in the militia to musicians and manual laborers. |
| **1739** | The Stono Rebellion in South Carolina, the largest slave revolt in the colonial era, results in the deaths of about 25 whites. |
| **1740** | South Carolina becomes the first colony to make it a crime to teach slaves to write. It also extends the authority of special slave courts to free blacks. |
| **1741** | In New York City, fear of a probably nonexistent slave conspiracy leads to the execution of 32 slaves, 14 by burning. |
| **1758** | The Philadelphia Yearly Meeting calls upon all Pennsylvania and New Jersey Quakers to free their slaves. |
| **1770** | Crispus Attucks is apparently the first to die in the Boston Massacre. |

| 1775 | Lord Dunmore, the royal governor of Virginia, offers freedom to all slaves joining British forces. |
|---|---|
| 1777 | Vermont becomes the first state to abolish slavery. |
| 1780 | Pennsylvania passes a gradual emancipation law. |
| 1782 | Virginia drops its 1723 requirement that masters receive government approval before freeing their slaves. |
| 1783 | A ruling by the chief justice of Massachusetts, based on the state's constitution of 1780, leads to the end of slavery in that state. |
| 1783 | A constitution is adopted in New Hampshire; its wording hastens the end of slavery in the state. |
| 1784 | Connecticut and Rhode Island pass gradual emancipation laws. |
| 1787 | Congress passes the Northwest Ordinance, banning the introduction of slaves north of the Ohio River and east of the Mississippi River. |
| 1787 | The U.S. Constitution recognizes slavery in three of its provisions while allowing Congress to ban the international slave trade beginning in 1808. |
| 1787 | Richard Allen leads blacks out of St. George's Episcopal Church in Philadelphia in a dispute over segregated seating. |
| 1793 | The Fugitive Slave Act provides for the return of slaves escaping across state boundaries, while giving free blacks few protections against whites falsely claiming them. |
| 1793 | Virginia bans free blacks from migrating into the state. |
| 1795 | North Carolina prohibits emancipation unless the freed slaves can post large bonds. |
| 1799 | New York passes a gradual emancipation law. |
| 1799 | Kentucky takes the vote away from free blacks. |
| 1800 | Heavy rains frustrate a planned slave revolt, known as Gabriel's Plot, in Virginia. |
| 1802 | President Thomas Jefferson signs a bill depriving free blacks in Washington, D.C., of the right to vote. |
| 1804 | New Jersey passes a gradual emancipation law. |
| 1806 | Virginia requires freed slaves to leave the state. |
| 1807 | Congress prohibits the importation of slaves effective January 1, 1808. |
| 1807 | New Jersey takes the vote away from free blacks. |
| 1810 | Maryland takes the vote away from free blacks. |
| 1813 | Virginia imposes a special poll tax on free blacks. |
| 1815 | Black merchant-shipbuilder Paul Cuffee of Massachusetts brings 38 black settlers from the United States to Sierra Leone, Africa. |
| 1816 | The African Methodist Episcopal (AME) church, the first black denomination in the United States, is founded. |
| 1816 | The American Colonization Society is founded by prominent whites to promote the settlement of free blacks in Africa. |
| 1817 | Spurred by the creation of the American Colonization Society in 1816, free blacks in Richmond, Virginia, and Philadelphia state their opposition to colonization abroad. |
| 1818 | Connecticut takes the vote away from free blacks. |
| 1820 | In the Missouri Compromise, Missouri is admitted to the Union as a slave state and Maine as a free state, while slavery is barred from the northern section of the Louisiana Purchase. |
| 1820 | New York takes the vote away from all free blacks except those who own real estate valued at $250 or more. |
| 1822 | A planned revolt known as the Denmark Vesey Conspiracy is foiled in Charleston, South Carolina. |

| 1827 | In New York City, John Russwurm and Samuel E. Cornish establish *Freedom's Journal*, the first black newspaper in the United States. |
|------|------|

1827    In New York City, John Russwurm and Samuel E. Cornish establish *Freedom's Journal*, the first black newspaper in the United States.

1829    *Walker's Appeal*, by Boston free black David Walker, is published. A militant pamphlet, it calls upon slaves to use violence if necessary to obtain their freedom.

1830    The first national black antislavery convention is held in Philadelphia.

1831    William Lloyd Garrison begins publishing the abolitionist newspaper the *Liberator*.

1831    The Nat Turner rebellion in Southampton County, Virginia, the bloodiest slave revolt in U.S. history, results in the deaths of 60 whites.

1831    A Maryland law provides that free blacks refusing to participate in the colonization movement will be expelled from the state. The law goes unenforced for lack of colonization funds and because of the need for black labor.

1832    The New England Anti-Slavery Society is formed under the leadership of William Lloyd Garrison.

1833    The American Anti-Slavery Society is formed, with William Lloyd Garrison among the leaders. The Female Anti-Slavery Society is founded as an affiliate.

1834    Tennessee takes the vote away from free blacks.

1835    North Carolina, the one remaining southern state where free blacks can vote, takes away that right.

1836    The House of Representatives adopts a "gag rule" to prevent consideration of antislavery petitions.

1837    Pennsylvania takes the vote away from free blacks.

1840    The American and Foreign Anti-Slavery Society is formed by critics of William Lloyd Garrison.

1840    Maryland authorizes sheriffs to hire out free black vagrants. Seven years later, Delaware passes a similar measure.

1841    Slaves on the ship *Creole*, being transported from Virginia to New Orleans, seize the vessel and bring it to the Bahamas.

1842    In *Prigg v. Pennsylvania*, the Supreme Court declares that laws in the northern states that hamper enforcement of the federal Fugitive Slave Act of 1793 are unconstitutional.

1845    The House of Representatives, led by John Quincy Adams, abolishes the "gag rule" against antislavery petitions.

1845    Frederick Douglass's *Narrative of the Life of Frederick Douglass* is published.

1847    Frederick Douglass founds the *North Star* (later *Frederick Douglass's Paper*) in Rochester, New York.

1848    Virginia bars free blacks who leave the state for educational purposes from ever returning.

1850    The Compromise of 1850 admits California as a free state, while applying no restrictions on slavery in other territories won in the Mexican War. Also, the slave trade in the District of Columbia is abolished, and a new Fugitive Slave Act—more favorable to slave owners than the Fugitive Slave Act of 1793—is passed.

1852    In his *Condition, Elevation, Emigration and Destiny of the Colored Race*, Martin R. Delany urges black abolitionists to depend less on their white colleagues.

1852    Harriet Beecher Stowe's antislavery novel, *Uncle Tom's Cabin*, is published.

1854    The Kansas-Nebraska Act permits residents of the Kansas and Nebraska territories to legalize slavery, although slavery had been barred from that area by the Missouri Compromise of 1820.

1857    In *Dred Scott v. Sanford*, the U.S. Supreme Court rules that blacks are not citizens and that Congress cannot bar slavery from the territories.

1859    White abolitionist John Brown leads an unsuccessful armed attack on the federal arsenal at Harper's Ferry, Virginia.

1860    Republican candidate Abraham Lincoln is elected president.

1861    The Civil War begins.

1861    The First Confiscation Act declares that any property used to advance the Confederate rebellion, including slaves, can be seized.

1862    At President Lincoln's request, Congress abolishes slavery in the District of Columbia.

1862    President Lincoln signs a bill abolishing slavery in the territories.

1862    The Second Confiscation Act frees all slaves belonging to persons supporting the Confederacy.

1863    President Lincoln issues the Emancipation Proclamation, which frees slaves in states or parts of states still in rebellion.

1863    Blacks are hunted down and attacked in the New York City Draft Riots. At least 105 persons are killed.

1863    President Lincoln issues his Ten Percent Plan for restoring the Confederate states to the Union on lenient terms.

1864    Confederate troops massacre 238 black soldiers at Fort Pillow, Tennessee, after capturing the fort.

1864    The Wade-Davis bill proposes strict terms for the restoration of the Confederate states into the Union, but President Lincoln refuses to sign it.

1865    The Freedmen's Bureau is established by Congress to assist former slaves.

1865    The Thirteenth Amendment, abolishing slavery, is ratified.

1866    The Civil Rights Act of 1866 gives blacks citizenship and equal protection of person and property.

1866    The Ku Klux Klan is founded in Tennessee.

1867    Congress gives the vote to blacks in Washington, D.C., and in the territories.

1867    A series of Reconstruction Acts imposes military occupation upon the unreconstructed Southern states and requires them to establish universal male suffrage and ratify the Fourteenth Amendment.

1868    The Fourteenth Amendment, giving blacks citizenship and "equal protection of the laws," is ratified.

1870    The Mississippi legislature elects Hiram R. Revels to the U.S. Senate, making him the first black to sit in that body.

1870    The Fifteenth Amendment, giving blacks the vote, is ratified.

1871    Congress passes the Ku Klux Klan Act, an attempt to stop the illegal activities of the Ku Klux Klan and other Southern vigilante groups.

1873    In the *Slaughterhouse Cases,* the Supreme Court reduces the federal government's authority to protect civil and political rights, giving most authority to the states.

1874    The Mississippi legislature elects Blanche K. Bruce to the U.S. Senate. He becomes the first black senator to serve a full six-year term.

1875    The Civil Rights Act of 1875 outlaws racial discrimination in hotels, public transport, places of amusement, and other facilities.

1877    The last federal troops in the former Confederate states are returned to their barracks as Reconstruction ends.

1879    Black conventions promote westward migration, and by the end of the year thousands of blacks leave the South for Kansas and other states.

1882    South Carolina passes the Eight-Box Ballot Act to make voting more difficult for the uneducated.

| 1883 | In *Civil Rights Cases* (1883), the Supreme Court declares the Civil Rights Act of 1875 unconstitutional. |
| 1887 | Florida becomes the first state to require separate first-class railroad compartments for blacks and whites. |
| 1890 | Mississippi becomes the first state after Reconstruction to disfranchise blacks. |
| 1895 | South Carolina becomes the second state after Reconstruction to disfranchise blacks. |
| 1895 | In an address at the Atlanta Cotton States and International Exhibition, Booker T. Washington urges blacks to put aside the struggle for civil and political rights and instead work for their economic well-being. |
| 1896 | In *Plessy v. Ferguson,* the Supreme Court establishes the "separate but equal" doctrine, permitting segregation of the races so long as they receive equivalent facilities. Over the next 20 years, segregation is established by law in the southern states in almost every area of public life. |
| 1898 | In *Williams v. Mississippi,* the Supreme Court helps clear the way for the disfranchisement of blacks by ruling that poll taxes and literacy requirements for voting are legal. |
| 1898 | Louisiana initiates a movement to disfranchise blacks that sweeps through the southern states in the following years. |
| 1901 | Booker T. Washington dines at the White House with President Theodore Roosevelt, upsetting southern white racists. |
| 1901 | William Monroe Trotter and George Forbes establish the *Boston Guardian* to oppose the views of Booker T. Washington. |
| 1903 | In *The Souls of Black Folk,* W. E. B. Du Bois criticizes the views of Booker T. Washington. |
| 1905 | Twenty-nine blacks led by W. E. B. Du Bois meet in Niagara Falls, Canada, to establish the Niagara Movement, dedicated to the goal of complete racial equality. |
| 1906 | Some 25 blacks are killed in an Atlanta race riot. |
| 1906 | Reacting against racial slurs, soldiers in three companies of the black 25th Infantry commit acts of violence against whites in Brownsville, Texas. Afterward, President Theodore Roosevelt dishonorably discharges the three companies. |
| 1908 | A race riot breaks out in Springfield, Illinois, with white mobs engaging in lynching, flogging, and the destruction of property. |
| 1910 | A gathering of blacks and whites in New York City establishes the National Association for the Advancement of Colored People (NAACP), committed to complete equality of the races before the law. |
| 1911 | The National Urban League is formed by white and black social workers to improve the employment opportunities and social services available to poor urban blacks. |
| 1913 | Segregated facilities are established in the U.S. Post Office and the Treasury Department after Democrat Woodrow Wilson becomes president. |
| 1915 | The NAACP leads protests against the showing of *The Birth of a Nation,* a movie based on a novel by Thomas Dixon that depicts blacks during Reconstruction as corrupt politicians and rapists of white women. |
| 1915 | In *Guinn v. United States,* the Supreme Court bans use of the grandfather clause in determining voter eligibility. |
| 1915 | A new Ku Klux Klan is formed. |
| 1916 | Heavy black migration from South to North begins during World War I. |

1917 A four-day racial clash occurs in East St. Louis, Illinois. Half of the black population flees the town. Several weeks later, thousands of blacks march silently in a New York City parade organized by the NAACP to protest the riot.

1917 Violence between black soldiers and white civilians in Houston leads to the deaths of 17 whites.

1917 In *Buchanan v. Warley*, the Supreme Court strikes down city ordinances establishing separate residential districts for whites and blacks.

1918 Marcus Garvey of Jamaica forms a branch of his black nationalist Universal Negro Improvement Association (UNIA) in Harlem, the first UNIA chapter in the United States.

1919 A meeting of the black Progressive Farmers and Household Union of America in Hot Spur, Arkansas, is attacked by white terrorists, who eventually kill more than 200 blacks.

1919 In Chicago, 23 blacks and 15 whites die in a 4-day race riot that highlights a summer of race riots around the country.

1920 James Weldon Johnson becomes NAACP executive secretary, the first black to hold an executive post in the organization.

1922 The U.S. House of Representatives passes the Dyer antilynching bill, but it is successfully filibustered in the Senate.

1923 In *Moore v. Dempsey*, the Supreme Court overturns the murder convictions of six blacks because no blacks sat on the jury and because the trial was conducted in an atmosphere of intimidation.

1923 Marcus Garvey is tried and sentenced to five years in prison for mail fraud.

1925 A. Philip Randolph forms the Brotherhood of Sleeping Car Porters.

1927 In *Nixon v. Herndon*, the Supreme Court bars white primaries under certain circumstances.

1928 Republican Oscar De Priest is elected to the U.S. House of Representatives from Chicago, becoming the first black elected to Congress from the North.

1930 NAACP lobbying helps persuade the U.S. Senate to reject the nomination of North Carolina judge John J. Parker for the U.S. Supreme Court.

1930 Walter White becomes NAACP executive secretary.

1931 At Scottsboro, Alabama, nine young black men are accused of raping two white women on a freight train. The case of the "Scottsboro boys" becomes famous during the 1930s; both the NAACP and the pro-Communist International Labor Defense work on the case.

1934 The Southern Tenant Farmers Union, bringing together black and white tenant farmers and sharecroppers, is formed in Tyronza, Arkansas.

1934 In Chicago, Arthur W. Mitchell defeats Republican U.S. representative Oscar De Priest to become the first black Democrat sent to Congress.

1935 The Costigan-Wagner antilynching bill is killed by a Senate filibuster.

1935 The National Negro Congress is founded by lawyer John P. Davis, labor leader A. Philip Randolph, political scientist Ralph Bunche, and others.

1936 In *University of Maryland v. Murray*, the Supreme Court orders the admission of a qualified black applicant to the previously all-white law school at the University of Maryland, a state institution. The Court states that since Maryland has no law school for blacks equal to the University of Maryland's law school, it is violating *Plessy v. Ferguson* (1896).

1936 Mary McLeod Bethune becomes director of the Division of Negro Affairs in the New Deal's National Youth Administration.

1936 An informal Black Cabinet, headed by Mary McLeod Bethune, is formed to pool the resources of black federal officials.

| 1937 | Mary McLeod Bethune founds the National Council of Negro Women. |
| 1937 | The Brotherhood of Sleeping Car Porters wins its first contract with the Pullman Company. |
| 1937 | William H. Hastie becomes the first black to win appointment as a federal judge. |
| 1938 | In *Missouri ex rel Gaines v. Canada,* the Supreme Court strikes down Missouri's policy of providing a law school for whites while paying the tuition for blacks to study law in a different state. The Court rules that a state must provide equal facilities for blacks and whites within its boundaries. |
| 1939 | Black opera singer Marian Anderson performs at the Lincoln Memorial on Easter Sunday before an unsegregated audience of 75,000, including prominent federal officials. |
| 1939 | The NAACP Legal Defense and Education Fund is established as a separate organization from the NAACP. |
| 1941 | The NAACP files a lawsuit for Yancey Williams, who wants to join the army air corps. Soon after, the Department of War opens a training base for black pilots at Tuskegee, Alabama. |
| 1941 | After A. Philip Randolph threatens a black march on Washington, President Franklin D. Roosevelt issues Executive Order 8802 banning racial discrimination by federal contractors, prohibiting discrimination in federal training programs for war production, and establishing a Fair Employment Practices Commission. |
| 1942 | The Congress of Racial Equality becomes a national organization. |
| 1943 | Detroit experiences the worst race riot of World War II; 25 blacks and 9 whites are killed. |
| 1943 | Blacks riot in Harlem over a rumor that a white policeman killed a black soldier. |
| 1944 | In *Smith v. Allwright,* the Supreme Court rules that white primaries violate the Fifteenth Amendment. |
| 1944 | The Southern Regional Council is formed in Atlanta by blacks and whites to work quietly against Jim Crow. |
| 1945 | After attempting to enter the all-white officers' club at Freeman Field in Indiana, 101 black army air corps officers are arrested. |
| 1945 | About 100 black WACs at Fort Devens, Massachusetts, stage a sit-down strike against being forced to do all of the menial work. |
| 1946 | In *Morgan v. Virginia,* the Supreme Court bans segregated seating on interstate buses. |
| 1947 | Jackie Robinson breaks major league baseball's color barrier by joining the Brooklyn Dodgers. |
| 1947 | Black and white members of the Congress of Racial Equality ride interstate buses in the Upper South in a challenge to segregated seating. |
| 1947 | A. Philip Randolph and Grant Reynolds form the Committee against Jim Crow in Military Service and Training, which in 1948 becomes the League for Nonviolent Civil Disobedience to the Draft. |
| 1948 | The Leadership Conference on Civil Rights, consisting of liberal, labor, and ethnic organizations, is created for joint lobbying efforts in Washington, D.C. |
| 1948 | Civil rights advocates, spearheaded by Minneapolis mayor Hubert H. Humphrey, persuade the Democratic National Convention to adopt a strong civil rights plank. |
| 1948 | President Truman issues Executive Order 9980 barring employment discrimination by the federal government. |

1948    President Truman issues Executive Order 9981, which requires "equality of treatment and opportunity" in the armed forces. When asked, Truman affirms that the order bars segregation.

1948    In *Shelley v. Kraemer*, the Supreme Court bars the enforcement of restrictive covenants.

1950    In *Sweatt v. Painter*, the Supreme Court rules that a new state law school for blacks, created to avoid integration of the state's all-white law school, cannot be equal to the white school because it lacks the prestige and traditions that develop over time.

1950    In *McLaurin v. Oklahoma State Regents for Higher Education*, the Supreme Court rules that a graduate school that segregates black students in the classroom, the library, and the cafeteria is denying their right to an equal education.

1953    A one-week black boycott of municipal buses in Baton Rouge, Louisiana, ends the system of segregated seating.

1954    In *Brown v. Board of Education of Topeka, Kansas*, a case involving the public schools, the Supreme Court asserts that "separate educational facilities are inherently unequal" and therefore violate the Fourteenth Amendment. The decision reverses *Plessy v. Ferguson* (1896) and spells the end of legal segregation.

1954    The first White Citizens Council is formed in Mississippi.

1955    Calling for "all deliberate speed," the Supreme Court issues orders for carrying out the desegregation of public schools required by *Brown v. Board of Education*.

1955    In Montgomery, Alabama, blacks led by Martin Luther King, Jr., begin a boycott of the city's buses, which have segregated seating.

1956    All but 27 of the 128 southerners in Congress sign the Southern Manifesto, which vows resistance to desegregation by all legal means.

1956    The Supreme Court voids segregated seating on the buses of Montgomery, Alabama, ending the Montgomery bus boycott.

1957    President Dwight D. Eisenhower sends federal troops to Little Rock, Arkansas, to protect black students integrating Central High School in the face of violence.

1957    The Civil Rights Act of 1957 takes small steps toward protecting black voting rights. It also creates the U.S. Civil Rights Commission to investigate discrimination. The measure is the first civil rights act passed since Reconstruction.

1957    Black ministers organize the Southern Christian Leadership Conference, with Martin Luther King, Jr., as its president.

1960    The Civil Rights Act of 1960 provides new but largely ineffective methods for defending the right of blacks to vote.

1960    The first sit-in demonstration occurs at a Greensboro, North Carolina, lunch counter.

1960    The Student Nonviolent Coordinating Committee (SNCC) is formed.

1960    In *Boynton v. Virginia*, the Supreme Court bans segregation in railroad stations and bus terminals handling interstate vehicles.

1961    CORE launches freedom rides to integrate southern bus terminal facilities.

1961    Martin Luther King, Jr., begins a civil rights campaign in Albany, Georgia.

1961    The Twenty-third Amendment allows residents of Washington, D.C., to vote for president and vice president.

1962    James Meredith integrates the University of Mississippi despite resistance by Governor Ross Barnett and campus rioting.

1962    President Kennedy issues an executive order banning racial discrimination in the sale or rental of federally financed housing.

1963    Martin Luther King, Jr., conducts a civil rights campaign in Birmingham, Alabama.

| | |
|---|---|
| 1963 | Governor George Wallace unsuccessfully tries to prevent the integration of the University of Alabama. |
| 1963 | President Kennedy sends a strong civil rights bill to Congress. |
| 1963 | NAACP field secretary Medgar Evers is assassinated in Jackson, Mississippi. |
| 1963 | More than 200,000 attend the March on Washington for Jobs and Freedom in Washington, D.C. |
| 1963 | A black church in Birmingham, Alabama, is bombed; four black girls are killed. |
| 1964 | President Lyndon B. Johnson initiates the War on Poverty. |
| 1964 | The Civil Rights Act of 1964 bars segregation in public facilities, prohibits employment discrimination and creates an Equal Employment Opportunity Commission, provides for a cutoff of federal funds to programs practicing racial discrimination, and promotes voting rights. |
| 1964 | SNCC's Robert Moses organizes the Freedom Summer Project, which brings northern college students into rural Mississippi to help blacks register to vote. Three Mississippi Freedom Summer volunteers—one black and two white—are killed near Philadelphia, Mississippi. |
| 1964 | The biracial Mississippi Freedom Democratic Party fails to oust the regular all-white Mississippi delegation at the Democratic National Convention. |
| 1964 | The Twenty-fourth Amendment, barring payment of a poll tax as a requirement of voting in federal elections, is ratified by the states. |
| 1964 | A riot in Harlem leaves 1 dead and 140 injured. |
| 1964 | Malcolm X forms the Organization for Afro-American Unity. |
| 1965 | Martin Luther King, Jr., leads a voting rights campaign in Selma, Alabama, ending with a march to Montgomery, the state capital. |
| 1965 | A Voting Rights Act is passed, providing strong protection of the right to vote in states where discrimination has been most common. |
| 1965 | Malcolm X is assassinated. |
| 1965 | After six days of rioting in the Watts section of Los Angeles, 34 are dead and more than 1,000 are injured. |
| 1966 | Martin Luther King, Jr., leads demonstrations against segregated housing in Chicago. |
| 1966 | Stokely Carmichael replaces John Lewis as leader of the Student Nonviolent Coordinating Committee and introduces the slogan, "Black power." Whites are expelled from the organization. |
| 1966 | Floyd McKissick replaces James Farmer as leader of the Congress of Racial Equality and introduces black nationalist policies. |
| 1966 | Republican Edward Brooke of Massachusetts becomes the first black to sit in the U.S. Senate since Reconstruction. |
| 1966 | The Office of Civil Rights is created to promote primary and secondary school desegregation. |
| 1966 | Riots break out in the black sections of Cleveland, Chicago, Atlanta, and other cities and towns. |
| 1966 | Huey Newton and Bobby Seale form the Black Panther Party for Self-Defense. |
| 1967 | Thurgood Marshall becomes the first black to sit on the U.S. Supreme Court. |
| 1967 | Carl Stokes of Cleveland and Richard Hatcher of Gary become the first blacks elected mayor in major cities. |
| 1967 | A race riot in Newark, New Jersey, leaves 23 dead, while 43 die and more than 2,000 are injured in Detroit rioting. |
| 1967 | A Black Power Conference is held in Newark, New Jersey. |
| 1968 | Martin Luther King, Jr., is shot and killed in Memphis. In reaction, riots in black neighborhoods occur in more than 100 cities. |

1968     The Poor People's Campaign, initiated the previous year by Martin Luther King, Jr., establishes an encampment in Washington, D.C., known as Resurrection City.

1968     The Office of Federal Contract Compliance Programs begins issuing affirmative action employment guidelines to federal contractors.

1968     In *Green v. County School Board*, the Supreme Court orders a faster pace for school desegregation in the South.

1968     The Fair Housing Act bans discrimination in most housing but does not provide for effective enforcement.

1968     Shirley Chisholm of New York City becomes the first black woman elected to the U.S. House of Representatives.

1968     Conflict in Brooklyn, New York, between the Ocean Hill–Brownsville school board and the United Federation of Teachers creates tensions between blacks and Jews.

1969     President Richard M. Nixon introduces the Philadelphia Plan to increase the number of blacks in construction unions.

1970     The Voting Rights Act of 1965 is renewed for five years.

1970     Kenneth Gibson is elected the first black mayor of Newark, New Jersey.

1970     The Office of Civil Rights rules that color-blind admissions policies of previously segregated state college systems will be considered discriminatory if they do not produce significant integration.

1971     In *Griggs v. Duke Power Company*, the Supreme Court invalidates seemingly color-blind job requirements when they perpetuate the results of previous discriminatory practices. The Court thereby creates a legal foundation for affirmative action employment policies.

1971     The Congressional Black Caucus is formed.

1972     The Equal Employment Opportunity Act empowers the Equal Employment Opportunity Commission to take employers to court. It also states that the Civil Rights Act of 1964 applies as much to private employers as to government agencies and federal contractors.

1972     Barbara Jordan of Texas and Andrew Young of Georgia become the first blacks to be elected to Congress from the South since 1900.

1972     Black U.S. Representative Shirley Chisholm runs for the Democratic presidential nomination.

1973     Congress passes a home rule bill for Washington, D.C., that allows residents to elect a mayor and city council.

1973     Thomas Bradley is elected the first black mayor of Los Angeles.

1973     Maynard Jackson is elected the first black mayor of Atlanta.

1973     Coleman Young is elected the first black mayor of Detroit.

1974     In *Milliken v. Bradley*, the Supreme Court sharply restricts the conditions under which students can be bused between cities and their suburbs to desegregate schools.

1975     The Voting Rights Act of 1965 is extended for seven years.

1975     The National Conference of Black Mayors is formed.

1977     In *Dayton Board of Education v. Brinkman*, the Supreme Court limits the conditions under which busing can be ordered for an entire school system.

1977     In *Teamsters v. United States*, the Supreme Court decides that affirmative action plans cannot be applied to union seniority systems.

1977     President Jimmy Carter names Patricia Harris as secretary of housing and urban development, making her the first black woman cabinet member.

1977    President Carter appoints black congressman Andrew Young as U.S. ambassador to the United Nations.

1977    Ernest R. Morial is elected the first black mayor of New Orleans.

1978    In *Regents of the University of California v. Bakke*, the Supreme Court rules that a state college cannot reserve a specific number of seats for minorities but can consider race, along with other factors, in selecting students.

1978    The Federal Communications Commission begins efforts to increase the number of minority-owned radio and television stations.

1979    In *United Steelworkers v. Weber*, the Supreme Court approves the temporary use of racial quotas in voluntary affirmative action agreements between employers and employees.

1979    Richard Arrington is elected the first black mayor of Birmingham, Alabama.

1980    In *City of Mobile v. Bolden*, the Supreme Court rules that the *results* of at-large elections cannot be used as proof of discrimination against black voters; instead, it must be shown that at-large districts were created with an *intent* to discriminate.

1980    In *Fullilove v. Klutznick*, the Supreme Court approves the use of set-asides for minority businesspeople in distributing federal contracts.

1980    A riot by blacks in Miami leaves 16 dead.

1982    The Voting Rights Act of 1965 is extended for 25 years. A new provision overrides the Supreme Court's decision in *City of Mobile v. Bolden* (1980).

1982    The Reagan administration reverses an Internal Revenue Service policy denying tax exemption to private colleges practicing racial discrimination, but then backs down when faced with protests.

1982    Secretary of Labor Ray Donovan unsuccessfully attempts to reduce the number of federal contractors covered by affirmative action employment guidelines.

1983    Harold Washington is elected the first black mayor of Chicago.

1983    Wilson Goode is elected the first black mayor of Philadelphia.

1983    The birthday of Martin Luther King, Jr., becomes a national holiday by act of Congress.

1984    Jesse Jackson becomes the first black to make a serious race for the U.S. presidency; he receives 3.3 million votes in the Democratic primaries.

1984    In *Grove City College v. Bell*, the Supreme Court states that if college programs engage in racial discrimination, the Office of Civil Rights can cut off federal funding only for those programs, not for the entire college.

1988    Jesse Jackson repeats his 1984 run for president of the United States, this time winning 6.8 million Democratic primary votes.

1988    The Civil Rights Restoration Act, passed over President Reagan's veto, expands the ability of the Office of Civil Rights to combat racial discrimination in higher education by overriding *Grove City College v. Bell*, a 1984 Supreme Court ruling.

1989    L. Douglas Wilder is elected governor of Virginia, the first black to become a governor by popular election.

1989    In *City of Richmond v. J. A. Croson*, the Supreme Court requires states and localities to show a history of intentional discrimination before enacting set-asides for minority businesspeople in the distribution of government contracts.

1989    In *Ward's Cove Packing Co. v. Atonio*, the Supreme Court requires employees to prove that personnel policies discriminate illegally against blacks. Previously, the burden of proof was on employers to show that the policies were legal.

1989    In *Martin v. Wilks*, the Supreme Court declines to set a time limit for white employees to challenge a voluntary, court-approved affirmative action plan on the grounds of reverse discrimination.

1989    In *Lorance v. AT&T*, the Supreme Court states that those claiming that a seniority system discriminates against minorities must file objections within 300 days after adoption of the seniority plan.

1989    Colin Powell becomes the first black chairman of the military's Joint Chiefs of Staff.

1989    Black U.S. Representative William Gray is chosen Democratic majority whip, the third-ranking House Democratic post.

1989    David Dinkins is elected the first black mayor of New York City.

1989    Ron Brown becomes Democratic Party chairman, the first black to head a major party.

1990    In *Metro Broadcasting, Inc. v. Federal Communications Commission*, the Supreme Court upholds set-asides for minority broadcasters.

1991    Clarence Thomas becomes the second black to sit on the Supreme Court.

1991    The Civil Rights Act sets aside a number of 1989 Supreme Court rulings making civil rights enforcement more difficult, especially in the area of employment.

1991    The Justice Department orders a number of southern states to create additional black-majority districts when redrawing district lines in accordance with the 1990 census.

1991    A Hasidic Jewish driver kills a black child in the Crown Heights section of Brooklyn; in the rioting that follows, a black mob kills a Hasidic Jew.

1992    After Los Angeles police officers are acquitted in the videotaped 1991 beating of black man Rodney King, massive rioting breaks out in the south-central Los Angeles ghetto. Thirty-eight are killed and 4,000 are arrested.

1992    Carol Moseley-Braun is elected to the U.S. Senate from Illinois, becoming the first black woman and the first black Democrat to sit in that body.

1992    In *United States v. Fordice*, the Supreme Court requires public colleges to adopt affirmative action programs if seemingly color-blind policies perpetuate past discrimination.

1993    President Bill Clinton names a record four blacks to the cabinet: Ron Brown as secretary of commerce; Mike Espy as secretary of agriculture; Hazel O'Leary as secretary of energy; and Jesse Brown as secretary of veterans affairs.

1993    President Clinton nominates black law professor Lani Guinier as assistant attorney general for civil rights, but then withdraws the nomination when it creates controversy.

1995    In *Adarand Constructors v. Peña*, the Supreme Court rules that federal affirmative action programs are unconstitutional unless they meet strict standards laid down by the Court.

1995    The Supreme Court lets stand a lower court ruling against blacks-only scholarships at the University of Maryland.

1995    In *Miller v. Johnson*, the Supreme Court declares that the racial composition of the population cannot be the "predominant factor" in creating congressional districts.

1995    Black former football star O. J. Simpson is acquitted of murdering his former wife and her friend, both white, in one of the most publicized and racially divisive American trials of the century.

1995    A "Million Man March" for black men only, initiated and led by Nation of Islam head Louis Farrakhan, draws over 500,000 to Washington, D.C.

1996    The Clinton administration suspends set-asides of federal contracts for minority businesspeople.

# GLOSSARY

• • • • • • • • •

A lthough some glossary entries have meanings that extend beyond African Americans, they are defined here as they apply to blacks in the United States.

**Abolitionism:** The principle that slavery should be eliminated. Abolitionist movements were influential at various times between the American Revolution and the Civil War.

**Affirmative action:** Race conscious efforts begun in the late 1960s to overcome racial discrimination by setting goals, or in some cases quotas, for black inclusion in the various activities and institutions of American society—the workplace, public schools, higher education, voting, and housing, for example.

**Black Codes:** Laws passed by the former Confederate states between 1865 and 1867 intended to return blacks to virtual slavery.

**Black nationalism:** A belief that blacks should develop independently of whites, particularly in the economic and cultural spheres. Some black nationalists, known as separatists, additionally favor political independence—the establishment of a separate black nation, usually in a territory carved out of the United States.

**Black power:** A term first used within the civil rights movement in 1966, signifying a desire among blacks to work together—independently of whites—to achieve political power and racial equality. Many black power advocates have gone further, favoring black nationalism. *See* **Black nationalism.**

**Blockbusting:** A practice by which realtors move blacks into an all-white neighborhood and then promote panic among white homeowners so that they sell their homes at a low price. The homes are then sold to blacks at a higher price.

*Brown v. Board of Education of Topeka* **(1954):** A U.S. Supreme Court ruling that "separate educational facilities are inherently unequal" and therefore violate the Fourteenth Amendment. The decision spelled the end of segregation. *See* ***Plessy v. Ferguson*** **(1896)** and **Segregation.**

**Busing:** The transporting of public school students outside their neighborhoods, usually by court order, to create racially integrated schools. Begun in the 1960s and expanded in the 1970s, it was widely opposed by whites.

**Civil rights:** The basic rights of citizenship: equality under the law and equal political rights. Except during Reconstruction, most blacks were denied these rights until the 1960s.

**Civil Rights Act of 1866:** Granted blacks U.S. citizenship and equal protection of person and property.

**Civil Rights Act of 1875:** Outlawed racial discrimination in hotels, public transport, places of amusement, and other facilities. The U.S. Supreme Court declared it unconstitutional in 1883.

**Civil Rights Act of 1957:** Took small steps toward protecting blacks' right to vote.

**Civil Rights Act of 1960:** A supplement to the Civil Rights Act of 1957, it took additional small steps toward enforcing the black franchise.

**Civil Rights Act of 1964:** Barred segregation in public facilities, prohibited employment discrimination and created an Equal Employment Opportunity Commission, provided for a cutoff of federal funds to institutions and activities practicing racial discrimination, and promoted voting rights.

**Civil Rights Act of 1991:** Set aside a series of U.S. Supreme Court decisions hampering civil rights enforcement, particularly in employment.

**Civil Rights Commission, U.S.:** Created by the Civil Rights Act of 1957 to investigate all forms of discrimination and make reports to the president and Congress.

**Civil Rights Restoration Act of 1988:** Restored the authority of the Office of Civil Rights to cut off all federal funding to colleges where discrimination took place, setting aside a U.S. Supreme Court ruling that the office could deny funds only to those individual programs that discriminated.

**Colonization:** Efforts—led sometimes by whites and sometimes by blacks—to settle blacks outside of the United States.

**Congress of Racial Equality (CORE):** Founded on a national basis in 1942, initially a biracial civil rights organization dedicated to direct, nonviolent action against racial discrimination. It is best known for its 1961 freedom rides to integrate Southern bus terminals, but in 1966–1967 CORE came under the control of black nationalists who expelled white members.

**Deindustrialization:** The sharp drop in U.S. manufacturing jobs during the 1970s and 1980s that sparked the growth of a chronically unemployed and heavily black underclass in the cities. *See* **Underclass.**

**Disfranchisement:** The practice of taking the right to vote away from blacks. Before the Civil War, disfranchisement was done openly by law in all slave states and many free states. After passage of the Fifteenth Amendment, it was done indirectly through new voting requirements that were supposedly unrelated to race but in reality applied mostly to blacks. *See* **Grandfather clause, Understanding clause,** and **White primary.**

**Disparate impact:** A policy or practice—in employment, for example—that has an unfavorable effect on blacks.

**Dred Scott v. Sanford (1857):** A U.S. Supreme Court ruling that blacks were not citizens and that Congress could not bar slavery from the western territories.

**Equal Employment Opportunity Commission (EEOC):** A federal panel established by the Civil Rights Act of 1964 to investigate employment discrimination and later authorized to take discriminating employers to court.

**Exclusionary zoning:** State and local regulations restricting low-income housing to poor neighborhoods, often used to perpetuate housing segregation.

**Fair Housing Act of 1968:** Banned housing discrimination by private lending institutions, but failed to define illegal practices clearly or provide strong enforcement procedures.

**Fifteenth Amendment:** Enfranchised blacks; ratified in 1870.

**Filibuster:** A practice by which a minority of the U.S. Senate often "talked to death" civil rights measures supported by a majority of senators. This was possible because of a Senate rule requiring more than a simple majority to cut off debate on a bill; without a cutoff of debate, no vote could be taken on the bill.

**Fourteenth Amendment:** Granted blacks U.S. citizenship and "equal protection of the laws"; ratified in 1868.

**Free blacks:** During the slavery era, blacks who were not slaves. Their rights, however, were severely limited.

**Freedom riders:** Black and white civil rights activists who rode buses into the South in the early 1960s in order to integrate bus terminals in that region.

**Gang system:** A method of organizing plantation labor by grouping slaves into crews that were supervised by drivers. *See* **Task system.**

**Ghetto:** A black section of a city or town, created by discriminatory housing practices preventing blacks from living in nonblack areas.

**Glass ceiling:** Unofficial discrimination limiting the extent to which blacks can advance in their workplaces; because the discrimination is "invisible" (not written down in a rule), the ceiling on advancement is said to be a glass one.

**Grandfather clause:** A legal provision used in Southern states for exempting whites from voting qualifications (such as literacy) meant to disfranchise blacks; it gave the franchise to all who had voted before 1867—when blacks were enfranchised in the ex-Confederate states—or whose father or grandfather had voted before then.

**Indentured servitude:** A labor system of the colonial era, under which Europeans wishing to come to British North America received free transportation and, in exchange, had to work without pay for a term of years. Until slavery became firmly established, some Africans were sold upon arrival as indentured servants rather than as slaves.

**Intent test:** A standard of proof for demonstrating that a policy discriminates illegally; it requires a showing that the policy was designed, or intended, to discriminate against blacks. *See* **Results test.**

**Jim Crow:** Practices that discriminate against blacks, most often used in reference to segregation.

**Ku Klux Klan:** The name of various white terrorist organizations using violence and intimidation against blacks and other groups. The first Klan emerged in the South during Reconstruction to prevent blacks from exercising their newly won rights. The second Klan appeared after World War I in both the Midwest and the South and targeted Jews, Catholics, and immigrants, as well as blacks. Starting in the 1950s, many smaller Klans have formed in the South in reaction against civil rights progress.

**Lynching:** The practice by which groups of whites, acting outside the judicial system, murdered blacks for supposed violations of the law or of unofficial racial codes; it occurred mostly in the South but also in the North, and most frequently in the late nineteenth and early twentieth centuries.

**Manumission:** The freeing of individual slaves or groups of slaves by their masters or by government, as opposed to a general emancipation of all slaves.

**Middle Passage:** The harsh ocean voyage from Africa to the Western Hemisphere forced upon Africans bought on their native continent to be sold as slaves in the Americas; around 12 million Africans endured the ordeal, which killed around 1.5 million of them.

**Nation of Islam:** Formed around 1930, a black separatist organization with an unorthodox Islamic doctrine, seeking a separate black nation carved from the United States.

**National Association for the Advancement of Colored People (NAACP):** Founded in 1910 by whites and blacks to promote equal rights for blacks. It quickly became the most important civil rights group in the country. Its most important work has been fighting discrimination in the courts and lobbying for civil rights legislation.

**National Urban League:** Founded by black and white social workers in 1911 to secure job opportunities and provide social services to blacks in Northern cities. In the 1960s it also became engaged in the civil rights struggle.

**Office of Civil Rights (OCR):** A federal agency created in 1966 to enforce primary and secondary school desegregation.

**Office of Federal Contract Compliance Programs (OFCCP):** A federal agency created in the mid-1960s to promote the hiring of blacks by federal contractors and subcontractors.

**Plessy v. Ferguson (1896):** A U.S. Supreme Court decision establishing the "separate-but-equal" doctrine by permitting segregation of the races so long as they received equivalent treatment. See **Segregation** and **Brown v. Board of Education of Topeka (1954).**

**Race-neutral:** A policy applied without regard to race; a color-blind policy. Under affirmative action, however, such policies are considered discriminatory if they perpetuate the results of past discrimination.

**Radical Reconstruction:** The era after the Civil War from the late 1860s to 1877, when blacks in the former Confederate states exercised civil rights under the protection of federal troops.

**Redeemers:** Southern white conservatives who led the fight against Radical Reconstruction and headed the post-Reconstruction governments in the last 30 years of the nineteenth century.

**Restrictive covenant:** Provision in a property deed or other legal document prohibiting homeowners from selling to blacks.

**Redlining:** Banking practices making it difficult for residents of black neighborhoods to get housing loans and other credit.

**Results test:** A standard of proof for demonstrating that a policy discriminates illegally, it requires a showing that the outcome of the policy is unfair to blacks. An easier test to meet than the intent test, it is the foundation for affirmative action. See **Affirmative action** and **Intent test.**

**Reverse discrimination:** Discrimination against nonblacks resulting from affirmative action programs.

**Second-generation discrimination:** Indirect attempts to discriminate against blacks after the end of legalized discrimination in the 1960s.

**Segregation:** A mostly, but not entirely, Southern policy of separating whites and blacks by creating separate facilities and institutions for the two races. Appearing around 1800, it was not systematically established until the Southern states legally required racial separation in most social situations during the late nineteenth and early twentieth centuries. Almost always, facilities for blacks were inferior to those provided for whites. See **Plessy v. Ferguson (1896).**

**Self-hiring:** A policy followed by some slaveholders of allowing slaves to find their own work, with the slaveowners receiving part of the slaves' wages.

**Set-asides:** A proportion or quota of government contracts reserved for black business people.

**Sharecropping:** A system of farming in the post-Civil War South, whereby landless farmers worked a piece of land in return for giving the landowner a share of the crop (usually cotton). The system developed because ex-slaves did not want to work as wage laborers in gangs supervised by whites.

**Slavery:** A system of servitude under which—from the late-seventeenth century to 1865—the great majority of blacks were the lifelong property of an owner or series of owners. With some exceptions in the colonial era, slave status was passed from generation to generation through the slave mother. With the exception of some American Indians in the seventeenth and early eighteenth centuries, all slaves were black; almost all masters were white.

**Southern Christian Leadership Conference (SCLC):** A civil rights group organized by black ministers in 1957, committed to racial equality achieved through nonviolent means. The SCLC was headed by Martin Luther King, Jr.

**Steering:** A practice of realtors for maintaining segregated housing by showing blacks only homes in all-black neighborhoods or neighborhoods changing from white to black.

**Student Nonviolent Coordinating Committee (SNCC):** Initially an integrated, nonviolent civil rights organization formed in 1960 by Southern black college students and best known for registering black voters in the rural Deep South. In 1966 it adopted the black power viewpoint and expelled all whites.

**Talented Tenth:** The educated black elite whose task was to elevate the condition of the remainder of the black population. The term was popularized by black historian W. E. B. Du Bois.

**Task system:** A method of organizing plantation labor, used mostly on rice plantations, by assigning each slave individual tasks to be completed during a day. *See* **Gang system.**

**Thirteenth Amendment:** Abolished slavery; ratified in 1865.

**Twenty-fourth Amendment:** Barred the use of poll taxes as a voting requirement in federal elections; ratified in 1964.

**Underclass:** Chronically unemployed persons, frequently black, living in the inner cities, having neither the skills nor the education to find decent work in the post-1970 era of deindustrialization. Social problems such as crime, drug abuse, alcoholism, and out-of-wedlock births are common within this class. *See* **Deindustrialization.**

**Understanding clause:** A method used in Southern states to exempt whites from voting qualifications meant to disfranchise blacks. It permitted election officials to use their judgment in determining whether prospective voters understood a written document submitted to them.

**Uncle Tom:** A black who serves white interests.

**Universal Negro Improvement Association (UNIA):** A black nationalist group and the first mass black organization in the United States, led by Marcus Garvey of Jamaica. Its membership peaked in the late 1910s and early 1920s at about 500,000.

**Urban League:** *See* **National Urban League.**

**Voting Rights Act of 1965:** In areas where voting discrimination was most severe, authorized federal examiners to determine the eligibility of voters, authorized federal observers to go to polling places to see if discrimination was occurring, suspended the use of literacy tests, and required approval by the U.S. attorney general of changes in election laws.

**White backlash:** Reaction against the movement for racial equality, usually by whites who believe they are victims of reverse discrimination resulting from affirmative action plans. *See* **Affirmative action** and **Reverse discrimination.**

**White primary:** Democratic party primary elections in Southern states that excluded black voters.

# FURTHER READING

•  •  •  •  •  •  •  •  •

his bibliography is intended to provide a starting point for reading or
research about the history of African Americans and civil rights in
America. It is not definitive because the published information on these
topics is vast and there are many thousands of books and articles in print; it is,
however, comprehensive in the sense that it covers a wide range of topics.

The bibliography is divided into categories, and books are listed alphabetically by
author's last name within the classifications. The titles are written for a general adult
audience, but those items most suitable for young adults are noted with an asterisk (*).

## BIBLIOGRAPHIES

Davis, Lenwood G., and George Hill. *Blacks in the American Armed Forces, 1776–1983.*
Westport, Conn.: Greenwood, 1985.

Dworaczek, Marian. *Affirmative Action and Minorities: A Bibliography.* Monticello, Ill.:
Vance Bibliographies, 1988.

Ham, Deborah Newman, ed. *The African American Mosaic: A Library of Congress Resource
Guide for the Study of Black History and Culture.* Washington, D.C.: Library of Congress,
1993.

Jenkins, Betty Lanier, and Susan Phillis, comps. *Black Separatism: A Bibliography.* Westport,
Conn.: Greenwood, 1976.

Miller, Joseph C. *Slavery: A Worldwide Bibliography, 1900–1991.* White Plains, N.Y.: Kraus
International, 1993. Supplemented annually in the journal *Slavery and Abolition.*

Smith, John D. *Black Slavery in the Americas: An Interdisciplinary Bibliography, 1865–1980.*
Westport, Conn.: Greenwood, 1980.

Wilson, Joseph. *Black Labor in America: 1865–1983.* New York: Greenwood, 1986.

## GENERAL

*Bennett, Lerone, Jr. *Before the Mayflower: A History of Black America.* 6th edition. New
York: Penguin, 1988.

Clark, Darlene Hine. *African Americans in U.S. History.* 2 vols. Englewood Cliffs, N.J.: Globe Books, 1989.

Clay, William L. *Just Permanent Interests: Black Americans in Congress, 1870–1991.* New York: Amistad Press, 1992.

Coniff, Michael L., and Thomas J. Davis. *Africans in the Americas: A History of the Black Diaspora.* New York: St. Martin's Press, 1994.

*Franklin, John Hope, and Alfred A. Moss, Jr. *From Slavery to Freedom: A History of African Americans.* 7th edition. New York: McGraw-Hill, 1994.

Frazier, E. Franklin. *The Negro Church in America.* New York: Schocken, 1963.

———. *The Negro Family in the United States.* Chicago: University of Chicago Press, 1939.

Giddings, Paula. *"When and Where I Enter . . .": The Impact of Black Women on Race and Sex in America.* New York: Morrow, 1984.

Greenberg, Jack. *Race Relations and American Law.* New York: Columbia University Press, 1959.

Gutman, Herbert G. *The Black Family in Slavery and Freedom, 1750–1925.* New York: Pantheon, 1976.

Hamilton, Virginia. *Many Thousand Gone: African Americans from Slavery to Freedom.* New York: Knopf, 1993.

Harding, Vincent. *There Is a River: The Black Struggle for Freedom in America.* New York: Harcourt Brace Jovanovich, 1981.

Jones, Jacqueline. *Labor of Love, Labor of Sorrow: Black Women, Work, and the Family from Slavery to the Present.* New York: Basic Books, 1985.

Lincoln, C. Eric, and Lawrence A. Mamiya. *The Black Church in the African American Experience.* Durham, N.C.: Duke University Press, 1990.

Lively, Donald E. *The Constitution and Race.* New York: Praeger, 1992.

Meier, August, and Elliot Rudwick. *From Plantation to Ghetto: An Interpretive History of American Negroes.* 3rd edition. New York: Hill & Wang, 1976.

Miller, Loren. *The Petitioners: The Story of the Supreme Court of the United States and the Negro.* New York: Pantheon, 1966.

Nieman, Donald G. *Promises to Keep: African Americans and the Constitutional Order, 1776 to the Present.* New York: Oxford University Press, 1991.

*Quarles, Benjamin. *The Negro in the Making of America.* 2nd revised edition. New York: Collier, 1987.

Williamson, Joel. *The Crucible of Race: Black-White Relations in the American South since Emancipation.* New York: Oxford University Press, 1984.

## REFERENCE

Asante, Molefi K., and Mark T. Mattson. *The Historical and Cultural Atlas of African Americans.* New York: Macmillan, 1991.

D'Emilio, John. *The Civil Rights Struggle: Leaders in Profile.* New York: Facts on File, 1979.

Estell, Kenneth, ed. *Reference Library of Black America.* 5 vols. Detroit: Gale Research, 1994.

Foner, Eric. *Freedom's Lawmakers: A Directory of Black Officeholders during Reconstruction.* New York: Oxford University Press, 1994.

Hawkins, Walter L. *African American Biographies: Profiles of 558 Current Men and Women.* Jefferson, N.C.: McFarland, 1992.

Hine, Darlene Clark. *Black Women in America: An Historical Encyclopedia.* 2 vols. Brooklyn, N.Y.: Carlson, 1993.

LaBlanc, Michael L., ed. *Contemporary Black Biography.* 6 vols. Detroit: Gale Research, 1992.

Logan, Rayford, and Michael R. Winston. *Dictionary of American Negro Biography*. New York: Norton, 1982.

Low, W. Augustus, ed. *Encyclopedia of Black America*. New York: McGraw-Hill, 1981.

Lowery, Charles D., and John F. Marszalek. *Encyclopedia of African-American Civil Rights: From Emancipation to the Present*. Westport, Conn.: Greenwood, 1992.

Miller, Randall M., and John David Smith. *Dictionary of Afro-American Slavery*. Westport, Conn.: Greenwood, 1988.

National Urban League. *The State of Black America 1995*. New York: National Urban League, 1995. Published annually beginning in 1976.

Rywell, Martin, comp. and ed. *Afro-American Encyclopedia*. 10 vols. North Miami, Fla.: Educational Book Publishers, 1974.

Salzman, Jack, and others, eds. *Encyclopedia of African-American Culture and History*. 5 vols. New York: Macmillan, 1996.

Trefousse, Hans L. *Historical Dictionary of Reconstruction*. New York: Greenwood, 1991.

## WEST AFRICA

Ajayi, J. F. A., and Michael Crowder, eds. *History of West Africa*. 2 vols. London: Longman, 1976.

Davidson, Basil. *Africa in History: Themes and Outlines*. Revised edition. New York: Collier, 1991.

———. *Black Mother: The Years of the African Slave Trade*. London: Victor Gollancz, 1961.

Fage, J. D. *An Atlas of African History*. 2nd revised edition. New York: African Publishing Co., 1978.

———. *A History of West Africa: An Introductory Survey*. 4th edition. Cambridge, Eng.: Cambridge University Press, 1969.

Fage, J. D., and Roland Oliver, eds. *Cambridge History of Africa*. Vols. 1 and 2. Cambridge, Eng.: Cambridge University Press, 1975, 1978.

Harris, Joseph E. *Africans and Their History*. Revised edition. New York: New American Library, 1987.

Hoyt, Edwin P. *African Slavery*. New York: Abelard-Schuman, 1973.

Lovejoy, Paul E. *Transformations in Slavery: A History of Slavery in Africa*. Cambridge, Eng.: Cambridge University Press, 1983.

Middleton, John, ed. *Encyclopedia of Sub-Saharan Africa*. New York: Scribner's, forthcoming.

Oliver, Roland, and Brian Fagan. *Africa in the Iron Age*. Cambridge, Eng.: Cambridge University Press, 1975.

Oliver, Roland, and J. D. Fage. *A Short History of Africa*. 6th edition. New York: Facts on File, 1988.

Robertson, Claire C. *Women and Slavery in Africa*. Madison: University of Wisconsin Press, 1983.

Willis, John Ralph. *Slaves and Slavery in Muslim Africa*. 2 vols. Totowa, N.J.: Frank Cass, 1985.

## THE ATLANTIC SLAVE TRADE

Anstey, Roger. *The Atlantic Slave Trade and British Abolition, 1710–1810*. Atlantic Highlands, N.J.: Humanities Press, 1975.

Bean, Richard. *The British Trans-Atlantic Slave Trade, 1650–1775*. New York: Arno Press, 1975.

Bethell, Leslie. *The Abolition of the Brazilian Slave Trade: Britain, Brazil, and the Slave Trade Question, 1807–1869.* Cambridge, Eng.: Cambridge University Press, 1970.

Coughtry, Jay Alan. *The Notorious Triangle: Rhode Island and the African Slave Trade, 1700–1807.* Philadelphia: Temple University Press, 1981.

Curtin, Philip D. *The Atlantic Slave Trade: A Census.* Madison: University of Wisconsin Press, 1969.

Duignan, Peter, and Clarence Clendenen. *The United States and the African Slave Trade, 1619–1862.* Stanford, Calif.: Hoover Institute, 1963.

Klein, Herbert S. *The Middle Passage: Comparative Studies in the Atlantic Slave Trade.* Princeton, N.J.: Princeton University Press, 1978.

Leveen, E. Phillip. *British Slave Trade Suppression Policies, 1821–1865.* New York: Arno Press, 1977.

Manning, Patrick. *Slavery and African Life: Occidental, Oriental, and African Slave Trades.* New York: Cambridge University Press, 1990.

*Mannix, Daniel R. *Black Cargoes: A History of the Atlantic Slave Trade, 1518–1865.* New York: Viking, 1962.

Miller, Joseph C. "The Slave Trade." In *Encyclopedia of the North American Colonies,* vol. 1, edited by Jacob Ernest Cooke. New York: Scribner's, 1993.

Pope-Hennessey, James. *Sins of the Fathers: A Study of the Atlantic Slave Traders, 1441–1807.* New York: Knopf, 1968.

Postma, Johannes Menne. *The Dutch in the Atlantic Slave Trade.* New York: Cambridge University Press, 1990.

Rawley, James A. *The Transatlantic Slave Trade: A History.* New York: Norton, 1981.

*Reynolds, Edward. *Stand the Storm: A History of the Atlantic Slave Trade.* Chicago: Ivan R. Dee, 1985.

Rodney, Walter. *West Africa and the Atlantic Slave-Trade.* Nairobi: Historical Association of Tanzania, 1967.

Stein, Robert Louis. *The French Slave Trade in the Eighteenth Century: An Old Regime Business.* Madison: University of Wisconsin Press, 1979.

Williams, Eric. *Capitalism and Slavery.* Chapel Hill: University of North Carolina Press, 1944.

## SLAVERY IN CENTRAL AMERICA, SOUTH AMERICA, AND THE CARIBBEAN

Boxer, Charles R. *Race Relations in the Portuguese Colonial Empire, 1415–1825.* Oxford: Clarendon, 1963.

Bush, Barbara. *Slave Women in Caribbean Society, 1650–1838.* Bloomington: Indiana University Press, 1990.

Cohen, David W., and Jack P. Greene, eds. *Neither Slave nor Free: The Freedmen of African Descent in the Slave Societies of the New World.* Baltimore: Johns Hopkins University Press, 1972.

Conrad, Robert. *The Destruction of Brazilian Slavery, 1850–1888.* 2nd edition. Melbourne, Fla.: Krieger, 1993.

Corwin, Arthur F. *Spain and the Abolition of Slavery in Cuba, 1817–1886.* Austin: University of Texas, 1967.

Craton, Michael, and others, eds. *Slavery, Abolition, and Emancipation: Black Slaves and the British Empire.* London: Longman, 1976.

Degler, Carl N. *Neither Black nor White: Slavery and Race Relations in Brazil and the United States.* New York: Macmillan, 1971.

Foner, Laura, and Eugene D. Genovese, eds. *Slavery in the New World: A Reader in Comparative History*. Englewood Cliffs, N.J.: Prentice-Hall, 1969.

Freyre, Gilberto. *The Masters and the Slaves: A Study in the Development of Brazilian Civilization*. Translated by Samuel Putnam. New York: Knopf, 1946.

Greene, William A. *British Slave Emancipation: The Sugar Colonies and the Great Experiment, 1830–1865*. Oxford: Clarendon, 1976.

Hall, Gwendolyn M. *Social Control in Slave Plantation Societies: A Comparison of St. Domingue and Cuba*. Baltimore: Johns Hopkins University Press, 1970.

Harris, Marvin. *Patterns of Race in the Americas*. New York: W. W. Norton, 1964.

James, C. L. R. *The Black Jacobins: Toussaint L'Ouverture and the San Domingo Revolution*. 2nd edition. New York: Vintage, 1963.

Johnson, Howard. *The Bahamas in Slavery and Freedom*. Kingston, Jamaica: Ian Randle Publishers, 1991.

Klein, Herbert S. *African Slavery in Latin America and the Caribbean*. New York: Oxford University Press, 1986.

———. *Slavery in the Americas: A Comparative Study of Virginia and Cuba*. Chicago: University of Chicago Press, 1967.

Lombardi, John V. *The Decline and Abolition of Slavery in Venezuela, 1820–1854*. Westport, Conn.: Greenwood, 1971.

McCloy, Shelby. *The Negro in the French West Indies*. Lexington: University of Kentucky Press, 1966.

Munford, Clarence J. *The Black Ordeal of Slavery and Slave Trading in the French West Indies, 1625–1715*. 3 vols. Lewiston, N.Y.: Edwin Mellen Press, 1991.

Ottley, Carlton Robert. *Slavery Days in Trinidad: A Social History of the Island, 1797–1838*. Trinidad: Ottley, 1974.

Packwood, Cyril R. *Chained on the Rock: Slavery in Bermuda*. New York: Eliseo Torres & Sons, 1975.

Price, Richard. *Maroon Societies: Rebel Slave Communities in the Americas*. New York: Anchor Press, 1973.

Rubin, Vera, and Arthur Tuden, eds. *Comparative Perspectives on Slavery in New World Plantation Societies*. New York: New York Academy of Sciences, 1977.

Schwartz, Stuart B. *Slaves, Peasants, and Rebels: Reconsidering Brazilian Slavery*. Urbana: University of Illinois Press, 1992.

Sharp, William F. *Slavery on the Spanish Frontier: The Colombian Choco, 1680–1810*. Norman: University of Oklahoma Press, 1976.

Tannenbaum, Frank. *Slave and Citizen*. New York: Vintage, 1947.

Thompson, V. B. *The Making of the African Diaspora in the Americas, 1441–1900*. London: Longman, 1984.

Toplin, Robert B., ed. *Slavery and Race Relations in Latin America*. Westport, Conn.: Greenwood, 1974.

Walvin, James. *Slaves and Slavery: The British Colonial Experience*. Manchester, Eng.: Manchester University Press, 1992.

## SLAVERY IN THE UNITED STATES

Abrahams, Roger. *Singing the Master: The Emergence of African American Culture in the Plantation South*. New York: Pantheon, 1992.

Berlin, Ira, and Ronald Hoffman, eds. *Slavery and Freedom in the Age of the American Revolution*. Charlottesville: University Press of Virginia, 1983.

Berlin, Ira, and Philip D. Morgan, eds. *Cultivation and Culture: Labor and the Shaping of Slave Life in the Americas*. Charlottesville: University Press of Virginia, 1993.

Blassingame, John. *The Slave Community: Plantation Life in the Old South*. Revised edition. New York: Oxford University Press, 1979.

Boles, John. *Black Southerners, 1619–1869*. Lexington: University Press of Kentucky, 1983.

Bracey, John H., and others, eds. *American Slavery: The Question of Resistance*. Belmont, Calif.: Wadsworth, 1971.

Breen, T. H., and Stephen Innes. *"Myne Owne Ground": Race and Freedom on Virginia's Eastern Shore, 1640–1676*. New York: Oxford University Press, 1980.

Campbell, Edward D. C., Jr., and Kim S. Rice, eds. *Before Freedom Came: Afro-American Life in the Antebellum South*. Charlottesville: University Press of Virginia, 1991.

Clayton, Ralph. *Slavery, Slaveholding, and the Free Black Population of Antebellum Baltimore*. Bowie, Md.: Heritage Books, 1993.

Davis, David Brion. *The Problem of Slavery in the Age of Revolution, 1770–1823*. Ithaca, N.Y.: Cornell University Press, 1975.

———. *The Problem of Slavery in Western Culture*. Ithaca, N.Y.: Cornell University Press, 1966.

Davis, Thomas J. *A Rumor of Revolt: The Great Negro Plot in Colonial New York*. New York: Free Press, 1985.

Duff, John B., and Peter M. Mitchell, eds. *The Nat Turner Rebellion: The Historical Event and the Modern Controversy*. New York: Harper & Row, 1971.

Egerton, Douglas R. *Gabriel's Rebellion: The Virginia Slave Conspiracies of 1800 and 1802*. Chapel Hill: University of North Carolina Press, 1993.

Fede, Andrew. *People without Rights: An Interpretation of the Fundamentals of the Law of Slavery in the U.S. South*. New York: Garland, 1992.

Fields, Barbara J. *Slavery and Freedom on the Middle Ground: Maryland during the Nineteenth Century*. New Haven, Conn.: Yale University Press, 1985.

Finkleman, Paul, ed. *Women and the Family in a Slave Society*. New York: Garland Publishing, 1989.

Foley, Robert William, and Stanley L. Engerman. *Time on the Cross: The Economics of American Negro Slavery*. Boston: Little, Brown, 1974.

Fox-Genovese, Elizabeth. *Within the Plantation Household: Black and White Women of the Old South*. Chapel Hill: University of North Carolina Press, 1989.

Frey, Sylvia. *Water from the Rock: Black Resistance in a Revolutionary Age*. Princeton, N.J.: Princeton University Press, 1991.

Genovese, Eugene D. *Roll, Jordan, Roll: The World the Slaves Made*. New York: Pantheon, 1974.

———. *The World the Slaveholders Made*. New York: Pantheon, 1969.

Goldin, Claudia D. *Urban Slavery in the American South, 1820–1860: A Quantitative History*. Chicago: University of Chicago Press, 1976.

*Greene, Lorenzo J. *The Negro in Colonial New England*. New York: Columbia University Press, 1942.

Halasz, Nicholas. *The Rattling Chains: Slave Unrest and Revolt in the Antebellum South*. New York: D. McKay, 1966.

Huggins, Nathan. *Black Odyssey: The Afro-American Ordeal in Slavery*. New York: Pantheon, 1977.

Johnston, James H. *Race Relations in Virginia and Miscegenation in the South, 1776–1860*. Amherst: University of Massachusetts Press, 1970.

Jordan, Winthrop D. *Tumult and Silence at Second Creek: An Inquiry into a Civil War Slave Conspiracy*. Baton Rouge: Louisiana State University Press, 1993.

———. *White over Black: American Attitudes Toward the Negro, 1550–1812*. Chapel Hill: University of North Carolina Press, 1968.

*Kaplan, Sidney, and Emma Rogrady Kaplan. *The Black Presence in the Era of the American Revolution*. Revised edition. Amherst: University of Massachusetts Press, 1989.

Kay, Marvin L. Michael, and Lorin Lee Cary. *Slavery in North Carolina, 1748–1775*. Chapel Hill, N.C.: University of North Carolina Press, 1995.

Kolchin, Peter. *American Slavery, 1691–1877*. New York: Hill & Wang, 1993.

Lofton, John M., Jr. *Insurrection in South Carolina: The Turbulent World of Denmark Vesey*. Yellow Springs, Ohio: Antioch Press, 1964.

McLaurin, Melton A. *Celia: A Slave*. Athens: University of Georgia Press, 1991.

McLeod, Duncan. *Slavery, Race and the American Revolution*. London: Cambridge University Press, 1974.

McManus, Edgar J. *Black Bondage in the North*. Syracuse, N.Y.: Syracuse University Press, 1973.

———. *A History of Negro Slavery in New York*. Syracuse, N.Y.: Syracuse University Press, 1966.

Miller, John C. *The Wolf by the Ears: Thomas Jefferson and Slavery*. New York: Free Press, 1975.

Mintz, Sidney, and Richard Price. *The Birth of African-American Culture*. Boston: Beacon, 1992.

Mohr, Clarence L. *On the Threshold of Freedom: Masters and Slaves in Civil War Georgia*. Athens: University of Georgia Press, 1985.

Mooney, Chase C. *Slavery in Tennessee*. Bloomington: Indiana University Press, 1957.

Morgan, Edmund. *American Slavery, American Freedom: The Ordeal of Colonial Virginia*. New York: Norton, 1975.

Mullin, Gerald W. *Flight and Rebellion: Slave Resistance in Eighteenth-Century Virginia*. New York: Oxford University Press, 1972.

Nash, Gary B., and Jean R. Soderlund. *Freedom by Degrees: Emancipation in Pennsylvania and Its Aftermath*. New York: Oxford University Press, 1991.

Newton, James E., and Ronald L. Lewis, eds. *The Other Slaves: Mechanics, Artisans, and Craftsmen*. Boston: G. K. Hall, 1978.

Oakes, James. *Slavery and Freedom: An Interpretation of the Old South*. New York: Knopf, 1990.

Oates, Stephen B. *The Fires of Jubilee: Nat Turner's Fierce Rebellion*. New York: Harper & Row, 1975.

Raboteau, Albert J. *Slave Religion: The "Invisible Institution" in the Antebellum South*. New York: Oxford University Press, 1978.

Ripley, C. Peter. *Slaves and Freedmen in Civil War Louisiana*. Baton Rouge: Louisiana State University Press, 1975.

Robinson, Donald. *Slavery in the Structure of American Politics, 1765–1820*. New York: Norton, 1971.

Rose, Willie Lee. *Slavery and Freedom*, edited by William W. Freehling. New York: Oxford University Press, 1982.

Scherer, Lester B. *Slavery and the Churches in Early America, 1619–1819*. Grand Rapids, Mich.: Eerdmans, 1975.

Scott, John Anthony. *Hard Trials on My Way: Slavery and the Struggle against It, 1800–1860*. New York: Knopf, 1974.

Sellers, James B. *Slavery in Alabama*. University, Ala.: University of Alabama Press, 1950.

Sobel, Mechal. *Trabelin' On: The Slave Journey to an Afro-Baptist Faith*. Westport, Conn.: Greenwood, 1979.

Soderland, Jean R. *Quakers and Slavery: A Divided Spirit*. Princeton, N.J.: Princeton University Press, 1985.

*Stampp, Kenneth. *The Peculiar Institution: Slavery in the Ante-Bellum South.* New York: Knopf, 1956.

Starobin, Robert S. *Industrial Slavery in the Old South.* New York: Oxford University Press, 1970.

Starobin, Robert S., ed. *Denmark Vesey: The Slave Conspiracy of 1822.* Englewood Cliffs, N.J.: Prentice-Hall, 1970.

Stuckey, Sterling. *Slave Culture: Nationalist Theory and the Foundations of Black America.* New York: Oxford University Press, 1987.

Sydnor, Charles Sackett. *Slavery in Mississippi.* New York: D. Appleton-Century, 1933.

Tadman, Michael. *Speculators and Slaves: Masters, Traders, and Slaves in the Old South.* Madison: University of Wisconsin Press, 1989.

Taylor, Joe. *Negro Slavery in Louisiana.* Baton Rouge: Louisiana Historical Association, 1963.

Taylor, Orville W. *Negro Slavery in Arkansas.* Durham, N.C.: Duke University Press, 1958.

Van Deburg, William L. *The Slave Drivers: Black Agricultural Labor Supervisors in the Ante-Bellum South.* Westport, Conn.: Greenwood, 1979.

Vlach, John Michael. *Back of the Big House: The Architecture of Plantation Slavery.* Chapel Hill: University of North Carolina Press, 1993.

Wade, Richard C. *Slavery in the Cities: The South, 1820–1860.* New York: Oxford University Press, 1964.

White, Deborah Gray. *Ar'n't I a Woman? Female Slaves in the Plantation South.* New York: Norton, 1985.

Wood, Peter H. *Black Majority: Negroes in Colonial South Carolina from 1670 through the Stono Rebellion.* New York: Knopf, 1974.

Wright, Donald R. *African Americans in the Colonial Era: From African Origins through the American Revolution.* Arlington Heights, Ill.: Harland Davidson, 1990.

———. *African Americans in the Early Republic, 1789–1831.* Arlington Heights, Ill.: Harland Davidson, 1993.

Zilversmit, Arthur. *The First Emancipation: The Abolition of Slavery in the North.* Chicago: University of Chicago Press, 1967.

## FREE BLACKS DURING THE SLAVERY ERA

Berlin, Ira. *Slaves without Masters: The Free Negro in the Antebellum South.* New York: New Press, 1974.

Bernstein, Iver. *The New York City Draft Riots: Their Significance for American Society and Politics in the Age of the Civil War.* New York: Oxford University Press, 1990.

Bracey, John H., and others, eds. *Free Blacks in America, 1800–1860.* Belmont, Calif.: Wadsworth, 1971.

Breen, T. H., and Stephen Innes. *"Myne Owne Ground": Race and Freedom on Virginia's Eastern Shore, 1640–1676.* New York: Oxford University Press, 1980.

Brown, Letitia Woods. *Free Negroes in the District of Columbia, 1790–1846.* New York: Oxford University Press, 1972.

Clayton, Ralph. *Slavery, Slaveholding, and the Free Black Population of Antebellum Baltimore.* Bowie, Md.: Heritage Books, 1993.

Cohen, David W., and Jack P. Greene, eds. *Neither Slave nor Free: The Freedmen of African Descent in the Slave Societies of the New World.* Baltimore: Johns Hopkins University Press, 1972.

Cook, Adrian. *The Armies of the Streets: The New York City Draft Riots of 1863.* Lexington, Ky.: University Press of Kentucky, 1974.

Curry, Leonard P. *The Free Black in Urban America, 1800–1850*. Chicago: University of Chicago Press, 1981.

Franklin, John Hope. *The Free Negro in North Carolina, 1790–1860*. Chapel Hill: University of North Carolina Press, 1943.

———. *A Southern Odyssey: Travelers in the Antebellum North*. Baton Rouge: Louisiana State University Press, 1976.

Harris, Sheldon H. *Paul Cuffee: Black America and the African Return*. New York: Simon & Schuster, 1972.

Horton, James Oliver. *Free People of Color: Inside the African American Community*. Washington, D.C.: Smithsonian Institution Press, 1993.

Horton, James Oliver, and Lois E. Horton. *Black Bostonians: Family Life and Community Struggle in the Ante-Bellum North*. New York: Holmes & Meier, 1979.

Jackson, Luther P. *Free Negro Labor and Property Holding in Virginia, 1830–1860*. New York: D. Appleton-Century, 1942.

Johnson, Michael P., and James L. Roark. *Black Masters: A Free Family of Color in the Old South*. New York: Norton, 1984.

———. *No Chariot Let Down: Charleston's Free People of Color on the Eve of the Civil War*. Chapel Hill: University of North Carolina Press, 1984.

Jordan, Winthrop D. *White over Black: American Attitudes toward the Negro, 1550–1812*. Chapel Hill: University of North Carolina Press, 1968.

*Kaplan, Sidney, and Emma Rogrady Kaplan. *The Black Presence in the Era of the American Revolution*. Revised edition. Amherst: University of Massachusetts Press, 1989.

Lebsock, Suzanne. *The Free Women of Petersburg: Status and Culture in a Southern Town, 1784–1860*. New York: Norton, 1984.

*Litwack, Leon F. *North of Slavery: The Negro in the Free States, 1790–1860*. Chicago: University of Chicago Press, 1961.

*Longworth, Polly. *I, Charlotte Forten, Black and Free*. New York: Crowell, 1970.

McCague, James. *The Second Rebellion: The Story of the New York Draft Riots of 1863*. New York: Dial, 1968.

McFeeley, William S. *Frederick Douglass*. New York: Norton, 1991.

Miller, Floyd John. *The Search for a Black Nationality: Black Emigration and Colonization, 1787–1863*. Urbana: University of Illinois Press, 1975.

Nash, Gary B. *Forging Freedom: The Formation of Philadelphia's Black Community, 1720–1840*. Cambridge, Mass.: Harvard University Press, 1988.

Nash, Gary B., and Jean R. Soderlund. *Freedom by Degrees: Emancipation in Pennsylvania and Its Aftermath*. New York: Oxford University Press, 1991.

Ripley, C. Peter. *Slaves and Freedmen in Civil War Louisiana*. Baton Rouge: Louisiana State University Press, 1975.

Russell, John H. *The Free Negro in Virginia, 1619–1865*. Baltimore: Johns Hopkins Press, 1913.

Staudenraus, Philip J. *The African Colonization Movement, 1816–1865*. New York: Columbia University Press, 1961.

Sterkx, H. E. *The Free Negro in Antebellum Louisiana*. Rutherford, N.J.: Farleigh Dickinson University Press, 1972.

Sweat, Edward F. *Economic Status of Free Blacks in Antebellum Georgia*. Atlanta: Southern Center for Studies in Public Policy, Clark College, 1974.

Thomas, Lamont D. *Paul Cuffee: Black Entrepreneur and Pan-Africanist*. Urbana: University of Illinois Press, 1988.

Walker, Juliet E. K. *Free Frank: A Black Pioneer on the Ante-Bellum Frontier*. Lexington: University Press of Kentucky, 1984.

Wesley, Charles H. *Richard Allen: Apostle of Freedom*. Washington, D.C.: Associated Publishers, 1935.

Wikramanayake, Marina. *A World in Shadow: The Free Black in Antebellum South Carolina*. Columbia: University of South Carolina Press, 1973.

Winch, Julie. *Philadelphia's Black Elite: Activism, Accommodation, and the Struggle for Autonomy, 1787–1848*. Philadelphia: Temple University Press, 1988.

Wright, Donald R. *African Americans in the Colonial Era: From African Origins through the American Revolution*. Arlington Heights, Ill.: Harland Davidson, 1990.

———. *African Americans in the Early Republic, 1789–1831*. Arlington Heights, Ill.: Harland Davidson, 1993.

Wright, James M. *The Free Negro in Maryland, 1634–1860*. New York: Longmans, Green & Co., 1921.

## ABOLITIONISM AND EMANCIPATION

Barnes, Gilbert H. *The Antislavery Impulse, 1830–1844*. New York: D. Appleton-Century, 1933.

Bell, Howard. *A Survey of the Negro Convention Movement, 1830–1864*. New York: Arno Press, 1969.

Blackett, R. J. M. *Building an Anti-Slavery Wall: Black Americans and the Atlantic Abolitionist Movement, 1830–1860*. Baton Rouge: Louisiana State University Press, 1983.

Bracey, John, and others. *Blacks in the Abolitionist Movement*. Belmont, Calif.: Wadsworth, 1971.

Buckmaster, Henrietta. *Let My People Go: The Story of the Underground Railroad and the Growth of the Abolition Movement*. New York: Harper & Brothers, 1941.

Campbell, Stanley W. *The Slave Catchers: Enforcement of the Fugitive Slave Law, 1850–1860*. Chapel Hill: University of North Carolina Press, 1970.

Cheek, William, and Aimee Lee Cheek. *John Mercer Langston and the Fight for Black Freedom*. Urbana: University of Illinois Press, 1989.

Conrad, Earl. *Harriet Tubman*. Washington, D.C.: Associated Publishers, 1943.

Cox, LaWanda. *Lincoln and Black Freedom: A Study in Presidential Leadership*. Columbia: University of South Carolina Press, 1981.

Dillon, Merton L. *Slavery Attacked: Southern Slaves and Their Allies, 1619–1865*. Baton Rouge: Louisiana State University Press, 1990.

Donald, David Herbert. *Lincoln*. New York: Simon and Schuster, 1995.

Drake, Thomas E. *Quakers and Slavery in America*. Gloucester, Mass.: Peter Smith, 1950.

Durden, Robert F. *The Gray and the Black: The Confederate Debate on Emancipation*. Baton Rouge: Louisiana State University Press, 1972.

Farrison, William E. *William Wells Brown: Author and Reformer*. Chicago: University of Chicago Press, 1969.

Fauset, Arthur H. *Sojourner Truth, God's Faithful Pilgrim*. Chapel Hill: University of North Carolina Press, 1938.

*Filler, Louis. *The Crusade against Slavery, 1830–1860*. New York: Harper & Brothers, 1960.

Gara, Larry. *The Liberty Line: The Legend of the Underground Railroad*. Lexington: University of Kentucky Press, 1961.

Gerteis, Louis. *From Contraband to Freedom: Federal Policy toward Southern Blacks, 1861–1865*. Westport, Conn.: Greenwood, 1973.

Graham, Shirley. *There Once Was a Slave: The Heroic Story of Frederick Douglass*. New York: Julian Messner, 1947.

Hansen, Ellen. *The Underground Railroad: Life on the Road to Freedom.* Lowell, Mass.: Discovery Enterprises, 1993.

Kraditor, Aileen. *Means and Ends in American Abolitionism: Garrison and His Critics on Strategy and Tactics, 1834–1850.* New York: Pantheon, 1969.

Lerner, Gerda. *The Grimké Sisters from South Carolina: Rebels Against Slavery.* Boston: Houghton Mifflin, 1967.

McFeely, William S. *Frederick Douglass.* New York: Norton, 1991.

McManus, Edgar J. *A History of Negro Slavery in the North.* Syracuse, N.Y.: Syracuse University Press, 1966.

Martin, Waldo E., Jr. *The Mind of Frederick Douglass.* Chapel Hill: University of North Carolina Press, 1984.

Mathews, Donald G. *Slavery and Methodism: A Chapter in American Morality, 1780–1845.* Princeton, N.J.: Princeton University Press, 1965.

Nash, Gary B., and Jean R. Soderlund. *Freedom by Degrees: Emancipation in Pennsylvania and Its Aftermath.* New York: Oxford University Press, 1991.

*Quarles, Benjamin. *Black Abolitionists.* New York: Oxford University Press, 1969.

*———. *Frederick Douglass.* Washington, D.C.: Associated Publishers, 1948.

Sterling, Barbara. *Ahead of Her Time: Abby Kelley and the Politics of Antislavery.* New York: Norton, 1991.

Thomas, John L. *The Liberator: William Lloyd Garrison.* Boston: Little, Brown, 1963.

Ullmann, Victor. *Martin Delany: The Beginnings of Black Nationalism.* Boston: Beacon, 1971.

Wagandt, Charles L. *The Mighty Revolution: Negro Emancipation in Maryland, 1862–1864.* Baltimore: Johns Hopkins University Press, 1964.

White, Shane. *Somewhat More Independent: The End of Slavery in New York City, 1770–1810.* Athens, Ga.: University of Georgia Press, 1991.

Wiley, Bell Irvin. *Southern Negroes, 1861–1865.* New York: Rinehart, 1938.

Yee, Shirley J. *Black Women Abolitionists: A Study in Activism, 1828–1860.* Knoxville: University of Tennessee Press, 1992.

Zilversmit, Arthur. *The First Emancipation: The Abolition of Slavery in the North.* Chicago: University of Chicago Press, 1967.

## RECONSTRUCTION, 1863–1877

Abbott, Richard H. *The Republican Party and the South, 1855–1877: The First Southern Strategy.* Chapel Hill: University of North Carolina Press, 1986.

Alexander, Roberta S. *North Carolina Faces the Freedmen: Race Relations during Presidential Reconstruction, 1865–1867.* Durham, N.C.: Duke University Press, 1985.

Benedict, Michael L. *A Compromise of Principle: Congressional Republicans and Reconstruction, 1863–1869.* New York: Norton, 1974.

Brown, David Warren. *Andrew Johnson and the Negro.* Knoxville: University of Tennessee Press, 1989.

Brown, Ira V. "Pennsylvania and the Rights of the Negro, 1865–1887." *Pennsylvania History,* vol. 28 (1961).

Butchart, Ronald E. *Northern Schools, Southern Blacks, and Reconstruction: Freedmen's Education, 1862–1875.* Westport, Conn.: Greenwood, 1980.

Conway, Alan. *The Reconstruction of Georgia.* Minneapolis: University of Minnesota Press, 1966.

Cruden, Robert. *The Negro in Reconstruction.* Englewood Cliffs, N.J.: Prentice-Hall, 1969.

Dawson, Joseph G., III. *Army Generals and Reconstruction: Louisiana, 1862–1877*. Baton Rouge: Louisiana State University Press, 1982.

Donald, David Herbert. *Charles Sumner and the Rights of Man*. New York: Knopf, 1970.

———. *Lincoln*. New York: Simon and Schuster, 1995.

Drago, Edmund L. *Black Politicians and Reconstruction in Georgia*. Baton Rouge: Louisiana State University Press, 1982.

Field, Phyllis F. *The Politics of Race in New York: The Struggle for Black Suffrage in the Civil War Era*. Ithaca, N.Y.: Cornell University Press, 1982.

Fischer, Roger A. *The Segregation Struggle in Louisiana, 1862–1877*. Urbana: University of Illinois Press, 1974.

Fitzgerald, Michael W. *The Union League Movement in the Deep South*. Baton Rouge: Louisiana State University Press, 1989.

Foner, Eric. *Reconstruction: America's Unfinished Revolution, 1863–1877*. New York: Harper & Row, 1988.

Gerber, David A. *Black Ohio and the Color Line, 1860–1915*. Urbana: University of Illinois Press, 1974.

Gillette, William. *Retreat from Reconstruction, 1869–1879*. Baton Rouge: Louisiana State University Press, 1979.

Grossman, Lawrence. *The Democratic Party and the Negro: Northern and National Politics, 1868–1892*. Urbana: University of Illinois Press, 1976.

Harris, William C. *The Day of the Carpetbagger: Republican Reconstruction in Mississippi*. Baton Rouge: Louisiana State University Press, 1979.

———. *Presidential Reconstruction in Mississippi*. Baton Rouge: Louisiana State University Press, 1967.

Holt, Thomas. *Black over White: Negro Political Leadership in South Carolina during Reconstruction*. Urbana: University of Illinois Press, 1977.

Horn, Stanley F. *Invisible Empire: The Story of the Ku Klux Klan, 1866–1871*. Boston: Houghton Mifflin, 1939.

James, Joseph B. *The Framing of the Fourteenth Amendment*. Urbana: University of Illinois Press, 1956.

———. *The Ratification of the Fourteenth Amendment*. Macon, Ga.: Mercer University Press, 1984.

Katzman, David M. *Before the Ghetto: Black Detroit in the Nineteenth Century*. Urbana: University of Illinois Press, 1973.

Litwack, Leon F. *Been in the Storm So Long: The Aftermath of Slavery*. New York: Knopf, 1979.

McPherson, James. *The Struggle for Equality: Abolitionists and the Negro in the Civil War and Reconstruction*. Princeton, N.J.: Princeton University Press, 1964.

Maltz, Earl M. *Civil Rights, the Constitution, and Congress, 1863–1869*. Lawrence: University Press of Kansas, 1990.

Mohr, James C., ed. *Radical Republicans in the North: State Politics during Reconstruction*. Baltimore: Johns Hopkins University Press, 1976.

Morris, Robert C. *Reading, 'Riting, and Reconstruction: The Education of Freedmen in the South, 1861–1870*. Chicago: University of Chicago Press, 1981.

Nieman, Donald G. *To Set the Law in Motion: The Freedmen's Bureau and the Legal Rights of Blacks, 1865–1868*. Millwood, N.Y.: KTO Press, 1979.

Novak, Daniel A. *The Wheel of Servitude: Black Forced Labor after Slavery*. Lexington: University of Kentucky Press, 1978.

Oubre, Claude F. *Forty Acres and a Mule: The Freedmen's Bureau and Black Land Ownership*. Baton Rouge: Louisiana State University Press, 1978.

Perman, Michael. *Reunion without Compromise: The South and Reconstruction, 1865–1868.* Cambridge, Eng.: Cambridge University Press, 1973.

———. *The Road to Redemption: Southern Politics, 1869–1879.* Chapel Hill: University of North Carolina Press, 1984.

Rabinowitz, Howard N. *Race Relations in the Urban South, 1865–1890.* Urbana: University of Illinois Press, 1976.

Rabinowitz, Howard N., ed. *Southern Black Leaders of the Reconstruction Era.* Urbana: University of Illinois Press, 1982.

Rable, George C. *But There Was No Peace: The Role of Violence in the Politics of Reconstruction.* Athens: University of Georgia Press, 1984.

Rose, Willie Lee. *Rehearsal for Reconstruction: The Port Royal Experiment.* Indianapolis, Ind.: Bobbs-Merrill, 1964.

Sefton, James E. *The United States Army and Reconstruction, 1865–1877.* Baton Rouge: Louisiana State University Press, 1967.

Singletary, Otis A. *Negro Militia and Reconstruction.* Austin: University of Texas Press, 1957.

*Stampp, Kenneth. *The Era of Reconstruction, 1865–1877.* New York: Knopf, 1965.

Thornbrough, Emma Lou. *Black Reconstructionists.* Englewood Cliffs, N.J.: Prentice-Hall, 1972.

Trelease, Allen W. *White Terror: The Ku Klux Klan Conspiracy and Southern Reconstruction.* New York: Harper & Row, 1971.

Uya, Okon E. *From Slavery to Public Service: Robert Smalls, 1839–1915.* New York: Oxford University Press, 1971.

Vaughan, William P. *Schools for All: The Blacks and Public Education in the South, 1865–1877.* Lexington: University Press of Kentucky, 1974.

Wilson, Theodore B. *The Black Codes of the South.* University, Ala.: University of Alabama Press, 1965.

Wood, Forrest G. *Black Scare: The Racist Response to Emancipation and Reconstruction.* Berkeley: University of California Press, 1968.

Woodward, C. Vann. *Reunion and Reaction: The Compromise of 1877 and the End of Reconstruction.* Boston: Little, Brown, 1951.

## THE TRIUMPH OF WHITE SUPREMACY, 1877–1945

Anderson, Eric. *Race and Politics in North Carolina, 1872–1901.* Baton Rouge: Louisiana State University Press, 1981.

Ayers, Edward L. *The Promise of the New South: Life After Reconstruction.* New York: Oxford University Press, 1992.

Cell, John W. *The Highest Stage of White Supremacy: The Origins of Segregation in South Africa and the American South.* New York: Cambridge University Press, 1982.

Cohen, William. *At Freedom's Edge: Black Mobility and the Southern White Quest for Racial Control, 1861–1915.* Baton Rouge: Louisiana State University Press, 1991.

Edmonds, Helen G. *The Negro and Fusion Politics in North Carolina, 1894–1901.* Chapel Hill: University of North Carolina Press, 1951.

Frederickson, George M. *The Black Image in the White Mind: The Debate on Afro-American Character and Destiny, 1817–1914.* New York: Harper & Row, 1971.

———. *White Supremacy: A Comparative Study in American and South African History.* New York: Oxford University Press, 1981.

Gerber, David A. *Black Ohio and the Color Line, 1860–1915.* Urbana: University of Illinois Press, 1976.

Harlan, Louis. *Separate and Unequal: Public School Campaigns and Racism in the Southern Seaboard States, 1901–1915.* Chapel Hill: University of North Carolina Press, 1958.

Hirshon, Stanley P. *Farewell to the Bloody Shirt: Northern Republicans and the Southern Negro, 1877–1893.* Bloomington, Ind.: Indiana University Press, 1962.

Kousser, J. Morgan. *The Shaping of Southern Politics: Suffrage Restriction and the Establishment of the One-Party South, 1880–1910.* New Haven, Conn.: Yale University Press, 1974.

Kusmer, Kenneth. *A Ghetto Takes Shape: Black Cleveland, 1870–1930.* Urbana: University of Illinois Press, 1976.

Lane, Ann J. *The Brownsville Affair: National Crisis and Black Reaction.* Port Washington, N.Y.: Kennikat Press, 1971.

Levine, David Allen. *Internal Combustion: The Races in Detroit, 1915–1926.* Westport, Conn.: Greenwood, 1976.

*Logan, Rayford W. *The Negro in American Life and Thought: The Nadir, 1877–1901.* New York: Dial Press, 1954.

McGovern, James R. *Anatomy of a Lynching: The Killing of Claude Neal.* Baton Rouge: Louisiana State University Press, 1982.

MacLean, Nancy. *Behind the Mask of Chivalry: The Making of the Second Ku Klux Klan.* New York: Oxford University Press, 1994.

McMillen, Neil R. *Dark Journey: Black Mississippians in the Age of Jim Crow.* Urbana: University of Illinois Press, 1989.

Newby, I. A. *Jim Crow's Defense: Anti-Negro Thought in America, 1900–1930.* Baton Rouge: Louisiana State University Press, 1965.

Nolen, Claude H. *The Negro's Image in the South: The Anatomy of White Supremacy.* Lexington: University of Kentucky Press, 1967.

Osofsky, Gilbert. *Harlem: The Making of a Ghetto: Negro New York, 1890–1930.* 2nd edition. New York: Harper & Row, 1971.

Prather, H. Leon. *We Have Taken a City: The Wilmington [North Carolina] Massacre and Coup of 1898.* Rutherford, N.J.: Farleigh Dickinson University Press, 1984.

Rabinowitz, Howard. *Race Relations in the Urban South, 1865–1890.* New York: Oxford University Press, 1978.

Rudwick, Elliott M. *Race Riot at East St. Louis, July 2, 1917.* Carbondale: Southern Illinois University Press, 1984.

Spear, Allan. *Black Chicago: The Making of a Negro Ghetto, 1890–1920.* Chicago: University of Chicago Press, 1967.

Tuttle, William M. *Race Riot: Chicago in the Red Summer of 1919.* New York: Atheneum, 1970.

Weinstein, Allen, and Frank Gatell, eds. *The Segregation Era, 1863–1954.* New York: Oxford University Press, 1970.

Williams, Lee E., and Lee E. Williams, II. *Anatomy of Four Race Riots: Racial Conflict in Knoxville, Elaine (Arkansas), Tulsa, and Chicago, 1919–1921.* Jackson: University and College Press of Mississippi, 1972.

Woodward, C. Vann. *Origins of the New South, 1877–1913.* Baton Rouge: Louisiana State University Press, 1951.

*———. *The Strange Career of Jim Crow.* 3rd edition. New York: Oxford University Press, 1974.

Wright, George C. *Racial Violence in Kentucky, 1865–1940: Lynchings, Mob Rule, and "Legal Lynchings."* Baton Rouge: Louisiana State University Press, 1990.

## RESISTING WHITE SUPREMACY, 1877–1945

Anderson, James D. *The Education of Blacks in the South, 1860–1935.* Chapel Hill: University of North Carolina Press, 1988.

*Anderson, Jervis. A. *Philip Randolph: A Biographical Portrait.* Berkeley: University of California Press, 1986.

Barnes, Catherine A. *Journey from Jim Crow: The Desegregation of Southern Transit.* New York: Columbia University Press, 1983.

Beatty, Bess. *A Revolution Gone Backwards: The Black Response to National Politics, 1876–1896.* Westport, Conn.: Greenwood, 1987.

Bunche, Ralph J. *The Political Status of the Negro in the Age of FDR.* Chicago: University of Chicago Press, 1973.

Cooper, Arnold. *Between Struggle and Hope: Four Black Educators in the South, 1894–1915.* Ames: Iowa State University Press, 1989.

Cronon, E. David. *Black Moses: The Story of Marcus Garvey and the Universal Negro Improvement Association.* 2nd edition. Madison: University of Wisconsin Press, 1969.

Egerton, John. *Speak Now against the Day: The Generation before the Civil Rights Movement in the South.* New York: Knopf, 1994.

Fox, Stephen R. *Guardian of Boston: William Monroe Trotter.* New York: Atheneum, 1971.

Gaither, Gerald H. *Blacks and the Populist Revolt: Ballots and Bigotry in the "New South."* University, Ala.: University of Alabama Press, 1977.

Goings, Kenneth W. *The NAACP Comes of Age: The Defeat of Judge John J. Parker.* Bloomington: Indiana University Press, 1990.

Grossman, James R. *Land of Hope: Chicago, Black Southerners, and the Great Migration.* Chicago: University of Chicago Press, 1989.

Harlan, Louis R. *Booker T. Washington.* Vol. 1, *The Making of a Black Leader, 1856–1901;* vol. 2, *The Wizard of Tuskegee, 1901–1915.* New York: Oxford University Press, 1972, 1983.

Henri, Florette. *Black Migration: Movement North, 1900–1920.* New York: Anchor Press, 1975.

Hine, Darlene Clark. *The Rise and Fall of the White Primary in Texas.* Millwood, N.Y.: KTO Press, 1979.

Kellogg, Charles F. *NAACP.* Baltimore: Johns Hopkins University Press, 1967.

Kirby, John H. *Black Americans and the Roosevelt Era: Liberalism and Race.* Knoxville: University of Tennessee Press, 1980.

Lemann, Nicholas. *The Promised Land: The Great Black Migration and How It Changed America.* New York: Knopf, 1991.

Lewis, David L. *W. E. B. DuBois: Biography of a Race, 1868–1919.* New York: Holt, 1993.

McGuire, Phillip. *He, Too, Spoke for Democracy: Judge Hastie, World War II, and the Black Soldier.* New York: Greenwood, 1988.

McNeil, Genna Rae. *Groundwork: Charles Hamilton Houston and the Struggle for Civil Rights.* Philadelphia: University of Pennsylvania Press, 1983.

McPherson, James M. *The Abolitionist Legacy: From Reconstruction to the NAACP.* Princeton, N.J.: Princeton University Press, 1975.

Marks, Carole. *Farewell, We're Good and Gone: The Great Black Migration.* Bloomington: Indiana University Press, 1989.

Martin, Tony. *Race First: The Ideological and Organizational Struggles of Marcus Garvey and the Universal Negro Improvement Association.* Westport, Conn.: Greenwood, 1976.

Meier, August. *Negro Thought in America, 1880–1915.* Ann Arbor: University of Michigan Press, 1963.

Moses, William Jeremiah. *The Golden Age of Black Nationalism, 1850–1925.* Hamden, Conn.: Anchor Books, 1978.

Naison, Mark. *Communists in Harlem during the Depression.* Urbana: University of Illinois Press, 1983.

Neverdon-Morton, Cynthia. *Afro-American Women of the South and the Advancement of the Race, 1895–1925.* Knoxville: University of Tennessee Press, 1989.

Painter, Nell Irvin. *Exodusters: Black Migration to Kansas after Reconstruction.* New York: Knopf, 1977.

Parris, Guichard, and Lester Brooks. *Blacks in the City: A History of the National Urban League.* Boston: Little, Brown, 1971.

Pfeffer, Paula F. *A. Philip Randolph, Pioneer of the Civil Rights Movement.* Baton Rouge: Louisiana State University Press, 1990.

Record, Wilson. *The Negro and the Communist Party.* Chapel Hill, N.C.: Atheneum, 1951.

Redkey, Edwin S. *Black Exodus: Black Nationalists and Back-to-Africa Movements, 1890–1910.* New Haven, Conn.: Yale University Press, 1969.

Ross, Barbara Joyce. *J. E. Spingarn and the Rise of the NAACP, 1911–1939.* New York: Atheneum, 1972.

Shapiro, Herbert. *White Violence and Black Response.* Amherst, Mass.: Amherst University Press, 1988.

Sitkoff, Harvard. *A New Deal for Blacks: The Emergence of Civil Rights as a National Issue—The Depression Decade.* New York: Oxford University Press, 1978.

Thornbrough, Emma Lou. *T. Thomas Fortune, Militant Journalist.* Chicago: University of Chicago Press, 1972.

*Trotter, Joe William. *From a Raw Deal to a New Deal? African Americans, 1929–45.* New York: Oxford University Press, 1995.

Tushnet, Mark V. *The NAACP's Legal Strategy against Segregated Education, 1925–1950.* Chapel Hill: University of North Carolina Press, 1987.

Weiss, Nancy. *Farewell to the Party of Lincoln: Black Politics in the Age of FDR.* Princeton, N.J.: Princeton University Press, 1983.

———. *The National Urban League, 1910–1940.* New York: Oxford University Press, 1974.

Wynn, Neil A. *The Afro-American and the Second World War.* New York: Holmes & Meier, 1975.

Zangrando, Robert L. *The NAACP's Crusade against Lynching, 1909–1950.* Philadelphia: Temple University Press, 1980.

## THE STRUGGLE FOR RACIAL EQUALITY, 1945–1968

Barnes, Catherine A. *Journey from Jim Crow: The Desegregation of Southern Transit.* New York: Columbia University Press, 1983.

Bartley, Numan V. *The Rise of Massive Resistance: Race and Politics in the South in the 1950s.* Baton Rouge: Louisiana State University Press, 1969.

Blumberg, Rhoda L. *Civil Rights: The 1960s Freedom Struggle.* Revised edition. Boston: Twayne, 1991.

Boesel, David, and Peter H. Rossi, eds. *Cities under Seige: An Anatomy of the Ghetto Riots, 1964–1968.* New York: Basic Books, 1971.

Bracey, John H., Jr., and others, eds. *Black Nationalism in America.* Indianapolis, Ind.: Bobbs-Merrill, 1970.

Branch, Taylor. *Parting the Waters: America in the King Years, 1954–1963.* New York: Simon & Schuster, 1988.

Brauer, Carl. *John F. Kennedy and the Second Reconstruction.* New York: Columbia University Press, 1977.

Burk, Robert F. *The Eisenhower Administration and Black Civil Rights.* Knoxville: University of Tennessee Press, 1984.

Button, James W. *Black Violence: Political Impact of the 1960s Riots.* Princeton, N.J.: Princeton University Press, 1978.

Carson, Clayborne. *In Struggle: SNCC and the Black Awakening of the 1960s.* Cambridge, Mass.: Harvard University Press, 1981.

Chafe, William H. *Civilities and Civil Rights: Greensboro, North Carolina, and the Black Struggle for Freedom.* New York: Oxford University Press, 1980.

Crawford, Vickie L., and others, eds. *Women in the Civil Rights Movement: 1941–1965.* Brooklyn, N.Y.: Carlson, 1990.

Dallard, Shyrle. *Ella Baker: A Leader behind the Scenes.* Englewood Cliffs, N.J.: Silver Burdett, 1990.

Egerton, John. *Speak Now against the Day: The Generation before the Civil Rights Movement in the South.* New York: Knopf, 1994.

Essien-Udom, Essien U. *Black Nationalism: A Search for Identity in America.* Chicago: Dell, 1962.

Fairclough, Adam. *To Redeem the Soul of America: The Southern Christian Leadership Conference and Martin Luther King, Jr.* Athens: University of Georgia Press, 1987.

Finch, Minnie. *The NAACP: Its Fight for Justice.* Metuchen, N.J.: Scarecrow, 1981.

Freyer, Tony. *The Little Rock Crisis: A Constitutional Interpretation.* Westport, Conn.: Greenwood, 1984.

Garrow, David J. *Bearing the Cross: Martin Luther King, Jr., and the Southern Christian Leadership Conference.* New York: Random House, 1986.

———. *Protest at Selma: Martin Luther King and the Voting Rights Act of 1965.* New Haven, Conn.: Yale University Press, 1978.

Graham, Hugh Davis. *The Civil Rights Era: Origins and Developments of National Policy, 1960–1972.* New York: Oxford University Press, 1990.

Greenberg, Jack. *Crusaders in the Courts: How a Dedicated Band of Lawyers Fought for the Civil Rights Revolution.* New York: Basic, 1994.

Hamilton, Charles V. *Adam Clayton Powell, Jr.: The Political Biography of an American Dilemma.* New York: Atheneum, 1991.

Jacoway, Elizabeth, and David R. Colbrun. *Southern Businessmen and Desegregation.* Baton Rouge: Louisiana State University Press, 1982.

Kaufman, Jonathan. *Broken Alliance: The Turbulent Times between Blacks and Jews in America.* New York: Scribner's, 1988.

Kluger, Richard. *Simple Justice: The History of Brown v. Board of Education and Black America's Struggle for Equality.* New York: Knopf, 1976.

Lawson, Stephen F. *Black Ballots: Voting Rights in the South, 1944–1969.* New York: Columbia University Press, 1976.

*———. *Running for Freedom: Civil Rights and Black Politics in America since 1941.* New York: McGraw-Hill, 1991.

*Levine, Ellen. *Freedom's Children: Young Civil Rights Activists Tell Their Own Stories.* Thorndike, Maine: Thorndike Press, 1993.

Lewis, David L. *King: A Critical Biography.* New York: Praeger, 1970.

Lincoln, C. Eric. *The Black Muslims in America.* Boston: Beacon, 1973.

McAdam, Doug. *Freedom Summer.* New York: Oxford University Press, 1988.

McCoy, Donald R., and Richard T. Ruetten. *Quest and Response: Minority Rights and the Truman Administration.* Lawrence: University of Kansas Press, 1973.

McMillen, Neil R. *The Citizens' Council: Organized Resistance to the Second Reconstuction, 1954–1964.* Urbana: University of Illinois Press, 1971.

Marable, Manning. *Race, Reform, and Rebellion: The Second Reconstruction, 1945–1982.* Jackson: University Press of Mississippi, 1984.

Meier, August, and Elliott Rudwick. *CORE: A Study in the Civil Rights Movement, 1942–1968.* New York: Oxford University Press, 1973.

Newman, Dorothy K., and others. *Protest, Politics, and Prosperity: Black Americans and White Institutions, 1940–75.* New York: Pantheon, 1978.

Oates, Stephen B. *Let the Trumpet Sound: The Life of Martin Luther King, Jr.* New York: Harper & Row, 1982.

Perry, Bruce. *Malcolm: The Life of a Man Who Changed America.* New York: Station Hill Press, 1991.

Ravitch, Diane. *The Great School Wars: New York City, 1805–1973.* New York: Basic Books, 1974.

*Sitkoff, Harvard. *The Struggle for Black Equality, 1954–1992.* Revised edition. New York: Hill & Wang, 1993.

Stanley, Harold W. *Voter Mobilization and the Politics of Race: The South and Universal Suffrage, 1952–1984.* New York: Praeger, 1987.

Tushnet, Mark V. *Making Civil Rights Law: Thurgood Marshall and the Supreme Court, 1936–1961.* New York: Oxford University Press, 1994.

Van Deburg, William L. *New Day in Babylon: The Black Power Movement and American Culture, 1965–1975.* Chicago: University of Chicago Press, 1994.

Watson, Denton L. *Lion in the Lobby: Clarence Mitchell, Jr.'s Struggle for the Passage of Civil Rights Laws.* New York: Morrow, 1990.

*Weisbrot, Robert. *Freedom Bound: A History of America's Civil Rights Movement.* New York: Penguin, 1990.

Weisbrot, Robert, and Arthur Stein. *Bittersweet Encounter: The Afro-American and the Jew.* Westport, Conn.: Negro Universities Press, 1970.

Weiss, Nancy J. *Whitney M. Young, Jr., and the Struggle for Civil Rights.* Princeton, N.J.: Princeton University Press, 1989.

Williams, Juan. *Eyes on the Prize: America's Civil Rights Years, 1954–1965.* New York: Viking, 1987.

## THE STRUGGLE FOR RACIAL EQUALITY, 1968–1996

Altschiller, Donald, ed. *Affirmative Action.* New York: H. W. Wilson, 1991.

Ball, Howard, Dale Krance, and Thomas P. Lauth. *Compromised Compliance: Implementation of the 1965 Voting Rights Act.* Westport, Conn.: Greenwood, 1982.

Belz, Herman. *Equality Transformed: A Quarter-Century of Affirmative Action.* New Brunswick, N.J.: Transaction Books, 1991.

Bullock, Charles S., III, and Charles M. Lamb, eds. *Implementation of Civil Rights Policy.* Monterey, Calif.: Brooks/Cole, 1984.

Button, James W. *Blacks and Social Change: Impact of the Civil Rights Movement on Southern Communities.* Princeton, N.J.: Princeton University Press, 1989.

Davidson, Chandler, ed. *Minority Vote Dilution.* Washington, D.C.: Howard University Press, 1984.

Edds, Margaret. *Free at Last: What Really Happened When Civil Rights Came to Southern Politics.* Bethesda, Md.: Adler & Adler, 1987.

Ezorsky, Gertrude. *Racism and Justice: The Case for Affirmative Action.* Ithaca, N.Y.: Cornell University Press, 1991.

Farley, Reynolds. *Blacks and Whites: Narrowing the Gap?* Cambridge, Mass.: Harvard University Press, 1984.

Formisano, Ronald P. *Boston against Busing: Race, Class, and Ethnicity in the 1960s and 1970s*. Chapel Hill: University of North Carolina Press, 1991.

Foster, Lorne S., ed. *The Voting Rights Act: Consequences and Implications*. New York: Praeger, 1985.

Franklin, John Hope. *The Color Line: Legacy for the Twenty-first Century*. Columbia: University of Missouri Press, 1993.

Greene, Kathanne W. *Affirmative Action and Principles of Justice*. New York: Greenwood, 1989.

Henry, Charles P. *Jesse Jackson: The Search for Common Ground*. Oakland, Calif.: Black Scholar Press, 1991.

Hochschild, Jennifer L. *Thirty Years after Brown*. Washington, D.C.: Joint Center for Political Studies, 1985.

Kaufman, Jonathan. *Broken Alliance: The Turbulent Times between Blacks and Jews in America*. New York: Scribners, 1988.

Landry, Bart. *The New Black Middle Class*. Berkeley: University of California Press, 1984.

Lawson, Stephen F. *In Pursuit of Power: Southern Blacks and Electoral Politics, 1965–1982*. New York: Columbia University Press, 1985.

*———. *Running for Freedom: Civil Rights and Black Politics in America since 1941*. New York: McGraw-Hill, 1991.

*Lucas, J. Anthony. *Common Ground: A Turbulent Decade in the Lives of Three American Families*. New York: Knopf, 1985.

Mills, Nicolaus, ed. *Debating Affirmative Action: Race, Gender, Ethnicity, and the Politics of Inclusion*. New York: Delta Trade Paperbacks, 1994.

Nelson, Willam E., Jr., and Philip J. Meranto. *Electing Black Mayors: Political Action in the Black Community*. Columbus: Ohio State University Press, 1977.

Nieli, Russell, ed. *Racial Preferences and Racial Justice: The New Affirmative Action Controversy*. Washington, D.C.: Ethics and Public Policy Center, 1991.

Orfield, Gary. *Must We Bus? Segregated Schools and National Policy*. Washington, D.C.: Brookings Institution, 1978.

Reed, Adolph, Jr. *The Jesse Jackson Phenomenon: The Crisis in Afro-American Politics*. New Haven, Conn.: Yale University Press, 1986.

Rosenfeld, Michel. *Affirmative Action and Justice: A Philosophical and Constitutional Inquiry*. New Haven, Conn.: Yale University Press, 1991.

Sindler, Alan P. *Bakke, DeFunis, and Minority Admissions: The Quest for Equal Opportunity*. New York: Longman, 1978.

*Sitkoff, Harvard. *The Struggle for Black Equality, 1954–1992*. Revised edition. New York: Hill & Wang, 1993.

Stanley, Harold W. *Voter Mobilization and the Politics of Race: The South and Universal Suffrage, 1952–1984*. New York: Praeger, 1987.

Swain, Carol M. *Black Faces, Black Interests: The Representation of African Americans in Congress*. Cambridge, Mass.: Harvard University Press, 1993.

Tate, Katherine. *From Protest to Politics: The New Black Voters in American Elections*. Cambridge, Mass.: Harvard University Press, 1993.

Taylor, Bron Raymond. *Affirmative Action at Work: Law, Politics, and Ethics*. Pittsburgh: University of Pittsburgh Press, 1991.

Thernstrom, Abigail M. *Whose Votes Count? Affirmative Action and Minority Voting Rights*. Cambridge, Mass.: Harvard University Press, 1987.

Urofsky, Mervin I. *A Conflict of Rights: The Supreme Court and Affirmative Action*. New York: Scribner's, 1991.

West, Cornel. *Race Matters*. Boston: Beacon, 1993.

Wolters, Raymond. *The Burden of Brown: Thirty Years of School Desegregation*. Knoxville: University of Tennessee Press, 1984.

## BLACKS IN THE ECONOMY SINCE THE CIVIL WAR

Arnesen, Eric. *Waterfront Workers of New Orleans: Race, Class, and Politics, 1863–1923*. New York: Oxford University Press, 1991.

Bracey, John H., Jr. *Black Workers and Organized Labor*. Belmont, Calif.: Wadsworth, 1971.

Cantor, Milton, ed. *Black Labor in America*. Westport, Conn.: Negro Universities Press, 1970.

Christian, Marcus. *Negro Ironworkers of Louisiana, 1718–1900*. Gretna, La.: Pelican, 1972.

Cobb, James C. *Industrialization and Southern Society, 1877–1984*. Lexington: University Press of Kentucky, 1984.

Daniel, Pete. *The Shadow of Slavery: Peonage in the South, 1901–1969*. Urbana: University of Illinois Press, 1972.

Davis, Ronald F. *Good and Faithful Labor: From Slavery to Sharecropping in the Natchez District, 1860–1890*. Westport, Conn.: Greenwood, 1982.

Dickerson, Dennis C. *Out of the Crucible: Black Steelworkers in Western Pennsylvania, 1875–1980*. Albany: State University of New York Press, 1986.

Fink, Gary M., and Merl E. Reed, eds. *Essays in Southern Labor History*. Westport, Conn.: Greenwood, 1977.

Flynn, Charles L. *White Land, Black Labor: Caste and Class in Late Nineteenth Century Georgia*. Baton Rouge: Louisiana State University Press, 1983.

*Foner, Philip S. *Organized Labor and the Black Worker, 1619–1973*. New York: Praeger, 1974.

Grubbs, Donald H. *Cry from the Cotton: The Southern Tenant Farmers Union and the New Deal*. Chapel Hill: University of North Carolina Press, 1971.

Hacker, Andrew. *Two Nations: Black and White, Separate, Hostile, Unequal*. New York: Scribner's, 1992.

Harris, William H. *The Harder We Run: Black Workers since the Civil War*. New York: Oxford University Press, 1982.

————. *Keeping the Faith: A. Philip Randolph, Milton P. Webster, and the Brotherhood of Sleeping Car Porters, 1925–1937*. Urbana: University of Illinois Press, 1977.

Henderson, Alexa Benson. *Atlanta Life Insurance Company: Guardian of Black Economic Dignity*. Tuscaloosa, Ala.: University of Alabama Press, 1990.

Jaynes, Gerald D. *Branches without Roots: Genesis of the Black Working Class in the American South, 1862–1882*. New York: Oxford University Press, 1986.

Landry, Bart. *The New Black Middle Class*. Berkeley: University of California Press, 1984.

Lewis, Ronald L. *Black Coal Miners in America: Race, Class, and Community Conflict, 1780–1980*. Lexington: University Press of Kentucky, 1987.

Meier, August, and Elliott Rudwick. *Black Detroit and the Rise of the UAW*. New York: Oxford University Press, 1979.

Nieman, Donald G., ed. *From Slavery to Sharecropping: White Land and Black Labor in the Rural South, 1865–1900*. New York: Garland, 1994.

*Northrup, Herbert R. *Organized Labor and the Negro*. New York: Harper & Brothers, 1944.

Novak, Daniel A. *The Wheel of Servitude: Black Forced Labor after Slavery*. Lexington: University Press of Kentucky, 1978.

Rachleff, Peter J. *Black Labor in the South: Richmond, Virginia, 1865–1890*. Philadelphia: Temple University Press, 1984.

Reed, Merl E., and others, *Southern Workers and Their Unions, 1880–1975.* Westport, Conn.: Greenwood, 1981.

Taft, Philip. *Organizing Dixie: Alabama Workers in the Industrial Era.* Revised edition. Westport, Conn.: Greenwood, 1981.

Trotter, Joe William. *Black Milwaukee: The Making of an Industrial Proletariat, 1915–1945.* Urbana: University of Illinois Press, 1985.

Wallace, Phyllis A. *Black Women in the Labor Force.* Cambridge, Mass.: MIT Press, 1980.

Washington, Joseph R., ed. *Dilemmas of the New Black Middle Class.* 1980.

Weare, Walter B. *Black Business in the New South: A Social History of the North Carolina Mutual Life Insurance Company.* Urbana: University of Illinois Press, 1973.

Wilson, William Julius. *The Declining Significance of Race: Blacks and Changing American Institutions.* 2nd edition. Chicago: University of Chicago Press, 1980.

————. *The Truly Disadvantaged: The Inner City, the Underclass, and Public Policy.* Chicago: University of Chicago Press, 1987.

Wolters, Raymond. *Negroes and the Great Depression: The Problem of Economic Recovery.* Westport, Conn.: Greenwood, 1970.

Woodward, C. Vann. *Origins of the New South, 1877–1913.* Baton Rouge: Louisiana State University Press, 1951.

Wright, Gavin. *Old South, New South: Revolutions in the Southern Economy since the Civil War.* New York: Basic Books, 1986.

## BLACKS IN THE ARMED FORCES

Barbeau, Arthur E., and Florette Henri. *Unknown Soldiers: Black American Troops in World War I.* Philadelphia: Temple University Press, 1974.

Berlin, Ira, and others. *The Black Military Experience.* New York: Cambridge University Press, 1982.

Brewer, James H. *The Confederate Negro: Virginia's Craftsmen and Military Laborers, 1861–1865.* Durham, N.C.: Duke University Press, 1969.

Buchanan, A. Russell. *Black Americans in World War II.* Santa Barbara, Calif.: Clio, 1983.

Caroll, John M. *The Black Military Experience in the American West.* New York: Liverwright, 1971.

Cornish, Dudley. *The Sable Arm: Negro Troops in the Union Army, 1861–1865.* New York: Norton, 1966.

Dalfiume, Richard M. *Desegregation of the U.S. Armed Forces: Fighting on Two Fronts, 1939–1953.* Columbia: University of Missouri Press, 1969.

Foner, Jack D. *Blacks and the Military in U.S. History: A New Perspective.* New York: Praeger, 1974.

Fowler, Arlen. *The Black Infantry in the West, 1869–1891.* Westport, Conn.: Greenwood, 1971.

Gatewood, Willard B. *Smoked Yankees and the Struggle for Empire.* Urbana: University of Illinois Press, 1971.

Glatthaar, Joseph T. *Forged in Battle: The Civil War Alliance of Black Soldiers and White Officers.* New York: Meridian, 1990.

Hargrove, Hondon B. *Black Union Soldiers in the Civil War.* Jefferson, N.C.: McFarland, 1988.

Henri, Florette. *Bitter Victory: A History of Black Soldiers in World War I.* Garden City, N.Y.: Doubleday, 1970.

*Kaplan, Sidney, and Emma Rogrady Kaplan. *The Black Presence in the Era of the American Revolution*. Revised edition. Amherst: University of Massachusetts Press, 1989.

MacGregor, Morris J., Jr. *Integration of the Armed Forces, 1940–1965*. Washington, D.C.: U.S. Government Printing Office, 1981.

*McPherson, James. *The Negro's Civil War: How America's Negroes Felt and Acted during the War for the Union*. New York: Pantheon, 1965.

Naltz, Bernard C. *Strength for the Fight: A History of Black Americans in the Military*. New York: Free Press, 1986.

*Quarles, Benjamin. *The Negro in the American Revolution*. Chapel Hill: University of North Carolina Press, 1961.

*————. *The Negro in the Civil War*. Boston: Little, Brown, 1969.

Stillman, Richard J. *Integration of the Negro into the U.S. Armed Forces*. New York: Praeger, 1968.

Wynn, Neil A. *The Afro-American and the Second World War*. New York: Holmes & Meier, 1976.

# INDEX

• • • • • • • • •

*by*
*James Minkin*